www.wadsworth.com

wadsworth.com is the World Wide Web site for Wadsworth Publishing Company and is your direct source to dozens of online resources.

At *wadsworth.com* you can find out about supplements, demonstration software, and student resources. You can also send e-mail to many of our authors and preview new publications and exciting new technologies.

wadsworth.com
Changing the way the world learns®

ETHICS

A Pluralistic Approach to Moral Theory

THIRD EDITION

LAWRENCE M. HINMAN
University of San Diego

THOMSON

WADSWORTH

Australia • Canada • Mexico • Singapore • Spain • United Kingdom • United States

For Laura, my daughter

THOMSON

WADSWORTH

Publisher: *Holly J. Allen*
Philosophy Editor: *Steve Wainwright*
Assistant Editor: *Lee McCracken*
Editorial Assistant: *Anna Lustig*
Technology Project Manager: *Susan DeVanna*
Marketing Manager: *Worth Hawes*
Advertising Project Manager: *Bryan Vann*
Print Buyer: *Rebecca Cross*

Permissions Editor: *Bob Kauser*
Production Service: *Matrix Productions*
Copy Editor: *Victoria Nelson*
Cover Designer: *Yvo Riezebos*
Cover Image: *Getty Images, Inc.*
Cover Printer: *Transcontinental-Louiseville*
Compositor: *Thompson Type*
Printer: *Transcontinental-Louiseville*

Printed in Canada
3 4 5 6 7 06 05 04

For more information about our products,
contact us at:
Thomson Learning Academic Resource Center
1-800-423-0563
For permission to use material from this text,
contact us by:
Phone: 1-800-730-2214
Fax: 1-800-730-2215
Web: http://www.thomsonrights.com

Library of Congress Control Number: 2002114389

ISBN 0 1550 62948

Wadsworth/Thomson Learning
10 Davis Drive
Belmont, CA 94002-3098
USA

Asia
Thomson Learning
5 Shenton Way #01-01
UIC Building
Singapore 068808

Australia
Nelson Thomson Learning
102 Dodds Street
South Melbourne, Victoria 3205
Australia

Canada
Nelson Thomson Learning
1120 Birchmount Road
Toronto, Ontario M1K 5G4
Canada

Europe/Middle East/Africa
Thomson Learning
High Holborn House
50/51 Bedford Row
London WC1R 4LR
United Kingdom

Latin America
Thomson Learning
Seneca, 53
Colonia Polanco
11560 Mexico D.F.
Mexico

Spain
Paraninfo Thomson Learning
Calle/Magallanes, 25
28015 Madrid, Spain

TABLE OF CONTENTS

CHAPTER 10   The Ethics of Diversity: Gender   306

CHAPTER 11   The Ethics of Diversity: Race, Ethnicity, and Multiculturalism   337

CHAPTER 12   Conclusion: Toward a Global Ethic of Peace   370

GLOSSARY   379

PHOTO CREDITS   384

INDEX   385

PREFACE

This third edition of *Ethics: A Pluralistic Approach to Moral Theory* has been shaped in important ways by the events of September 11, 2001. The section on Islamic ethics, which dates back to the first edition in 1994, has been expanded and specifically addresses the issue of Islam and tolerance. The chapter on relativism and pluralism has been revised to address more directly questions of where the line must be drawn in regard to ethical tolerance. A new chapter on theories of justice not only explores this concept from Plato to Rawls, but also includes a discussion of traditional just war theory and the notion of a just peace. A concluding chapter, "Toward a Global Ethic of World Peace," points the way toward some of the key ethical concerns that can guide us in perilous times.

Numerous revisions have been made throughout the rest of the book as well. All the bibliographical essays have been edited and brought up to date. The glossary has been expanded. Additional discussion questions about recent movies, from *Amélie* to *Gladiator* and *Black Hawk Down*, have been added. The chapter on egoism has been significantly revised, and now includes a new account of the egoism-altruism debate and an extended discussion of theories of moral motivation. Throughout the book, discussions have been streamlined and more emphasis has been placed on major distinctions. The chapter on "Theories Against Theories" has been dropped; although it raised interesting questions, even I did not actually include it in my courses. (It will be available on my web site, *Ethics Updates* (http://ethics.sandiego.edu) for anyone who wants to download it and use it in class.) The chapter on gender and ethics has been updated to include more recent work in this area. The chapter on "Race, Ethnicity, and Multiculturalism" has been expanded and integrated with the discussion of relativism and pluralism in Chapter Two. Numerous other, smaller changes have been made throughout the book.

Despite these changes, the heart of the book remains the same. It attempts to do two things. First, it provides students with a clear and reliable guide to the major theories and concepts in moral philosophy and helps them to understand the critical discussions surrounding these issues. Second, it provides a conceptual framework—ethical pluralism—for understanding the diversity of ethical theories and the persistence of moral disagreements. I worry that students, in the face of such pervasive disagreement, might simply give up and lapse into a kind of moral nihilism, believing that one position is as good as any other because there are arguments that can be advanced on all sides of a moral issue. Ethical pluralism offers a way of understanding this disagreement as a sign of strength in the moral life, not weakness. Furthermore, it offers a reasonable account of moral tolerance that does not lapse into some kind of moral *laissez-faire* form of ethical relativism. Finally, it provides a structure within which we can understand the relationship between traditional moral theories and what has come to be known as the politics of difference.

When the first edition of this book was published in 1994, I began a small web site, *Ethics Updates* (http://ethics.sandiego.edu), to keep the bibliographies up to date. It has grown steadily since then in both size and popularity, and received over one million visits in the first half of 2002. This site provides extensive resources on the topics covered in this book. It includes PowerPoint presentations on the material in each chapter, streaming video (RealVideo and Windows Media) of lectures on the topics in this book, videos of paper presentations, panels, and interviews on those topics, on-line texts of major works in moral philosophy (by Aristotle, Bentham, Mill, Kant, etc.), discussion forums, and links to helpful materials elsewhere on the Web. You are cordially invited to visit the site and make use of its resources.

Several features of this book are intended to make the journey easier as the reader moves through these often complex matters. *Extended examples* from real life have been used throughout the book to illustrate theoretical matters, and these have been updated in this new edition. *Discussion questions* have been provided for every chapter that encourage students to apply theoretical points to their own experience. *Movie questions* focus on the ways in which insights from the chapter can be applied to contemporary films, and a number of questions on recently released movies have been added to the third edition. The *glossary* at the end of this book has been expanded. *Bibliographical essays* provide a guide through the thicket of primary and secondary literature, and these have been extensively updated for this third edition. The *appendix* on writing ethics papers—which offers stylistic, technical, and substantive help on such things as choosing a topic, finding resources, and refining arguments—has been moved to my web site, *Ethics Updates.*

Despite all these changes, the original assumptions underlying this book remain largely unchanged. Three principal assumptions have guided me throughout.

First, *we can learn from tradition.* Each of the major ethical traditions has important truths to contribute to our understanding of the moral life, even if none of them is able to capture all the truths about that life. This book approaches each tradition in this spirit, asking what light it can shed on the moral life. This does not mean that criticism will be absent—far from it. However, even the criticism is designed to help us to see what is right, not just what is wrong, in each tradition.

Second, *we can learn from each other.* Diversity is a source of strength in the moral life, and this book provides a conceptual foundation for understanding and appreciating diversity. This is explicitly present in the treatment of relativism, absolutism, and pluralism in Chapter Two, and the discussion of both gender and ethnic diversity in Chapters Ten and Eleven. It is implicitly present in the choice of examples and the discussion of particular topics throughout the book.

Third and finally, *we can learn from ourselves*. This book begins with an ethical inventory that is intended to provide each student with the opportunity to take stock of his or her own moral beliefs. The discussion questions at the end of each chapter follow up on those initial responses, stressing the examination and refinement of the arguments underlying each student's initial position. Ultimately, each of us must make a personal assessment of the theories and arguments presented in this book.

In conclusion, I wish to thank some of the many people who have contributed to this book. My students at the University of San Diego have been a constant source of support and inspiration, and this book originally came out of a course that I continue to teach there every year. My new editor at Wadsworth, Steve Wainwright, has provided steady and enthusiastic support for this project. Merrill Peterson guided the book with a skilled hand through the production process. Karma Lekshe Tsomo, Ali Gheissari, Gary Macy, Lance Nelson, and Elaine Tagliaferri have made helpful suggestions for this new edition. I also wish to thank the manuscript reviewers for Wadsworth: Stanley M. Browne, Alabama A&M University; Joan Whitman Hoff, Lock Haven University of Pennsylvania; Mario Morelli, Western Illinois University; and Hal Walberg, Minnesota State University at Mankato. They provided insightful and constructive criticisms that have significantly improved this book, and I appreciate their help. My wife, Virginia Lewis, has been a source of continuing love and support, intellectual as well as emotional, throughout the entire project. Without her, this book would never have been written. Our daughter, Laura, has been a constant inspiration, and this book is dedicated to her.

ETHICS

A Pluralistic Approach to Moral Theory

THE MORAL POINT OF VIEW

WHY STUDY ETHICS?

There are many areas of life that we can avoid studying without any dire consequences. Few of us study, for example, molecular biology or quantum mechanics, but most of us (except for scientists in certain fields) are able to live quite well without any of the knowledge that comprises such disciplines. Yet there are other areas that we neglect only at hazard to ourselves and others. Consider nutrition. Most of us, myself included, have never had a course in nutrition or even read much about it. Yet many of us do have some general knowledge of the field. We know, for example, that there are six basic food groups, that a well-balanced diet involves items from each of these different groups, that we need a certain amount of protein each day, and that certain foods (usually ones we like) are bad for us. But we also realize that we make mistakes about these things. We discover that certain foods that we originally thought to be nutritious are actually quite harmful to us, sometimes in subtle ways that are evident only over a period of many years. We may also realize that there are foods we do not like that are nevertheless quite healthful. Even though we are not naturally inclined to eat them, we may find that we include some of them in our diet because in the long run we are going to feel better and be healthier because of it.

The Inevitability of Moral Questions

Morality is a lot like nutrition. We cannot avoid confronting moral problems because acting in ways that affect the well-being of ourselves and others is as unavoidable as acting in ways that affect the physical health of our own bodies. We inevitably face choices that hurt or help other people, choices that may infringe on their rights or violate their dignity or use them as mere tools to our own ends. We may choose not to pay attention to the concerns of morality such as compassion or justice or respect, just as we may choose to ignore the concerns of nutrition. However, that does not mean we can avoid making decisions about morality any more than we can evade deciding what foods to eat. We can ignore morality, but we cannot sidestep the choices to which morality is relevant, just as we cannot avoid the decisions to which nutrition is relevant even when we ignore the information that nutritionists provide for us. Morality is about living, and as long as we continue living, we will inevitably be confronted with moral questions—and if we choose to stop living, that, too, is a moral issue.

The Role of Moral Experts

There is a second respect in which ethics is like nutrition. We all have some general nutritional information that is part of our everyday stock of knowledge. We know, for example, that an ice cream cone is less healthful than a fresh garden salad, and we really do not need to consult a specialist to figure that out. Similarly, we know that torturing a little baby is morally wrong—and we do not need to ask a philosopher's advice to see that. Yet in both fields there are whole groups of specialists who spend their entire lives trying to refine and provide a solid foundation for the everyday beliefs that we do have. Sometimes nutritionists, for example, discover things that are surprising (such as the health benefits of fish oil), sometimes things that are disturbing (such as the harmful effects of certain food additives). At other times they just confirm our everyday beliefs, but they do so in a way that gives those beliefs a more solid foundation than they had before. The relation between our everyday moral beliefs and the work done by professional ethicists (that is, philosophers and others who specialize in ethics) seems to follow this same pattern. At times they provide a secure foundation for things that we already know, such as the fact that we should not torture other people for our own amusement. At other times they may discover unsettling things, such as the idea that we may have stronger obligations to people starving in other countries than we originally thought or that our society in general may not be treating the elderly with sufficient respect. Thus we consult these moral experts for at least two reasons: They provide a firmer foundation for many of our existing beliefs, and they provide new insight into some moral issues that confront us in our everyday lives.

Moral Disagreement

There are several other points to note in the analogy between research in nutrition and the specialized knowledge of ethicists. The first of these concerns the problem of moral disagreement. Just as there is disagreement among nutritionists about the health value of certain foods and just as their opinions change as they understand nutritional matters better, so it is with ethicists. They may disagree about some important matters, and their views may change over time. The best we can do is listen to them, understand their arguments, weigh their relative merits, and come to the best decision we can. Just as we should not give up on nutrition because the final answers are not yet completely available, so, too, we should not abandon ethics just because there is not complete agreement on all the important issues. We shall return to this issue in more detail in several of the following chapters, especially in Chapter 2.

Ethics as an Ongoing Conversation

The comparison with research in nutrition is enlightening in another respect. If we were to pick up a recent issue of a professional journal devoted solely to nutrition, we might well be lost. Not only would there probably be an extensive technical vocabulary that was largely foreign to us, but also the articles would be dealing with questions that seem so minute or detailed that they are hardly helpful to us in the daily business of eating well. We might also feel as though we suddenly were thrown into the middle of a set of discussions that had been going on for a long time—and no one had bothered to fill us in on what had been said before.

Reading the work of professional ethicists can have the same effect on us, and it is easy to understand why this is so. Philosophers have been discussing these issues, sometimes in great detail, for decades if not centuries. As happens in any discipline, the discussion becomes more finely tuned. Distinctions are drawn, concepts refined, arguments criticized and reconstructed, rebuttals developed, rejoinders to the rebuttals framed. All of this dialogue makes perfect sense to those engaged in the conversation over a long period of time, but to newcomers it will often seem overly technical, much too picky, and too removed from everyday experience. If you are new to ethics, you may feel that you have just walked into a room where a conversation has been going on for a very long time. The people already in the room understand one another's positions well and have been working on these issues for quite a while. They may be right in the middle of a heated debate about some small point in an argument advanced by one of the participants. One of the functions of this book is to be the good host: to introduce you to the people in the room, to fill you in on what has been said, and to ease you into participating in the conversation yourself. A portion of each chapter of this book will be devoted to supplying you with the background knowledge necessary to participate in the ongoing conversation among philosophers about the particular moral issues found in that chapter.

Ethics as an Ongoing Task

There is another way in which reading an ethics book is rather like reading a nutrition book: We inevitably are confronted with more information than we could possibly absorb in a single sitting. This is simply to be expected, and again, should not be a source of discouragement. Just as we would not change our eating habits overnight after reading a nutrition book but instead would gradually become more aware of nutritional concerns and perhaps change our diet in certain areas over a period of time, so, too, with reading an ethics book. It forces us to notice things we have not noticed before and to pay attention to issues that we previously had been unaware of or had ignored. Generally, however, it will not result in a total and immediate change in our lives—and with good reason. Most of us live basically good lives, and it is unlikely that an exposure to formal work in ethics would necessitate a complete revamping of our moral outlook. Moreover, we need to test these ideas through our own experience, and that is a gradual process of living with a new idea and beginning to get a feel for how our daily experiences are changed when seen through the lens of that new insight. This back-and-forth process, in which both the idea and our experience gradually become refined, and changed, and developed, is a process that we will examine more closely later in this book when we discuss moral change. For the moment, however, it is sufficient to remember that reading a good ethics book is like reading a good nutrition book: If it is really good, we will not absorb it all at once but will continually come back to it, refining and developing our ideas and reshaping our lives.

Morality and Ethics

Playing the good host, let me mention at this point a distinction between morality and ethics that recurs throughout this book. Philosophers generally draw this distinction in the following way. Every society has its set of moral rules or guidelines that set the boundaries of acceptable behavior. Often these rules are about behavior that might harm other people (killing, stealing), behavior that is concerned with the well-being of others (helping those in need, responding to the suffering of others), or actions that touch on issues of respect for other persons (segregation, using other people for one's own ends without concern for their welfare). Often the rules about such behavior are expressed in statements about what you *ought* to do or *should* do. These rules fit together, more or less consistently, to form the moral code by which a society lives.

Moral codes are seldom completely consistent. Our everyday life raises moral questions that we cannot answer immediately. Sometimes that is because there are contradictions among our different values, and we are uncertain about which value should be given priority. For example, Oliver North was caught in a conflict between what he saw as the value of loyalty to his country and the value of telling the truth, even to Congress. At other times, our traditional values do not cover new situations, and we have to figure out how to extend them. We believe in the value of privacy, but in an age of increasing computerization, what rules should we establish to govern access to information in computer data banks about private individuals? When we step back and consciously reflect on our moral beliefs, we are engaging in ethical reflection. **Ethics,** then, **is the conscious reflection on our moral beliefs** with the aim of improving, extending, or refining those beliefs in some way. This book is an invitation for you to participate in the activity of ethical reflection.

Public and Private Moral Beliefs

Let us take our analogy with nutrition a step further. If people are at a party with many health food fanatics, it is unlikely that most people will volunteer that their favorite breakfast food is Hostess Twinkies and Pepsi-Cola or that they would like to have pizza and beer for dinner every night. For most people, the atmosphere is not conducive to such confessions, although there are certainly some people who would not hesitate to make such unwelcome statements.

We encounter a similar situation in regard to our moral beliefs. There are certain things that are acceptable to say, others that are not. In most circles, it is socially quite acceptable to say that you are in favor of honesty, fairness, respect for other people, and so on; it is frowned upon to claim that lying, cheating, or using other people as mere means may sometimes be quite acceptable to you. Indeed, for many of us there may be a difference between our public (overt, official) moral beliefs and our private (covert, personal) moral beliefs. We may publicly endorse paying one's debts, but if a major purchase on our credit card never shows up on our bill, we may be quite content not to call it to the company's attention. We may proclaim the importance of truthfulness, but lie to a friend about what we did last weekend.

This discrepancy between overt and covert moral beliefs causes a problem for ethics. Imagine that you went to a nutritionist to get some information on a better diet, and, in response to questions about what you ate during a typical day, you lied and said, for example, that you had tofu and a spinach salad for dinner instead of pizza and beer. If your goal is to change your eating habits, lying in this way simply keeps you from dealing with reality and thus prevents you from changing. Similarly, if we are going to enter into the ongoing conversation that constitutes ethical reflection, we have to become clear what our real (at times, covert or unacknowledged) moral beliefs are and then examine those actual beliefs, rather than simply talk about the overt, publicly acceptable moral values that most of us espouse as a matter of course. This refocus may be quite difficult. Not only is there social pressure against expressing some of our personal values, but also sometimes we do not know what our actual beliefs and values are. At times we must look at our behavior to see what we actually believe. We say that honesty is the best policy, but do we in fact act in that fashion? We talk about the importance of respect for other persons, but how do we actually treat those around us? Coming to know ourselves is a difficult but essential step in ethical reflection.

This book is an invitation to enter into a discussion about your own beliefs, the private as well as the public. It is an invitation to examine, develop, and perhaps even improve those beliefs as you see fit in light of the insights that others have had into the moral life. In order for that process to be most meaningful to you, you need to examine the private as well as the public values you hold. This reflection may be work that you want to do in complete privacy, looking at those personal values alone. Or you may want to discuss them with classmates, friends, or professors. Those are choices each of us must make as an individual. I would urge you, however, to dig for those real values by which you actually live and—in whatever way you find appropriate—bring them into the ongoing conversation that constitutes ethical reflection. It is in this way that the material contained in this book will be most meaningful to you.

Moral Health

There is one final point to make in our comparison between nutrition and ethics: Both are concerned with good health. This point is obvious in the case of nutrition, which focuses on our physical health. Ethics has a corresponding focus on our *moral* health. It seeks to help us determine what will nourish our moral life and what will poison it. As such, it seeks to enhance our lives, to help us to live better lives. Just as nutrition sometimes is experienced primarily as telling us what we cannot eat, so ethics may seem to be concerned mainly with telling us what we cannot do. But this negative aspect is simply a by-product of a more positive focus. In the case of nutrition, the central question is how we should eat in order to experience more of the vibrancy associated with genuine physical healthiness. Similarly, in the case of ethics, our principal concern is how we should live in order to experience the joy and satisfaction of a morally good life. The negative prohibitions arise not out of a desire to be negative, but rather as by-products of a much more positive concern about moral health.

AN ETHICAL INVENTORY: DISCOVERING YOUR OWN MORAL BELIEFS

All of us already have some idea of what our moral beliefs are, but often there is no need to make these explicit. Because the rest of this book provides you with an opportunity for developing and refining your views on moral theory, it is helpful to begin by taking stock of the views with which you begin this investigation. The following checklist is intended to provide you with the opportunity to make an initial survey of your views. Read each of the following statements carefully and indicate whether you strongly agree, agree, are undecided or do not know, disagree, or strongly disagree with each statement.

ETHICAL INVENTORY

Strongly Agree
Agree
Undecided
Disagree
Strongly Disagree

Relativism, Absolutism, and Pluralism

1. ❑ ❑ ❑ ❑ ❑ What's right depends on the culture you are in.

2. ❑ ❑ ❑ ❑ ❑ No one has the right to judge what's right or wrong for another person.

3. ❑ ❑ ❑ ❑ ❑ No one has the right to intervene when he or she thinks someone else has done something morally wrong.

4. ❑ ❑ ❑ ❑ ❑ It's hopeless to try to arrive at a final answer to ethical questions.

5. ❑ ❑ ❑ ❑ ❑ Ultimately, there is one and only one right standard of moral evaluation.

Religion and Ethics

6. ❑ ❑ ❑ ❑ ❑ What is right depends on what God says is right.

7. ❑ ❑ ❑ ❑ ❑ There is only one true religion.

8. ❑ ❑ ❑ ❑ ❑ What my religion says (in the Bible, the Qur'an, or other sacred scripture) is literally true.

9. ❑ ❑ ❑ ❑ ❑ All major religions have something important to tell us about what is right and what is wrong.

10. ❑ ❑ ❑ ❑ ❑ We do not need to depend on religion in order to have a solid foundation for our moral values.

Psychological and Ethical Egoism

11. ❑ ❑ ❑ ❑ ❑ Everyone is just out for himself or herself.

12. ❑ ❑ ❑ ❑ ❑ Some people think that they are genuinely concerned about the welfare of others, but they are just deceiving themselves.

13. ❑ ❑ ❑ ❑ ❑ People are not really free. They are just products of their environment, upbringing, and other factors.

14. ❑ ❑ ❑ ❑ ❑ Everyone should watch out just for himself or herself.

15. ❑ ❑ ❑ ❑ ❑ You can't be both altruistic and selfish at the same time.

Strongly Agree	Agree	Undecided	Disagree	Strongly Disagree	

Utilitarianism

16. ❑ ❑ ❑ ❑ ❑ When I am trying to decide what the right thing to do is, I look at the consequences of the various alternatives open to me.

17. ❑ ❑ ❑ ❑ ❑ The right thing to do is whatever is best for everyone.

18. ❑ ❑ ❑ ❑ ❑ If someone tries to do the right thing but it works out badly, they still deserve moral credit for trying.

19. ❑ ❑ ❑ ❑ ❑ Pleasure is the most important thing in life.

20. ❑ ❑ ❑ ❑ ❑ Happiness is the most important thing in life.

Kant, Duty, and Respect

21. ❑ ❑ ❑ ❑ ❑ If someone tries to do the right thing but it works out badly, that person still deserves moral credit for trying

22. ❑ ❑ ❑ ❑ ❑ It is important to do the right thing *for the right reason*.

23. ❑ ❑ ❑ ❑ ❑ What is fair for one is fair for all.

24. ❑ ❑ ❑ ❑ ❑ People should always be treated with respect.

25. ❑ ❑ ❑ ❑ ❑ We should never use other people merely as a means to our own goals.

Rights Theories

26. ❑ ❑ ❑ ❑ ❑ Morality is basically a matter of respecting people's rights.

27. ❑ ❑ ❑ ❑ ❑ Some rights are absolute.

28. ❑ ❑ ❑ ❑ ❑ I have a right to do whatever I want as long as it does not impinge on other people's rights.

29. ❑ ❑ ❑ ❑ ❑ People have a right to health care, even if they can't afford to pay for it.

30. ❑ ❑ ❑ ❑ ❑ Animals have rights.

Justice

31. ❑ ❑ ❑ ❑ ❑ Justice is the most important characteristic of a society.

32. ❑ ❑ ❑ ❑ ❑ Might makes right.

33. ❑ ❑ ❑ ❑ ❑ Justice consists of treating everybody exactly the same.

34. ❑ ❑ ❑ ❑ ❑ A just society is one in which everyone has the maximal amount of liberty.

Strongly Agree
Agree
Undecided
Disagree
Strongly Disagree

35. ❑ ❑ ❑ ❑ ❑ Sometimes strict justice is bad for society.

Virtue Ethics

36. ❑ ❑ ❑ ❑ ❑ Morality is mainly a matter of what kind of person you are.

37. ❑ ❑ ❑ ❑ ❑ Sometimes courage seems to go too far.

38. ❑ ❑ ❑ ❑ ❑ Compassion for the suffering of others is an important character trait.

39. ❑ ❑ ❑ ❑ ❑ It's important to care about yourself.

40. ❑ ❑ ❑ ❑ ❑ Virtues are the same for males and females.

Gender and Ethics

41. ❑ ❑ ❑ ❑ ❑ Men and women often view morality differently.

42. ❑ ❑ ❑ ❑ ❑ Emotions have no place in morality.

43. ❑ ❑ ❑ ❑ ❑ Morality is primarily a matter of following the rules.

44. ❑ ❑ ❑ ❑ ❑ The more masculine someone is, the less feminine that person is.

45. ❑ ❑ ❑ ❑ ❑ There are often unjust relationships in the modern family.

Race, Ethnicity, and Ethics

46. ❑ ❑ ❑ ❑ ❑ Morality should reflect an individual's ethnic and cultural background.

47. ❑ ❑ ❑ ❑ ❑ Some ethnic and racial groups deserve reparations for the wrongs done to them in the past.

48. ❑ ❑ ❑ ❑ ❑ Moral disagreement is a good thing in society.

49. ❑ ❑ ❑ ❑ ❑ Compromise is bad.

50. ❑ ❑ ❑ ❑ ❑ Minorities have special rights by virtue of their status as minorities.

In the discussion questions at the end of each chapter, we shall return to your responses to these statements. At this juncture, however, it is helpful to have some initial idea of the issues raised by these statements and the place of those issues in this book. I will briefly comment on each group of statements in turn.

Relativism, Absolutism, and Pluralism

We live in a world of differing and sometimes conflicting values. How do we deal with differences in value? Is there a single moral standard that is correct for everyone? Are standards completely relative to each culture? To each individual? What right do we have to make moral judgments about other people, whether in our own culture or in another culture? If we can make moral judgments about the behavior of others, are we ever justified in intervening in their affairs? If so, when? These are crucial questions about how we understand the relationship between our own moral values and the moral values of others. We shall deal with them in detail in chapter 2, where I shall sketch out a middle ground between the two extremes of relativism and absolutism.

If you find yourself agreeing or strongly agreeing with **statement 1,** your initial position is most compatible with *ethical relativism*. Chapter 2 is primarily concerned with a clarification and assessment of this position. A corollary of ethical relativism is the belief that we ought not to judge others. **Statement 2** indicates your position on that issue. Finally, relativists and subjectivists also often maintain that one cannot intervene in the affairs of others, an issue dealt with in **statement 3.** If you agree or strongly agree with statements 2 and 3, you will find Chapter 2 interesting because it presents some reasons for reconsidering and revising your agreement with these items. **Statement 4** deals with how much you think we can know about moral matters; if you strongly agree with statement 4, you will be very sympathetic to the moral skeptic. **Statement 5** deals with the issue of whether there is some single standard of moral value *(ethical monism)* or whether there are several different and legitimate standards *(ethical pluralism)*. If you agreed with statement 5, you will find the approach articulated in this book very challenging, for it defends an explicitly pluralistic account of morality.

Religion and Ethics

Chapter 3 discusses the relationship between our moral values and our religious beliefs. For many people, religion plays a crucial role in their moral values, whether as a formative factor in their development or as their principal foundation. Your response to **statement 6** gives a partial indication of where you stand on this issue; those who agree with it are often called *divine command theorists*. Some people, often called *fundamentalists*, hold that their religious beliefs are literally true **(statement 8)** and are the only truth **(statement 7)**; others maintain that the truths of their religion are better understood as metaphorical. Those who see religious truth as metaphorical are more likely to see all major religions as being sources of moral truth **(statement 9)**.

In contrast to those who hold that there is a positive and supportive relationship between religion and ethics, many people maintain that moral questions should be resolved independently of any religious beliefs. Those who agree or strongly agree with **statement 10** would hold this position, which is called the *autonomy of ethics* theory.

The Ethics of Selfishness: Egoism

Some thinkers have maintained that the only thing that matters in the moral life is the self. This position, called *egoism*, encompasses two distinct beliefs. *Psychological egoists* maintain that we all act selfishly all of the time (**statement 11**) and that those who think they don't are just deceiving themselves (**statement 12**). Often, in order to support their belief, psychological egoists invoke some version of *determinism*, that is, the claim that human behavior is causally determined rather than freely chosen (**statement 13**). Other egoists—called *ethical egoists*—admit that people can act altruistically, but argue that people *ought* to act selfishly. **Statement 14** measures the degree to which you agree with this position. Perhaps the best-known advocate of this position is Ayn Rand. Chapter 4 is concerned with evaluating this theory and showing that, although it does contain an important insight into the moral life, it falls far short of giving a comprehensive account of how we ought to act. **Statement 15 shows whether you think altruism and selfishness are incompatible; we will examine this question in Chapter 4.**

The Ethics of Consequences: Utilitarianism

When we address ourselves to moral issues, many of us are particularly concerned with evaluating the *consequences* of specific actions or rules. Both ethical egoists and utilitarians are consequentialists, but there is a crucial difference between the two. The ethical egoist is concerned only with the consequences for the individual agent; the *utilitarian* is concerned with the consequences for everyone. The extent to which you agree with **statement 16** indicates the extent to which you are a *consequentialist*. If you agree or strongly agree with **statement 17,** this indicates that utilitarian considerations are a significant part of your moral theory. If you agree or strongly agree with **statement 18,** you will find that Kantian criticisms of utilitarianism are appealing to you. **Statements 19 and 20** deal with the standard that utilitarians use to judge consequences. *Hedonistic utilitarians* (statement 19) say that consequences must be judged in terms of their ability to produce pleasure, whereas *eudaimonistic utilitarians* (statement 20) maintain that happiness is the proper standard by which consequences should be judged.

The Ethics of Intentions: Duty and Respect

Whereas utilitarians concentrate on consequences, many ethical theorists—Immanuel Kant is the most famous representative of this tradition—claim that *intentions* are what really count in the moral life. If you found yourself strongly agreeing or even agreeing with **statements 21 and 22,** you will probably find the Kantian viewpoint initially attractive. As we shall see in Chapter 6, Kant held that everyday life is simply too unpredictable to allow the moral worth of an action to depend on consequences. After we have performed an action, it is out of our control; anything might happen as a result. The only thing for which we are truly responsible, and the only thing for which we can take moral credit, is the intention behind our action.

Kant used several criteria in evaluating intentions, and your response to **statement 22** indicates how you view those criteria. For Kant, rules must be applied impartially to everyone. Your response to **statement 23** indicates the extent to which you agree with Kant on this issue. In addition to fairness, Kant emphasized the importance of *respect*. **Statements 24 and 25** measure the degree to which you agree with Kant that we should always treat people with respect and never use them merely as a means to our own goals.

The Ethics of Rights

During the last fifty years, philosophers and political leaders have come to see *rights* as occupying an increasingly important place in the moral life. We shall discuss this movement in Chapter 7. Your response to **statement 26** indicates the degree to which you agree with this trend; if you strongly agree with this statement, you will be among those thinkers who hold that morality is *only* a matter of rights. **Statement 27** highlights a central issue for rights theorists: Are there any rights that are absolute, that can never legitimately be violated? Some thinkers—in the political realm, these are often libertarians—hold that the only restriction on our actions should be the rights of others to noninterference; **statement 28** shows the extent to which you initially agree with this claim. **Statement 29** indicates your position on an important and controversial issue of positive rights. **Statement 30** indicates the extent to which you believe animals have rights.

The Ethics of Justice

Your answer to **statement 31** indicates the extent to which you agree with Rawls and others about how important the concept of justice is in society. **Statement 32** measures the extent to which you agree with Thrasymachus in Plato's *Republic*. If you agree with **statement 33,** you hold a very egalitarian notion of justice; if you agree with **statement 34,** your position has libertarian elements in it. **Statement 35** indicates that you think justice has to be tempered or supplemented by something else. These issues will be explored in Chapter 8.

The Ethics of Character: Virtues and Vices

Although much of ethical theory centers around the evaluation of actions (in terms of intentions or consequences or both), ever since Aristotle there has been another tradition in ethics that concentrates on the development of *character*. If you agree or strongly agree with **statement 36,** you will probably find this tradition compatible with your own ideas. Your responses to **statements 37, 38, and 39** indicate where you stand on several specific virtues (courage, compassion, and self-love, respectively) which are discussed in detail in Chapter 9. **Statement 40** measures the extent to which you think virtue and gender are linked.

The Ethics of Diversity: Gender

During the past two decades, there has been a rapidly growing interest in the relationship between morality and gender. Some thinkers, such as Carol Gilligan, have argued that males and females view morality differently. **Statement 41** measures your initial position on this issue, whereas **statements 42 and 43** indicate your position on the place of emotions and of rules in the moral life. If you agree with **Statement 44,** you find masculinity and femininity mutually exclusive; we will offer an alternative perspective on this issue in Chapter 10. **Statement 45** indicates the extent to which you see issues of justice and gender as important within the family. These issues will all be discussed in Chapter 10, which focuses on the ethics of diversity in regard to gender.

The Ethics of Diversity: Race and Ethnicity

In recent years, some philosophers have maintained that race and ethnicity not only do but should place an important role in ethical theory. **Statement 46** elicits your position on this issue. **Statement 47** examines the issue of group reparations. Diversity often brings disagreement, and the **statements 48 and 49** are intended to gauge your initial attitude toward disagreements and your initial position on how they are to be resolved. Finally, **statement 50** indicates your position on the question of whether minorities have special rights as such. This is particularly an issue for indigenous people, for whom special protection (i.e., special rights) is necessary to preserve their cultural identity.

Save your answers to these questions. We will return to them throughout the course of this book, and at the end of the semester you will be asked to take this ethical inventory again (see pp. 7–9) to see if your views on these issues have changed.

THE MORAL POINT OF VIEW

When I was on vacation a few years ago, I visited a farm in Pennsylvania where chickens were raised. Although I had heard about the conditions under which chickens are kept for laying eggs, I had never seen them first-hand. I was appalled. The chickens were squeezed so tightly into the cages that they could not move at all. They would spend their entire lives in the particular cage in which they were confined, which struck me as a terribly *cruel* thing to do to the chickens, and I found myself going outside just to avoid looking at them. For the first time, I could appreciate on an emotional level one of the reasons why some people in our society are strict vegetarians. They refuse to be a part of a process that they consider cruel and inhumane. I found myself wondering whether it was immoral for me to eat chicken or even to eat eggs. Was I participating in something morally bad by doing so? Let's look more closely at some of the elements in this example. Was it even a moral issue? What puts something in the **moral ballpark,** that is, makes it an issue within the moral domain rather than a non-moral issue.

Consider, first, the process through which we usually recognize that something is a nutritional issue. When we call something a nutritional issue, we are singling it out both in terms of its *content* (that is, it has to do with food or other sources of bodily nourishment) and in terms of the *perspective* we take on that content (that is, we consider food in terms of its effect on health rather than primarily in terms of its color, price, and so on). Similarly, when we claim that something is a moral issue, we usually are indicating that:

- Its content is of a particular type (duties, rights, human welfare and suffering, and so on).
- We are approaching it from a particular point of view (impartial, caring, and so on).

Moral issues are thus a matter both of *what* we see and *how* we see it.

Let's look at an example of a typical moral issue and then outline some of the major theories about what makes it a moral issue.

An Example

Imagine that you are a student in a very large undergraduate course at a university that has a clear honor code about cheating and the duty to report cheating to appropriate authorities. During a very difficult midterm exam, you notice that many students—including one of your best friends—are cheating on the exam. The proctor, a teaching assistant for one of the sections, is reading a novel and seems oblivious to the cheating. At one point, a friend of yours even leans over to ask you the answer to one of the questions. You pretend not to hear the request for help. A week later, the professor returns the exams. A number of students, including some of your close friends, receive *A*s and *B*s, higher grades than they otherwise would have gotten if they had not cheated. You would have received a *B*, which you feel is a reasonably accurate assessment of your grasp of the material, but because of the high curve you actually receive a *C* on the exam.

The Moral Content

Consider those things in the *content* of this situation that make this a moral issue. Several things stand out. First, some people are *hurt* in the situation. They receive lower grades than they otherwise would because of the cheating and the fact that grading is done on a curve. Second, there is *deception* in the situation, which is usually a moral "red flag," an indication that moral scrutiny is in order. Third, it seems *unfair* that people who cheat get ahead because of their cheating, whereas those who are honest seemingly are penalized because of their honesty. Fourth, there are questions of *conflicting values,* and these are usually principal sources of moral questions. In this case, loyalty to friends conflicts with possible duties to inform a professor about cheating. Finally, there may be a concern about *character* and the effects that cheating or informing on cheaters has on a person's character. All of these are elements that typically are recognized as part of the moral content of this situation.

The Moral Standpoint

For something to be a moral issue, it is not enough for it simply to have a certain content. We must also approach it in a particular way. If we approached this cheating example solely as sociologists interested in describing the various social forces at work in the situation, we would not be raising a moral issue. For something to be a moral issue, we have to raise it from a particular standpoint or point of view. If, for example, we are asking what is *right* to do in the situation, we are approaching it from a moral point of view. So, too, our concern is a moral one if we ask what our duty is in a particular situation. Similarly, if we are concerned with what makes a person a *good* person rather than popular or witty, we are approaching the issue of character from a moral point of view. We will examine several attempts to describe the moral standpoint later.

Nonmoral Concerns

There are a number of questions you could ask about this situation that would *not* be specifically or directly moral in character. For example, you might ask questions about what the correct answers were, about which pages from the textbook were covered in the exam, about how many people missed a particular question, and the like. None of these questions is specifically moral in character.

The Language of Moral Concerns

Many philosophers have attempted to specify the nature of the moral point of view by looking at the language we typically employ when we are talking about moral issues. Recall the cheating example just given. We may ask whether it is our *duty* to inform on students who cheat. Is the proctor *obligated* to pay close attention to signs of cheating? Is cheating *bad* or *wrong* or *immoral*? Is it always *right* or *good* to be honest? *Ought* we to always be honest? Do students have a *right* to demand that cheating not be permitted? Will a policy of strict honesty have the greatest *overall amount of good consequences for everybody*? Who will be *hurt* by such a policy?

These are questions that are characteristically moral questions that you could ask about this situation, and the italicized words are characteristically moral vocabulary. Indeed, one of the ways that philosophers describe the moral point of view is that it typically employs the kind of moral vocabulary emphasized in the previous paragraph. We will look at this concept in more detail later in this book, so for the moment you need to get only a rough idea of what type of language usually is associated with the moral point of view.

Impartiality

There is another characteristic of each of these approaches to morality, one that many philosophers take to be at the heart of the moral point of view. Typically, the moral point of view is an *impartial* one. When we make a moral judgment, we do not ask just what would be good for ourselves. We set aside our own personal, selfish interests and attempt to do what is right, even if it involves sacrifice on our part. (One ethical system, ethical egoism, disagrees with this notion and defends the moral value of selfishness. We shall examine this position in Chapter 4.) We all have certainly experienced this phenomenon: doing the right thing even when it hurts, even when it would be easier to do the selfish thing. For example, consider what happens when a salesperson gives you back too much change in the store. Especially if you know that the clerk will have to pay for any shortages at the end of the day, you may give back the extra money, even though you could use the additional cash. You may do so because it is the right thing to do, or because it would hurt the other person not to do it, but in any case you set aside your self-interest to do what morally is demanded of you. Many philosophers maintain that setting aside narrow personal interests in this way is at the heart of the moral point of view.

Compassion

Some philosophers have described the moral point of view in quite a different way, a way that initially seems far from the impartiality just discussed. Morality, they maintain, is essentially about *compassion*, about the ability to understand and to help alleviate the suffering of other people. (Indeed, the etymology of *compassion* is from the Latin, meaning "suffering with.") The moral point of view, according to this approach, is characterized by our ability to understand, appreciate, and help relieve the suffering of others.

Although compassion may initially seem quite distant from impartiality, there is actually an important underlying link between the two. Josiah Royce, an American philosopher, once characterized the essential moral insight as the realization that "such as that is for me, so is it for him, nothing less." Compassion is the ability to appreciate that all suffering is equal, that my own suffering counts for no more than the suffering of any other person. Compassion is a unique combination of the impartial and the personal: It is an intensely personal concern for the suffering of others, but it is applied impartially to the suffering of everyone.

Universally Binding

There is yet another way in which some philosophers characterize the moral point of view. They see morality as being primarily a matter of commands or, as they usually put it, *imperatives* that are binding on everyone in an impartial manner. We encounter many imperatives in life. Some of them are *hypothetical* in character, that is, they say that we should do some particular thing only *if* we want to achieve a specific goal. "If you want to see an enjoyable movie, see the new James Bond film." "If you want to get an *A* in this course, you must write an excellent term paper." These are everyday examples of hypothetical imperatives. Yet some imperatives are not hypothetical in character. They claim to be binding without qualification. According to Immanuel Kant, an eighteenth-century philosopher whose work has had a profound impact on ethics, these unconditional or **categorical imperatives** are at the heart of ethics. Kant maintains that the moral point of view is distinguished by the fact that its imperatives are categorical rather than merely hypothetical in character. "Never treat people merely as a means to your own ends." "Always respect people as ends in themselves." "Always act in such a way that you could will that everyone follow the same rule that you are following." These are examples of typical moral categorical imperatives. Notice that none of them is hypothetical; none begins with an "If . . ." clause. Morality is not a matter of choice. It binds us absolutely. Part of the moral point of view, according to many philosophers, is that we feel bound by moral imperatives, not just hypothetically, but categorically.

Our everyday experience of morality often confirms this claim that morality is universally binding, especially in serious moral matters. Think, for example, of our moral prohibitions against sexually abusing children. Virtually none of us thinks that this is just a matter of personal opinion. We feel that it is wrong to sexually abuse children, and we feel that this prohibition is binding on *everyone*. Morality, at least at its core, is universally binding.

Concern for Character

Each of the previous ways of characterizing morality (moral language, impartiality, and categorical imperatives) presumes that morality is primarily concerned with the assessment of particular *acts*. But as we have already mentioned, there is another tradition in ethics, stretching back at least to Aristotle's time over twenty-two hundred years ago. This tradition, called **virtue ethics,** suggests that **morality is primarily a matter of individual character.** Within this tradition, the moral point of view is primarily concerned with the question of what it means to be a good person. The focus is on excellence of character. Indeed, the Greek word for *virtue (areté)* originally meant just "excellence." Courage, compassion, self-love, and generosity are some of the moral virtues that we will be discussing in this book. Along with these, we will also be looking at the opposite of virtues: vices such as hatred, envy, jealousy, and cowardice.

THE POINT OF ETHICAL REFLECTION

In the preceding sections, we have discussed the question of why we should study ethics and looked at various answers to the question of what puts an issue into the moral ballpark. There is one final topic to consider here: What is the *point* of ethical reflection? More specifically, is it primarily supposed to help us judge others or to better understand and guide our own lives?

Ethics as the Evaluation of Other People's Behavior

We are certainly aware of those who see ethical reflection primarily as a means of making judgments about the morality (or the immorality) of other people. Think, for example, of some of the nastier debates about the morality of abortion, euthanasia, the death penalty, or nuclear armaments. Very often, advocates on all sides of these issues use ethical arguments to press a case against their opponents, to show their audience that the course of action recommended by their opponents is morally objectionable. Sometimes they will attack even the moral character of their opponents, claiming that they are bad people. Ethics, in this context, is often used to condemn other people, or at least to denounce the actions that they advocate.

Mistrust about Moral Judgments

This is certainly an important and legitimate use for ethics, and I have no desire to urge its elimination. However, some people feel a certain mistrust about this aspect of ethics. There seem to be several sources of this mistrust, and I would like to discuss five of them here.

Hypocrisy. The first source of mistrust centers on the issue of consistency and motivation. Some people wonder whether ethics isn't being used, when it is convenient to do so, to attack others but being ignored when it raises difficult questions about one's own conduct. They mistrust, in other words, the *motives* of those who advance such arguments and are concerned that ethical arguments may be being used selectively to support particular positions. Such critics do not necessarily deny the soundness of the arguments, but rather they have doubts about the motives behind their use.

Sometimes such mistrust about motivation may be justified, but it certainly does not need to be extended to all moral judgments. Not all persons who make moral judgments are unwilling to look at themselves and apply the same moral standards to themselves that they apply to others. Moreover, we need to distinguish between the motivation for making a moral judgment and its validity. Moral judgments may be self-serving, but that doesn't mean that they necessarily lack any validity. Indeed, the converse is also true. The fact that a particular moral judgment is not self-serving does not mean that it is valid. There is no shortage of well-intentioned mistakes.

Knowing Other People. The second source of mistrust that I have encountered is primarily *epistemological,* that is, it has to do with how much we can *know* about other people. (Epistemology is a branch of philosophy that deals with the nature and justification of our knowledge claims.) How, many people ask, can we ever know enough about what other people are thinking or feeling to pass judgment on their actions?

This argument has merit, but perhaps not as much as its proponents believe. We probably can never *completely* know and understand another person. (Indeed, we can probably never completely know and understand ourselves, either.) But this is a matter of degree. We can partially know and understand some people, just as they can at least partially know and understand us. Moreover, we can increase our knowledge and understanding of another person—this is a natural part of the process of getting to know someone. Indeed, think of what an incredibly lonely world we would inhabit if we could never really know or understand another person at all.

There is another problem with these epistemological doubts. Sometimes we don't need to know another person's inner beliefs and feelings and motives in order to make a judgment about the moral worth of an act. Sometimes our concern is with the act and its consequences, not with motives or intentions. It is primarily when we are making moral judgments about persons rather than actions or consequences that we need to know about the person's intentions and feelings.

The Right to Judge. The third source of mistrust is captured in the question, "Who am I to judge other people's actions?" By what right, in other words, do I claim to be in a position to pass judgment on someone else's life? This is a good question—and, like all good questions, it deserves an answer. Clearly, we are not entitled to make such judgments simply because we want to. It would seem, in order to exercise the right to make moral judgments (about oneself as well as others), that at least two conditions must be met. First, we must have some standards that we don't think are arbitrary. The standards must, in other words, be justified. Much of the rest of this book is an exploration of how such standards may be justified. Second, we must have some knowledge of the situation we are judging. Moral judgments, in other words, must be well grounded in both justified moral standards and in appropriate knowledge of the situation. Of course, when some people ask the question, "Who am I to judge?" they aren't really looking for an answer. They are using a rhetorical question to assert that no one has a right to make moral judgments. This is a strong, important claim that must be examined directly. We will do so in the next chapters when we discuss moral skepticism and moral nihilism.

Intervention. Another source of mistrust centers on the issue of intervention. What good, it is often asked, does it do to try to change the way someone else lives? We can't live other people's lives for them. They have to do it themselves.

Several things need to be said about this mistrust. First, judgment is not the same thing as intervention. Therefore, even if it is true that intervention is not justified in a particular case, that does not mean that judgment is impossible. We may very well say that what someone is doing is wrong but decide that the best thing for us to do is not to intervene. Second, although it may often be true that intervention is not effective, that is not *always* true. Intervention can sometimes both be justified and effective. Certainly there are times when we intervene in order to protect innocent people from the potentially harmful effects of someone's actions. Think about drunk driving. We may refuse to let someone drive home drunk after a party because we do not want to see anyone hurt or killed by such driving, whether it be the driver or any unsuspecting victims. Such intervention may well be effective. It may not ultimately eliminate the behavior, but it will prevent it on that occasion and reduce the chance that anyone will be hurt or killed that evening by that drunk driver.

Finally, we should emphasize that intervention is an art that often requires quite a bit of skill. Most of us have been in situations where we knew that we ought to do something, but we didn't know what—and we were afraid that if we did the wrong thing, it would make matters only worse. Part of the moral life is learning how to intervene in ways that are both caring and effective. That is not an easy or a simple task.

Judging and Caring. There is a final possible source of mistrust about making moral judgments that deserves special attention here. Making moral judgments sometimes feels harsh and uncaring. To judge people seems equivalent to condemning them, which seems antithetical to caring about them.

Once again, we can safely say that sometimes this is true. At times people do judge one another harshly and uncaringly. But two points need to be noted about this. First, people do not *always* judge in an uncaring and harsh way. Second, if moral judgments are sometimes objectionably harsh and uncaring, that does not mean that we should get rid of the entire process of making moral judgments. Rather than throw out the baby with the bath water, we need reject only the objectionable part—the harsh, uncaring part. The moral challenge in this regard is to learn how to *make* moral judgments in a caring, sometimes even loving, fashion and to *express* them when appropriate in a similar way.

Ethics as the Search for the Meaning of Our Own Lives

There is, however, another tradition in ethics that has a quite different focus. Within this tradition, ethics is primarily concerned with reflection about the quality of one's own life. Here ethics is less a matter of judging and more a matter of understanding and seeing things more clearly. It is less concerned with other people's lives than with our own. Finally, it is less concerned with the negative than with the positive. Let me illustrate this difference first by means of an example.

Most of us have probably had the following kind of experience, one that illustrates this difference well. Imagine that we are facing a difficult moral choice—let's say, about removing life-support equipment for a loved one. We can easily imagine going to someone who has very firm views on the subject and who tells us there is only one thing to do. Often we go away from such conversations with a feeling of dissatisfaction, because the other person's advice does not seem to have anything to do with us personally. We realize that anyone would have gotten the same answer. Contrast that to the experience of talking with someone who does not give us an immediate and absolute answer, but rather joins with us in the search for what will be the right answer for us. Such discussions involve probing the details of the situation, trying to see one's own motives more clearly, looking for additional courses of action that might have been neglected, and searching for an answer that reconciles the various moral challenges we experience in the situation. Often the participants are not primarily concerned with determining what is the moral minimum that anyone must do in the situation, but rather with figuring out what is the morally appropriate course of action for us as unique individuals to do. This may well involve more than what is minimally necessary.

WHAT TO EXPECT FROM A MORAL THEORY

The Power of Theory

Theories attract and fascinate us. The extent to which they ultimately satisfy us as well depends at least in part on our expectations of a moral theory. What do we think moral theories are able to do? Our expectations center on five areas.

Description and Explanation

Theories help us to understand how things actually work, how apparently diverse elements fit together into a single whole. Moral theories are no exception to this general rule. They help us to understand the ways in which people structure their lives, the ways in which their diverse actions fit together into a coherent whole. These theories are primarily *descriptive* in character, that is, they focus on describing how people actually act and thus on understanding the underlying coherence of their actions.

In the next chapter, we will see one example of such a theory—descriptive ethical relativism. In Chapter 3, we will examine another example of this type of theory—descriptive psychological egoism, which maintains that people always act in their own self-interest. In Chapter 10, we will consider two contemporary descriptive theories that aim to increase our understanding of moral development: Lawrence Kohlberg's cognitive-developmental model and Carol Gilligan's account of female moral development. Other descriptive accounts are structured in terms of narratives about individual lives. For example, Robert Bellah and colleagues' *Habits of the Heart: Individualism and Commitment in American Life* describes and helps explain the moral interplay between the strong current of individualism in American life and the difficulty of developing an adequate language of commitment in our society. Robert Coles, a child psychiatrist at Harvard Medical School, has written with particular insight into the moral lives of children in many of his works, including his *Children of Crisis* and most explicitly in his *The Moral Life of Children*.

Strength

When Captain James Stockdale was shot down over North Vietnam and taken prisoner, he began three years of hell. He was tortured frequently and ruthlessly in an attempt to get him to confess to war crimes against the Vietnamese people and to collaborate with the enemy. (Because he was the senior officer in captivity, he was the commanding officer of all the American prisoners of war in North Vietnam; a confession from him would have been a tremendous public relations coup for his captors.) He spent months in solitary confinement, and throughout his ordeal one of his principal sources of strength was the Roman Stoic philosophers, especially Epictetus. Their philosophy provided him with wisdom and solace in a time of desperate need. As such, Stockdale was simply continuing a long tradition, beginning with Plato's *Apology* and immortalized in Boethius' *The Consolations of Philosophy*, of turning to philosophy in times of adversity to find comfort and moral security.

Critique

Moral theories also help us to see moral blind spots, both our own and those of other people. For example, I was once working out an example of what Marx meant by the alienation of capitalist society by writing about education as a commodity. In the course of the article, I found myself seeing grades in a new light. They are, I realized, like money. Part of the alienation we find in societies like our own arises when people work simply for the sake of money, not caring about the value of the job they do or the quality of the product they produce. They work only in order to be paid. Similarly, part of the alienation of education occurs when people start working only for the grades themselves rather than for anything inherently meaningful or interesting in the work itself.

As I began to play with the example, I also started to reflect on the curve in grading and began to see a moral dimension to the curve that I had not appreciated before. When grades in a class are curved in such a way that a certain percentage of the class must receive *A*s, *B*s, *C*s, *D*s, and *F*s, we set up a competitive model of learning in which one person's progress is necessarily bought at the price of someone else's (relative) failure. In other words, if you are a student in a course with such a curve, it is not in your best interest to have your fellow students learn well. Indeed, there are two ways in which you can improve your own grade: Either score higher on your own exams, or else see to it that your classmates score lower on their exams! It is far preferable, from a moral point of view, to establish in the classroom a model that permits all students to do well (if they are able to do so) and that encourages cooperation rather than competition in learning.

New Possibilities

One of the most striking characteristics of the twentieth century, one that will undoubtedly be carried over into the next century, is the sheer amount of *newness* in our lives. We are continually confronted with new problems and new possibilities. Good theories work to unveil new possibilities for us and to offer solutions to new problems.

Consider the perplexities posed by advances in reproductive medicine. It is now possible for a woman to have one of her eggs fertilized outside her body and then implanted in another woman for the period of the pregnancy and birth. Who, then, would be the mother? Genetically, the baby has nothing in common with the woman who gives birth to her or him. On the other hand, the fetus has not spent any time at all in the womb of the woman from whose egg it sprang. Developments such as these force us to develop our theories in two ways. First, when disagreements arise and turn into court cases, we must reflect on the rights of the various parties. Second, even when no disputes occur, we need to reflect on our notion of a family. What is the source of its coherence? What does it mean, for example, to be a mother? Is it a genetic concept, a social one, or some combination of both?

Wonder

Aristotle claimed that philosophy begins in wonder, and there has always been a dimension to philosophy that values it as an activity done for its own sake. Philosophy done in this way is pursued for its own sake, for the sheer joy of discovery and exploration.

All of us must determine what we as individuals expect moral theories to do and then use these expectations as a focus for our investigations of the theories presented in the following chapters.

Ethics and Moral Health

Let me conclude with an invitation. We have seen some of the ways in which ethics is concerned with moral health. In the following chapters, we shall consider some of the major theories that have been advanced to help us understand what the morally good life is like. I invite you to approach this in the same spirit in which you might approach the study of nutrition. Most of us want to live a healthier life, even if we don't always want to eat in the ways necessary to achieve this end. Similarly, most of us want to live a morally better life, but we may also be reluctant to do what is necessary to achieve this. Yet in both cases we often encounter pleasant surprises, discovering that there is a greater overlap between what is good and what is ultimately enjoyable than we suspected. Just as we are sometimes surprised that something can taste great and still be good for us, so we may be pleasantly surprised to discover that there is joy in doing the right thing.

And in both cases we discover that there is no unanimity on how we can achieve health. There are conflicting theories, and all of them contribute in varying degrees to our understanding how to live a healthy life. Similarly, the various theories discussed throughout the rest of this book help us to understand how to live a good life, but none of them provides the single and exhaustive answer to our questions. That's hardly surprising because the moral life is no less complex than the life of the body. Yet despite the fact that none of these theories provides the complete answer, each does provide a part of the answer.

There is a final point in our comparison between nutrition and ethics. In the last analysis, no matter how much we know about nutrition, it can make no difference if we don't act on that knowledge. Similarly, our knowledge of moral theories will be of little benefit to us unless we are willing to incorporate it into our own lives. This book cannot make that decision for any of us. It can only provide knowledge and insights that will be useful if we decide to live a moral life. All of us must decide individually the extent to which we want to do so or not. The invitation of this book is a simple one: Take the insights offered by the theories presented in the following chapters and use them in making your own life a better one. Use them in your own quest for a better life.

DISCUSSION QUESTIONS

1. Imagine that you are a hospital administrator and that you have been asked to set up an ethics committee in the hospital. The committee will deal with moral dilemmas that may confront hospital staff and advise in establishing ethical guidelines for the treatment of patients. (a) What kind of persons would you look for to fill this position? What values would you want them to hold? What types of moral sensitivity would you be looking for? (b) What basic moral principles would you advise the committee to follow?

2. Imagine that you have been charged with the same task described in question 1, but this time for an advertising agency instead of a hospital. What would the differences be? If there are any differences, what conclusions would you draw about the way we define the moral ballpark?

3. What are your own deepest moral values? What moral qualities do you look for in other people as well as in yourself? Are these values that you think everyone shares, or are some of your values ones that you feel are not always observed by our culture as a whole? How have your values changed, if at all? What influenced their development?

4. A friend asks you to pick out a tie for him to wear at a social occasion. Is this a moral issue? Why or why not? If you refuse, is that immoral, or just rude? If you pick out the wrong tie (one that causes him shame or great embarrassment in public), is that immoral, or just a mistake? Does

it make a difference if you pick out the wrong tie intentionally or accidentally? The same friend asks you to transport some merchandise across state lines so that he can avoid paying sales tax on it. Is this a moral issue? Why or why not?

5. When (under what circumstances) is it right to tell a lie? Give some examples from everyday life. What does your answer reveal about the scope (or relevance) of morality in general?

6. A few years ago, an undergraduate student from Rutgers published *Cheating 101,* a guidebook to help students learn how to cheat. What moral issues do you see associated with publishing such a book? Should the campus bookstore carry it? What or why not? Should the campus newspaper carry advertisements for the book? Similarly, should the campus newspaper carry advertisements for companies that will write students' research papers for them? Again, what are the relevant moral considerations here? Are these issues in the moral ballpark? Why or why not?

8. What is the moral issue that you are most undecided about? Describe the pros and cons in regard to this issue. How do you go about arriving at a decision when it is unavoidable?

9. We have suggested that ethics is about moral health. When you think of a morally healthful life, what sort of a life do you imagine? What would be some examples of lives that (at least in some respect) are not morally healthy? Give examples from your own experience.

10. When asked to explain his batting technique, Yankee catcher Yogi Berra said, "Just watch me do it." To what extent is this statement true of morality as well? Can we convey morality to others or learn it by following someone's example? Or must we teach it to ourselves?

BIBLIOGRAPHICAL ESSAY

There are a number of other good **introductions to ethics** that present this some of this same material in other ways. Among the best are James Rachels, *The Elements of Moral Philosophy,* 3rd ed. (New York: McGraw-Hill, 2002); Louis Pojman, *Ethics: Discovering Right and Wrong,* 4th ed. (Belmont, CA: Wadsworth, 2002) and his anthology, *Ethical Theory: Classical and Contemporary Readings,* 3rd ed. (Belmont, CA: Wadsworth, 1997); and J. L. Mackie, *Ethics: Inventing Right and Wrong* (Harmondsworth, UK: Penguin Books, 1977). For a short but exceptionally nuanced view of the place of ethics in contemporary thought (including the social sciences and the humanities), see Frederick A. Olafson, *Ethics and Twentieth Century Thought* (Englewood Cliffs, NJ: Prentice-Hall, 1973). For an excellent introductory approach that emphasizes moral realism and the development of moral sensitivity, see David McNaughton, *Moral Vision: An Introduction to Ethics* (Oxford: Blackwell, 1988).

Several excellent **reference works** in ethics may be helpful to those who wish to pursue the ideas presented in this book further. Among the most helpful are the excellent *Encyclopedia of Ethics,* edited by Lawrence and Charlotte Becker (New York: Garland Press, 1992); the Beckers' *Encyclopedia* has articles covering virtually all the major topics in ethics and has just appeared in a third edition. Also see Peter Singer, ed., *A Companion to Ethics,* (Oxford: Blackwell, 1991); Robert L. Arrington, ed., *A Companion to the Philosophers* (Oxford: Blackwell, 1999); Hugh LaFollette, ed., *The Blackwell Guide to Ethical Theory* (Oxford: Blackwell, 2000); and R. G. Frey and Christopher Heath Wellman, eds., *Companion to Applied Ethics* (Oxford: Blackwell, 2002). Also see Steven Darwall, *Philosophical Ethics* (Boulder, CO: Westview Press, 1998); Stephen L. Darwall, Allan Gibbard, and Peter Railton, eds., *Moral Discourse and Practice: Some Philosophic Approaches* (New York: Oxford University Press, 1995). Also see the series of anthologies edited by Steven Darwall on *Consequentialism*; *Contractarianism, Contractualism*; *Deontology*; and *Virtue Ethics* (all published by Blackwell in 2002). For three philosophers representing three different moral traditions discussed in this book, see Marcia Baron, Philip Pettit, and Michael Slote, *Ethical Theory: For and Against: Consequences, Maxims, and Virtues* (Oxford: Blackwell, 1999). Several **histories of ethics** are also available. Vernon Bourke, S.J.'s *A History of Ethics* (Garden City, NJ: Doubleday, 1968) provides a solid, reliable historical guide. Alasdair MacIntyre's *A Short History of Ethics,* 2nd ed (South Bend, IN: University of Notre Dame Press, 1998) is more tendentious and insightful. For a brief survey of contemporary Anglo-American ethical theories, see Mary Warnock, *Ethics since 1900,* 2nd ed. (Oxford: Oxford University Press, 1966) and G. J. Warnock, *Contemporary Moral Philosophy* (New York: St. Martin's Press, 1967). Frederick A. Olafson's *Principles and Persons: An Ethical Interpretation of Existentialism* (Baltimore, MD: The Johns Hopkins Press, 1967) is an exceptionally insightful treatment of existentialist ethics. Among the anthologies in this area, see J. B. Schneewind, *Moral Philosophy from Montaigne to Kant,* 2 vols. (Cambridge: Cambridge University Press, 1990) and Michael Wagner, *An Historical Introduction to Moral Philosophy* (Englewood Cliffs, NJ: Prentice-Hall, 1990).

On the **definition of the moral point of view,** see Paul Taylor's "On Taking the Moral Point of View," *Midwest Studies in Philosophy* 3 (1978): 35–61 which argues that six characteristics are necessary for a standard or rule to be a moral one: (1) generality, (2) universality, (3) priority, (4) disinterestedness, (5) publicity, and (6) substantive impartiality. Gerald Wallace and A. D. M. Walker's excellent anthology, *The Definition of Morality* (London: Methuen, 1970) contains reprints of important papers on the definition and limits of morality by Alasdair MacIntyre, William Frankena, Neil Cooper, Peter Strawson, Philippa Foot, Kurt Baier, G. E. M. Anscombe, David Gauthier, and others. For a more detailed presentation of Baier's views, see Kurt Baier, *The Moral Point of View* (Ithaca, NY: Cornell University Press, 1958). For a strong defense of the rationality of the moral life, see Bernard Gert, *Morality: A New Justification of Moral Rules* (New York: Oxford, 1988). For a vigorous defense of the claim that the moral point of view is impartial, see Thomas Nagel, *Equality and Partiality* (New York: Oxford, 1991). Josiah Royce's characterization of the moral insight is found in his *The Religious Aspects of Philosophy* (Boston: Houghton Mifflin, 1885), reprinted in part in Sommers and Sommers, *Vice and Virtue in Everyday Life,* 3rd ed. (San Diego, CA: Harcourt, Brace and Jovanovich, 1992).

For a sustained argument that the **moral ballpark** is smaller than often believed, see Peter A. French, *The Scope of Morality* (Minneapolis: University of Minnesota Press, 1979). Shelly Kagan's *The Limits of Morality* (Oxford: Clarendon Press, 1989) provides a forceful critique of those who see morality's demands as very limited. For an excellent discussion of the notion of **moral health,** see Martha Nussbaum, "Aristotle on Emotions and Ethical Health," in her *The Therapy of Desire* (Princeton: Princeton University Press, 1994), pp. 78–103.

CHAPTER
2

Understanding the Diversity of Moral Beliefs: Relativism, Absolutism, and Pluralism

"The era of moral relativism," Mayor Rudy Giuliani told the U.N. General Assembly in the aftermath of the World Trade Center attacks, "between those who practice or condone terrorism, and those nations who stand up against it, must end." (*New York Times,* October 2, 2001, p. A1)

Cultures clash, and when they do we must decide how to deal with the resulting conflict. **Ethical absolutists maintain that there is a single standard in terms of assessments can be made, and that standard is usually their own.** In a clash of cultures, they often see the other culture as simply wrong insofar as it deviates from their own. **Ethical relativists see each culture as an island unto itself, right in its own world, and they deny that there is any overarching standard in terms of which conflicting cultures can be judged.** This chapter seeks to stake out a middle ground for dealing with moral conflicts, one which retains the legitimacy of cross-cultural judgments (something the absolutists are correct in believing) but one which does not claim that we necessarily have a monopoly on the truth. **Ethical pluralism acknowledges that cultures can legitimately pass judgments on one another and encourages us to listen to what other cultures say about us as well as what we say about them.** In addition, it encourages toleration when possible, recognizing that cultures may legitimately differ,

27

even on the most important of issues. Finally, it shows that there are situations where we must simply stand up to evil and oppose it, and in this respect it differs from ethical relativism. Wisdom consists in knowing where to draw the line between the tolerable and the intolerable.

The events of September 11, 2001 provide a powerful example of the clash of cultures. In Chapter 3 we will be looking at Islam, including its notion of *jihad*, so some of the issues raised by the September 11 attacks can be postponed until that chapter. Even before looking in detail at Islam, however, we can see the way in which the attacks of September 11 highlight this chapter's central issue of deep, and sometimes fundamental disagreements in our world. The question we face is how we should deal with those disagreements. In some cases, we might adopt a "live and let live" attitude, acknowledging differences but not passing judgment on them. (This position is typical of the ethical relativist.) Some cultures practice polygamy, for example, but we seldom single them out for criticism. In other cases, we may criticize practices outside our borders, sometimes even sharply. When the Taliban destroyed the giant statues of the Buddha that had watched over the Bamiyan valley in Afghanistan for over fifteen centuries, claiming that the images were offensive to Islam, leaders from many countries spoke out against their actions. The Taliban destroyed many works of art in museums as well, especially the Kabul Museum, which saw over three-quarters of its collection destroyed. No one, however, actively intervened by using force to prevent the destruction of the Buddhas, although several museums in the West offered to buy the works of art (including the giant Buddhas) and remove them to safer locations.

In some cases, active intervention using force may be judged necessary. Sometimes this occurs in response to direct attacks, as did the U.S. intervention in WW II after Pearl Harbor; at other times, we intervene in response to large-scale atrocities that do not affect us directly but are so horrible that it becomes morally unacceptable to stand by and allow them to occur, as was the case in the Balkans. The practice of "ethnic cleansing" by the Serbian forces to eliminate Muslims from "their" territory motivated the U.S. to send peacekeepers to Bosnia. Both absolutists and pluralists might condone such interventions, but there are two important differences between them on this issue. Absolutists are more likely to find a greater number of such situations that justify intervention, and absolutists are less likely to reflect on ways in which they might have contributed to the situation. Pluralists, in contrast, consider intervention as a last resort, are much more interested in exploring ways of resolving the situation that acknowledge to some extent the interests of all the involved parties, and are willing to examine ways in which their own actions (perhaps inadvertently) contributed to the conflict.

In this chapter, we will be looking at these three possible responses to moral conflicts (relativism, absolutism, and pluralism), assessing their respective merits and seeing how they are applied to actual cases. In doing so, we will be looking at two kinds of moral conflict. First, we will be attempting to understand how we can best deal with concrete moral conflicts. Second, we will be looking at how we can best understand the conflict of moral theories. In the course of this book, we will be looking at a number of those theories. How are we to understand their conflict? Are we to say one is right and all the others wrong, as the absolutist is inclined to do? This response seems improbable to me, since these theories have been developed by good and thoughtful people and have stood the test of time. Are we to say that somehow they are all right? This too seems improbable, since the theories appear to contradict one another in important instances. The pluralist's response to this type of moral conflict is to suggest that there is much of value in moral diversity and yet to acknowledge that there are instances in which we must say that a given moral theory falls short of the mark. The entirety of this book is intended as a pluralist's answer to the question of how this moral conflict is to be resolved on the level of theory.

TWO LEVELS OF MORAL CONFLICT

Concrete Conflicts

One of the most controversial cases of moral conflict in recent years has been the issue of forced clitoridectomies. Yael Tamir describes it as "an extremely painful, traumatizing mutilation of young girls that leaves them permanently disfigured and deprived of sexual enjoyment." The procedure is often done in unsanitary conditions and without the use of any kind of anesthesia; in some cases, at least, it is done against the will of the young girls. This surgical procedure is widely practiced in a number of countries in the Middle East and Africa.

This is not an issue that we can simply ignore, saying that it happens in other cultures and that, at least for reasons of respecting national sovereignty, we certainly do not want to intervene in those cultures to stop such practices. But it does become an issue within the United States in two ways. First, some women ask for asylum in this country to avoid forced clitoridectomy, either for themselves or for their daughters. In 1994, an immigration judge in Oregon prevented a Nigerian woman from being deported because she claimed that she would be subjected to involuntary genital mutilation if sent back to Nigeria (in Matter of Oluloro, A72-147-491, March 23, 1994). Many similar cases have followed, making the issue unavoidable. Second, in some cases immigrant families in the United States continue to engage in this practice in a clandestine way, sometimes importing circumcisers from their home country for this expressed purpose.

Consider a second example. In the heartland of America, the bridegrooms thought it was a joyous occasion—not just a wedding, but a double wedding in which the brides were sisters. The men, refugees from persecution in their native Iraq, felt that they were indeed fortunate. Latif Al-Hussani and Majed Al–Tamimy had fled Iraq to a series of refugee camps in Saudi Arabia.

In one of those camps, the two men came to know Salim, the father of their future brides. The acquaintance was rekindled when Latif and Majed met Salim in Lincoln, Nebraska, where they had all resettled. Eventually the two men asked Salim for permission to marry his two daughters. The marriage, a religious ceremony, took place at home; no one bothered with a civil ceremony. Shortly after the wedding, one of the newly married wives ran away, apparently to a boyfriend's house. Her husband and her father went to the police together to report her disappearance. Soon both husbands and the father were in jail, and the mother of the girls was charged as well. The girls themselves were placed in protective custody. They were thirteen and fourteen years old.

The two men, twenty-eight and thirty-two years old, maintained that they didn't know that they had done anything wrong. Would they have gone to the police, they ask, if they thought they had done something illegal? In Iraq, it is legal for thirteen-year-old girls to marry; and in the rural part of Iraq where these men grew up, it was not uncommon. The men thought that by asking the father's permission, they were following the proper form. But marriages of girls that age, although once legal in America, are now against the law. Indeed, the consummation of such a marriage counts as statutory rape. Both new husbands were in fact charged with statutory rape, and the girls' parents were both charged with contributing to the delinquency of a minor.

How do we react to such situations? Something that is legally and morally permissible in one culture is illegal and immoral in another. Who is right? Pursuing this question not only brings us directly to the heart of the issue of ethical relativism; it also raises a core issue in multiculturalism. Given a multiplicity of cultures, each with somewhat different moral standards, how do we understand the relationship among them? **Ethical relativists** would say that each culture is right unto itself, so such practices would be morally permissible in some countries and morally wrong in the United States. But the difficulty with this position is that cultures often overlap, as in the case of women seeking asylum. Conversely, would we want to say that it is morally permissible for Americans in other cultures to engage in these practices? How do we adjudicate moral differences when such overlaps occur? **Ethical absolutists,** in contrast, maintain that there is a single moral truth in terms of which all cultures and individuals are to be judged. This absolute moral standard usually happens to coincide with the absolutist's own personal beliefs. American absolutists, for example, would maintain that not only are such practices illegal here, but they should be banned everywhere. The moral issue, in their minds, would be clear: this is an extreme form of child abuse.

Ethical pluralism attempts to find some middle ground here in two ways. First, unlike both absolutists and relativists, ethical pluralists would be interested in looking at the practices in our own culture that may raise similar questions, such as tattooing, body piercing, and "cosmetic" surgery. The difference between the pluralist and the absolutist is that the pluralist is much less likely to assume a "holier than thou" attitude, less likely to use examples such as this just to acquire the moral high ground. Second, ethical pluralists may well be open to examining the goals of the practice and, if those goals appear legitimate, exploring other ways in which they could be attained without the associated harms of clitoridectomy. Whether there are such legitimate goals in this case remains unclear.

Conflicting Theories

Our opening example posed the issue of moral conflict in terms of a specific moral incident, but another type of conflict is equally relevant here: the conflict between opposing moral theories. Much of the rest of this book is devoted to a consideration of various moral theories, each of which claims to provide the best account of the moral life and each of which claims to exclude all the others. In Chapter 3, we will discuss **divine command theories** of morality that maintain that we ought to do whatever God wills. In our opening example, we are still left with a conflict. Not only do Muslim and Christian differ on what God wills in this type of situation, but also believers differ among themselves about its acceptability. In each faith community there might be disagreement about how to understand and to interpret God's command. For example, in the marriage case being discussed here, the men involved were from rural Iraq, where this practice is more acceptable than it is in the cities. Conversely, it was not too many decades ago that rural Mormons in our own country accepted and practiced polygamy, and there was no strictly enforced minimum age of sixteen for girls to be married. **Ethical egoism,** which we shall consider in Chapter 4, tells us that each person ought to act selfishly, seeking to maximize self-interest. The ethical egoist would thus recommend to all parties in the situation that they should act in the way that will best promote their own interests. There are, as we shall see, several difficulties with such a recommendation, not the least of which is that self-interest may dictate that the various parties act in conflicting ways. **Utilitarians,** as we shall see in Chapter 5, will argue that we should always act in such a way as to produce the greatest overall amount of pleasure or happiness. Faced with the question of whether such marriages should be allowed, a utilitarian would look at the potential benefits and drawbacks for society as a whole. **Immanuel Kant,** whose ethics is discussed in Chapter 6, maintains that we ought always to act in ways that respect the autonomy and dignity of ourselves and of other persons. A Kantian might very well conclude that such marriages involve using the girls as a mere means because girls in such situations are often deprived of the opportunity to decide for themselves whether to accept or reject the request for marriage. Furthermore, they may simply be too young to exercise informed consent, even if it was asked of them. **Rights** theorists contend that there is a certain universal moral minimum with which all people must comply. In recent decades, there has been a growing awareness among rights theorists that children have rights by virtue of the vulnerability of their position in society. Most rights theorists would see the arranged marriages of such young girls as violating those rights. Human rights activists have taken a strong position against female genital mutilation. Finally, **virtue** theorists concentrate on issues of character, on the role of virtues and vices in the moral life. They would have little to say directly about the morality of this practice, but they would certainly be very interested in the issues of character and relationship that it raises.

Thus we see that there are two levels of moral disagreement that we must explain: moral conflicts about specific cases and moral conflicts among competing moral theories. Ethics needs a way of making sense out of both of these types of moral conflict. For reasons that will be shown later in this chapter, neither relativism nor absolutism succeeds in adequately making sense out of either of these levels of conflict. The relativists say, in effect, that everyone is right, but this position is of little help in resolving cases where cultures overlap. Nor does this provide a foundation for opposing flagrantly bad practices in other cultures. The absolutists, on the other hand, find it easy to say that others are wrong, but they are often unable to understand and appreciate the legitimate moral diversity of cultures. What we need is a middle ground between relativism and absolutism, and that middle ground is ethical pluralism.

The Fundamental Intuitions of Ethical Pluralism

This book arises out of my own conviction that neither relativism nor absolutism tells the whole story about moral conflict, either on the level of specific moral problems or on the level of moral theory. There is, I think, **a middle ground between relativism and absolutism that combines the attractions of both without their attendant liabilities.** We can call this middle ground **ethical pluralism.** It recognizes the importance of understanding other cultures and respecting their autonomy, yet it also recognizes that we live in an increasingly shared world in which moral differences often cannot simply be left unresolved. It also recognizes that if cultures are to be subject to moral judgment, it may well be *our own* culture that is found morally wanting. In developing this account of ethical pluralism, I am trying to do justice to several basic intuitions about the moral life:

- **The Principle of Understanding:** Whenever we look at the moral practices of another culture, we must seek to understand the meaning of those practices within the culture as a whole. Understanding does not necessarily imply approval.

- **The Principle of Tolerance:** It is important, whenever possible, to leave different cultures as much room as possible to pursue their own moral vision, even though it might be quite different from our own. Tolerance is an important value for pluralists, but not the highest value.

- **The Principle of Standing Up against Evil:** It is also important, at least in cases of egregious moral wrongdoing, to speak out against offenses wherever they may occur, whether in one's own culture or another culture. Here pluralism differs from ethical relativism.

- **The Principle of Fallibility:** When examining moral differences between ourselves and other cultures, we may sometimes discover it is we, not they, who are found morally wanting. Here pluralism differs from moral absolutism.

Neither ethical relativism nor ethical absolutism, at least in its simpler versions, captures all of these principles. Ethical pluralism, as developed in this book, in fact attempts to incorporate all four of these intuitions. Before looking at pluralism, however, let's take a closer look at relativism and then at absolutism.

ETHICAL RELATIVISM

We all have heard the old saying, "When in Rome, do as the Romans do." Yet what do you do if you are an American executive of a multinational corporation in Rome and income tax time comes around? Many Italians consider an income tax report to be like an opening bid in what often prove to be complex and challenging negotiations. It would be silly to give away your entire hand on the first bid, so typically much is initially concealed. Nor would the Italian government expect complete honesty at this stage. To an Italian, this does not feel like cheating; it is simply the way business is done. Yet to an American businessperson, to file a false tax return is to cheat. When in Rome, what does the American executive do?

Nor, obviously, is this just an issue about Rome. What should American business people with factories in South Africa have done during the decades of apartheid? When in South Africa, did one do as the Afrikaners did and exploit the native population? Should one have actively participated in the oppression, or perhaps just benefited economically from it? Or, to shift locations, how should the American businessperson behave in countries in which a bribe, *la mordida* or the *baksheesh,* is considered a normal and acceptable part of almost any business deal? How are we to act in such situations, especially given the moral restrictions against bribes in our own culture?

Nor are these questions faced just outside of our own country. Consider our opening example of arranged marriages of young girls. Or think of the problems faced by our State Department when a man from Saudi Arabia applies for a visa for himself and his wives. Polygamy is forbidden morally as well as legally in our country, but it is both legally and morally acceptable in Saudi Arabia. Do we issue visas for all his wives, for just one (if so, who chooses which one), or for none? Indeed, do we issue him a visa even though he is a polygamist? Even closer to home, how would we have dealt with polygamous Mormon families in the United States a hundred years ago when this was still sanctioned by some of their leaders? More recently, consider the question of the religious use of peyote in Native American religious ceremonies. Should the moral standards of the dominant white society in the United States override the moral and religious standards of the indigenous population?

These are difficult questions, and we will not be able to answer them all in this chapter. However, we will answer that part of the questions that relates to the issue of ethical relativism. **Ethical relativism** is a doctrine that is expressed (inadequately and misleadingly) in adages such as, "When in Rome, do as the Romans do." More precisely, **ethical relativism is the belief that moral values are relative to a particular culture and cannot be judged outside that culture.** In examining ethical relativism, we shall be concerned with understanding what makes it attractive to many of us because it is a doctrine that many people accept, or at least *think* they accept. Yet we shall also ask whether ethical relativism actually succeeds in delivering on its promises, in providing the things that seem to make it attractive. Then we shall look at the standard alternative, moral absolutism, and examine some of its strengths and weaknesses. Finally, we shall suggest a middle ground between relativism and absolutism, one that combines the attractions of both without their liabilities.

The Attractions of Ethical Relativism

Ethical relativism is an attractive doctrine, and in this section we shall see some of the reasons *why* it is attractive. People are drawn to it for any of several possible reasons. First, ethical relativism seems to encourage moral tolerance and understanding, attitudes that most of us find highly desirable. Second, it seems to fit the facts about moral diversity much better than does any alternative. Third, it seems that no one has produced a moral system that has commanded universal assent, and it seems unlikely that anyone will in the foreseeable future. Fourth, some people hold that everything is relative, and for them ethical relativism is just a corollary of a more general relativism about all beliefs. Finally, we often feel that we have no right to make moral judgments about other people because we ourselves have led far from perfect moral lives. Ethical relativism is often a way of saying, "Don't judge me, and I won't judge you." Let's examine each of these lines of argument.

The Need for Tolerance and Understanding

Ethical relativism is initially attractive to many of us because it offers the promise of *tolerance* and *understanding,* attitudes that most of us value highly. All too often in the past, we have rushed to judgment, letting condemnation eliminate the need for tolerance, allowing superiority to substitute for understanding. Ethical relativism holds the promise of a tolerant attitude of "live and let live."

Ethical absolutism, on the other hand, can be a morally intolerant and insensitive position, one that is all too willing to condemn what it does not understand. This argument is sometimes placed within the context of the history of anthropology, which is one of the disciplines most directly involved with issues of cultural relativism. Early anthropology, so the argument goes, was absolutist, measuring the entire world in terms of its own standards and generally finding the rest of the world lacking. So, for example, anthropologists would often refer to the peoples they studied as "barbarians" or "primitive societies." Anthropology made progress, they contend, when it moved toward a more relativistic stance, when it recognized that societies that are different from our own are not necessarily primitive or inferior. Indeed, *we* often appear barbaric to these so-called primitive societies. (When Europeans first reached China, the Chinese were appalled at the Westerners' lack of cleanliness and manners; to the Chinese, it was the Europeans who were the barbarians.) Each society, relativism suggests, should be judged in terms of its own standards rather than be judged in terms of our ethnocentric expectations. We shall return to this comparison with anthropology in the final part of this chapter, and at that point I want again to argue in favor of a third possibility. We shall consider some of the problems with this argument about tolerance shortly.

Oddly, given that relativism is frequently associated with a plea for greater understanding as well as tolerance, it is often associated with a belief that we can *not* understand other cultures. Indeed, it is often the conclusion of an argument that begins with a premise such as, "We can never (fully) understand another culture." The conclusion then drawn is that we ought not to judge any other culture, and the implicit premise is, "We ought not to judge anything that we do not (fully) understand." We will discuss the merits of this argument later.

The Fact of Moral Diversity

Initially, one of the most attractive aspects of the relativist's position is that it gives adequate recognition to moral diversity. Different cultures apparently have such widely divergent moral codes that the notion of a universal morality of any kind simply seems to fly in the face of the facts: There is radical moral diversity in our world. Anthropology seems to provide plenty of evidence for this claim. Indeed, even individuals within a single society seem to exhibit great diversity in the range of moral values they accept. The only adequate way of recognizing this fact, according to the relativist, is by accepting ethical relativism.

The Lack of a Plausible Alternative

Relativists have another argument at their disposal, one that seems to supplement and strengthen the first argument. They issue the following challenge: "If you claim that ethical relativism is mistaken, then show me a plausible alternative. Show me a set of moral values that everyone accepts, or even that everyone plausibly could accept." In other words, they are suggesting, we may come to agree with ethical relativism by default: No alternative moral system has really managed to carry the day. Not only, they continue, is this true of the world at large, but it is also true of moral philosophers. These are the people whom one would expect to agree on basic moral principles, if anyone could, because they spend their lives thinking and talking and writing about such things. Yet when we look at the opinions of many moral philosophers today, we see that there is a tremendous amount of disagreement, even about fundamental moral values. Finally, relativists argue, this situation is in sharp contrast to science and medicine. Certainly there is disagreement in those areas, but there is also widespread agreement on many fundamentals. Because morality has never exhibited that kind of consensus, it is pointless to expect that it ever will.

The Relativity of All Understanding

There is yet a fourth route that leads to ethical relativism, and it begins with the conviction that *all* knowledge and understanding are relative. In its strongest version, this position claims that all truth, even in the natural sciences, is relative to the culture and conceptual framework within which it is expressed. Other cultures may develop quite different ways of understanding and controlling the natural world. In some cultures, magic occupies the place that science occupies in our society. Strong relativists would claim that we cannot say that science is right and magic wrong; rather, each is appropriate to, and to be judged only in terms of, the culture in which it is situated.

Other, more moderate versions of relativism make a slightly more modest claim. They say that *the meaning of human behavior is always relative to the culture in which it occurs.* In one desert society, it is a sign of friendship and respect to spit at the foot of another person; such behavior means something quite different in our own society. In some cultures, eating dogs is as acceptable as eating cows is in Western societies. In our society, we consider killing dogs cruelty to animals; in India, killing cows is a sacrilege. The meaning of the act is different, depending on the society. In India, how we act toward cows is a *religious* issue, and this is what gives it special meaning. In our country, how we treat dogs is a matter of how we relate to pets, which is almost an issue of *friendship.* More generally, the meaning of any action depends on the cultural context within which it is performed. Consequently, the relativist argues, the moral dimension of our actions is similarly dependent on cultural context for meaning.

Don't Cast the First Stone

There is a final consideration that often weighs in favor of relativism, and it centers on doubts about whether we have the *right* to judge other people. Often people are hesitant to pass judgment on someone else's actions because they feel that, if they had been in that same situation, they might have done the same thing. Because few people like to condemn themselves, it is just a short step to saying that they should not condemn other people, either. In one sense, this is a self-protective strategy: If I don't condemn other people, then they can't condemn me. Yet in another sense, it is a position that emphasizes consistency: If I am unwilling to judge myself harshly, then I forfeit my right to judge others in such a manner. In yet a third sense, it is a position of humility, recalling Jesus's injunction, "Let one who is without sin cast the first stone." Whatever way one takes it, it is a position that denies that one has a *right* to pass judgment on other people. It is, moreover, a position that becomes even more plausible in times when there seems to be fundamental disagreement about basic moral values. "Who," my students often ask, "am I to judge someone else?" We will discuss possible answers to this important question later.

The Definition of Ethical Relativism

We've begun to consider some of the reasons why ethical relativism is attractive, but we haven't really looked closely at what ethical relativism maintains. As we shall see, there are several different positions that are often lumped together under this single name. It will be important to distinguish among these various positions because some may prove to be true, whereas others turn out to be false.

Descriptive and Normative Ethical Relativism

There is a sense in which there is little disagreement among philosophers about the truth of one type of ethical relativism. It is clear, simply as a matter of fact, that different people have some different moral beliefs—sometimes radically so. Various societies in the past have engaged in such practices as cannibalism or sacrificing human beings to the gods, and those practices were viewed within those societies as morally acceptable, often even as morally commendable. Indeed, even in our own day, there exist some isolated societies that until recently have approved of such actions.

Simply to state that different people in fact have different moral beliefs, without taking any stand on the rightness or wrongness of those beliefs, is to accept **descriptive ethical relativism.** This is, as I have already implied, a rather uncontroversial claim because it does not in any way commit us to saying that these other moral beliefs are also *correct*. Thus, someone could be a moral absolutist (that is, someone who believes that there is one and only one true morality) and still accept descriptive ethical relativism because the absolutist would simply say that those who do not accept this true moral code are wrong. Descriptive ethical relativism does not entail any beliefs about whether the moral codes of various societies are right or wrong.

The more controversial and interesting position is what we can call **normative ethical relativism.** The normative ethical relativist puts forward a crucial additional claim not found in descriptive ethical relativism, namely, that each moral code is *valid* relative only to the culture in which it exists. Thus, for example, if cannibalism is acceptable according to the moral code of society X, then members of that society are right in permitting their people to practice cannibalism, even though it would not be permissible for people in

TYPES OF ETHICAL RELATIVISM

Descriptive	Claims as a matter of fact that different cultures have different values
Normative	Claims that each culture's values are right for that culture

our society to do so. This is the controversial claim because it suggests that what is right in one culture is not right in another and that members of one culture either should not pass any moral judgments on any other culture or else must endorse the moral judgments of other cultures as right for those cultures. (Because normative ethical relativism is both the interesting and controversial claim and the one that our discussion will center on, when I refer to *relativism* or *ethical relativism* I will mean *normative ethical relativism* unless otherwise noted.)

If normative ethical relativism is correct, then the kind of truth that we find in morality is far different than the kind of truth characteristic of everyday factual knowledge, scientific knowledge, or mathematics. If I know that the Morning Star and the Evening Star are the same celestial body (Venus), then I know that that is true for everyone. If some society believes that they are two different stars, that society is simply wrong. Similarly, many societies in the past have held that the earth is flat, but we would not hesitate today to state that their belief is false. So, too, we can say with assurance that 2 + 2 = 4 absolutely, even if some societies do not believe that to be the case. Those who don't believe it are just mistaken. However, if the normative ethical relativist is correct, we cannot say that intentionally killing innocent human beings is always wrong in the same way because if members of some society believe that sacrificing innocent victims to the gods is a morally good thing to do, then it is not wrong *for them*, according to the normative ethical relativist.

We have now seen one of the basic ambiguities in the claim that morality is relative: It may be either a descriptive or a normative claim. Now we need to get a clearer idea of precisely what we may mean by *ethical relativism*. We can do this by looking more closely at two important questions: What is morality relative *to*, and *what portion* of our morality is relative? We shall see that there are widely divergent answers to these questions.

Relative to What? The Problem of Individuating Cultures

So far, we have presumed that the ethical relativist believes that morality is relative to a particular *culture*. That, however, is no easy notion. What, precisely, do we mean by a culture? Typically, we tend to think of some isolated tribe in New Guinea or some other such secluded place, and this does provide a clear-cut example of another culture that is radically different than our own and that is generally isolated from our own. However, such examples are quickly becoming the exceptions. Few such isolated cultures remain in the world today, and it is likely that their number and degree of isolation will rapidly diminish in the near future. The simple fact of the matter is that most cultures interact with and mutually influence other cultures. In fact, the issue is even more complicated than this because cultures often seem to contain quite a bit of internal diversity.

Consider American culture. We may refer to it as though there were some single culture, but when we look more closely, we uncover a lot of diversity. A generation ago there were many neighborhoods in major cities where one did not need to know English. German, Lithuanian, Polish, Italian, Greek, or any number of other European languages might have sufficed. Were these part of American culture, or should they be seen as part of the culture of their original country? Today Vietnamese, Korean, Tagalog, Cambodian, Laotian, and other Asian and Pacific languages predominate, some in these same neighborhoods. Again, should we see the culture as American or as belonging to another country? We can refer to this as the problem of how we *individuate a culture,* that is, how we draw the lines to separate one culture from another. It's rare, in these days of shifting political systems and mass migrations of people, that cultural boundaries coincide strictly with geographical ones. Furthermore, in an age of increasing mass communication and ever-expanding international trade, individual cultures are less and less likely to remain isolated.

The problem of individuating a culture is by no means an abstract issue created solely by philosophers who enjoy drawing logical distinctions. It is very much a problem of everyday living. Consider the moral conflicts that individuals encounter when they find themselves on the borderline of two such cultures. For instance, imagine that you were teaching grammar school in an area of the Southwest where a number of the students came from Hopi Indian families. When one student doesn't know the answer to a question in grammar school, the teacher often calls on other students until one comes up with the correct answer. Yet Hopi schoolchildren would regard it as an insult to provide the answer when the first student did not know it because they have quite different views on the morality of competition. As a teacher, do you follow the morality of the dominant white group or the morality of the minority Native American group? (Indeed, do we determine which group is "dominant" by sheer numbers or by the power that it has in the political and economic system?) Do we have one culture here or two?

In a similar way, think of the problems encountered by American business people in other countries. In South Africa, for example, until very recently much of the white population supported apartheid; some of the white population and virtually all of the black and mixed-race population oppose it strongly. If we have businesses with branch offices there, whose values do we follow? Our own? The values of the majority of whites? Those of the majority of blacks and a minority of whites? Again, do we have one culture here or two? These are the questions about the individuation of cultures that are faced everyday by people and that directly raise the question of ethical relativism.

From Relativism to Subjectivism

It is easy to see one direction in which this can lead. Some people have taken the question, "What are our moral values relative to?" and given increasingly specific answers to it until they finally conclude that those values are relative to each individual person. If our values are partially shaped by the culture in which we live, are not our own individual values also shaped by more specific factors such as geographical location, period in history, family background, religion, schooling, early childhood experiences, and so forth? Isn't it plausible to believe that if our values are shaped by our culture, they are just as significantly shaped by our individual life histories? Soon we reach the point where, instead of seeing values as relative to a culture, we see them as relative primarily to individual life histories. Those who maintain this position claim that *cultural ethical relativism collapses into ethical subjectivism.* They maintain, in other words, that cultural ethical relativism inevitably leads to a more radical position, **ethical subjectivism,** which claims that **moral values are relative to each unique individual.** People are, as it were, moral islands unto themselves, each individual separate from everyone else. This is the most extreme form of relativism, and today it is often conveyed through a shrug of the shoulders and a "whatever."

One of the reasons given in support of this claim that relativism leads to subjectivism has already been discussed: the difficulty in individuating cultures. The other reason usually given has also been hinted at: A number of individual factors (such as family background, religious training, economic status, and education) seem to be at least as powerful as general cultural factors in shaping an individual's moral beliefs. Yet when our argument is stated in this way, something very interesting starts to emerge. We see that the relativist's claim is at least in part about the *causes* of our moral beliefs. Indeed, as we look more closely, we shall see that the relativist can be making several different claims—one about *understanding* and *judging* moral values, one about the *causes* of those values, one about their *justification,* and one about how to *act.* We will look more closely at this distinction when we discuss the nature of the relativist's claim, but first we must address the question of how much of our morality is relative according to the relativist.

When we claim that morality is relative, our claim is still vague. We have not answered the question of *how much* of morality is relative. This is the question of the *scope* of the relativist's claim. There are at least three ways of defining the scope of relativism. It is important to distinguish among these three because it may well turn out that only one or two of these claims are true.

The Relativity of Behavior

The first thing that the relativist could be saying is that *moral behavior is relative to a particular culture* (or some other aspect of a person's background). This is certainly true in nonmoral areas. In some cultures, for example, the polite way of expressing approval of the dinner is to belch; in our own society, such behavior would be considered ill mannered. Approval would properly be expressed in some other way, such as complimenting the host on the meal. Similarly, spitting at another person's feet is a way of expressing respect in some desert cultures; the same behavior in our culture expresses contempt. Notice that there may be agreement here that it is a good thing to show appreciation of a meal, but the *way* in which that is expressed (that is, the behavior) differs from culture to culture. It seems uncontroversial to say that polite behavior is often relative to a particular culture.

The Relativity of Peripheral Values

The second thing that may be said to be relative is what I shall call *peripheral values*. By this I mean the nonfundamental or somewhat secondary values of a culture. In our own culture, for example, respect for innocent human life is taken to be a fundamental moral value; individual privacy is a less fundamental one; freedom to smoke cigarettes is becoming comparatively peripheral and low level. Here, then, is the second claim that the relativist could be making: *Peripheral values vary from culture to culture.* So, for example, the value of private property may be quite important in one society and of relatively little significance in another. One culture may value monogamy quite strongly, another may endorse polygamy, but both might value the basic family, especially for childrearing, even though they differ in their respective definitions of the family unit.

Of course, there is no clear-cut line that separates low-level values from fundamental ones, and one point of disagreement between two cultures may be precisely whether a particular value should be taken as fundamental or as peripheral. The distinction is unavoidably vague, but nonetheless useful, as we shall now see.

The Relativity of Fundamental Values

Imagine, in discussing ethical relativism, that someone supports the relativist's position by claiming that morally acceptable behavior varies from culture to culture and that, furthermore, moral values such as privacy or monogamy are different in various cultures. You could easily imagine someone replying to this in the following way.

> Yes, I agree that there are these differences among cultures. However, although many things are relative, there are some things that are absolute. Virtually no culture believes in torturing and killing innocent children—and if it does, it is simply wrong in holding that value. There are some values, such as respect for innocent human life, that, though they may be few in number, are not relative. Cultures that do not accept these values are simply wrong.

The person who maintains this position is conceding the first two forms of relativism discussed in this section (the relativity of behavior and the relativity of low-level moral values), but disputing the relativity of fundamental values. There are, as I hope to show, good reasons for rejecting the relativist's claim when it comes to fundamental values.

WHAT IS RELATIVE?

Behavior	How different values are expressed in action varies from one culture to another.
Peripheral values	Secondary or peripheral values vary from one culture to another.
Fundamental values	Basic values vary from one culture to another.

What Kind of Doctrine Is Ethical Relativism?

There is another kind of ambiguity in the relativist's position, one that can cause serious confusion if not brought to light. When relativists say, "Moral values are relative to culture," they may mean several rather different things. Once again, it's necessary to distinguish among these different meanings because one or two of them may be true, whereas the other(s) may be false. For the sake of clarity, I will present this in terms of different versions of the adage, "When in Rome, do as the Romans do." In this adage, "Rome" stands for any culture different than one's own.

Action

The first sense in which ethical relativism may be intended is as a doctrine about action, a doctrine that tells us how to act. Here we see the full and straightforward force of the saying, "When in Rome, do as the Romans do." It tells us to *always act in a way that is consistent with local customs and values.* This in fact turns out to be a guide not only to behaving in other cultures, but also in our own. It says that we should act in a way that is consistent with the moral standards of whatever culture we are in, including our own when we are at home.

As a doctrine of action, relativism is incomplete in three ways. First, it does not tell us how to act when two cultures overlap—an increasingly important issue, as we shall see. Second, it does not tell us *why* we should act in this way. In order to do this, relativism as a doctrine of action usually depends on one of the other following versions of relativism for its justification. Third, it does not provide any leverage to convince the majority to change because by definition whatever the majority believes to be right simply is right.

Understanding

The second claim that the relativist may be making is that *in order to understand a person's values and behavior, we must understand the cultural background out of which they arise.* We must, in other words, understand the Roman's behavior in terms of Roman society. This is a relatively uncontroversial claim, at least in regard to behavior. The meaning of most behavior is embedded in a context of social meanings that at least to some extent vary from one culture to another. If we are to understand what a particular action or value means to a person in another culture, it is often necessary to understand that stock of background meanings that underlie its significance. To fail to do so is often to misunderstand and distort the meaning of the behavior that we observe in another society.

There is an ambiguity in relativism as a doctrine of understanding, and it is one that is important in our assessment of the relativist's claim. When the relativist claims that behavior can be understood only relative to the specific cultural context within which it occurs, it is unclear whether an outsider to the culture can understand the behavior at all. In its **strong version,** this doctrine claims not only that all behavior must be understood relative to the cultural context, but also that the cultural context can be understood only by participants; consequently, outsiders cannot genuinely understand behavior in a society in which they are not participants, and thus they are not entitled to make value judgments about that behavior. In its **weak version,** this doctrine claims that meaning is relative to culture but that outsiders can understand other cultures. This weaker version leaves the door open for dialogue between cultures and for mutual understanding. The stronger version seems to close the door to such dialogue and perhaps even precludes the possibility of anthropology.

Judgment

At this juncture, we encounter another ambiguity within relativism as a doctrine of understanding, and this ambiguity rests on the relation between understanding and judgment. Assuming that behavior must be understood relative to its cultural context, what does this tell us about the moral judgments that we make about the actions and values of other societies? There are three possibilities: Such behavior may not be judged at all by outsiders; it may be judged by outsiders only in relation to the society's own values; it may be judged by outsiders even in relation to values that the society itself does not share. Relativism as a doctrine of judgment maintains that behavior within a society can be judged only by the standards of that society. We should judge Romans only by Roman standards. Again, this has a strong version and a weak version. The **strong version** maintains that only Romans can judge Romans by their own standards; the **weak version** allows anyone in principle to judge Romans as long as he or she employs Roman standards.

Explanation

In arguing in favor of relativism, some people claim to explain the origins of our moral values by showing that *moral values are caused or determined by cultural forces.* This, our fourth possible claim, is equivalent to saying that if you were raised in Rome, you would have the values that the Romans have. The fact that people grew up in a particular culture explains *why* they have the specific values they do. Our own culture determines us to accept particular values, whereas living in another culture would cause us to believe in a different set of values. This is closely related to what philosophers call **determinism,** that is, **the belief that (in this case) our moral values are causally determined.** In contrast to this, some philosophers claim that our values are, at least to some extent, *freely chosen.* They maintain that, although our culture may initially shape our values, as we mature we come to make our own independent choices about what our values will be. This is a version of the dispute between freedom and determinism, which will be discussed in Chapter 4 in our consideration of psychological egoism.

There is little chance that we will be able to unravel all the knotty issues surrounding freedom and determinism here, but we can at least note the following objection to the determinist's position. If we have no choice in our moral values, then there really isn't much point in talking about them at all because we will believe whatever we are determined to believe anyway. If there isn't *some* room for freedom of choice, then we will have just whatever values we are determined to have. Yet the whole point of these discussions is that we have to make choices, and making choices presumes some degree of freedom. If determinism is true, there is no point in discussing what we ought to do. (This will be discussed in more detail in the chapter on egoism.)

Justification

There is a fifth claim that the relativist may be making: *Moral values may be justified only relative to the standards of a particular culture.* In other words, when values are challenged or called into question in some way, the only appropriate way of justifying them is by an appeal to the standards of the culture. When in Rome, the only way of justifying one's actions and values is to appeal to fundamental values accepted by Roman society. This claim is distinct from any of the four preceding claims. One could, for example, maintain that values may initially be understood within the context of a particular culture and yet deny that they can be justified only in relation to that culture.

The question of justification of values is a tricky one, and it is important to realize what the alternatives are here. Those who support the claim that moral values can be justified only in terms of the values of that culture encounter a possible problem: The fundamental values of the culture themselves are not open to justification. Those values simply have to be accepted as they are. Yet we can imagine cases, at least as outsiders to a particular culture, where we would want to question some of a society's values and claim that they should *not* be accepted as they are. The anti-Semitism of Nazi Germany, for example, became a fundamental value for a number of people in that society, but most of us today would want to deny that that value was justified, even for those in that situation. Yet the relativist's position on justification would seem to leave no basis for those in Nazi Germany to have questioned that value. We shall consider this problem in more detail when we discuss relativism and moral change.

We have now seen some of the important distinctions that need to be drawn in talking about relativism. We could summarize them in the following chart.

ETHICAL RELATIVISM AS A DOCTRINE ABOUT:

Action	People ought to act according to the values of the culture in which they live.
Understanding	People's values must be understood within their cultural context.
Judgment	People's values can be judged only within their cultural context.
Explanation	People's values are causally determined by cultural forces.
Justification	People's values can be justified only in terms of their own culture.

As we shall see by the end of this chapter, relativism as a doctrine of action is largely useless, unable to answer the questions that confront us today. Relativism as a doctrine of understanding has a lot of merit and should be accepted. Finally, relativism as a doctrine of judgment, of explanation, and of justification is seriously incomplete. Let's now turn to a consideration of some of the reasons why ethical relativism will not suffice as a doctrine of action or justification, even though it is partially valid as a doctrine of understanding.

The Limits of Ethical Relativism

Despite its attractiveness, many philosophers have been hesitant to accept ethical relativism. A number of arguments have been advanced against it, some of which are primarily put forward by philosophers, others of which are shared by the more general public. In this section, we shall consider five of these arguments: (1) the facts of moral diversity do not actually justify ethical relativism, (2) the refutation of relativism through the defense of one's own absolutist position, (3) the claim that relativism is self-defeating, leading to the acceptance of absolutism or intolerance, (4) the concern that ethical relativism is really a form of moral isolationism or indifference that ignores the fact that moral judgments are unavoidable, and (5) the claim that relativism is unable to provide an adequate basis for moral change. Let's consider each of these arguments in turn.

The Facts of Moral Diversity Reconsidered

We can already see, in light of some of the distinctions just drawn, that the argument from moral diversity is less strong than it originally appeared to be. First, the fact of moral diversity is certainly sufficient to establish *descriptive ethical relativism*, but taken by itself it does not necessarily commit us to *normative ethical relativism*. We could argue, for example, that there are many bizarre scientific views in the world (today as well as in the past), but the mere fact of different views does not entail the conclusion that each of them is right within its own culture or context. Similarly, a lot of people hold unusual medical beliefs, but we do not hesitate to label at least some of them quacks. The mere fact of diversity alone, in other words, does not suffice to support the conclusion that we cannot make judgments about the moral values held by other cultures.

Second, we have to be wary of the level of generality on which the relativist's argument is stated. Recall the earlier distinction among behavior, low-level values, and fundamental values. We may well want to concede that respect for the dignity of the person is shown in different ways in different cultures and that other cultures should not necessarily be compelled to manifest this value through the same kinds of behavior that we find appropriate. But most of us would certainly draw the line at *some* point. The Nazis' attempted extermination of Jews, Gypsies, homosexuals, and others is certainly one such point. It may have *seemed* right to some of them within their culture, but I would clearly want to say that they were wrong if they held that belief.

The Appeal to an Absolute Position

Perhaps the most common way of arguing against ethical relativism is to present an alternative, and usually this is a position that one claims is absolute. We find this in everyday life quite often. Sometimes it is a religiously based viewpoint that is being advocated to the exclusion of all others, at other times it may be grounded in a particular political ideology. Sometimes it is rooted in philosophical systems, and in the following chapters we shall critically assess five of the primary attempts to provide a philosophical basis for an absolutist morality: the libertarian program of the ethical egoist, Kant's ethics of duty, a utilitarian ethics of consequences, modern attempts to see ethics primarily as rights, and recent attempts to revive Aristotle's approach to the ethics of character. Certainly the strongest refutation of relativism would be the introduction of a moral system that not only claimed to be absolute, but also that everyone actually accepted as such.

There is no simple way of evaluating here all of these attempts at an absolutist morality, although we shall examine several of the strictly philosophical positions in subsequent chapters. Yet there are many other absolutist positions that have not received elaborate philosophical expression, and an examination of these is simply beyond the scope of this book. It is important to note, however, what relativists would say to all of these attempted refutations. None, they would claim, has *in fact* achieved anything approaching universality. Although there are groups of people who believe strongly that each of these positions is absolute, relativists see this as simply supporting their claim. Different groups, they would argue, have different sets of moral beliefs, and relativism is the only plausible way of accounting for these differences.

Relativists are demanding not only that an absolutist system of morality *claim* to be absolute, but they are demanding also that it be *accepted* by everyone (or at least a very large percentage of people) as absolute if it is to count as a refutation of relativism. Claiming to be absolute is simply not enough because many moral systems already do that. Indeed, it is precisely the fact that many such systems *claim* to be absolute that creates the problem that relativism tries to solve. Until we all agree about which system of morality is absolute, the absolutist refutation of relativism falls short of the mark.

Is Relativism Self-Defeating?

There is a paradoxical implication in relativism as a doctrine of action. If you should do in Rome as the Romans do, what happens if the Romans assume a very absolutist attitude toward everyone else in the world? What if the Romans turn out to be highly ethnocentric, taking their own culture's values and customs as the absolute measure of everyone else's? Then, it would seem, if we are in Rome, and if the Romans are absolutist and ethnocentric, then we should be absolutist and ethnocentric. Yet this is precisely the kind of culturally chauvinistic attitude that the relativist is trying to convince us to give up. If relativism tells us to do as the Romans do, and if the Romans are not relativists, then relativism tells us to act like nonrelativists. Such an injunction appears to be self-defeating.

There is another, closely related difficulty with relativism as a doctrine of action. One of the principal attractions of relativism is that it seems to promise tolerance. Yet what if the other culture is intolerant? Do we then accept intolerance as one of our values when we are in that culture? If, to return to our standard example, the Romans are intolerant, should we also be intolerant when we are in Rome? It would seem that relativism as a doctrine of action commits us to this position, and that fact threatens to undermine one of its attractions.

This is also true of relativism as a doctrine of understanding and judgment, but in a slightly different way. As a doctrine of understanding and judgment, relativism seems to be the clearest example of tolerance imaginable. It recommends a highly tolerant attitude toward others, and yet this becomes a problem when those others are themselves intolerant. If relativism says don't judge the Romans, be tolerant of them, and if the Romans themselves are very judgmental and intolerant, then relativism commits us to being tolerant toward intolerance.

The Value of Tolerance

As we have seen, one aspect of relativism that makes it initially so attractive is that it promises a more tolerant attitude toward other cultures. We have also seen that this promise may at times be illusory because relativism as a doctrine of action might oblige us to adopt intolerant values if we were in a society that valued intolerance. Yet there is another difficulty with tolerance that we have not yet addressed here. Granting that tolerance should be an important value for us, should we place it above all others? Should tolerance be our *highest* value?

There are clearly some areas in which most of us are inclined to be tolerant. Other cultures may have different moral codes governing—say, business relations or family obligations—and most of us would probably tolerate and respect those differences, even if we would not personally want to live by these codes. Yet in other areas, we are more likely to draw the line. Racism in South Africa, for example, was something that called forth protest from many of us. The Nazis' attempted genocide of the Jews, the Turkish massacre of the Armenians, and Pol Pot's attempt at genocide in Cambodia are but a few examples of the wanton killing that outrages almost all of us. When faced with atrocities such as these, tolerance has to take second place to other, more important values, such as respect for innocent human life and justice. Tolerance, in other words, is an important value—it just isn't appropriate as our *highest* value.

Relativism as Moral Isolationism

There is yet another difficulty with ethical relativism: All too often, it seems to lead to a kind of moral isolationism in which we simply do not care about the rest of the world. There are several aspects to this.

Relativism as a Conversation Stopper

In order to understand relativism, we need to consider not only what relativism actually says, but also the *function* of the appeal to relativism in moral discourse. Consider, in this regard, the typical way that appeals to relativism function in a conversation. Imagine two persons discussing and disagreeing about some moral issue such as abortion or capital punishment. If one of them says, "Well, after all, it's all relative, isn't it?" this serves to bring the conversation to a halt. What, after all, can you say *after* you've said it's all relative? It is crucial to see how the appeal to relativism works in such situations. When people say, "It's all relative," they are often also *implicitly* saying that something follows from this claim, namely, "therefore, we cannot criticize it." It is this implication that is, I think, most doubtful. If the appeal to relativism were used to begin a conversation rather than to end it, we would have quite a different picture of its rhetorical function.

Relativism as a Protection from Criticism

There is another aspect of the way in which relativism is used in conversation that is the opposite side of the implicit claim that we cannot criticize others. If we cannot criticize others because "it's all relative," then neither can *they* criticize *us*. In a sense, this may be the payoff that relativism has for many people: It insulates them against criticism from the outside. It nullifies in advance any possible objection to their behavior or values that anyone outside their culture could present.

The full force of this hidden implication of relativism becomes apparent when we recall that relativism often collapses into subjectivism, namely, the belief that values are relative to each individual person. If this is true, then the hidden implication of relativism may be that no one has a right to criticize us. We are each, as it were, worlds unto ourselves, and no one is entitled to criticize a person's choices because no one is in the same situation. The appeal to relativism thereby becomes an insulation against possible criticism, a way of protecting oneself against any possible moral objections to one's behavior or values.

Relativism as Care-Less

Carol Gilligan, a psychologist whose work on women's moral voices has been extraordinarily influential, sees another aspect of the isolating character of moral relativism. It is, she suggests, care-less. When relativists assert that "it's relative," this is often a way of saying that they simply don't care about what the other person thinks or does. Indeed, we rarely adopt an attitude of relativism toward those we love the most, dismissing our moral differences with a theoretical shrug of the shoulders and saying, "Whatever." When moral differences arise between us and those we love, we seek to understand those differences, to build a bridge between our beliefs and theirs. We question ourselves as well as those we care about.

What's Wrong with Moral Isolationism?

What, one might plausibly ask, is wrong with this hidden implication of the appeal to relativism? There are at least three problems with this isolationist attitude: It fails to provide an answer about how we should resolve moral disagreements between cultures; it ignores the fact that we live in a constantly shrinking world that necessitates intercultural moral judgments; and it overlooks the ways in which intracultural as well as intercultural moral judgments are necessary parts of everyday life.

The Absence of an Answer

First, the appeal to relativism claims to function as a way of dealing with moral conflict, with disagreements about moral values. But the difficulty is that often relativism is not an answer to the question of how to deal with such differences, but rather *the absence of an answer.* Faced with moral disagreements, the relativist says, in effect, "Let's not talk about it." This is not an answer, but rather the refusal even to search for an answer. But why, we may well ask, are answers necessary?

Relativism in a Shrinking World

Relativism as an attitude toward other cultures made more sense when cultures were in fact much more isolated from one another. A century ago, it was not uncommon to find isolated cultures, often tribes that lived in remote jungles or mountains, that had had virtually no contact with our own culture. In such instances, relativism might have expressed an attitude of respect toward those cultures, an unwillingness to interfere with the culture or to judge it too quickly. Such an attitude of noninterference would be particularly appropriate to a scientific, anthropological approach to such a society.

Such societies are increasingly rare today, and it seems highly improbable that they can escape interacting with other, more powerful societies. When interaction occurs, the problem is to decide whose values should prevail. And here, precisely where it is needed most, ethical relativism fails to deliver an answer. As different cultures interact more and more, we need to develop rules that govern the *intersection* of two cultures, and such guidelines are what relativism fails to offer. When in Rome, relativism as a doctrine of action suggests that we do as the Romans do. Yet there is an area of overlap, an area that is neither purely Roman nor purely American, in which the two cultures meet—and it is here that we need guidance. This overlap emerges most clearly in our world in two ways. First, cultures overlap through trade and commerce. They have to deal with each other, and consequently they must develop rules of interaction that are acceptable to *both* cultures. Second, the rapid growth of communications and of the news and entertainment media has increased the amount of influences that cultures have on one another. In both of these areas, the larger, more powerful, and more productive cultures threaten to overwhelm the smaller, weaker, and less productive ones. German children grow up watching a number of American television programs; American children watch American programs. We are, in other words, living in a shrinking world, and we need guidance about how to interact with other cultures. To the extent that relativism says that each culture simply is a world unto itself, it fails to give us such guidance.

The Unavoidability of Moral Judgments

Relativism, we have seen, often collapses into subjectivism. Just as cross-cultural moral judgments are increasingly unavoidable in our world, so, too, is it impossible to avoid interpersonal moral judgments. Yet when ethical relativism collapses into moral subjectivism, it is precisely such judgments that it seeks to avoid. To the extent that interpersonal moral judgments are unavoidable, and to the extent that ethical relativism fails to offer us any guidance in making those judgments, relativism does not provide us with an answer to the moral questions that face us.

There can be no doubt that interpersonal moral judgments are unavoidable. We continually make decisions that affect other people, just as their decisions affect us—and in both cases, we need to make moral judgments about the acceptability of such decisions. Nor can we remain neutral about such issues because we are often forced to make decisions that implicitly take a stance on moral issues. Consider abortion, for example. We may not have to make a personal decision about whether to have an abortion, but we often make decisions that either support or condemn such a practice. The allocation of our tax dollars, the political candidates we support, the kind of sex education we encourage in schools—these are but a few of the ways in which we indirectly take a stand on the morality of abortion.

Even in matters that do not require a decision, we make moral judgments. Recall that moral judgments do not need to be negative. When we say that someone is good, we are making a moral judgment just as much as if we were condemning the person. If we try to avoid moral judgments, then we have to give up positive judgments as well as negative ones. We have to give up even such things as blaming or gossiping, both of which have a significant component of moral judgment. Moral judgments, in other words, permeate our everyday life, and it is hard to imagine what life would be without them.

Relativism and Moral Change

There is an additional set of difficulties associated with ethical relativism, and these relate to the issue of moral progress. Let's examine each of these.

Pressure to Change

A cartoon years ago in the *New Yorker* captured well one of the difficulties with relativism. It showed a group of people marching down a street, carrying signs such as, "It's a point of view," "This is just my opinion," "My perspective," and "This is just another way of looking at things." Although the signs were not explicit appeals to relativism, they were close enough to illustrate one of its drawbacks. When we claim that everything is relative, we say that our own point of view is valid only for ourselves. After we do this, we lose any moral leverage for claiming that other people ought to heed what we say.

Consider the civil rights movement in America. If Martin Luther King, Jr. had been a relativist, in effect he would have said, "I have a dream—but, of course, that's only my limited point of view, valid within my context but not binding on anyone outside that context." For the full-fledged moral relativist, there is no vantage point from which to exert moral pressure because each person is considered right relative to his or her culture.

There is, of course, one way in which relativists do have some moral leverage: They are justified in objecting to anything that is *not* consistent with the values of the culture. Yet this stance makes relativism a profoundly conservative doctrine in ways that may be unacceptable. In a racist society, relativists are justified in objecting only to those who are *opposed* to racism, those who are in favor of equal treatment. This is not to suggest, of course, that relativists are necessarily racists, or anything of the kind. Rather, it is to say that relativists in a racist society can offer no *reasons* why someone should not be a racist, no *justification* for rejecting racism.

Moral Progress

Another difficulty that relates to this issue is whether the relativist can offer a satisfactory account of moral progress. When relativists say that morality is relative to a culture, they are usually also saying that a culture changes over time. Consequently, what might be morally right at one time might be morally wrong at some other time. Just as we cannot legitimately impose one culture's values on another, so, too, we are not permitted to impose one *epoch's* values on another epoch. Each epoch must be understood and judged in terms of its own values.

The difficulty with this claim is that each epoch is, in effect, right unto itself; consequently, it is impossible to say that one is any better than any other. Yet if we cannot say this, then it makes no sense to talk about moral progress (or moral decline, either). Just as we cannot say that one society is better than another, neither can we say that one historical period is better than another. Each has to be judged only in relation to itself. For the relativist, there is no overarching standard in terms of which the various epochs could be judged.

This contrasts sharply to our attitude toward, say, science or medicine. A century ago, people were bled with leeches when they had infections; now physicians administer antibiotics. This is progress. Antibiotics are more effective than leeches in eliminating infections. Yet the relativist cannot make similar judgments about moral progress. If we used to hang pickpockets and now we give them a jail sentence, the relativist can say only that we now have different standards, not that we have *better* standards. Similarly, if we used to condone slavery and we now value and strive toward genuine freedom and equality, the relativist can see this only as a change, not as progress. To claim that these changes are improvements would be to claim that there is some standard in terms of which they both could be judged—and it is precisely this claim that relativism precludes. Each age can be judged only by its own standards.

Where Do We Go from Here?

Where, then, are we left in our attempt to decide whether ethical relativism is true or not? Clearly, *ethical relativism is simply inadequate*. As a doctrine of action, it fails to provide us with guidance precisely where we need it most—at the intersection of two cultures. As a doctrine of judgment, it leads to an unacceptable and unrealistic moral isolationism. As a doctrine of causal explanation, it commits us to a determinism that creates more problems than it solves. Yet as a doctrine of understanding, it makes an important contribution, especially through its emphasis on tolerance and the contextuality of our understanding of moral practices. It is precisely this dual emphasis on tolerance and contextuality that we must retain.

ETHICAL ABSOLUTISM

There is a curious asymmetry, or imbalance, in the relationship between moral relativism and moral absolutism. Moral relativism is itself a position, and as such there are specific arguments for and against it. **Moral absolutism, in contrast, is not a position in itself; rather, it is a characteristic of other, more specific positions.** Defenses of human rights, for example, can be made in absolutist terms, as can defenses of religious-based ethical systems, ethical egoism, utilitarianism, and Kantian moral philosophy.

One of the curious results of this situation is that absolutism cannot be refuted directly in the same way that relativism can; rather, only specific *versions* of absolutism can be refuted. Indeed, this is precisely what will happen in Chapters 4 through 7, where we will see both the strengths and shortcomings of several major moral theories. None of these theories will have a sufficient basis for claiming to be absolute. Readers who are understandably reluctant to accept this promissory note about the inadequacy of these various claims to absolutism will have to await our discussion of the individual theories before this note can be fully redeemed. Saying that no major moral theory is justified in its claim to absolutism is, of course, not the same thing as proving it. Readers will want to consider the chapters on egoism, utilitarianism, Kant, and rights theory to see whether they, too, find that each of these theories provides only a partial account of the moral life.

It is helpful to distinguish between what can be called everyday absolutism and philosophical absolutism. Many of the preceding comments refer to everyday absolutism, whose adherents usually couple the belief that there is a single, objective truth with the conviction that this objective truth coincides perfectly with their own personal beliefs. Philosophical absolutism is usually much more sophisticated in both form and content. Philosophical absolutism claims that there is an absolute truth, but it may recognize that we are all fallible in our attempts to grasp that truth. Moreover, philosophical absolutists are not necessarily monists; they may recognize the possibility that there is a plurality of values.

It is certainly worth adding that absolutism has its attendant dangers, ones that relativism avoids. The twin dangers of intolerance and lack of understanding, although not a necessary part of absolutism, are certainly liabilities that often accompany it. Those who believe that they have the absolute truth are rarely motivated to look beyond their own beliefs for further enlightenment, and too often they feel little motivation to understand the moral worldviews of other cultures from within. It is precisely these liabilities that we want to avoid.

ETHICAL PLURALISM

How, then, are we to make sense of the fact that moral disagreements seem to be unavoidable? I have suggested that we reject two possible responses to the persistence of such disagreements. First, the moral relativist declares that each culture is right unto itself, but this is of little help in determining how we can live together in a shared world. The presence of moral disagreement is thus quite understandable for the relativist, but the possibility of resolution seems absent. Second, the moral absolutist declares that there is a single truth, that all the other positions are mistaken except for the absolutist's own view. This offers little or no foundation for understanding legitimate diversity in the moral life, and agreement is often purchased at the price of condemnation of those who disagree. Interestingly, relativism and absolutism have something in common: Neither sees disagreement as something that we can learn from, as a positive source of understanding.

Ethical pluralism offers a very different view of the nature and significance of moral disagreements. The pluralist assumes that we will continue to have moral disagreements for the foreseeable future and that, given the shrinking character of our world, such disagreements will become increasingly unavoidable. *Disagreement and difference are standard features of the moral landscape and can be sources of moral strength.* Let's first look more closely at ethical pluralism itself and then return to the issue of moral disagreement.

Ethical Pluralism

Ethical pluralism is simply the conviction that the truth, at least in the moral life, is not singular or unitary. There are many truths, sometimes partial and sometimes conflicting. This does not mean that there is no truth, as the subjectivist claims. Nor does it mean that all truth is relative, as the relativist claims. But it does mean that, at least in some situations, there is not just a single truth.

A Baseball Analogy

The best example of this type of pluralism comes from Bernard Gert, a philosopher who teaches at Dartmouth. He asks his students, "Who is the best hitter in major league baseball today?" Invariably, he gets several different answers. As the discussion proceeds, it becomes evident that there are different standards for judging who the "best hitter" is. Some point to the number of hits per year, others to the number of runs batted in (RBIs), and some even point to the number of home runs a year. This is a perfect example of pluralism. There are several different standards, each of which is reasonable, none of which is exhaustive. Notice, though, that pluralism does not mean that "anything goes." There is room for mistakes in two ways. First, despite the plurality of standards, clearly most baseball players do not qualify as the best hitter. Second, not every standard is legitimate. If someone tried to define "best hitter" as "batter most often hit by a pitched ball" or "batter most often in a television commercial," we would immediately reject those proposed definitions. Pluralism does not mean that anything goes.

The Plurality of Moral Values

Ethical pluralism is similar but somewhat more complicated. Imagine that someone asked, "Who's the best baseball player today?" Several answers would be possible, depending on whether one focuses on hitting, fielding, team spirit, or some other criterion. Similarly in ethics: If we asked an abstract question such as, "What is goodness?" we might get several different answers. Most philosophers would focus on actions, although some would look primarily at moral agents. Some would consider a combination of both. Among philosophers who concentrate primarily on the *morality of actions,* some are primarily concerned with *formal characteristics* of the acts, whereas others look at the acts' *consequences.* Among those who focus principally on the formal characteristics of acts are Kant, some divine command theorists, and many human rights theorists. Kant is concerned with whether the maxim behind an action can be consistently willed as a universal law. Some divine command theorists ask whether acts conform to God's law. Rights theorists concentrate on whether actions avoid infringing on the rights of other persons. Other act-oriented approaches consider the way in which actions produce consequences of a particular type, such as increasing the overall amount of happiness in a society (utilitarianism) or maximizing one's own self-interest (ethical egoism). All of these approaches take acts as the principal focus of moral evaluation, but there is another way of approaching the moral life. Some philosophers take the *morality of the agent* as the principal focus. Among those who focus on the agent are Kantians who ask if an act is being done for the sake of duty and those divine command theorists who are concerned that actions are done for God's sake. Both of these approaches look primarily to the agent's *intention* as the key moral factor. Other philosophers such as Aristotle see the agent's *character* as the primary focus. Such theorists see virtues as those strengths of character that promote human flourishing and see vices as those weaknesses of character that restrict human flourishing. Thus the different traditions illuminate a plurality of values.

Some of these standards of value, as we shall see in later chapters, are better than others, but all have some merit. The good is not some single factor, but rather a plurality of factors. There are different standards of moral value. Each is reasonable; none is the only reasonable standard.

Just as in the case of "best baseball player," this does not mean that anything goes. There are lots of baseball players who will never qualify for the title of best player, no matter what standard we use. There are also plenty of standards (for example, most foul balls hit in a single season) that no reasonable person would accept as legitimate. Pluralism means simply that not all moral situations admit of a single evaluation. Several moral standards may

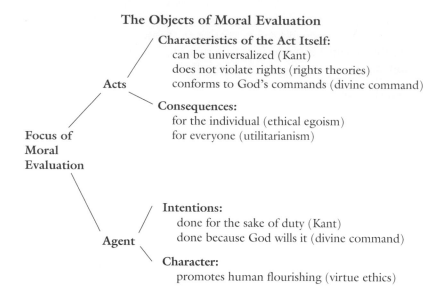

be relevant. Sometimes these various standards may yield the same results, sometimes they may produce conflicting results.

We learn from both the agreements and the disagreements. In the "best baseball player" case, we sometimes find that there is one player who excels in all areas. Then there is no doubt who deserves the title, and we are delighted to acknowledge that the choice was so clear cut. At other times, various players will have strengths in a particular area, but none of them will be best in all areas. Then we have genuine ambiguity about who the best player is, and we may be willing to acknowledge that others are almost as deserving of the title as the one we chose. When someone edges out the competition by a small margin, it is appropriate to acknowledge that the margin was a small one. Reporting the final score of a tennis match, a sports commentator once captured this distinction well by prefacing the score with the phrase, "In a match that neither opponent deserved to lose. . . ."

It is similar in the moral life. When all the standards agree—for example, in prohibiting the torture of innocent children for fun—we usually discover that we have a very clear-cut moral issue and acknowledge it as such. When the standards disagree—for example, in judging the morality of voluntary euthanasia—we discover that we have a genuinely complex moral problem. This is precisely the complexity of the moral life, and it is appropriate to acknowledge it as such. The fact that some moral issues are difficult does not mean that moral theory is useless. It simply tells us that there are times in the moral life when we have to make close calls.

Pluralism entertains the possibility not only that we may have many standards of value, but also that they are not necessarily consistent with one another. This position does not give up the hope of compatibility, but neither does it make compatibility a necessary requirement.

Pluralism is best captured by a metaphor suggested by Amélie Rorty in another context. We might imagine these various theories in a relationship similar to that of the three branches of government. The legislative, executive, and judicial branches exist in a network of *checks and balances* with one another. Not only are they not necessarily in harmony, but also their disagreement is often a good thing. So, too, with moral theories. Each, as it were, keeps the others honest. Just as we should not hope for the eventual victory of one branch of government over the other two, so we should not hope that one moral theory will finally vanquish all competitors from the field.

One of the intriguing aspects of this metaphor is that it suggests that disagreement can be positive. The fact that different moral theories point to different courses of action is not necessarily bad; indeed, the disagreement can help us ultimately to arrive at the best course of action. Yet we should not be misled by this metaphor because the American political system has certainly known periods of relative paralysis that was in part due to the check-and-balances system. Sometimes, if the disagreements are too great and the possibility of genuine dialogue and compromise too small, the system of checks and balances can immobilize us, preventing us from choosing any course of action at all.

This book approaches moral theory within the context of ethical pluralism. It assumes that there are many standards of value and that these are not necessarily consistent with one another.

The Principle of Fallibility

The principle of fallibility is an essential component of the type of ethical pluralism outlined in this chapter. Essentially, this principle urges us toward moral humility, the realization that we might be mistaken in moral matters. No matter how strong our beliefs are, we might be mistaken. Consequently, we are always open to the possibility that we have to reconsider and revise those beliefs. Open-mindedness is the corollary of the principle of fallibility.

This principle does not exclude commitments to theories, even deep and passionate commitments. We may still have strong, deep beliefs, but we are always aware of the possibility that they might be mistaken or incomplete. Although moral fallibilists may be passionate about their beliefs, they are not dogmatic. Their passion is for finding the truth, for uncovering the morally most enlightening way of understanding a given situation or problem. They may be devoted to their moral beliefs, but their devotion does not stem from the fact that those beliefs are *their* beliefs, but rather from their conviction that they are the *best* beliefs available. Moral fallibilists are open to the possibility that if someone can present good reasons for revising those beliefs, they should then be revised. The moral pluralist who accepts the principle of fallibility thus treads a narrow line between open-mindedness and commitment, managing to combine the best elements of both.

CONCLUSION

We must, I have suggested, figure out a way of making sense out of both specific moral conflicts and the conflict among moral theories. Neither relativism nor absolutism succeeds in doing this. Ethical pluralism does. In particular, it allows us to endorse four key intuitions about how we should respond to moral conflicts.

The Principle of Understanding

If there is one thing that centuries of absolutism and cultural chauvinism have taught us, it is the danger of judging others before we understand them. Whenever we look at the moral practices of another culture, we must seek to understand the meaning of those practices within the culture as a whole. Any approach to moral conflict that does not seriously enjoin us to understand before we judge is inadequate.

The Principle of Tolerance

One of the key insights of multiculturalism is that there are many ways of achieving moral excellence. Our own way of doing so may be most familiar, but its familiarity does not invalidate other ways. It is important, whenever possible, to leave different cultures as much room as possible to pursue their own moral vision, even though it might be quite different than our own. An account of morality that does not allow for genuine diversity and multiculturalism misses the mark.

The Principle of Standing Up against Evil

The understanding and tolerance urged by these first two principles must not lead to a moral laissez-faire policy: We ought not to conclude that therefore anything goes, morally speaking. It is also important, at least in cases of egregious moral wrongdoing, to speak out against offenses wherever they may occur, whether in one's own culture or another culture. This is of particular importance because often the most outrageous wrongdoing is directed against the powerless of the world: children, women, and minorities (whether these be racial, ethnic, or religious minorities). An account of morality that provides no moral foundation for opposing such wrongdoing falls far short of the mark.

The Principle of Fallibility

Moral judgment across cultures is necessary, but we must approach it in a spirit of humility and self-reflection. We must be prepared to learn from other cultures and to have some of our own moral shortcomings revealed to us by them. Cross-cultural moral dialogue is a necessity, but we must not forget that it is also a two-way conversation. When examining moral differ-ences between ourselves and other cultures, we may sometimes discover that it is we, not they, who are found morally wanting. We must remain steadfast in our commitment to self-examination, to understanding the ways in which we can learn from other cultures. This is the spirit in which we will approach the diversity of moral theories discussed in subsequent chapters of this book, and it is also the spirit that I hope will underlie our approach to particular cases of moral diversity. We must always seek first to understand. We should seek to tolerate and learn from differences whenever possible, but still stand up against evil when we see it. Finally, we should judge and act with humil-ity, always aware of our own fallibility.

DISCUSSION QUESTIONS

1. Recall **statement 1** in your Ethical Inventory ("What's right depends on the culture you are in").
   (a) How would you reformulate this statement in order to make it more precise?
   (b) Has your rating of this statement changed after reading this chap-ter? If so, in what way? If your rating has not changed, are your rea-sons for your rating any different now than they were when you first responded to this statement?
2. **Statement 2** of the Ethical Inventory ("No one has the right to judge what's right or wrong for another person") concentrates on our right to make moral judgments about other people.
   (a) Has your rating of this statement changed after reading this chap-ter? If so, in what way? If your rating has not changed, are your rea-sons for your rating any different now than they were when you first responded to this statement?
   (b) Take a specific example of someone who has committed a morally extreme act, whether extremely good or bad. What argu-ments could be advanced to claim that we are not entitled to make a judgment about that act? What replies could be offered?
3. Recall **statement 3** of the Ethical Inventory ("No one has the right to intervene when he or she thinks someone else has done something morally wrong").
   (a) When, if ever, do you think intervention is morally justified? Morally required? Give examples of actual situations.
   (b) Has your rating of this statement changed after reading this chap-ter? If so, in what way? If your rating has not changed, are your rea-sons for your rating any different now than they were when you first responded to this statement?
4. Recall **statement 5** in your Ethical Inventory ("Ultimately, there is one and only one right standard of moral evaluation").

(a) Has your rating of this statement changed after reading this chapter? If so, in what way? If your rating has not changed, are your reasons for your rating any different now than they were when you first responded to this statement?

(b) Contrast **statement 11** with the account of ethical pluralism given in this chapter. Which position do you think is stronger? Why?

5. A friend of mine taught English as a second language to a group of Southeast Asian students in southern California. Over the months she developed an excellent rapport with the students. When she became pregnant, they all were happy for her and her husband, even hosting a baby shower after class one night. My friend was delighted when she delivered a beautiful, healthy, seven-pound girl. She was shocked and puzzled when, several days after the students in her class had heard of the birth, she began to receive cards of *condolence* from them! It soon became clear. In their culture, having a son as a first child is a matter of great joy, and they all sympathized with what they presumed was her sense of deep disappointment that she had given birth to a girl.

Discuss the issues that this example raises about moral relativism. If you were in my friend's position, how would you deal with the situation?

6. Near the Taos pueblo of New Mexico, Native Americans for centuries have considered Blue Lake, on the slopes of Mount Wheeler, a sacred place, as holy to them as a church is to Christians. During the 1970s, residents of the pueblo engaged in a long and ultimately successful judicial and legislative battle to regain control of Blue Lake. Whereas Blue Lake meant one thing to Native Americans, it meant something quite different to most non-Native Americans. How do you think such differences should be resolved? What principles do you appeal to in deciding who should have control of the land?

7. In some countries, thieves are still punished by having a hand chopped off. In the United States, we punish thieves quite differently. In light of our discussion of ethical relativism, how should we proceed in a discussion of the morality of punishments such as chopping off a hand?

8. MOVIE In Peter Weir's movie *Witness* (1985), we find an interesting clash of two cultures: the pacifist world of the Amish and the violence-ridden world of a Philadelphia police detective played by Harrison Ford. What would the normative ethical relativist have to say about their interaction, and especially about how Harrison Ford should behave while living with the Amish? Do you agree with the relativist's normative recommendations? Why or why not?

9. MOVIE In *The Mission*, (1986), Jeremy Irons plays a Jesuit missionary in South America, and Robert de Niro depicts a slave trader who gives up his former life and becomes a Jesuit as well. Both bring foreign values to the native inhabitants. What would the normative ethical relativist say about Jeremy Iron's activities among the natives as a missionary? What would the same relativist say about Robert de Niro's

slave trading among the natives? In the eyes of the relativist, are there any morally relevant differences between the two? If so, what are they? If not, why not? How would you assess the behavior of both men in light of our discussion of moral relativism?

10. Imagine that you are the Undersecretary of State for refugees seeking asylum in the United States. In recent years, a number of women have sought political asylum in the United States, claming that if they remained in their home country, they would become the victims of forced genital mutilation. In at least some of those home countries, female genital mutilation is a common and widely accepted practice. You have been asked to develop a policy to guide the State Department in dealing with these cases. What would you say? Place your recommendations within the context of our discussion of ethical relativism, absolutism, and pluralism.

11. Imagine that you are an ethics advisor to the Secretary of State. The United States has been asked to intervene in a small Eastern European country after repeated reports, some of which have been confirmed by United Nations observers, of persecution of an ethnic minority, including rape and murder. This country is of little strategic interest to the United States. You have been asked to prepare a white paper for the Secretary of State outlining the ethical issues surrounding intervention and giving your own recommendation about what the United States ought to do.

BIBLIOGRAPHICAL ESSAY

Relativism and Anthropology. Ruth Benedict's "A Defense of Moral Relativism," *Journal of General Psychology* 10 (1934): 59–82, is one of the most influential and often reprinted contemporary defenses of ethical relativism by a leading figure in twentieth-century anthropology. Also see Edward Westermarck, *The Origin and Development of the Moral Ideas* (London: Macmillan, 1912) and, much more recently, Richard A. Shweder, "Anthropology's Romantic Rebellion against the Enlightenment: Or There's More to Thinking than Reason and Evidence," in R. A. Shweder and R. A. Levine, eds., *Culture Theory: Essays on Mind, Self and Emotion* (Cambridge: Cambridge University Press, 1984). For an anthropologist's critique of cultural relativism, see Robert B. Edgerton, *Sick Societies. Challenging the Myth of Primitive Harmony* (New York: Free Press, 1992). For a middle ground between relativism and absolutism, see John W. Cook, Morality and Cultural Differences (New York: Oxford, 1999). For a fascinating study of the history and morality of **bribes,** see John T. Noonan, Jr.'s *Bribes* (Berkeley, CA: University of California Press, 1984). For a critique of relativism within a medical context, see Ruth Macklin, *Against Relativism. Cultural Diversity and the Search for Ethical Universals in Medicine* (New York: Oxford, 1999). On the question of incommensurability in a moral context, see the essays in Ruth Chang, ed., *Incommensurability, Incomparability, and Practical Reason* (Cambridge: Harvard University Press, 1997). One of the most interesting contributions to this discussion is Michelle Moody-Adams, *Fieldwork in Familiar Places: Morality, Culture, and Philosophy* (Cambridge, MA: Harvard University Press, 2002).

There are several good **introductory anthologies** containing a number of the basic articles on moral relativism, including Paul K. Moser and Thomas L. Carson, eds. *Moral Relativism: A Reader* (Oxford University Press, 2001); Michael Krausz and Jack W. Meiland, eds. *Relativism: Cognitive and Moral* (Notre Dame, IN: University of Notre Dame Press, 1982), which contains essays by Philippa Foot, Bernard Williams, Gilbert Harman, David Lyons, and Geoffrey Harrison; and Michael Krausz, ed., *Relativism: Interpretation and Conflict* (Notre Dame, IN: University of Notre Dame Press, 1989) contains an excellent selection of articles primarily by philosophers but also contains articles by two eminent anthropologists, Clifford Geertz and Richard Shweder. Also see S. C. Brown, ed., *Objectivity and Cultural Divergence* (Cambridge: Cambridge University Press, 1984), which contains a number of insightful papers on the possibility of objectivity (including, but not limited to, moral objectivity) in light of cultural differences. For an excellent **survey of recent work on moral relativism,** see Robert M. Stewart and Lynn L. Thomas, "Recent Work on Ethical Relativism.," *American Philosophical Quarterly* 28 (April, 1991): 85–100; also see the extensive bibliography on relativism in Harvey Siegel, *Relativism Refuted* (Dordrecht: Reidel, 1987).

On the relationship between **relativism and tolerance,** see Joshua Halberstam's "The Paradox of Tolerance," *Philosophical Forum,* 14 (1982/83): 190–206; Geoffrey Harrison's "Relativism and Tolerance," *Ethics,* 86 (1976): 122–135; Max Hocutt's "Must Relativists Tolerate Evil?" *The Philosophical Forum* 17 (Spring 1986): 188–200; Nicholas Unwin's "Relativism and Moral Complacency," *Philosophy* 60 (1985): 205–214; Also see J. Budziszewski, *True Tolerance. Liberalism and the Necessity of Judgment* (New Brunswick, NJ: Transaction, 1992) for a critique of the liberal notion of tolerance and Nick Fotion and Gerard Elfstrom, *Toleration* (Tuscaloosa: University of Alabama Press, 1992) for a strong defense of the moral importance of tolerance, and Michael Walzer, *On Toleration* (New Haven, CT: Yale University Press, 1997) On the related notions of **compromise and accommodation,** see Martin Benjamin, *Splitting the Difference: Compromise and Integrity in Ethics and Politics* (Lawrence, KS: University of Kansas Press, 1990) and David Wong, "Coping with Moral Conflict and Ambiguity," *Ethics* 102, no. 4 (July, 1992): 763–784. The classic text is John Locke's *A Letter Concerning Toleration*, which is available in numerous editions.

One of the more persuasive arguments in favor of relativism from the fact of **moral disagreement** is to be found in J. L. Mackie's *Ethics: Inventing Right and Wrong* (New York: Penguin Books, 1976). Also see Judith Wagner DeCew, "Moral Conflicts and Ethical Relativism," *Ethics* 101 (October 1990): 27–41; Amy Gutmann and Dennis Thompson, "Moral Conflict and Political Consensus," *Ethics* 101 (October 1990): 64–88 and their *Democracy and Disagreement* (Cambridge, MA: Harvard University Press, 1996); James D. Wallace, *Moral Relevance and Moral Conflict* (Ithaca, NY: Cornell University Press, 1988); and Michael Stocker, *Plural and Conflicting Values* (Oxford: Clarendon Press, 1990). For a defense of a middle ground on moral realism, see Richard W. Miller, *Moral Differences: Truth, Justice, and Conscience in a World of Conflict* (Princeton: Princeton University Press, 1992).

For critical assessments of Mackie's position, especially in regard to the question of **moral realism,** see David O. Brink's "Moral Realism and the Skeptical Arguments from Disagreement and Queerness," *Australasian Journal of Philosophy* 62 (1984):

111–125 and William Tolhurst, "The Argument from Moral Disagreement," *Ethics* 87 (April 1987): 610–621. The anthology edited by Ted Honderich *Morality and Objectivity: A Tribute to J. L. Mackie* (London: Routledge & Kegan Paul, 1985) contains essays by Blackburn, Foot, Hare, Hurley, Lukes, McDowell, Sen, Wiggins, and Williams on the issues raised by Mackie. Geoffrey Sayre-McCord's *Essays on Moral Realism* (Ithaca, NY: Cornell, 1988) contains a number of excellent essays (including one by Mackie) for and against moral realism. Also see Robert L. Arrington, *Rationalism, Realism, and Relativism: Perspectives in Contemporary Moral Epistemology* (Ithaca, NY: Cornell University Press, 1989) for an overview of recent work in this area; and Daniel N. Robinson, *Praise and Blame: Moral Realism and Its Application* (Princeton: Princeton University Press, 2002).

Some of the most interesting work on the issue of ethical relativism stems from **Alasdair MacIntyre**'s *After Virtue,* 2nd ed. (Notre Dame, IN: University of Notre Dame Press, 1984). He has carried this work forward in two later books: *Three Rival Versions of Moral Inquiry* (Notre Dame, IN: University of Notre Dame Press, 1990), which examines competing conceptions of moral discourse, and *Whose Justice? Whose Rationality?* (Notre Dame, IN: University of Notre Dame Press, 1988), which is devoted to an examination of changing conceptions of justice and rationality. Also see his "Relativism, Power and Philosophy," *Proceedings and Addresses of the American Philosophical Association* 59 (September 1985): 5–22. In this same tradition, also see Jeffrey Stout's *Ethics after Babel. The Languages of Morals and Their Discontents* (Boston: Beacon Press, 1988); and James Boyd White's *When Words Lose Their Meaning: Constitutions and Reconstitutions of Language, Character, and Community* (Chicago: University of Chicago Press, 1984).

Gilbert Harman has offered a vigorous **defense of ethical relativism** in Gilbert Harman, Explaining Values and Other Essays in Moral Philosophy (Oxford: Clarendon Press, 2000); Steven Darwall's "Harman and Moral Relativism," *The Personalist* 58 (1977): 199–207 and Louis P. Pojman's "Gilbert Harman's Internalist Moral Relativism," *The Modern Schoolman* 68 (November 1990): 19–39 present some insightful criticisms of Harman's position. For an excellent debate on this issue, see Gilbert Harman and Judith Jarvis Thomson, *Moral Relativism and Moral Objectivity* (Oxford: Blackwell, 1996).

For a subtle account of the ways in which philosophical theories are connected to certain **contexts of questions,** see Virginia Held, *Rights and Goods: Justifying Social Action* (New York: The Free Press, 1984). For a variant of the **spotlight metaphor,** see Dorothy Emmet, *The Moral Prism* (New York: St. Martin's Press, 1979). On the **checks and balances metaphor,** see Amélie Rorty's essay, "Two Faces of Courage," in her *Mind in Action* (Boston: Beacon Press, 1988), where this metaphor is used to a different purpose, and her essay, "The Advantages of Moral Diversity," *Social Philosophy & Policy* 9, no. 2 (Summer 1992): 38–62.

For a number of perceptive essays on **ethical pluralism,** see the Symposium on Pluralism and Ethical Theory in *Ethics* 102, no. 4 (July 1992), especially Susan Wolf's "Two Levels of Pluralism," pp. 785–798 and Dennis Wong's "Coping with Moral Conflict and Ambiguity," pp. 763–784. I am indebted to Wolf's essay for the reference to Gert and his "best hitter" analogy. Also see William A. Galston, *Liberal Pluralism: The Implications of Value Pluralism for Political Theory and Practice* (Cambridge: Cambridge University Press, 2002); Nancy L. Rosenblum, *Membership and Morals. The Personal Uses of Pluralism in America* (Princeton: Princeton University Press, 1998); Ralph Grillo, *Pluralism and the Politics of Difference* (New York: Oxford, 1998); John Kekes, "Pluralism and Conflict in Morality," *Journal of Value*

Inquiry 26 (1992): 37–50 for an insightful discussion of this issue, as well as his *The Morality of Pluralism* (Princeton: Princeton University Press, 1993). Michael Walzer's *Spheres of Justice: A Defense of Pluralism and Equality* (New York: Basic Books, 1983) develops a pluralistic approach to distributive justice; for further discussion of Walzer's position, see David Miller and Michael Walzer, eds., *Pluralism, Justice, and Equality* (Oxford: Oxford University Press, 1995). Neil Cooper's *The Diversity of Moral Thinking* (Oxford: Clarendon Press, 1981) presents a justification of the rationality of altruism within the context of a theory of diversity in moral judgments. Michael Stocker's *Plural and Conflicting Values* (Oxford: Clarendon Press, 1990) presents a subtle account of the relationship between pluralism and conflict in morality and a perceptive analysis of the reasons why contemporary moral philosophers find such conflict so disturbing. Nicholas Rescher defends a pragmatic version of pluralism in *Pluralism: Against the Demand for Consensus* (Oxford: Clarendon Press, 1993).

Citation. The Iraqi example is drawn primarily from a news story by Alex Chadwick and Bib Edwards on National Public Radio's *Morning Edition* on December 23, 1996. For Yael Tamir's position, see Yael Tamir, "Hands Off Clitoridectomy," *Boston Review* 21, no. 5 October/November 1996 and the replies and rejoinder in the following issue. These are available on the Web at http://bostonreview.mit.edu/BR21.3/Tamir.html and http://bostonreview.mit.edu/BR21.5/.

Further Information. For additional resources relating to these issues, see the page on relativism, absolutism, and pluralism (http://ethics.acusd.edu/theories/relativism/) on my *Ethics Updates* website.

THE ETHICS OF DIVINE COMMANDS: RELIGIOUS MORALITIES

In the twenty-second chapter of Genesis, God talks to Abraham and tells him that he must sacrifice his son Isaac, who was born very late in Abraham's life when he had given up all hope of having children. Abraham had longed for children for years, and Isaac meant almost everything to him. Thus, imagine Abraham's dismay when God said to him:

> Take now thy son, thine only son Isaac, whom thou lovest, and get thee into the land of Moriah; and offer him there for a burnt offering upon one of the mountains which I will tell thee of.

Abraham took his son Isaac to the mountain, prepared to offer the sacrifice. Isaac, who did not know what God had said to his father, was puzzled because he noticed that his father seemed to have everything for the sacrifice but the offering itself. When his father actually tied him up and put him on the sacrificial altar to be sacrificed, Isaac presumably realized what was going on. Eventually, just before Abraham was ready to sacrifice Isaac, God told him to stop. "Lay not a hand upon the lad," God told Abraham, "neither do thou any thing unto him: for now I know that thou fearest God, seeing thou hast not withheld thy son, thine only son, from me."

Many of us may feel that such a case could never happen in our own society. Today, Abraham would probably be taken into custody and sent for an (involuntary) psychiatric evaluation. The fact that he heard voices might be sufficient in some states to hold him for several days; the fact that the voices told him to sacrifice his only son would often be sufficient to justify a much longer period of restraint and involuntary treatment.

Is this example really so far removed from what some people accept today? In our society there are individuals who still feel the essential tension that Abraham experienced: the tension between the officially sanctioned morality of our society and the commands that come to them from some higher power. Consider two types of cases that have received a lot of media attention. Christian Scientists are required by their religious beliefs to refuse medical treatment, even for their own children. The essential tension that they experience appears similar to Abraham's: The (apparent) commands of God require them to act in ways that (apparently) conflict with their love for their children. To turn to modern medicine is to betray their faith in God. Similarly, when religiously motivated opponents of abortion disobey civil laws in order to disrupt the practice of abortion, they believe they are responding to a higher law that requires them to disobey the laws of the state.

What all three of these examples have in common is the conviction that religion tells us how to act. As such, religion either replaces or overrides the demands of society's morality. This issue is at the heart of a heated, long-standing debate on the relationship between religion and ethics, a debate that in the Christian tradition has its roots in centuries of discussion and disagreement about the nature and limits of religious morality. Yet Christianity is not by any means the only tradition within which this issue exists. Although it is impossible in the short space available here to survey even the major religious traditions, we can look briefly at some of the diverse ways in which the relationship between religion and ethics has been understood in various religious traditions. Then we can turn to an examination of the general conceptual issues raised by these examples.

THE DIVERSITY OF RELIGIOUS TRADITIONS

It is misleading to talk about the relationship between *religion* and *ethics* as if each of these words referred to a single, uniform phenomenon. In fact, neither of them does. Most of this book will be devoted to a discussion of the diversity of traditions contained within the single word *ethics* in traditional Western thought from Aristotle to the present. In this section, we will examine the ways in which religion and ethics are related to each other in three quite different traditions: the Navajo view of the harmony between human beings and the natural world; the Muslim (Islam) vision of a religious state that unifies religion, ethics, law, and politics; and the Buddhist view of the place of a morality of compassion in the eightfold path. In the process of doing so, we will see that the term *religion* can refer to as widely diverse a set of practices and beliefs as the word *ethics* does.

Each of these three traditions presents us with a distinctive ethical perspective, and each provides a different view of the relationship between religion and ethics. The Navajo provide us with an *ethic of harmony,* in which a balance in the relationship between human beings and the natural world is central. Islam offers us an *ethic of law,* based on the Qur'an and other sacred texts, in which obedience to the will of Allah is the highest good. Buddhism presents an *ethic of compassion* in which the alleviation of suffering and the purification of the soul become principal concerns. In the Navajo worldview, there is little need to draw a line between religion and ethics because the natural and the supernatural permeate one another much more than in scientifically oriented cultures. Islam, in contrast, makes ethics clearly depend on religion—indeed, the good is ultimately whatever Allah wills it to be. For the Buddhist, the path to enlightenment or *nirvana* is one that blurs traditional Western distinctions between faith and reason, between religion and ethics. Buddhism provides a model in which enlightenment lies beyond rationality.

Each of these religious traditions is also distinctive in another sense. The Navajo worldview contains a plurality of Gods and spirits, and these are not necessarily in agreement with one another or with human beings. The Islamic worldview, in contrast to this, is starkly monotheistic. There is only one God, and Allah is his name. Buddhism presents yet a third model because it is virtually a nontheistic religion. It has no notion of a personal or individual God at all. Each of these religions thus exemplifies a different relationship between God and the world. In the polytheistic model, different Gods may issue different, and at times conflicting, moral commands to human beings. In a monotheistic model, the possibility of such conflict is eliminated. Presumably one cannot be caught between conflicting divine commands within a monotheistic worldview. Finally, the nontheistic model offered by Buddhism necessitates the grounding of moral commands in some kind of order outside of God—in this case, in the order of *karma.* Thus, we see quite different ways in which religion and ethics can be related.

Let's begin by considering the Navajo worldview. Be aware in our considerations of each of these traditions that it is difficult to avoid oversimplifying in such brief presentations. Consider the following discussions of Navajo, Muslim, and Buddhist ethics as a first step toward understanding these traditions rather than as the final word, as an invitation to learn more rather than a guarantee of understanding.

The Navajo Holy Wind

One of the benefits of studying other cultures is that we come to see and understand our own assumptions more clearly. Rarely is this more clearly shown than in the contrast between the Navajo understanding of the moral life and our own. There are a number of key points of divergence, points that help us to see our own world more clearly just as we come to understand theirs better. Before we consider some of those points of contrast, let's begin with a brief consideration of the distinctive character of an ethic that for centuries existed in a comparatively small society with an oral tradition.

Traditions and Societies

Initially, one of the most obvious differences between the Navajo and many white cultures is simply one of size. For centuries, Navajo ethics was largely oriented toward guiding the actions of Navajo toward Navajo, that is, toward guiding the actions of people who usually knew one another or at least knew one another's families. This is in sharp contrast to much of Western European ethical thought, which—as we shall see in Chapter 8—is primarily directed toward regulating the behavior of people who are strangers to one another.

There is a second, related difference. Navajo ethics is almost exclusively practical; there is virtually no interest in theory. Part of the reason for this is that it is passed from one person to another. There is nothing impersonal about the process of transmission of moral values for the Navajo. This was even more strongly the case before the development of a written language. Abstract theories rarely exist without the support of the written word. A corollary of this is that it is more difficult for outsiders to come to understand the Navajo worldview insofar as the tradition is still an oral one.

Dualisms and Antagonisms

Whereas classical modern European ethical thought has been dominated for the past several centuries by fundamental dualisms, the Navajo understanding of morality is generally free of such dualities. As we shall see in later chapters, dualism is pervasive in these European traditions: Body versus spirit, emotion versus reason, and sensuous inclination versus duty are but a few of the dualities that recur continually in these traditions. Typically, these traditions try to resolve such dualities by choosing one side—usually spirit, reason, and duty—over the other.

Not only are these classical European dualities foreign to the Navajo way of understanding the world, but also the idea of choosing one side of a duality would be completely out of keeping with their way of dealing with tensions and antagonisms in their world. Like the Chinese *yin* and *yang*, each side of any antagonism needs the other. When one exists without the other, it is incomplete. The principal tension is that of male and female, and virtually everything in the Navajo's world is either male or female. Together, both sides create a dynamic union in tension. Good and evil do not exclude one another. Each needs the other. The Navajo idea of harmony thus involves embracing both sides of an antithesis rather than choosing one and banishing the other.

The difference between Western medicine and Navajo medicine illustrates the way in which the Navajo worldview simply has no trace of the mind-body dualism so prevalent in Western medicine. Navajo medicine is directed toward the whole person, what we (as non-Navajo) would call body and spirit. Western medicine, in contrast, strictly separates body and spirit. Indeed, the body itself is compartmentalized through medical specialization. Healing, in the Navajo tradition, is a process that involves the entire person.

A corollary of this antagonistic worldview is to be found in the Navajo attitude toward evil, which is often puzzling to the outsider. In large measure, evil—like good—just "is" for the Navajo. This is found both in their view of a person's character and in their view of the everyday world. People are a mixture of good and evil, and there is very little that one can do to adjust the balance in any given individual. Similarly, evil exists in the world, and its presence is as necessary as the presence of goodness. A Navajo might well look for ways to avoid evil but would not think of trying to create a world free from it.

Hozho. In the Navajo worldview, the principal goal toward which they strive is *hozho,* which is variously translated as harmony, beauty, peace of mind, goodness, health, well-being, or success. Although some scholars have interpreted this concept in a dualistic way in which *hozho* is contrasted with its opposite *(hochxq),* this does not seem to be the way in which the Navajo themselves have traditionally understood it. Rather, they seek a dynamic harmony with their environment that is characterized by a proper balance of all things. The function of morality is to guide individuals toward achieving such a balance by marking out alternatives that prevent the achievement or maintenance of such harmony.

Three levels must be harmonized in the Navajo world: the natural, the human, and the supernatural. Rather than trying to control nature, the Navajo tries to achieve harmony with it. Again, we find a sharp contrast here to Western views that emphasize the technological subjugation of the natural world. Where representatives of Western technology would deal with flooding on a river by building a dam, the Navajo would simply move to higher ground.

The Holy Wind

How, then, do the Navajo determine how they should act? Clearly they learn patterns of behavior from the myths and stories that comprise their oral tradition, but that tradition also tells us that there is another source of guidance: the Holy Wind. The wind is a major force in the Navajo worldview, and it provides a superb example of a concept that escapes traditional dualities. The wind is physical (we can feel it on our faces when it blows), yet strangely ephemeral (we cannot hold it or capture it like we can physical objects). It is pervasive, but shifting in its direction and intensity. It is both one (there is one wind, just as there is one ocean) and many (we distinguish among several different oceans even though they are all connected). The winds come from the four principal directions, are associated with the four mountains where the gods dwell, and in some Navajo creation stories are even responsible for the creation of the world.

The wind, moreover, acts in a way similar to the Christian conscience. It becomes a Messenger Wind, often called a Little Wind or Wind's Child, that swirls around and enters the individual through a hidden point in the ear. The wind then warns individuals of impeding dangers, discouraging them from pursuing courses of action that would upset their *hozho*. Like Socrates' *daimon* and the Christian conscience, this Little Wind is primarily a negative voice. Rarely does it provide positive guidance about what we must do, but rather just negative warnings about possibilities that could lead to disaster. The individual is free to pay attention to those warnings or to disregard them. In a striking contrast to most Western worldviews, the wind does not punish. Individuals suffer the natural consequences of their own actions, but there is no divine final reckoning that punishes the evil and rewards the good.

One Who Lacks Faults

The person who heeds these Messenger Winds becomes what the Navajo call "one who lacks faults." Their concept of a person without faults gives us a clear idea of what they consider a good person to be. Here are two representative Navajo descriptions (by speakers designated as "HB" and "CM") of what such a person is like.

> This person who lacks faults thinks in a good way, he thinks well of one, one thinks well of him. He usually smiles, comes up to one slowly and, showing his relationship, shakes one's hand. (HB)
> "One lacks faults" means . . . he does not argue with a person. He does not steal. He is not mean. . . . Nothing bad is said about him. He is obliging towards everything. (CM)

The person who is without faults thinks in a good way and because of this talks and acts in a good way.

Practical Ethics

As we have already mentioned, the Navajo do not have a theory of ethics. Their ethics is purely practical. It may help to get the flavor of their ethics to consider some of their typical guidelines. Many of them follow closely from one of the basic premises of Navajo life, namely, that *"life is very, very dangerous."* Kluckholm and Leighton describe some of the practical directives that follow from this view of life for the Navajo.

- "Maintain orderliness [i.e., harmony] in those sectors of life which are little subject to human control."
- "Be wary of nonrelatives."
- "Avoid excesses."
- "When you are in a new situation, do nothing."
- "Escape."

The practical value of some of these directives is obvious to outsiders. In other cases, it is initially harder to see. Wariness toward nonrelatives, for example, is partially a function of the strength of kinship ties, but it is intensified by a fear of witches, who are more likely to go unrecognized among strangers. Similarly, the idea of doing nothing in a new situation derives from a deep mistrust of the unknown. Safety is to be found in remaining still and quiet—or escaping. Instead of taking control of a situation, one tries to remain untouched by it. Again, we see the connection to the idea of harmony. If you find yourself in a new situation, then *you* are the foreign, potentially disharmonious element. As such, you need to do as little as possible until you understand how to act in a way that will restore harmony.

The Role of Ritual

The preceding directives help the Navajo to avoid disrupting harmony whenever possible. Sometimes, however, such disruptions are impossible. Illness, death (especially sudden and violent death), and other catastrophic events may disrupt that harmony. When that occurs, harmony must be reestablished. One of the principal ways in which that is accomplished is through rituals. Indeed, the very repetitive character of the chants of rituals contributes greatly to restoring a sense of orderliness to the Navajo world. Whereas to an outsider this might appear monotonous, to a Navajo the repetitiveness of the chants is a source of order and safety. The role of the rituals such as the Blessingway *(hozhooji)* is crucial in the reestablishment of a harmony *(hozho)* that has been disrupted in one way or another. When the Blessingway is performed, the Holy People who first brought the Navajo out onto the surface of the earth are present through the Holy Wind. Through their presence, moral harmony is reestablished in the world.

An Ethic of Harmony

Thus we see the central focus of Navajo ethics is the establishment of balance and harmony among the natural, the human, and the supernatural worlds. Rather than seeking to control by brute force or to flee into an otherworldly existence, the Navajo seek to establish a harmony and balance in their lives. Their ethics is intended to promote precisely this balance.

The Islamic Shari'ah

After the attacks of September 11, 2001, no discussion of Islamic ethics can fail to address the issues raised by those attacks and others. In this section, I shall sketch out some of the basic tenets of Islamic ethics (*akhlaq*) and describe the way in which it represents a strong version of divine command theory. Especially in the sections on "Islam and Tolerance" and "Jihad," I will address some of the ethical issues raised by these attacks. But first we must sketch out a bit of background.

Background

The world of Islam is vast, with over 900 million believers, and of long standing, stretching back fourteen centuries to Mohammed himself in the seventh century. Within a century after Mohammed's death, the Islamic empire had already become larger than the Holy Roman Empire ever was.

The world of Islam is also vastly different than our own Western tradition, especially in regard to the place of religion in the moral and political lives of its believers. Since the Enlightenment in modern Europe, the West has usually maintained a tradition of separation of church and state, a tradition that has found one of its strongest expressions in the political system of the United States. The image of the late Ayatollah Khomeini, dressed in stark black clerical garb, is in sharp contrast to the secular images of Western leaders such as George Bush or Margaret Thatcher or Helmut Kohl. In Iran, there is no separation of church and state, and in fact that state has an explicitly religious mandate to support the growth of Islam.

Not only does Islam wipe out the traditional Western separation of church and state, but also it eliminates the distinction between ethics and religion. Two factors account for this. First, Islam is concerned primarily with behavior rather than dogma. Whereas Christians are intensely concerned with theology, which deals with the proper interpretation of dogma, Muslims are primarily concerned with *law*, which deals with proper action. Indeed, the very word *islam* means "surrender to the will of God." Second, Muslims are concerned not only with behavior, but also with almost all behavior. Their code of behavior is a remarkably extensive one, covering practically every area of daily life. Islam thus provides a striking model of a worldview in which religion completely determines ethics. However, it is important to note that neither the Christian separation of church and state nor Islam's fusion of the two was always reflected in history. Christians during the Holy Roman Empire fused religion and politics in "Caesaropapism," whereas Muslims separated the affairs of *sultans,* the secular leaders, from those of the *ulama,* the clergy.

The Three Canonical Elements of Islam

In suggesting that Islam emphasizes the importance of right action, we do not mean to claim that this is all that comprises Islam. Traditionally, there are three canonical elements to Islam: belief or faith *(imam),* practice or action *(islam),* and virtue *(ihsan).* Islam is staunchly monotheistic in its faith, and its central belief is in a single God (Allah) and in Mohammed as God's prophet. Yet Islamic belief also encompasses faith in God's angels, revelations, and prophets. We shall consider the Muslim concept of virtue later.

As we shall see later in this chapter, Islam exemplifies what we will call the *divine command theory of moral goodness.* Actions are right in Islam because God commands them. The question, "What should I do?" is seen as equivalent to the question, "What is Allah's will?" The will of Allah is embodied in Shari'ah, the religious and civil law that governs Muslim life. An action is good simply because Allah wills it, and there is comparatively little room in mainstream traditional Islam for reason to determine Allah's will. It is the authority of revelation, contained in the Qur'an and the other sacred texts comprising the Shari'ah, that determines what is good.

There are two other traditions in Islam. One, the mystical tradition of the Sufis, is beyond our scope here. There is, however, another tradition in

Islam, dating from the ninth century and deeply affected by the Greek rationalism of Aristotle, that maintained that reason is crucial to the interpretation of the Qur'an. Those in this tradition, the Mutazila, emphasized the importance of philosophy and rational reflection upon belief. They further argued that God is not absolutely omnipotent and unconstrained by any limitations at all; rather, because God's nature is good and just, God is able to act only in ways that are good and just. Although the Mutazila did not survive as a distinct group in Islam any more than the Gnostics did in Christianity, the philosophical tradition as a whole did. This soon proved, however, to be a minority position in Islam, and proponents of Greek rationalism and philosophy came to be seen as infidels, unbelievers, and thus as not true Muslims. (This same dispute, as we shall see later in this chapter, also occurred in Christianity with quite a different outcome.) This has profound implications for ethics because it removes any possible rational restrictions on what can be taken to be God's will. There is no foundation in principle for denying that God could command us to torture or kill other human beings. (None of this, of course, denies that Allah can be compassionate; indeed, Allah commands believers to be compassionate, to care for widows and orphans, etc.)

Shari'ah: The Islamic Law

Muslim religious law covers virtually all areas of human behavior, telling believers in great detail what behavior is (1) required, (2) recommended, (3) permitted, (4) discouraged, and (5) forbidden. As members of a religion that places very strong emphasis on the importance of right action, Islamic scholars have devoted tremendous energy to articulating laws that govern actions. These fall, roughly, into two categories. On one hand, there is that body of law that governs the behavior of Muslims toward God. These include laws about prayers, fasting, alms giving (which is principally a duty to God, although the alms themselves are given to human beings), pilgrimages, and the like. These are not directly comparable to Western ethical codes because they are not primarily about the interactions of human beings among one another but rather of the actions of human beings toward a transcendent God. The most important of these laws are described in the Five Pillars. The second category of Islamic law directly regulates the ways in which human beings treat one another, and for this reason it covers approximately the same territory as Western ethical systems and can be seen as a direct counterpart to them. These laws include the penal code, regulations governing commercial interactions, and laws structuring family life. Let's first consider the Five Pillars, which govern how believers should act toward God.

The Five Pillars

Central to Islam's understanding of itself are the Five Pillars of Islam, the five elements that comprise the core of the Muslim religion. No true Muslim is allowed to openly disavow any of these Five Pillars, although in practice it is only the first of these that every Muslim has to observe actively. The pillars are

- *Shahadah:* The profession of faith that "there is no god but God (Allah) and that Mohammed is the Messenger of God"
- *Salah:* Ritual prayer and ablutions, undertaken five times a day while facing the holy city of Mecca
- *Zakah:* The obligatory giving of alms (at an annual rate of approximately 2.5 percent of one's net worth) to the poor to alleviate suffering and promote the spread of Islam
- *Saum:* Ritual fasting and abstinence from sexual intercourse and smoking, especially the obligatory month-long fast from sunup to sundown during the month of Ramadan to commemorate the first revelations to Mohammed
- *Hajj:* A ritual pilgrimage, especially the journey to Mecca that traditionally occurs in the month after Ramadan and that Muslims should undertake at least once in a lifetime

Detailed and elaborate rules govern every aspect of the believer's behavior in each of these areas. In a *hajj,* for example, the pilgrims are supposed to wear very plain, unsewn clothes that resemble burial shrouds, and they must wear nothing that distinguishes social or economic class. Similarly, there are detailed rules governing the ritual ablutions and prayer that Muslims participate in five times a day. All of these are part of the Shari'ah that governs the way in which believers relate to God.

Muslim Civil and Family Law

One of the most striking developments in Islamic countries during recent years has been a gradual return to Shari'ah as the basis of criminal, civil, and family law. In contrast to Western nations, in which the separation of church and state is usually taken for granted, this movement establishes a religious state under which all citizens are subject to a religiously based civil law. The contrast between Islamic and Western states is not, of course, complete in this regard. Christian religious groups in Western countries often push for bans on abortion and homosexuality on primarily religious grounds.

The family is central to traditional Islamic society, and much of Muslim law is devoted to strengthening the Islamic conception of the family. Although to contemporary Westerners Islam often seems to diminish the status of women, we get a somewhat different picture when Islamic practices are seen against the tribal background to which they were in part a reaction. Generally, Islamic family law raised and ensured the status of women in Islamic society as compared with the tribal cultures of the Middle East. Prior to Islam, there were no limitations on the number of wives a man might take, and a woman had no right to refuse an offer of marriage and did not receive the dower that the man gave. All of this changed with the advent of

Islam. Centuries before their rights to inheritance were recognized in the West in the nineteenth century, Islamic family law guaranteed inheritance rights for women in families. Similarly, when we place contemporary Islamic practices next to classical Judaic and Christian practices in treating women, the similarities may be more striking than the differences.

Virtue

Ihsan, or virtue, constitutes the third essential element of Islam in addition to faith and action. Traditionally, there have been two quite different ways of characterizing virtue. On one hand, virtue has been defined in terms of worshipping God. In this sense, virtue is roughly equivalent to piety or holiness. On the other hand, virtue is sometimes also defined in a way strikingly reminiscent of Aristotle as excellence in the pursuit of some end or goal. Thus, Mohammed said, "Allah has prescribed *ihsan* for everything; hence if you kill, do it well; and if you slaughter, do it well; and let each one of you sharpen his knife and let his victim die at once" (quoted in Glassé, p. 182). As we shall see toward the end of this book, this is remarkably similar to Aristotle's conception of virtue.

The Role of the *Ulama*

Any worldview that sees right actions as depending on God's will needs some way of determining what God's will is, and traditional Islam deals with this issue by stressing the role of the clergy, the *ulama,* in providing a way of giving definitive interpretations of God's will. Although the clergy often occupy a similar interpretive role in Christianity, what sets Islam apart from Christianity in this respect is that the *ulama* provide interpretations that have political as well as theological implications.

One of the most striking examples of the changing role of the *ulama* in contemporary Islam was Ayatollah Khomeini's rise to political power in Iran, which signaled a growing Islamic conviction that Muslim clergy should assume positions of political power in order to promote the development of Islam. Thus the *ulama* have not only an interpretive role, but also an executive role in implementing the law.

Jihad

The word *jihad* often conjures up frightening images in the minds of Westerners, and the popular press has not hesitated to exploit the sensationalism associated with this in the past. Although there may be occasional justification for such fears, in large measure the Islamic concept of *jihad* is much different than the popularly feared concept of a "holy war." The word *jihad* literally means "striving," and its focus is on resisting evil. Muslims commonly distinguish between the internal striving against evil desires within oneself and the external striving against forces that threaten the way of Islam. The former, internal striving is called the Greater Jihad, and the latter, externally directed striving is usually referred to as the Lesser Jihad. What is common to both types of *jihad* is the conviction that the path to holiness requires a constant vigilance and striving against the forces of evil.

Just as there is a clearly articulated tradition in the West about the conditions of just war, so too in Islam there are clearly defined limits on when someone may go to war and on the conduct of war. These are spelled out in the Qur'an. The killing of noncombatants, including women and children, is clearly forbidden by the Qur'an. The Qur'an also forbids the poisoning of wells, which Islamic scholars interpret as including a ban on biological and chemical weapons and warfare. Yet like many other religions (including Christianity), the Qur'an is open to many interpretations. Unlike many Christian churches, Islam does not have a central interpretative body that decides on the official interpretation of its sacred texts. This is in sharp contrast to the Catholic Church, for example, which has a well-defined hierarchical structure for providing definitive interpretations of the Bible. In Islam, the Qur'an is supreme and there is no single organizational structure that provides definitive interpretations of it. As a result, when radical groups such as the Taliban and al Queda lay claim to the mantle of Islam there is no single authority to dispute such claims.

Although most Muslim traditionalists have focused on the Greater Jihad, in recent years some Islamic radicals have emphasized the connection between the Lesser Jihad and revolutionary movements toward social justice. Although traditionally *jihad* has been seen as almost exclusively defensive in character, a few have begun to interpret it in a more aggressive manner. Some commentators maintain that such interpretations are not representative of traditional Islam, whereas others argue that the early spread of Islam depended directly on conquest. This leads directly to our final topic in our consideration of Islam: the place of tolerance in Islam.

Islam and Tolerance

For centuries Islam stood out as a friend to other cultures. In the Middle Ages, it was Islamic scholars who saved the works of the ancient Greeks, scientific as well as philosophical, for the West. The ancient sources on mathematics, astronomy, hydraulics, optics, and medicine were all preserved and enhanced by Islamic scholars. (Indeed, our English word *algebra* comes from the Arabic *al-jabru,* the science of restoration and balancing.) Ibn Sina (Avicenna) was best known for his work in medicine and produced the basic handbook (*The Canons of Medicine*) on medicine that was over a million words in length, but he also wrote detailed works synthesizing Aristotle, the Neoplatonic tradition, and Islamic theology. Ibn Rushd (Averroes), a twelfth-century jurist, was one of the most influential commentators on Aristotle and was a significant influence on St. Thomas Aquinas and many other medieval theologians.

Nor was Muslim culture friendly only to ideas. Muslim civilization provided a safe haven to Jews and even to Christians who experienced intolerance at home. Indeed, at the same time that Muslim leaders were showing tolerance and a cosmopolitan openness to the world, some Christian leaders were exhibiting the same intolerance that we find so unacceptable among right-wing Muslim fundamentalists. The Crusades arose as a holy war against the "infidels," and Pope Urban II at the Council of Clermont in 1095 urged Christians to attack "a despised and base race, which worships demons." He promised them complete remission of their sins (and thus immediate entry into heaven) if they died in the course of the crusade, even if they died on the road before they had begun to fight. Nor did the Pope seem overly selective about whom he invited to take up arms: "Let those who have been accustomed unjustly to wage private warfare against the faithful now go against the infidels and end with victory this war which should have been begun long ago. Let those who for a long time, have been robbers, now become knights. Let those who have been fighting against their brothers and relatives now fight in a proper way against the barbarians. Let those who have been serving as mercenaries for small pay now obtain the eternal reward."

Today the roles seem to have been reversed. In recent years we have seen the spread of Islamic fundamentalism in a number of countries, especially in the Middle East and neighboring countries. Often this trend has been accompanied by intolerance of anything that is not part of the fundamentalists' very narrow interpretation of the proper Islamic life. In its extreme forms, this fundamentalism leads to the destruction of anything seen as undermining that vision of Islamic life. Thus, have we seen not only fundamentalist-inspired attacks against the United States and other Western democracies, but even the destruction of centuries-old giant statues of the Buddha in Afghanistan, where fundamentalists waged a war against anything seen as inconsistent with their version of Islam.

Although there are certainly Islamic voices of tolerance, we also hear strident voices of intolerance clambering for center stage. Thinkers both East and West, Muslim and non-Muslim, have asked themselves what went wrong. Khaled Abou El Fadl, a Muslim professor at UCLA's law school who has written extensively on Islam and tolerance, asks himself this same question. He maintains that in the past, extremist factions in Islam—what he calls "Muslim puritans"—were marginalized and eventually came to be seen as not representative of the Islamic message. Today, however, the situation has changed, he says: "The Islamic civilization has crumbled, and the traditional institutions that once sustained and propagated Islamic orthodoxy—and marginalized Islamic extremism—have been dismantled." Thus when extremist views emerge—Osama bin Laden, the Taliban/Jihad organizations, Wahhabism—there is no structure sufficiently strong to marginalize them. In El Fadl's eyes, Islam faces a fundamental challenge: ". . . the burden and blessing of sustaining . . . the Qur'anic message of tolerance and openness to the other . . . falls squarely on the shoulders of contemporary Muslim interpreters of the tradition."

Recent events such as 9/11 present a challenge to non-Muslims as well. We can treat Islam as a single monolithic entity locked in a life-and-death

The Buddha (563–483 B.C.E.) gave his followers a message of deep compassion for all living things.

struggle against Western values. Or we can see Islam as a rich, internally divided tradition and lend our support to those voices of moderation and reconciliation that seek to live in peace with the West while retaining their distinctive way of life.

Morality, Compassion, and the Eightfold Path

The moral code of the Buddha is best understood against two background beliefs that profoundly shape the Buddhist's perception of the moral life: the character of existence and reincarnation. Only within this context can we understand the Eightfold Path and the central role of compassion in Buddhism. Buddhists traditionally emphasize the importance of the ethic of renunciation for the clergy (monks and nuns) and stress the ethic of *karma* and reincarnation for laypersons. We will begin by considering this ethic of renunciation and then turn to the ethic of *karma*.

The Four Noble Truths and the Character of Existence

Life, according to the Buddha in his sermon in "The Deer Park," inevitably involves *suffering*. Indeed, suffering is the principal fact of existence that we must recognize—the inevitability of suffering is the first of the Four Noble Truths preached by the Buddha, and the remaining three truths deal with the sources of suffering, the elimination of suffering, and the path that leads to its elimination. In an analysis that bears striking resemblances to the philosophy of the Stoics, the Buddha saw suffering as arising from a discrepancy between the way things are and our desires for how we want things to be.

Desire: **External Reality:**
"I want it to be cool." ◄——————► It's 95° outside!

SUFFERING

When we understand suffering in this way, we see that it can be alleviated or eliminated only if we are able to reduce or eliminate this discrepancy.

There are two ways of reducing this discrepancy between reality and desire. On one hand, we can attempt to transform reality so that it matches our desires, thereby reducing suffering. Typically, this is the path that the West has taken, especially insofar as it has become a technological society. Each approach to suffering has its characteristic strengths and weaknesses. We in the West seek to eliminate suffering by transforming the material world through technology. If we are suffering because the weather is hot and we want it to be cool, we invent air conditioning. This attitude, on the other hand, stands in stark contrast to the Buddha's approach to ameliorating suffering. He saw the same discrepancy but tried to change the other pole of the relationship by reducing human desire. If we can eliminate our desire to have the climate be cool, then we can eliminate our suffering as well. The path to overcoming suffering, for the Buddha, lies in overcoming our desires—and the purpose of morality is to help us in this task. Of course, Buddhists recognize the importance of changing external conditions as well. Indeed, there are well-developed traditions of Buddhist medicine, often practiced by Buddhist monks. But the crucial point is that externals can never be totally controlled to our advantage, and even if they could be, this would not deal with our deeper frustrations, dissatisfactions, and sufferings.

Each of these approaches to suffering has its merits, and each leads to a different moral outlook. The Western understanding of suffering seems particularly well suited to certain kinds of suffering that arise from physical conditions, such as excessive heat, that are subject to change. It leads to an ethic of action that emphasizes intervention and control. There are several limitations of this approach. First, some physical conditions, such as death, are not subject to such change. Second, some kinds of suffering (such as the pain that comes from losing the love of someone close) are not primarily about physical conditions, but rather center on psychological or spiritual issues. Third, the Western approach has a tendency to treat all issues as physical, even when they are not. Western medicine exemplifies this because it often equates healing the body with healing the person. Such an approach increases dependence on technology, leading to what some critics see as the technological "quick fix." On the other hand, the Buddhist approach also has its limitations. It is well suited to the psychological and spiritual aspects of suffering, but it is more likely to neglect the ways in which changes in physical conditions can ameliorate suffering. Whereas the Western attitude focuses on the morality of action and leads to an ethic of activism, the Buddhist approach to suffering is more likely to emphasize the morality of desire and to lead to an ethic of acceptance.

Reincarnation

There is a second key background belief that shapes the Buddhist understanding of morality, and that is the belief in reincarnation. The dominant metaphor that Buddhists use is that of the passing of a flame from one candle to another. The personal self moves through the wheel of existence in the same way in which the flame moves from one candle to another: It is both the same flame and yet a different flame. So the same personal ego is not reborn in a different body; instead, some spark of life passes on to a new individual. Hence, Buddhists do not believe in an eternal personal soul, and this sets them apart from Christians. Christians typically believe in the immortality of each individual soul, and often within Christian religions the function of morality is to ensure the salvation of the soul. Each individual soul, after a single life on earth, thus gains eternal existence, either in heaven or in hell. Yet Buddhists are typically striving to *extinguish* the personal self through the overcoming of desire. It is hardly surprising, then, that they do not believe in an eternal self. The self is but a fleeting bundle of sensations, and wisdom lies in the recognition of the ephemeral character of the self. Instead of seeking to strengthen a purified self as Christians do, Buddhists take the extinguishing of the individual self as their goal.

Yet the doctrine of *karma* still plays an important role for Buddhists and has important ethical implications. Each individual action either helps to free us from the personal self or to increase our attachment to it. Because *nirvana* is achieved through a detachment from that personal self, actions that increase that attachment—greed, jealousy, and envy are some of the possible motives for such actions—force us to remain in the cycle of existence longer, until we can break the attachment. The cycle of reincarnation is a gradual process through which we struggle to free ourselves from our past, unwholesome acts and to achieve a state of ever-increasing detachment that culminates in the extinguishing of the personal self, *nirvana*. Thus the goal is not the salvation of the individual soul, but rather its extinction.

The Eightfold Path

The moral teachings of the Buddha offer a way of extinguishing that self, a way of reducing suffering by overcoming the desires that conflict with the facts of existence. This path to *nirvana* is the Fourth Noble Truth, and the path is an eightfold one. It consists of

- Right views
- Right intention
- Right speech
- Right action
- Right livelihood
- Right effort
- Right mindfulness
- Right concentration

The first two of these paths require the development of wisdom *(Prajna)*; the next three are the proper domain of morality *(Sila)*, whereas the final three are developed through concentration *(Samadhi)*. The emphasis in the eightfold path is on right understanding and right thought because right speaking and acting follow from this. Right meditation provides the mental discipline necessary to overcome desire. Anything that clouds the mind's true perception of itself is to be avoided. Thus, drugs and alcohol, for example, are to be shunned. So, too, powerful emotions such as anger should be avoided because they also cloud our perceptions and fetter us to the everyday world of illusion. Thus Buddhism preaches an *ethic of detachment,* one that claims that the ultimate state is one in which the personal self has been overcome and left behind.

Compassion

After the Buddha's death, Buddhism developed along two distinctive paths. In Mahayana Buddhism, which is the Buddhist path followed in many northern Asian countries, the realization of the fact of suffering leads in a different direction than is found in the Theravada Buddhism of southern countries such as Cambodia, Laos, and Sri Lanka. Whereas Theravada Buddhism stresses the importance of self-purification and a striving for detachment from this world, Mahayana Buddhism stresses the way in which compassion for the suffering of others leads one back into the world in order to help others to overcome their own suffering. In Mahayana Buddhism, compassion for the suffering of others leads the Buddhist back into the world, relinquishing the possibility of immanent *nirvana* in order to help others free themselves from their earthly bounds, from the wheel of life and death. Indeed, we find here one of the strongest statements of *altruism* imaginable. In the Diamond Banner Sutra, for example, followers of the Buddha are urged to take the entire suffering of the world onto themselves. The rationale is simple if daunting: How much better the world would be if all its suffering fell on me alone, and everyone else was without woe.

Nowhere is this emphasis on compassion more prominent than in Tibetan Buddhism, where training in compassion and loving kindness is one of the mainstays of Buddhist disciplines. Indeed, the fourteenth Dalai Lama, who is the spiritual leader of many Buddhists, is one of the most powerful voices today for compassion, kindness, and world peace. This message of compassion, kindness, and peace extends to all living creatures, including animals, which are not to be killed. All suffering, not just the suffering of human beings, deserves our compassion.

Religious Ethics without God

One of the distinctive characteristics of Buddhism is that there is no reference to a personal God of any sort. Indeed, some have even characterized Buddhism as a "nontheistic religion." This distinction has profound implications for our understanding of the relationship between religion and ethics. In monotheistic religions, God's commands are often seen as the basis of right and wrong. Islam provides an excellent example of this because in Islamic thought "morally right" is simply equivalent to "willed by Allah." Yet Buddhism allows no such foundation for morality because it contains no idea of an individual God who could be a source of ethical commands.

Instead of grounding moral commands in God's will, Buddhism ultimately grounds them in the notion of *karma*, a doctrine of ethical causation whose operation is almost akin to the laws of Western physics. In a sense, this is a consequentialist moral doctrine, that is, it maintains that the rightness or wrongness of actions depends on their consequences. But two points need to be noted here. First, consequences are not judged by the same standards that many versions of Western utilitarianism (which we shall examine in Chapter 5) employ. Second, the motives behind our actions are not irrelevant to the consequences, as they are in Western utilitarianism. Indeed, a common Buddhist saying is, "I call the motive to be the deed." The rightness or wrongness of actions (including their accompanying intentions) depends on their karmic consequences.

How, then, are karmic consequences determined? Here we find a fundamental tension in Buddhism already alluded to. On one hand, karmic consequences are determined by the extent to which they contribute to individual self-purification, to the attainment of *nirvana*. Actions that purify us, that loosen our ties to bodily pleasures and distorting emotions, are thus good precisely because they move us along the path to self-extinction. This is the tradition of Theravada Buddhism. On the other hand, Mahayana Buddhism understands karmic consequences much more in terms of an action's contribution to reducing the overall amount of suffering in the world for all creatures. Thus, for the Mahayana Buddhist, the right action may well be to forgo immediate salvation and go back into the world in order to help to free others from the wheel of life and death.

The sayings of the Buddha and the numerous commentaries upon them have, of course, a central place in the moral life of Buddhists. However, in most versions of Buddhism, the moral truths enunciated in these texts are not true *because* the Buddha said them; rather, they are true because they express the fundamental and inexorable character of existence. Similar considerations apply to the precepts (which are different for monastics and laypersons) and the *vinaya* (the monastic rule).

Respecting Religious Diversity

The preceding examples bring to light an important aspect of the relationship between religion and morality. In many cultures, moral codes are either directly or indirectly dependent on religious beliefs. Religion either dictates certain behavior as good or bad, or else at least provides the background beliefs about the character of existence within which moral codes are then developed. Moreover, religion often provides or supplements the motivation to be moral, especially in difficult times. Finally, religion may provide the consolation necessary to deal with the unavoidable injustices of our world.

One of the central moral issues that we all face, whether we espouse religious beliefs or not, is how we ought to deal with the diversity of religious beliefs. Let me make several suggestions here. First, we ought to respect the religious beliefs of others and their right to hold those beliefs. (Respect, it should be noted, is not synonymous with approval.) Second, because religious beliefs are often essential components of fundamental worldviews, we should try to understand and appreciate those worldviews and thereby understand more about our own view of the world. Third, it is important to seek out common ground between different religious traditions. Even when the differences are great, the similarities may be greater. An awareness of common elements, such as the importance of respect and compassion, can provide the basis for developing agreements about how we can live together with our differences. Fourth, it seems appropriate in certain circumstances to make judgments about how deeply we are willing to let other people's religious beliefs impinge on our own behavior. This is perhaps the most difficult issue raised by religious pluralism because it is the area in which the possibility of conflict is highest and in which there are often no shared rules for negotiating disagreements.

RELIGIOUS BELIEF AND MORAL RULES

Those who have been involved in the discussion of the relation between religion and ethics have focused on questions about the morality of specific types of *actions* (war, abortion, euthanasia, etc.), but the underlying issue has always been about whether reason or religious sources (revelation, tradition, the word of religious leaders, etc.) tell us what the right thing to do is.

POSSIBLE RELATIONSHIPS BETWEEN RELIGION AND REASON IN ETHICS

	Supremacy of Religion	Compatibilist Theories	Supremacy of Reason
Strong version	All morality based on divine commands	Reason and religion are identical.	Ethics based only on reason; atheistic or agnostic
Weak version	Teleological suspension of the ethical	Reason and religion may be different but do not conflict.	Even God must follow dictates of reason.

There are, broadly speaking, three possible answers to the question of whether reason or religion takes precedence in ethics. First, some have maintained that, whenever there is a moral conflict between religion and reason, *religion* provides the correct guide for our behavior and *should take precedence over reason*. The most notable example of this position is the claim that God's commands determine what we ought to do. We shall consider two representatives of this tradition, *divine command theorists* and those who admit that ethics is usually determined by reason but claim that in some cases of conflict *the ethical (i.e., reason) is suspended in favor of the divine*. At the other end of the spectrum are those who maintain that in cases of such moral conflict, reason ought to take precedence over religion. Reason provides the criterion for judging which actions are right and wrong. Some in this tradition, whom we shall call the *priority of reason theorists,* are theists who claim that even God must do what is right simply because it is right, whereas others *(atheistic ethicists)* reject any religiously based morality whatsoever. There is a middle ground between these two traditions that we shall refer to as *compatibilist theories*. **Compatibilism** claims that **religion and reason are compatible with each other in moral matters, that they do not conflict.** The *strong version* of this position claims that ethics and religion are saying the same thing, although perhaps in different language; the *weak version* claims that religion and ethics may be saying different, but not incompatible, things.

Let's examine each of these positions.

Theories That Give Priority to Religion over Reason in Ethics

Those who claim that God's commands take precedence over reason-based morality fall into two distinct groups. On the one hand, there are those **(divine command theorists)** who maintain that there is no real conflict between God's commands and genuine morality because *whatever God commands is what is right simply because God commands it*. In other words, the only reason something is right is that God commands it. Conversely, the only reason something is wrong is that God forbids it. Thus, those in this tradition claim that there can never be a genuine conflict between religion and ethics because ethics just *is* what God commands. A corollary of this is that if God does not exist, then neither does ethics. This is the sense of Dostoyevsky's dictum, "If God does not exist, then everything is permitted." On the other hand, there are those (advocates of what Søren Kierkegaard called the **teleological suspension of the ethical**) who maintain that ethics has an independent foundation (usually in reason) but that God's commands override the rules of morality in those cases where a conflict occurs. Representatives of this position are willing to accord an independent validity to ethics, so they would not say that if God does not exist, everything is permitted. However, they do maintain that there is a higher law than the ethical, that God's word takes precedence over the commands of morality. Let's consider both of these traditions more closely.

Divine Command Theorists

In his dialogue *Euthyphro,* Plato poses the question of whether the gods love what is holy because it is holy or whether it is holy because the gods love it. The corresponding question in the realm of ethics is whether God loves the good because it is good or whether it is good because God loves it. Divine command theorists give a clear and unequivocal answer to this question in the area of ethics: They maintain that whatever is good is good only because God wills it to be good.

This position has serious implications for how divine command theorists live their everyday lives. Moral decisions are ultimately made on the basis of what God commands, not on what reason tells us. We have to turn to God for the answer to all our questions about how to act. No matter what God commands, it is right just because God commands it. There simply is nothing more to say about it.

Divine command theories fit best within a monotheistic religion in which God is all good. Christianity and Islam both meet this requirement. Yet divine command theories make little or no sense within either a Navajo or a Buddhist worldview. For the Navajo, two things count against the divine command view of ethics. First, for the Navajo there are many gods (what they call the Holy People), not just one, and they are not necessarily in agreement with one another. Second, the gods are not all good; they, too, are a mixture of good and evil. Despite the fact that they are called the "Holy People," the gods of the Navajo neither always act good nor always give good advice to The People. Indeed, Kluckholm and Leighton, whose *The Navaho* is one of the finest studies of The People by outsiders, report no trace of the belief that an action is right simply because God commands it. The situation is quite different in Buddhism because there simply is no personal God in the Buddhist religion. Consequently, the idea that something is good because God wills it simply has no place.

The Teleological Suspension of the Ethical

Abraham believed that God's commands take precedence over morality. Many today share this belief in the priority of religious convictions over moral rules, even if they disagree about which religious convictions are to be given precedence. Fundamentalist Muslims believe very strongly that their religious beliefs take precedence over any demands of secular morality. Similarly, Christian religious fundamentalists take a comparable position, although it is the commands of Jesus rather than Allah that override secular morality for them. Orthodox Jews hold comparable beliefs about the commands of the God of the Old Testament. What all of these positions have in common is the conviction that God's commands, not human reason or local *mores*, are the ultimate guide to human behavior.

Kierkegaard, a nineteenth-century Danish philosopher who is often seen as one of the founders of the religious strain of existentialism, devoted much of his work to a discussion of the relation between religion and ethics. In *Fear and Trembling*, his analysis of the case of Abraham, Kierkegaard argues that there are times when God's commands override the demands of morality. In contrast to divine command theorists who maintain that morality is simply a matter of God's commands, Kierkegaard acknowledges that morality has its own independent basis in reason. Thus, for Kierkegaard, if God did not exist, morality would not be eliminated. It would still have its own independent foundation. However, if we genuinely believe in God, we must believe that God has ultimate supremacy, even over reason. If God commands something, then it overrides the commands of morality.

Criticisms of Divine Command Theories

Divine command theories of ethics have been subjected to strong criticisms from both theistic and atheistic philosophers who maintain that God's commands cannot override an ethics based on reason. Let's consider three of these criticisms.

How Can We Know God's Will?

One of the most difficult questions for divine command theorists to answer is the question of how we can come to know God's will. The difficulty is not that no one claims to know God's will. Rather, the problem is just the opposite: *Too many* people claim to know God's will, and they have quite different ideas of what it is. Why, critics ask, should we believe that any one of them has any greater claim to being right than any other? Perhaps God's will is revealed in sacred texts—but which ones? Do we look to the Bible, the Qur'an, or the writings of Mary Baker Eddy? Although the answer is clear to the believer, to the outsider there appears to be no reason to think that one group has any greater access to God's genuine commands than any other group. Even if one accepts a particular religious tradition, there is still a significant problem in determining exactly what God's will is. Typically, sacred texts tell us too much and too little: too much because they often contain contradictory statements; too little because they are often not specific enough.

Sacred texts are not the only way in which people claim to know God's will. Many religious thinkers claim that God speaks to individuals through some kind of voice. In the Christian tradition, this is the voice of conscience; among the Navajo, the Holy Wind speaks to individuals by means of a Messenger Wind that enters through the person's ear. In most religions, there is an institutionalized code of conduct that is refined, transmitted, and often enforced by an institutionalized clergy. The *ulama*, the Muslim clergy, are in charge of the interpretation of the Shari'ah. Similar structures are found in most organized religions.

Some religions still see signs in the natural world as indications of God's will, although these are usually religious traditions that remain largely untouched by Western natural science. Animistic religions, for example, often see many natural events, ranging from cataclysmic occurrences such as volcanic eruptions to much less noticeable things such as the appearance of a brown owl, as giving clues to God's will and the course of future events. These perspectives depend on a concept of nature that is far different than that found in Western thought since Descartes. Remnants of this view remain, for example, in the Christian belief in miracles, in astrology, and sometimes in superstitions.

The difficulty with all of these sources is not that they tell us too little, but that they claim to tell us too much. If they all are correct, they give us a wealth of varied and often contradictory information—and no way of resolving the contradictions satisfactorily.

God and Criteria for the Divine

The example of God asking Abraham to sacrifice his only son offers an interesting and difficult challenge to divine command theorists. Some philosophers, such as Robert Adams at Yale, have argued that God cannot require cruelty for its own sake because this contradicts the notion that God is love. If we did not have some concept of God, and with this some criteria (such as love) for what legitimately counts as the divine and what doesn't (such as cruelty), the door would be open for saying that God could command us to do *anything*, even rape or pillage or kill. But the difficulty is that if we do establish some criteria for the divine, such as love or compassion, then it seems that these stand above God's commands, thereby limiting them. Consequently, these no longer seem to be divine command theories, that is, they no longer maintain that actions are good solely because God commands them. There is a higher standard to which even God must conform. The divine command theorists seem to be caught on the horns of Euthyphro's dilemma. Either they maintain that a good action simply is whatever God commands, in which case they permit the possibility that God might command us to kill or pillage; or they maintain that there are some limits on what God can legitimately command, in which case they aren't genuine divine command theorists any longer because they say that there are independent limits on God's commands.

This issue is sometimes seen as a comparatively abstract one with little real import for our behavior. William of Ockham, for example, held a strong version of the divine command theory in which he believed that whatever God might command was good simply by virtue of the fact that God commanded it, but he never seriously entertained the possibility that God might command murder or mayhem. Yet this issue becomes absolutely crucial when religious authorities command in God's name a course of action that involves actions that would usually be considered immoral. Holy wars, whether crusades or *jihads,* would be but one example of this. The Holy Inquisition is certainly another, as is persecution of any kind that appeals to religion for its foundation. If one is a believer and a strong divine command theorist, there is little basis for opposing such actions unless it is to challenge the legitimacy of the religious authority's claim to be speaking in God's voice. The one thing that opponents cannot say, if they believe in the divine command theory, is that God would never condone a particular type of activity. Strong divine command theories eliminate such appeals because they hold that whatever God wills is good simply because God wills it. Thus, if God wills war or torture or even genocide, then it must be good. The divine command theory removes any kind of moral leverage that others, whether believers or nonbelievers, could use to convince authorities that such actions were not good.

Divine Commands and Human Autonomy

The third major difficulty faced by divine command theories centers on the issue of human autonomy. By saying that the good is simply whatever God wills it to be, this position makes human moral life depend solely on God's will. What place, then, does human reason have? Are human beings simply reduced to the role of obedient puppets, to pets that respond to whatever the master's will is at the moment? In their strongest forms, divine command theories of ethics seem to leave human beings little room for independent thought or reasoned choice.

Defenders of divine command theories are also concerned about autonomy, but not primarily the autonomy of human beings. One of the principal motivating concerns in their position is to preserve God's autonomy, the divine sovereignty. The guiding insight for divine command theorists is that God is all-powerful; consequently, there is no reason to think that there are any necessary limits on God's power that are imposed from the outside. They seek to preserve the omnipotence of God at all costs.

Autonomy of Ethics Theories

Many philosophers have been unwilling to accept the claims of divine command theorists and have argued that the justification of ethics does not depend on God's will and that, in cases of conflict between the dictates of reason and God's commands, reason ought to override apparently divine commands.

Defenders of the **autonomy of ethics** may be either theists or atheists. Among theists, *autonomy of ethics philosophers* argue that even God must do what is right. God's choices are constrained by what is morally right. Theists are attracted to this position for at least two reasons. First, it provides a way—the appeal to reasoned arguments—for settling moral disputes with- · out an appeal to religious authority. Furthermore, it provides a bridge to the nonbeliever, a common ground for moral deliberation that would not be available to the divine command theorist. *Agnostic and atheistic philosophers* are also attracted to the autonomy of ethics position because it gives ethics an independent existence and justification in a world without God.

Before looking at both the theistic and atheistic versions of the supremacy of ethics position, it is helpful to consider the historical and conceptual background against which they arose.

The Heritage of the Enlightenment

The principal characteristic of the **Enlightenment** in seventeenth- and eighteenth-century Europe was the *belief in the power of reason*. Developing against the background of the rise of modern science, Enlightenment thought was captured by the dream that it could provide an absolute and presuppositionless starting point for itself. The model was geometry, which seemed to offer absolute certitude in its proofs. The Enlightenment captured a rising faith in the power of the human intellect, especially through modern science, to understand the world and to provide a meaning to life. Enlightenment philosophers hoped that philosophy could emulate mathematics and achieve an absolute foundation for its belief. Reason could then at last be free from dependence on religion.

The principal heritage of the Enlightenment is its beliefs in the power and the autonomy of reason. These two beliefs about reason—its autonomy and its efficacy—lie at the foundation of much of modern ethical thought. To understand our Enlightenment heritage in this regard is to better understand ourselves. Let's consider each of these two beliefs.

The Autonomy of Reason

The belief in the *autonomy* of reason is the belief that reason does not need to take anything outside of itself for granted. This belief, which pervades the history of modern thought, is most evident in the various attempts of modern philosophers to start anew and provide a solid foundation for all our ideas. René Descartes, a precursor of the Enlightenment, provides a perfect example of this in his *Meditations*. At the beginning of his *Meditations,* he casts everything into doubt in order to avoid inadvertently assuming something that is not true. Then, purely through the power of reason, he tries to establish a solid foundation for all our well-founded beliefs (especially those of mathematics and physics). From the indisputable truth of the statement that "I think, therefore I am" (*Cogito, ergo sum*), Descartes hoped to build a foundation for knowledge that is absolutely certain and secure without taking anything for granted at all. This includes, but is not limited to, religious beliefs. Three hundred years later, at the beginning of the twentieth century, we find essentially the same dream still alive, this time in logical positivism. Once again, philosophers sought a presuppositionless starting point for grounding all our knowledge claims. Reason, now reduced to the laws of logic, was thought to provide precisely that foundation.

It is precisely this belief in the role that reason should play that provides the background for much contemporary thinking about the relationship between reason and religion. Even those who have lost their faith in the autonomy of reason are still children of the Enlightenment in the sense that they believe that reason *should* have been autonomous. This expectation that reason should be autonomous is a principal heritage of the Enlightenment, even among those who feel that reason has failed to fulfill this expectation.

The Efficacy of Reason

The other principal heritage of the Enlightenment is the belief in the *efficacy* of reason. This belief is an understandable correlate of the tremendous advances of modern science. The Enlightenment belief was that reason could change the world and could change us. Reason could motivate, could move us to action. Immanuel Kant, for example, firmly believed that reason not only could tell us what is good, but also could motivate us to act in accord with its demands. Georg Wilhelm Hegel saw the whole of human history as the gradual unfolding and development of reason throughout history.

Theistic Versions of the Autonomy of Reason in Ethics

When Immanuel Kant developed his ethics, his guiding belief was that reason alone could tell us what to do and could motivate us to do it. As a theistic adherent of the belief in the autonomy of ethics, Kant believed that reason is the same for everyone, both God and human beings alike, and that both are obligated to follow its dictates.

In the eyes of many theists, the advantage of this approach to ethics is that it eliminates any necessary barrier between believers and nonbelievers in regard to their moral convictions. Because everyone has the same access to reasoned arguments, both theists and nontheists stand on equal footing in their search for the moral life.

Agnostic and Atheistic Versions of the Supremacy of Reason in Ethics

Many philosophers who maintain an agnostic or atheistic position as the basis for their views on the autonomy of ethics simply do not address the issue of the relationship between reason and religion in ethics because in their eyes there is no relationship. They are *de facto* agnostics or atheists. Some philosophers have, however, spoken out directly against the influence of religion on ethics. In the final section of this chapter, we will consider two nineteenth-century philosophers in this tradition, Friedrich Nietzsche and

Karl Marx. In the twentieth century, two of the most eloquent voices in this tradition were the French existentialist Jean-Paul Sartre and the British logician and analytical philosopher Bertrand Russell. Sartre saw God as the ultimate threat to human freedom, and in his "Letter on Humanism" he argued that God had to die in order to make room for human freedom. Similarly, Russell saw belief in God as a pernicious fiction that, if believed, could rob human beings of their freedom.

Both Russell and Sartre see human beings as existing in a natural world that is essentially indifferent to them and see morality as a purely human phenomenon that has no deeper roots in either a natural or a transcendent order. This stands in sharp contrast to theistic positions, which often claim that there is a continuity between the moral order and the natural world and which see morality as woven more deeply into the fabric of existence. Recall, for example, the Navajo vision of moral harmony, which includes harmony with nature as an essential dimension of *hozho*. Nature and morality reflect one another. In a quite different way, the Christian traditions often see the natural order as fundamentally good and condemn that which runs counter to nature. When contrasted to their theistic counterparts, agnostic and atheistic accounts of ethics typically seem to be much less deeply rooted in any order outside that of purely human creation.

Compatibilist Theories

Among those who maintain that there is no conflict between religion and ethics are some, like the eighteenth-century philosopher Hegel, who argued that faith and reason could not conflict. According to Hegel, they are simply saying the same thing in different languages. Whereas religion speaks in the language of symbolism and myth, philosophy speaks in the language of reason. The basis of such positions, which we will refer to as **strong compatibilism,** is a deeply rooted metaphysical conviction that the divine and the natural are in fundamental harmony and profoundly reflect one another. According to the strong compatibilist, God would not create a universe in which reason is at odds with God's thinking, nor would God create a world in which the natural order is opposed to the divine. Rather, according to the strong compatibilist, the natural order is a reflection of the divine. Reason and revelation are but two paths to the same truth.

Weak compatibilism is more modest in its claims. It begins with the conviction that God would not create a natural or a moral order that is opposed to the divine or a human reason that is contradicted by revelation. Yet even though they are not in conflict, revelation (according to the weak compatibilist) may tell us more than reason is ever able to disclose. A weak compatibilist, like the medieval Christian theologian Thomas Aquinas, maintains that there may well be religious beliefs that are not reducible to reason, that cannot be achieved through any means except revelation. Although this content does not contradict reason, it does go beyond it. For example, reason may establish that we treat our neighbors with respect; Christianity might go further and enjoin us to love our neighbors. Indeed, the philosopher Philip Quinn, in one of his arguments in favor of a Christian Divine Command Theory, has argued that the distinctive message of Jesus is that we should love everyone; this, Quinn maintains, goes beyond what morality based on reason can demand of us. These are not contradictory demands, but religion in this case requires more of us than does reason alone. Weak compatibilism thus combines some of the strengths of both divine command theories and autonomy of ethics positions. It recognizes that religion has some distinctive contribution to the moral life that is not completely reducible to reason, yet at the same time it recognizes that reason has its own proper domain.

SAINTS AND MORAL EXEMPLARS

In the previous section, the focus of our discussion was the morality of specific actions and whether the rightness or wrongness of such actions ultimately depends on an appeal to God or not. Yet as we shall see in much more detail in Chapter 9, there is another approach to morality that focuses on the morality of *character* rather than on specific actions. Its principal question is about what kind of persons we ought to be, rather than about how we should act. Good actions are seen as flowing from good character.

Saints

Consider the religious traditions that we discussed at the beginning of this chapter and their religious leaders. We see very different models of moral goodness and of the relationship between religion and morality. In Christianity and Buddhism, there are strong monastic traditions that see the pursuit of holiness as involving a renunciation of the world. This stands in sharp contrast to Islam, where there is much more emphasis on the establishment of Muslim states and the pursuit of religious goals through political power. In Native American religions, there is a long tradition that maintains that spiritual leaders do not seek positions of power.

Despite these differences, we see a greater level of fundamental compatibility among religious leaders than we find among religious dogmas. Imagine, for example, the Dalai Lama, Mother Teresa, Bishop Tutu, and Black Elk coming together. They all are deeply religious persons of goodwill, and it is difficult to believe that they could not find common moral ground. We will discuss the issue of saints in more detail in Chapter 8.

Stories

So, too, is the method of teaching different when the focus is on persons rather than on dogmas. We learn about people through stories, and there is less of a chance of attributing an absolute and exclusive quality to stories than there is to dogma. Furthermore, stories often make it easier for individuals to identify with those outside their own tradition. Certain elemental stories—about love, loss, and death—allow cross-cultural identification that is more difficult to achieve when doctrine is at issue.

This tradition promises greater compatibility between religion and ethics, primarily because the focus is on individual persons rather than on principles. Principles stand in logical relations to one another: They can be identical, compatible, or inconsistent. The relations among people have an elasticity not found in theories. Indeed, even in this book on moral theories, many of the chapters begin with stories and provide extended narrative examples. Furthermore, in the interviews with major theorists in this book, I have tried to place their theories to some extent within the context of their lives. As we shall see in Chapter 9, Aristotle's ethics of character offers a helpful framework for understanding the place of stories in the moral life.

THE ROLE OF RELIGION IN THE MORAL LIFE

Philosophers through the centuries have been strongly divided over whether religion is a positive or a negative influence in the moral life, whether it enhances or diminishes morality. Let's begin with those who argue that religion is a threat to the moral life.

Is Religion Harmful to Morality?

The last hundred and fifty years in the West have witnessed a number of scathing critiques of religion and, in particular, of the effects of religion on the moral life of humanity. The claim that has been made is that religion undermines human dignity and robs people of the autonomy necessary for making moral decisions. Let's briefly examine the ideas of two major representatives of this line of argument: Karl Marx and Friedrich Nietzsche.

Marx and the "Opiate of the People"

Over a century ago, Karl Marx claimed that religion is the "opiate of the people." Like opium, religion—in Marx's eyes—dulls the senses, lulls people into a false sense of security, and undermines their motivation to bring about effective social change to remedy conditions of injustice. When virtues such as humility and meekness are extolled, when people are told that injustices will be righted in the afterlife, and when suffering in this world is praised as preparation for salvation, few people will be motivated to challenge the existing social, political, and economic order.

Indeed, there is some historical justification for Marx's charges. In many countries in Latin America, for example, peasant populations were kept in a state of virtual slavery for generations, and religion played an important role in maintaining a very oppressive socioeconomic system. Whereas a large percentage of the population lived in staggering poverty and often worked under brutal conditions, a privileged few reaped great profits. To the extent that Christianity was used—or abused—to sanction this situation, it certainly functioned as an opiate for the people and as an enemy of social justice.

Nietzsche, Morality, and the Death of God

Friedrich Nietzsche, the other major nineteenth-century voice against religion, also criticized Christianity for its effects on people, including the way in which it has prevented the development of a genuine morality of strength. According to Nietzsche, Christianity is founded on *ressentiment,* the desire of the weak to gain control over the strong without themselves developing strengths. It is an example of what Nietzsche called the "herd morality" or "slave morality." The Christian virtue of humility provides a perfect example of this in Nietzsche's eyes. Humility, according to Nietzsche, is a sign of weakness, of lack of power, of a failure to believe in oneself. Christianity takes this weakness and pretends that it is a strength and then criticizes those with genuine strength—in this case, those with pride—as bad. Thus, Christianity inverts the moral world, making the weak strong and the strong weak. The result, Nietzsche argues, is a world of mediocrity and sameness, a weak world from which genuine individuality has vanished.

When Nietzsche proclaimed that "God is dead," he was also making a statement about morality. In the traditional Christian worldview, moral values had an ultimate guarantee in God. This had at least two important implications for ethics. First, because God is good, goodness is not just a human creation. It has an objectivity independent of human choice. Second, God's goodness guarantees that justice will ultimately prevail, that the wicked will be punished and the good will be rewarded. This provides an important answer to the question, "Why should I be moral?" God's goodness ensures that a lifetime of being good will be rewarded in the long run. When Nietzsche said that God is dead, he meant (among other things) that morality has lost any transcendent foundation for its values and any guarantee that the scales of justice will be righted in a later life. In Nietzsche's view, morality must cease to be other-worldly. It must become purely a morality of this world, a morality of strength and self-affirmation that does not depend on a God or an afterworld.

Historical Accidents versus Necessary Connections

The common message in this criticism is that religion is harmful to morality. It encourages a false morality and undermines human autonomy.

The central question that these critiques pose is whether religion *necessarily* has the effects that Marx and Nietzsche attribute to it. It may well be that religion has at least to some extent in fact had the negative influence that Marx and Nietzsche identified, but religious thinkers could well join

Marx and Nietzsche in condemning such effects. Insofar as religion does undermine an individual's sense of autonomy, then religion is contradicting its own goals, falling short of its potential for human liberation. Far from shackling human beings, religion can liberate them to achieve a more fulfilling life in this existence as well as in the next. In order to examine the merits of this reply, let us now turn to a consideration of the arguments that claim that, without religion, morality would be impoverished.

Does Morality Need Religion?

Although arguments have been advanced in support of divine command theories, there is a sense in which such arguments are beside the point. Divine command theories claim that God's word takes precedence over reason, so there would be something logically odd if they were to appeal to reason to support their position. Divine command theorists can, however, point to several advantages or strengths of their position. They do not claim that they accept the position for this reason—rather, they accept it because it is the word of God. Nonetheless, they can point to strengths in their position that defenders of the autonomy of ethics cannot claim. Let's examine two of these strengths.

Ultimate Justice

One of the most vexing difficulties for moral philosophers is that morality demands on some occasions that we set personal advantage aside and act for the sake of some larger good. Morality may require, for example, that we behave honestly, even when those around us are accepting bribes and never getting caught for it. Why should we behave morally when we lose by doing so? Divine command theorists have an answer to this question that is not available to others: They claim that ultimately God will balance the scales. The just will be rewarded, and the unjust punished. If this is true, it certainly provides followers of divine command theories with a motivation to be moral that is not present for others. All of this presumes, of course, that God is just.

Religion as a Motivation to Be Good

In considering the relation between religion and ethics, we have seen that there are really two distinct issues, one relating to the *content* of morality, the other pertaining to its *motivation*. Our discussion has focused primarily on whether the content of morality derives from divine commandments or from reason. Yet even philosophers like Kant, who concluded that reason is the source of morality, were troubled by whether reason alone could provide a sufficient motivation to be moral. Kant himself vacillated on this issue. On one hand, he argued that reason does provide a sufficient motivation in the feeling of respect for the law that it creates. On the other hand, he felt that from a practical point of view it is necessary to postulate the existence of

God and the immortality of the soul in order to make sense of morality. There are several senses in which religion is able to provide that motivation. First, as we have seen, the thought that the just will be rewarded may often be a sustaining motivating thought for people in morally difficult times, guaranteeing that their virtue will be rewarded. Second, the other side of this same motivational coin is the threat of punishment and damnation, which also can be a powerful motivating force. Both of these factors presuppose a religion containing beliefs about personal immortality and some divinely administered system of rewards and sanctions. Third, in addition to these factors, we should note that religion provides practices and structures that support its values. There is usually a church of some kind and a community of faithful who provide mutual support to one another. Ethics lacks a comparable support structure. Even religions that lack a belief in personal immortality can provide such communal support.

Religion as Liberating

Critics of religion such as Marx and Nietzsche saw religion as a profound source of social conformity, as a means of maintaining the status quo and keeping people confined to their existing social and economic positions. Yet there is another face of religion, one that was perhaps less visible in the nineteenth century, that suggests that religion may be a profoundly liberating force in individuals' lives and an important force for social change.

Consider the role of religion in some of the most important moral transformations of our day. In the civil rights movement in America, religious faith was a central source of both vision and motivation for those involved in the fight for equality. Many of the black leaders of the civil rights movement, both major figures such as Reverend Martin Luther King, Jr. and countless minor figures such as local pastors and preachers, were ordained ministers. Similarly, throughout the world religious leaders have been tremendously important forces for peaceful change. The story of Archbishop Romero in El Salvador is a powerful example of the transformation from a conservatively minded view of religion to a much more radical, liberation-oriented perspective. Initially a strong supporter of the repressive government and its institutions, Romero gradually became committed to the cause of the poor and the oppressed. He eventually was killed for his beliefs. Much of liberation theology in Latin America is an eloquent testimony to the way in which religion can allow people to escape the status quo and to develop a vision of genuine human equality. So, too, in other parts of the world. Bishop Desmond Tutu remains one of the most eloquent and powerful voices for peaceful change in South Africa. Mohendas Gandhi certainly sought to bring an equality and respect to India that changed the face of that subcontinent—again, without resorting to violence. Although religion may sometimes serve the functions that Marx and Nietzsche attributed to it, the evidence of the twentieth century is that it can also be a powerful force for moral progress and human dignity.

RELIGIOUS BELIEF: DIVERSITY AND DIALOGUE

Benjamin Barber, a professor of political science at Rutgers, has suggested that our world is torn between two tendencies, which he calls Jihad and Mac-World. On the one hand, there is "a Jihad in the name of a hundred narrowly conceived faiths against every kind of interdependence, every kind of artificial social cooperation and civic mutuality." On the other hand, we find ourselves increasingly in "one MacWorld tied together by technology, ecology, communications, and commerce." We are caught up in both these opposing trends. "The planet," Barber continues, "is falling precipitately apart *and* coming reluctantly together at the very same moment." One of the central challenges facing us within this context is to create ways of living together that respect diversity but that provide a sufficiently broad common ground to ensure comparatively peaceful and harmonious interaction. The movement toward MacWorld threatens to obliterate most differences in favor of a homogeneity without moral substance, and this is hardly respectful of diversity. The movement toward Jihad, on the other hand, threatens to pull us back toward regional, warring tribes, each pitted ferociously against all the others.

Where does religion fit in this picture? Clearly there is a strain—present in most religions, but stronger in some than in others—toward proclaiming its truth as universal. This is the strain in religion that is convinced that it has found the absolute truth and, all too often, that those who deny this truth are not to be tolerated. It is the spirit of the Inquisition, which tried and executed people for heresy. It is the spirit of all those who have died—and killed—for religion. We can call this the *fundamentalist* tradition in religion.

Fundamentalism is not limited to any single religion, and it is not itself a religious belief; rather, it is better described in this context as a way of holding particular beliefs. As such, it has three characteristics. First, it tends to see its beliefs in *literal* rather than metaphorical or allegorical terms. Fundamentalists of all religious persuasions usually have a very specific, explicitly spelled-out set of beliefs. Second, fundamentalism tends to take its beliefs as *absolute*. It sees its beliefs as true for everyone and for all times. Fundamentalism usually sees itself as incompatible with relativism. Third, fundamentalism tends to be *intolerant* of those who do not agree with its beliefs. This is, of course, a matter of degree. In some cases, it is simply an intolerance that emerges when its dogmas are directly challenged. In other, more extreme cases, it is an intolerance that demands that everyone accept its beliefs, even if others present no direct or indirect challenge. In such cases, fundamentalism goes out into the world to convert it—or, in its most extreme forms, to destroy the world of the infidels. Fundamentalism is, to a greater or lesser degree, intolerant of differences and disagreements. Many religions have fundamentalist sects or groups, and their place in their respective religious traditions may vary from one period of history to the next.

There is, however, another strain in most religious traditions that is quite different than the fundamentalist approach. I shall refer to this as the **ecumenical tradition,** although it may go by different names in different religious contexts. It differs from fundamentalism in regard to each of the three characteristics mentioned. First, it tends to treat its statements of belief as more metaphorical or allegorical in character. This alone opens the door to tolerating greater diversity because metaphors and allegories cannot contradict one another in the same direct way that literal statements can. Because of this, ecumenism usually does not hold its own beliefs to be absolute in the same way that fundamentalism does. It is more likely, for example, to be aware that any language it uses inevitably distorts and fails to completely capture the reality to which it refers. Finally, at least in part because of the first two differences, ecumenism tends to be more tolerant toward disagreements, often holding that there are many paths to the same God.

The ecumenical spirit in religion corresponds to the pluralistic and fallibilistic approach to ethics that is developed in this book. Both see diverse traditions as containing important truths, and both emphasize the ways in which we can learn from one another. Indeed, both see diversity as an opportunity for learning and insight, rather than as an impediment to them. Both ecumenism and pluralism recognize that none of us has the whole truth and that all of us can learn from one another in our continuing search for greater insight.

DISCUSSION QUESTIONS

1. Recall **statement 6** in the Ethical Inventory: "What is right depends on what God says is right."
    (a) What is the proper name for the theory that this statement exemplifies?
    (b) Has your rating of this statement changed after reading this chapter? If so, in what way? If your rating has not changed, are your reasons for your rating any different now than they were when you first responded to this statement?
2. Recall **statement 10** in the Ethical Inventory: "We do not need to depend on religion in order to have a solid foundation for our moral values."
    (a) What is the proper name for the theory that this statement exemplifies?
    (b) Has your rating of this statement changed after reading this chapter? If so, in what way? If your rating has not changed, are your reasons for your rating any different now than they were when you first responded to this statement?
3. Review your response to **statement 9** in the Ethical Inventory: "All major religions have something important to tell us about what is right and what is wrong."

(a) If you agree with this statement, discuss a moral insight that you have gained from a religious tradition other than your own.

(b) Has your rating of this statement changed after reading this chapter? If so, in what way? If your rating has not changed, are your reasons for your rating any different now than they were when you first responded to this statement?

4. The Russian novelist Fyodor Dostoyevsky (1821–1881) often said that "if God is dead, everything is permitted." What does this mean? How does it affect divine command morality? Would you live your own life any differently if you concluded that God is dead?

5. Many cultures, such as ancient Greece, are polytheistic—that is, they believe in many different gods. How would a polytheist interpret a divine command? What problems would the polytheistic divine command theorists encounter that their monotheistic counterparts do not have to confront? Is the (alleged) existence of more than one god an argument for moral relativity? (cf. Chapter 2)

6. In Genesis, chapter 22, God orders Abraham to sacrifice his only son Isaac. Should Abraham (or any father) obey such a command? Why or why not? In your own experience, have you ever encountered a conflict between your religious beliefs and your moral convictions? If so, how did you resolve the conflict? What does your way of resolving that conflict say about your position on the autonomy of ethics?

7. Does religion provide believers with consolations not available to the nontheist? For example, is there a difference between the ways in which theists and nontheists deal with injustices and the suffering of the innocent? Is there a difference between the ways in which they experience guilt and forgiveness? What are the strengths and weaknesses of each perspective?

8. In the Amish and Mennonite sections of Pennsylvania, you can often see black horse-drawn buggies on the highways. Not only do Amish and Mennonite religious beliefs dictate using horse-drawn buggies instead of cars powered by mechanical engines, but their religious convictions also prohibit the Amish and Mennonites from displaying images—including the image of the red reflective triangle that the state requires that they put on the rear of their carriages to lessen the danger of collision with cars. How do you think we should resolve conflicts such as these? What does your answer reveal about your more general beliefs about the relationship between religious beliefs and moral standards?

9. **MOVIE** The movie *The Mission* (1986) presents a subtle and complex portrait of the relationship between religion and ethics. Which characters in the movie advocate the divine command theory of ethics? Which oppose it? What reasons do they have in both cases? One of the principal issues in divine command theories of ethics is the question of how one determines what God's will is. Different characters in the movie deal with this in different ways. Which characters claim to know what

God's will is? Which don't? What is the position of the character played by Jeremy Irons?

10.   **MOVIE**   In the movie *Gandhi,* (1982), Gandhi at one point says, "I am a Moslem; I am a Hindu; I am a Christian; I am a Jew." What did he mean by that? In what sense, if any, was it true? In what sense, if any, do you feel that it is true about you?

11.   **MOVIE**   We have seen the way in which some philosophers have argued that religion is harmful to the moral life, whereas others have claimed that it is necessary to it. What view of the relationship between religion and ethics do you find in the movie *Gandhi?* Do you agree with this view? Why or why not?

BIBLIOGRAPHICAL ESSAY

For an introduction to **Navajo ethics,** see especially James Kale McNeley, *Holy Wind in Navajo Philosophy* (Tucson: University of Arizona Press, 1981); John R. Farella, *The Main Stalk: A Synthesis of Navajo Philosophy* (Tucson: University of Arizona Press, 1984); and Leland C. Wyman, *Blessingway* (Tucson: University of Arizona Press, 1970). For a classic and insightful introduction to Navajo culture, see Clyde Kluckhohn and Dorothea Leighton, *The Navaho* (Cambridge: Harvard University Press, 1946). There are several excellent essays on Navajo culture, language, worldviews, religion, and culture in the *Handbook of North American Indians,* edited by William C. Sturtevant (Washington: Smithsonian Institution, 1983), vol. 10: *Southwest,* edited by Alfonso Ortiz; unfortunately, none of the essays deals directly with morality or ethics. Gladys A. Reichard's *Navajo Religion: A Study of Symbolism* (Princeton: Princeton University Press, 1977) contains a helpful chapter on Navajo ethics. John Ladd's *The Structure of a Moral Code* (Cambridge: Harvard University Press, 1957), a study of Navajo ethics, is one of the few studies of Native American ethics by an American philosopher; Richard Brandt's *Hopi Ethics: A Theoretical Analysis* (Chicago: University of Chicago Press, 1954) is the only other such book-length work that I have been able to find. Much more recently, see Barbara E. Wall, "Navajo Conceptions of Justice in the Peacemaker Court," *Journal of Social Philosophy* 32, no. 4 (Winter 2001): 532–546. One of the principal sources for information about the Navajo is the manuscripts of Fr. Bernard Haile, many of which are available at the superb Museum of Northern Arizona in Flagstaff. Mention should also be made of the mystery novels of **Tony Hillerman,** which have done much to bring an appreciation of Navajo culture to a wider audience; see especially *The Blessing Way.* For an eloquent statement of the plight of contemporary native Americans, see especially Peter Matthiessen, *Indian Country* (New York: Penguin Books, 1979), and his *In the Spirit of Crazy Horse* (New York: Penguin Books, 1992). Mourning Dove's *Coyote Stories* (Lincoln: University of Nebraska Press, 1990) is an excellent collection of stories about the coyote figure.

On **Islamic ethics,** see John L. Esposito, *Islam: The Straight Path,* 3rd ed. (New York: Oxford University Press, 1998), and also Seyyed Hossein Nasr's works, especially his *History of Islamic Philosophy* (New York: Routledge, 2001). Cyril Glassé's *The Concise Encyclopedia of Islam* (New York: HarperCollins, 1991) is an excellent reference work. Azim Nanji's "Islamic Ethics," in Peter Singer, ed., *A Companion to*

Ethics (Oxford: Blackwell, 1991), pp. 106–120, discusses Islamic ethics specifically within the context of Western thought. Also see G. Hourani, *Reason and Tradition in Islamic Ethics* (Cambridge: Cambridge University Press, 1985); Michael A. Cook, *Commanding Right and Forbidding Wrong in Islamic Thought* (Cambridge: Cambridge University Press, 2001); Majid Khadduri, *The Islamic Conception of Justice* (Baltimore: Johns Hopkins University Press, 1984); and the essays in R. Houvannisian, ed., *Ethics in Islam* (Malibu, CA: Undena Publications, 1985). For a short survey of recent developments in Islam, see John L. Esposito, *Islam and Politics,* 4th ed. (Syracuse: Syracuse University Press, 1998); Nazih Ayubi, *Political Islam* (New York: Routledge, 1991), Emmanuel Sivan, *Radical Islam,* 2nd ed. (New Haven: Yale University Press, 1991); and Bernard Lewis, *What Went Wrong: Western Impact and Middle Eastern Response* (New York: Oxford University Press, 2001). For a comparison of **just war and jihad,** see John Kelsay and James Turner Johnson, eds., *Just War and Jihad* (Westport, CN: Greenwood Press, 1991) and Hilmi Zawati, *Is Jihad a Just War? War, Peace, and Human Rights Under Islamic and Public International Law,* Studies in Religion and Society (Lewiston, NY: Edwin Mellen Press, 2002); Kahled Abou El Fadl, *Rebellion and Violence in Islamic Law* (Cambridge: Cambridge University Press, 2001) and John L. Esposito, *Unholy War: Terror in the Name of Islam* (New York: Oxford University Press, 2002). On the issue of *Islam and tolerance,* see the exchange in the *Boston Review of Books,* beginning with Khaled Abou El Fadl's "The Place of Tolerance in Islam," vol. 26, no. 6 (December 2001/January 2002) and the replies by Sohail H. Hashmi, Amina Wadud, and John L. Esposito, plus the rejoinder by El Fadl in vol. 27, no. 1 (February-March 2002); these are available online at http://bostonreview.mit.edu/archives.html. For Islamic resources on the Web, see the listings at the Islamic Texts and Resources MetaPage (http://wings.buffalo.edu/student-life/sa/muslim/isl/isl.html); this includes links to online translations of the Qur'an. Also see Islamic Ethics.com (http://islamic-finance.net/islamic-ethics/ethindex.html), which emphasizes business ethics, and Islamset (http://www.islamset.com/introd.html), which also contains a section on Islamic bioethics.

There are numerous collections of texts from, and articles about, **Buddhism.** For an excellent introduction to Buddhism, see Peter Harvey, *An Introduction to Buddhism: Teachings, History, and Practices* (New York: Cambridge University Press, 1990) The first place to start for contemporary Buddhist ethics is His Holiness the Dalai Lama, *Ethics for the New Millenium* (New York: Putnam, 2001). Also see the works of Damien Keown, especially *The Nature of Buddhist Ethics* (New York: St. Martin's Press, 2001) and *Contemporary Buddhist Ethics* (Copenhagen: Curzon Press, 2001), and Peter Harvey's *An Introduction to Buddhist Ethics* (Cambridge: Cambridge University Press, 2000). For a discussion of Buddhist ethics that relates it to the categories of Western philosophy, see Padmasiri de Silva, "Buddhist Ethics," in Peter Singer, ed., *A Companion to Ethics,* (Oxford: Blackwell, 1991), pp. 58–68, and Ninian Smart, *Worldviews: Crosscultural Explorations of Human Beliefs* (New York: Scribner's Sons, 1983), especially Chapter 6, "The Ethical Dimension," which contains an excellent discussion of comparative religious ethics. Additional works on Buddhist ethics include *Buddhist Ethics and Modern Society: An International Symposium,* edited by Charles Wei-hsun Fu and Sandra A. Wawrytko (New York: Greenwood Press, 1991) and Charles S. Prebish, *Buddhist Ethics: A Cross-Cultural Approach* (Dubuque, IA: Kendall/Hunt, 1992). See Lenore Friedman, *Meetings with Remarkable Women: Buddhist Teachers in America* (Boston and London: Shambhala Publications, 1987), and Karma Lekshe Tsomo, *Sisters in Solitude: Two Traditions of*

Buddhist Monastic Ethics for Women (Albany: State University of New York Press, 1996), for the distinctive and often-neglected voice of women in Buddhism. There is now an excellent online journal, *The Journal of Buddhist Ethics* (http://jbe.gold.ac.uk/), which contains both articles and book reviews relevant to this chapter. On the notion of *karma*, see especially Wendy Doniger O. Flaherty, ed., *Karma and Rebirth in Classical Indian Traditions* (Berkeley: University of California Press, 1980) and Christopher Chapple, *Karma and Creativity* (Albany, NY: State University of New York Press, 1986). For web resources on Buddhism, see Buddhist Studies WWW Virtual Library (http://www.ciolek.com/WWWVL-Buddhism.html), BuddhaNet (http://www.buddhanet.net/), and DharmaNet (http://www.dharmanet.org/).

Much of the contemporary discussion of the **divine command theory of ethics** stems from the contemporary defense of this theory by Robert Merrihew Adams; see his *The Virtue of Faith and Other Essays in Philosophical Theology* (New York: Oxford, 1993) and *Finite and Infinite Goods: A Framework for Ethics* (New York: Oxford, 2002); also see Paul Rooney, *Divine Command Morality* (Aldershot: Avebury Press, 1996). On this same topic, see the essays in J. Idziak, ed., *Divine Command Morality: Historical and Contemporary Readings* (Lewiston, NY: The Edwin Mellen Press, 1980); John Chandler, "Is the Divine Command Theory Defensible?" *Religious Studies* 20 (1984), 443–52, and his "Divine Command Theories and the Appeal to Love," *American Philosophical Quarterly*, Vol. 22, no. 3 (July 1985), pp. 231–39. Also see Philip Quinn, *Divine Commands and Moral Requirements* (Oxford: Clarendon Press, 1978). Many of the most influential articles on this topic are gathered in Paul Helm, ed., *Divine Commands and Morality*, (Oxford: Oxford University Press, 1981); and R. G. Swinburne, "Duty and the Will of God," *Canadian Journal of Philosophy* 4, no. 2 (December 1974). For an insightful discussion of whether God's omnipotence entails the claim that God is able to sin, see Nelson Pike, "Omnipotence and God's Ability to Sin," *American Philosophical Quarterly* 6, no. 3 (July 1969): 208–216. On the relationship of divine command theories to utilitarianism, see Edward Wierenga, "Utilitarianism and the Divine Command Theory," *American Philosophical Quarterly* 21, No. 4 (October 1984): 311–318.

On the question of whether it is possible to have **morality without religion,** see William K. Frankena, "Is Morality Logically Dependent on Religion?" in Gene Outka and J. P. Reeder, Jr., eds., *Religion and Morality: A Collection of Essays* (New York: Doubleday, 1973); E. D. Klemke, "On the Alleged Inseparability of Religion and Morality," *Religious Studies* (1975); Kai Nielsen, *Ethics without God* (Pemberton Books, 1973); Alasdair MacIntyre and Paul Ricoeur, *The Religious Significance of Atheism* (New York: Columbia University Press, 1969); George Mavrodes, "Religion and the Queerness of Morality," Robert Audi and W. Wainwright, eds., *Rationality, Religious Belief and Moral Commitment: New Essays in the Philosophy of Religion,* (Ithaca, NY: Cornell University Press, 1986); Patrick Nowell-Smith, "Religion and Morality," *Encyclopedia of Philosophy,* edited by Paul Edwards (New York: Macmillan, 1967), pp. 150–58; Robert Young, "Theism and Morality," *Canadian Journal of Philosophy* 7, no. 2 (1977): 341–351. For an argument that worshipping God is incompatible with human dignity and autonomy, see James Rachels, "God and Human Attitudes," *Religious Studies* 7 (1971): 325–337, and the reply by Philip Quinn, "Religious Obedience and Moral Autonomy," *Religious Studies* 11 (1975): 265–281.

On the **Marxist critique of religion,** see the excellent anthology of Marx's own writings in Karl Marx, *On Religion,* edited by Saul Kussiel Padover (New York: McGraw-Hill, 1974). Robert B. Tucker's *Religion and Myth in the Philosophy of Karl Marx* (Cambridge: Cambridge University Press, 1972) offers an insightful discussion of Marx's views on religion; the best discussion of religious alienation is still the untranslated work by Jean-Yves Calvez, *La pensée de Karl Marx* (Paris: Éditions du Seuil, 1956). Also see Bertell Ollman, *Alienation: Marx's View of Man in Capitalist Society* (Cambridge: Cambridge University Press, 1976). Nietzsche's **critique of religion** is found throughout his writings, but especially his *Genealogy of Morals* and *Beyond Good and Evil,* both available in paperback translations by Walter Kaufmann. On the relationship among **religion, narrative, and character,** see especially Stanley Hauerwas, *Vision and Virtue: Essays in Christian Ethical Reflection* (Notre Dame: Notre Dame University Press, 1981), and Richard J. Regan, "Virtue, Religion, and Civic Culture," *Midwest Studies in Philosophy—Ethical Theory: Character and Virtue* 13 (1988): 342–351. On the **emotive dimension of religious experience,** see especially Gareth Matthews, "Ritual and the Religious Feelings," *Explaining Emotions,* edited by Amélie O. Rorty (Berkeley: University of California Press, 1980), pp. 339–354.

Citations. The Navajo descriptions of the person who lacks faults come from McNeley, *Holy Wind in Navajo Philosophy,* p. 42. The practical ethical guidelines are found in Kluckhohn and Leighton, *The Navaho,* pp. 304–307. The quote by Benjamin Barber is found in "Jihad vs. MacWorld," *The Atlantic Monthly* 269, no. 3 (March 1991): 53. The quote from Pope Urban II is taken from Urban II, "Speech at Council of Clermont, 1095," according to Fulcher of Chartres from Bongars, *Gesta Dei per Francos,* 1, pp. 382 f., trans in Oliver J. Thatcher, and Edgar Holmes McNeal, eds., *A Source Book for Medieval History* (New York: Scribners, 1905), 513–17; online at http://www.fordham.edu/halsall/source/urban2-fulcher.html.

Further Information. For further resources on the material covered in this chapter, see page on religion and ethics (http://ethics.sandiego.edu/theories/religion/) on my *Ethics Update* site.

The Ethics of Selfishness: Egoism

"As a basic step of self-esteem, learn to treat as the mark of a cannibal any man's *demand* for your help. To demand it is to claim that your life is his property—and loathsome as such claim might be, there's something still more loathsome: your agreement. Do you ask if it's ever proper to help another man? No—if he claims it as his right or as a moral duty that you owe him. Yes—if such is your own desire based on your own selfish pleasure in the value of his person and his struggle. Suffering as such is not a value; only man's fight against suffering, is. If you choose to help a man who suffers, do it only on the ground of his virtues, of his fight to recover, of his rational record, or of the fact that he suffers unjustly; then your action is still a trade, and his virtue is the payment for your help. But to help a man who has no virtues, to help him on the ground of his suffering as such, to accept his faults, his need, as a claim—is to accept the mortgage of a zero on your values. A man who has no virtues is a hater of existence who acts on the premise of death; to help him is to sanction his evil and to support his career of destruction. . . .

"I swear—by my life and my love of it—that I will never live for the sake of another man, nor ask another man to live for mine."

—A speech by John Galt in
Ayn Rand, Atlas Shrugged

In her novel *Atlas Shrugged,* Ayn Rand presents a portrait of a man who lives his entire life for himself alone, asking nothing of other people, feeling no obligation to help anyone else. Her hero, John Galt, is a model of the person who practices what she calls the virtue of selfishness. Every man is an island, responsible for himself and for no one else, and genuine morality consists precisely in striving not to give in to temptations such as compassion. In the fictional figure of John Galt, egoism has become a moral ideal. This chapter is devoted to a consideration of the value of that ideal.

Egoism has two forms that we will consider in this chapter, both of which center around the concept of acting in one's own self-interest. **Psychological egoism,** which advances a purely descriptive claim, **maintains that people always act in their own self-interest.** In contrast to this purely descriptive thesis, **ethical egoism maintains that people *should* always act in their own self-interest.** This is a normative claim because it tells us how we *ought* to act. (Recall the distinction between descriptive and normative claims that we drew in our discussion of moral relativism.)

TYPES OF EGOISM

Type of Egoism	Type of Claim	Main Thesis
Psychological	Descriptive	Claims that everyone acts in their own self-interest
Ethical	Normative	Claims that everyone ought to act in their own self-interest

Let's look at both of these versions.

PSYCHOLOGICAL EGOISM

At first glance, psychological egoism is a plausible and appealing doctrine to many. Indeed, it is so plausible that many economic analyses of human behavior take psychological egoism as their basic premise. It also seems to be a fairly straightforward theory. What, after all, could be clearer than saying that people act out of their own self-interest?

Some Initial Distinctions

This initial clarity is deceptive. Psychological egoists claim that *people act out of their own self-interest.* Yet exactly what are they asserting when they make this claim? Several questions need to be posed.

- Do people *always* act *only* out of their own self-interest?
- Do people act out of their *genuine* self-interest or what they (perhaps mistakenly) *think* is their self-interest?
- How do we define the "self" in "self-interest?"

The plausibility of the psychologist's thesis will depend on how each of these questions is answered. Let's examine each of them.

Do People *Always* Act *Only* Out of Their Own Self-Interest?

In its stronger versions, psychological egoism claims that people *always* act *only* out of self-interest. This is an interesting claim, because it entails that altruistic behavior (behavior done solely for the sake of the other person) does not exist. Even when someone like Mother Teresa appears to be acting for the sake of other people, in actuality she is doing what she does because—according to the psychological egoist—it makes her feel better. Everyone, the psychological egoist claims, always acts solely out of self-interest.

Some psychological egoists advance a much more restricted claim. According to these egoists, "self-interest tends to be overriding in people's motivational structures . . . at least until they have reached a stable and satisfactory level of well-being and security." For most people in most situations, except where the ratio of altruistic gain to personal loss is very large or where they are dealing with people or projects that they care deeply about, self-interest will override any altruistic motives.

Which of these two versions of psychological egoism is better? The strong version of egoism is by far the more controversial and interesting position, for if it is true then some of our most deeply held beliefs about human goodness, compassion, and love must be revised. The weaker version is much more likely to be true, but precisely because it is not an extreme position, its truth will be of much less interest to most people. If this weaker version is true, most people's basic beliefs about human motivation will be largely unaffected.

Do People Act Out of Their *Genuine* Self-Interest or What They (Perhaps Mistakenly) *Think* Is Their Self-Interest?

Psychological egoists claim that people act out of self-interest, but what do they say about people who smoke three packs of cigarettes a day? Are they acting out of self-interest? Clearly, most of us would say that heavy smoking is not in fact in anyone's self-interest. Does that prove that psychological egoism is false, since a number of people are heavy smokers?

The psychological egoist replies to this question by drawing a distinction between genuine self-interest and apparent self-interest. Everyone, the psychological egoist may claim, does what he or she *believes* is in his or her self-interest, even though that belief may be mistaken. Yet does this really solve the problem? Many smokers willingly admit that their continued smoking is not in their self-interest, and yet they do it anyway. (Some say things like, "I know this is bad for my health and I should quit . . .") Does the egoist have to deny the validity of first-person testimony? If so, egoists are saying that they know what a person's real motivation is—even better than the person herself knows it. Psychological egoists must make a similar claim when talking about people who claim to act out of love for others. Psychological egoists must doubt those claims and instead offer an account of apparently altruistic behavior in terms of selfish motivations.

How Do We Define the "Self" in "Self-Interest"?

When psychological egoists claim that human beings act out of self-interest, they usually presuppose a particular notion of the self which is the basis of that self-interest. Although there are a number of possibilities, we will consider only two of them here; a third will be added when we consider ethical egoism.

The Hedonistic Self

In its most primitive form, the "self" of "self-interest" is a hedonistic self, that is, a self that seeks pleasure and tries to avoid pain. This self is also a largely unconscious self, that is, we can imagine people seeking pleasure and avoiding pain without even consciously realizing what they are doing. Moreover, this self is situated almost exclusively in the present and the immediate future. It is not a long-range planner and usually has no awareness of long-term self-interest. This is the self that Freud identified as the *id*, a blind groping for pleasure.

The appeal to the hedonistic self most neatly resolves the difficulties about the difference between genuine and apparent self-interest without any reference to states of belief. The distinction between genuine and apparent self-interest depends on the distinction between what one believes is best (i.e., maximizes self-interest) and what actually is best. By grounding self-interest in the hedonistic self, the psychological egoist bypasses this entire issue. Self-interest simply is whatever in the moment increases pleasure and reduces pain. There is simply no issue of "genuine" self-interest. The issue is simply whether something increases pleasure or not. Because there is no distinction between apparent pleasure and genuine pleasure, there is no distinction between apparent self-interest and genuine self-interest for the hedonistic self.

The difficulty with interpreting self-interest exclusively in hedonistic terms is that it makes psychological egoism much less likely to be true. The claim that people act solely to increase pleasure and reduce pain seems to fly in the face of the facts. There are numerous cases in which people we know choose a course of action that at least in the short term causes them more pain and less pleasure (e.g., training for a marathon instead of staying in bed in the morning and sleeping late), but they do so in order to achieve some goal or purpose that they have. This may ultimately be in the person's self-interest, but it is certainly not something which increases the immediate pleasure that the person experiences.

The Project-Bearing Self

It is precisely difficulties such as these with the hedonistic concept of the self that have led many psychological egoists to revise their view of the self in such a way that the self is seen primarily as the *bearer of projects*. Self-interest then comes to be defined as that which promotes the individual's projects, and that which is contrary to self-interest is that which is detrimental to those projects. Psychological egoism then asserts that people act in ways that they believe will promote (or maximize) their own projects.

The shift from hedonistic self-interest to project self-interest seem to be a move toward a more defensible but less interesting form of egoism. Once self-interest is seen in terms of projects, it is no longer as narrow, as blind, or as selfish as it was when it was interpreted in purely hedonistic terms. Project self-interest encompasses a wider range of possible motivations than hedonistic self-interest, including altruistic projects, and thus seems more compatible with our experience of the range of people's motivations.

The flexibility of the concept of a project is at once both a strength and a weakness. It is a strength, as we have already seen, because it recognizes that human beings have a wider range of motivations than simple pleasure and pain. Yet this flexibility also threatens to be a liability if it becomes too great. Can *anything* count as an egoistic project? If so, then the notion of egoistic motivation is so broad as to be useless. Egoists—as Kavka has pointed out in *Hobbesian Moral and Political Theory* (1986)—must, therefore, place some limitations on the notion of what counts as a self-interested project. Some of these restrictions are negative, others positive. Clearly, it cannot be a project that is (1) self-destructive, (2) done for the sake of duty or some other moral motivation, or (3) done for the sake of others (i.e., altruistic). Many other motivations, however, are acceptable because they do count as personal benefits. Kavka lists the following aims as self-directed: "the agent's pleasure, pain, wealth, power, security, liberty, glory, possession of particular objects, fame, health, longevity, status, self-respect, self-development, self-assertion, reputation, honor, and affection" (p. 42). Typically, projects done for any of these purposes will count as self-interested in the relevant, egoist's sense.

Support for Psychological Egoism

What evidence can be presented in support of the claim that people always act out of self-interest? Let us consider here three possible sources of support for the egoist's position: (1) the argument that people always derive pleasure or satisfaction from their actions, (2) the claim that we often deceive ourselves about our actual motives, and (3) the evidence of the social sciences.

The Pleasure Argument

Some psychological egoists advance an argument that initially may appear fairly strong. Everyone, they claim, derives pleasure (or satisfaction) from what they do; therefore, they conclude, their behavior is done for the sake of pleasure and is thus self-interested. I will call this the *pleasure argument*.

As soon as the argument is stated clearly, we can see the hole in it. It may be true that people feel pleasure in what they do, but that does not mean that they do it *in order to* experience that pleasure. Often during times of natural disasters, people perform genuinely heroic acts, saving other people at great risk to themselves. Presumably, when such rescues are successful,

THE RING OF GYGES

Imagine that you were given a magic ring—the ring of Gyges, the Greeks called it—that would allow you to be invisible to everyone surrounding you. No one could see that you were there, and no one could punish you for anything that you did. How would you act with the threats of detection and punishment removed? Would you act like an egoist? Is it only our fear of embarrassment or punishment that restrains us from acting like egoists?

   This is what philosophers often call a thought experiment—imagine a situation and then see what follows from it. But there is something tricky about this experiment: By imagining us cloaked behind a veil of invisibility, the example portrays us as without relationships, isolated and devoid of genuine human interaction. It may be that, given these conditions, egoism follows as a result—or, conversely, that egoism best fits a world in which individuals see themselves as isolated and hidden from others, as devoid of relationships.   ▪

they feel a deep sense of pleasure and satisfaction. But it is a big—and unwarranted—step from saying this to conclude that they performed the rescues *in order to* feel pleasure. Yet that is precisely what the psychological egoist claims. Recall those who risked—and often lost—their lives trying to save others at the World Trade Center. The egoist has to say that they did this for selfish motives, and that claim seems patently false.

   Two other points should be noted about this argument. First, all too often people do not feel pleasure or satisfaction in what they do. The world would certainly be a happier place if this were not true, but unfortunately many people fail to find pleasure or satisfaction in at least some of what they do. Second, people may experience pleasure or satisfaction in performing altruistic actions. Far from counting against the altruistic character of such actions, this fact simply suggests that, at least in this regard, our world is well constructed. How much less happy the world would be if altruistic behavior never carried any pleasure or satisfaction with it!

The Self-Deception Argument

The second source of support for psychological egoism is one that most of us are familiar with. We have all had the experience of initially believing that we are acting out of purely altruistic motives and subsequently, perhaps in the quietude of solitary reflection, realized that there were self-serving motives buried beneath the surface. It is much more acceptable in our society—and in most other societies as well—to cloak our selfish motives in the garb of altruism. Moreover, this is not simply a matter of concealing selfish motives from other people. There is a good reason for concealing them from ourselves as well. Insofar as our society defines a good person as one who acts altruistically, and insofar as all of us naturally want to think of ourselves as good people, we need to think of ourselves as having altruistic motives, even when we don't. Self-deception, so the psychological egoist claims, helps us to have a better opinion of ourselves.

There is undoubtedly an element of truth in this argument, perhaps even a large element. The difficulty with the argument is that there is no evidence to suggest that *all* apparently altruistic actions really have this structure below the surface. Moreover, this argument suggests that our apparent motives aren't our real motives, that our genuine motives lie beneath the surface. If this is so, are these actions really free? Is the egoist saying that some unconscious force makes us act selfishly, even when we think we are acting altruistically? This question raises difficulties about free will and determinism that we will consider in the second part of this chapter.

Self-Interest, Altruism, and the Behavioral Social Sciences

It would be much easier to reach a decision about the validity of psychological egoism if the social sciences offered a single, conclusive picture of the motives of human behavior. Unfortunately, this is not the case. Although there is certainly no shortage of empirical research showing that human beings often act out of self-interest, a sufficient number of studies indicate that at least some people act morally or altruistically at least some of the time. Moreover, some theories *begin* with the premise that everyone acts out of self-interest. Yet such a starting-point can hardly provide conclusive evidence that all behavior must be self-interested, for that belief is built into the starting point of the theory rather than arrived at through empirical investigation. In general, the sciences of human behavior do not provide a strong, unequivocal case to support strong psychological egoism.

Some of the most interesting evidence in this area has come from a relatively new area of study, *sociobiology*, a discipline that studies social behavior in light of genetics. Sociobiologists have found that altruistic behavior exists, not only in human beings, but throughout the animal world. Animals often share food and take care of each other in ways that would count as altruistic if done by human beings. In some species, such as worker bees, the behavior is almost completely altruistic, done solely for the sake of the other with little or no concern for one's own interests. Most instances, however, are less extreme than this, involving a mixture of altruistic and self-interested behavior. Natural selection, so sociobiologists hypothesize, favors altruistic behavior in at least two situations: close kinship relationships and cooperative behavior in which all participants benefit (reciprocal altruism). The evidence of sociobiology suggests that strong psychological egoism is wrong. Behavior is *not* always self-interested. However, sociobiology is consistent with weaker versions of psychological egoism that claim that behavior is *usually* self-interested.

Indeed, in some instances individuals have not only acted altruistically, but have done so at great personal risk. The firefighters who risked (and often lost) their lives trying to help others to safety in the aftermath of the attacks on the World Trade Center are a prime example of individuals who acted altruistically, putting the welfare of others ahead of their own safety and survival. All that is necessary to defeat strong psychological egoism empirically is one instance of someone who does not act exclusively in terms of self-interest, and there is no shortage of such examples. Weak psychological egoism, on the other hand, is not as easily disproved empirically, since it simply maintains that people generally act out of self-interest. A few instances of altruistic behavior are not enough to undermine weak psychological egoism.

Does Psychological Egoism Depend on an Unfalsifiable Hypothesis?

At this point in our argument, many dedicated psychological egoists will ask, "But was the firefighters' behavior *really* altruistic? Or did they really get something out of it for themselves, even if it was only a feeling of satisfaction about acting like a good person?" Indeed, psychological egoists could question whether the firefighters and other safety workers were being honest in their accounts of their own behavior or whether, even if they were honest, they might have been deceiving themselves about their own motives. It is always possible to ask questions such as these about any example of apparently altruistic behavior. The interesting issue that this raises is whether any possible empirical example could undermine the psychological egoist's faith in egoism. Would the committed psychological egoist doubt that the Dalai Lama, Mother Teresa, Bishop Desmond Tutu, or some other apparent saint was really altruistic? If so, we have to question whether psychological egoism is a genuine empirical belief or an unfalsifiable belief for such a person.

Karl Popper, one of the most influential figures in twentieth-century philosophy of science, was impressed by the apparent explanatory power of the unfalsifiable beliefs characteristic of Freudian, Marxist, and many religious frameworks. No matter what happened, these perspectives had an explanation for it. Consider psychoanalytic theory. If behavior exhibited overt sexual motivation, that showed that the Freudian theory was sound. If behavior did not show any signs of sexual motivation, then that simply showed that repression or sublimation was at work. Again, this explanation showed that the theory was sound. Yet Popper became suspicious of such frameworks, for he quickly saw that there was *no* empirical evidence that could count against the theory. Such theories, or pseudotheories, are what he calls **unfalsifiable hypotheses.** They appear to be grounded in empirical evidence but in fact are not. In principle, there is no empirical instance that could invalidate the hypothesis.

Is psychological egoism a doctrine that people accept or reject on the basis of the empirical evidence available to them, or is it a viewpoint that is largely accepted or rejected in advance of any empirical evidence? Is it, in other words, usually an unfalsifiable hypothesis? Rather than attempting to answer this question on a general level, reflect for yourself on whether your own acceptance or rejection of psychological egoism is based on empirical evidence or is simply an unfalsifiable hypothesis for you.

Does Psychological Egoism Rest on a Tautology?

There is another way in which psychological egoism can appear to be an empirical claim but in actuality is not based on empirical evidence at all. Some people have claimed that all human behavior is self-interested because, after all, it all stems from our own motives. If we do something, so this line of thinking goes, we are doing it because we want to; our motives are our own, so we must be acting for ourselves. Mother Teresa, for example, is doing what she wants (i.e., helping others) because she wants to do it; therefore, she is acting out of her own interests and thus is acting egoistically. This type of argument appears to make an empirical claim about people's motives, but when we look at it more closely we see that in fact it is simply a matter of establishing the egoist's case by definition. Any motive that a person has is defined to be self-interested because it is the person's own motive. Following Bernard Gert, we shall call this **tautological egoism** because it is based on a tautology:

• self-interest = any interest that the self has

There are two difficulties with this type of egoism. First, it tells us nothing about the world, nothing about actual people's real motivations. It simply tells us about how we have defined certain words. Second, the definition is in fact misleading since most people (including egoists) understand "self-interest" in a narrower, more specific way that is almost synonymous with "selfish." When tautological egoism is used as support for psychological egoism, it gives the appearance of providing empirical evidence when in fact it is simply establishing its case by definition of key terms.

Does Psychological Egoism Rest on a False Dichotomy?

Psychological egoism presupposes that human behavior is either altruistic or selfish. The implicit conceptual map underlying egoism looks something like this:

Selfish ←————————————→ Altruistic
Human action

Egoism and altruism appear to be opposite ends of a single spectrum: The more selfish a person is, the less altruistic, and vice versa.

This view of human behavior may, however, rest on a false dichotomy. Instead of seeing selfishness and altruism as mutually exclusive, we can imagine them as independent axes. Then we would get a diagram like this:

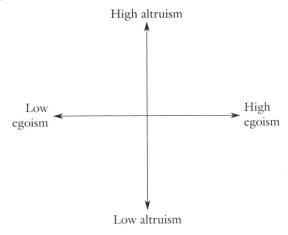

In this diagram, we can rank an action according to how much it helps other people (the altruism axis) or how much it helps the individual performing the action (the egoism axis). The interesting thing about conceptualizing behavior in this way is that we can see precisely the category of actions that we want to encourage in a well-ordered society: those which help both other people and the self. Certainly there will be examples of behavior that is highly altruistic and low on the egoism scale—heroic acts of self-sacrifice belong here—but the long-term operation of society requires that there be some balance between self-interest and concern for others. The more we are able to structure society in ways that encourage actions that are both altruistic and egoistic, the better off everyone will be.

There is one final ambiguity is this picture: It does not distinguish between intentions and consequences. If we add that distinction, we have the following diagram:

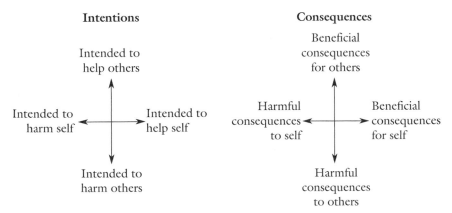

This diagram provides us with a more accurate picture of both the intentions and the consequences of human behavior and suggests that the psychological egoist's picture is misleadingly simple. Some behavior can be intended to help others but actually harm others; conversely, some actions intended to harm may actually have beneficial consequences.

So far, the evidence we have considered does not support strong psychological egoism, although much of it is consistent with weak psychological egoism. Yet there is a whole range of arguments to consider that proceed from a quite different premise than any considered in this section: the premise that human behavior is causally determined. Since it raises distinct conceptual issues that touch not only on psychological egoism but also on certain versions of moral relativism and moral skepticism, we will consider this issue separately.

DETERMINISM AND FREEDOM

We have seen a recurring theme throughout the last three chapters. Psychological egoism, certain causal versions of descriptive ethical relativism, and even a few divine command theories of ethics that involve predestination all presuppose *determinism*. Psychological egoists say that we are causally determined to act solely in our own pleasure or self-interest. Some descriptive ethical relativists claim that our moral values are causally determined by our culture. Certain divine command theorists claim that our behavior is determined by God's foreknowledge. What all of these positions have in common is the conviction that human behavior is causally determined by certain types of factors and that human behavior is therefore not free.

Nor are there only these three versions of determinism. Various types of *psychological determinism* achieved prominence in the twentieth century. Some followers of Freud saw him as maintaining that human behavior is determined by *unconscious forces* in the human psyche. B. F. Skinner and his radical behaviorist followers maintained that human behavior is completely determined, primarily by positive and negative reinforcers in the environment. Skinner's *Beyond Freedom and Dignity* (1971) is a manifesto for contemporary radical behaviorists. A comparable claim on behalf of *genetics* has been central to sociobiology, which maintains that human behavior is determined by genetic factors. Edward Wilson's *On Human Nature* (1980) is the comparable manifesto for sociobiologists. What all these positions have in common is the belief that *human behavior is causally determined;* they differ only in their specification of which kinds of causes play the dominant role in shaping such behavior.

The Actor and the Spectator

Human behavior exhibits two faces, the face that is shown to the external world and the face that is turned in on itself. When we look at human behavior from the sidelines of life, as it were, we are viewing it as spectators. Often, the spectator's viewpoint sees human behavior in causal terms. Radical behaviorists, for example, look at human behavior and attempt to uncover the psychological reinforcers which shape that behavior. When behaviorists see people mindlessly feeding coins into slot machines in Las Vegas, they look for the intermittent reinforcers (the occasional small payoff, the very infrequent large jackpot) that promote such behavior. When they do that, behaviorists are being spectators, looking at the external face of human behavior. All scientific studies of human behavior assume the stance of the spectator, the impartial observer. As spectators, such scientists are continually asking the question, "What caused this behavior to happen?" They never ask whether the behavior was caused; that is simply taken for granted. The only question is what particular factor caused it. The claim that human behavior is causally determined is not a conclusion that such scientific approaches reach; rather, it is the starting point from which they proceed.

Yet when we act, we are unable to assume the spectator's standpoint. We must necessarily assume the standpoint of the actor, and a central element in that standpoint is the assumption that we are free. Imagine, for a moment, that you are faced with a decision about which movie to go to see tonight. Even if you were a radical behaviorist, you couldn't help but use the language of choice, of freedom. You could hardly say, "Well, I'll go to the movie that is most positively reinforcing." How do you know which is most reinforcing? Even if you did know, you would find yourself saying that you are deciding to go to the most positively reinforcing one. Indeed, you hardly feel your body being moved toward the correct movie theater like a magnet moves a piece of iron around. From the viewpoint of the actor, you feel yourself make up your mind. You feel that you yourself decide what to do. The claim that human behavior is free is not the result of reflection on our behavior as actors; rather, it is the premise from which such reflection begins.

This, then, is the dilemma we face about freedom and determinism. From the viewpoint of disinterested scientific spectators, we have to assume that human behavior is causally determined. Yet from the viewpoint of people who act, we have to assume that we have freedom of choice. Moreover, we have to be both spectators and actors in life. There are times when we must all be spectators, observing the behavior of other people, trying to understand why they act the way they do. Yet we are also actors, and as such we have to make decisions about what we are going to do at any given moment. A hardcore determinist, working long hours in the lab, still has to decide whether to order a pizza with pepperoni or mushrooms or both for dinner. The language of choice is as inescapable an element in the actor's standpoint as the language of causality is in the spectator's perspective.

Most of the issues surrounding the problem of freedom and determinism lie outside the scope of ethics itself. They are usually considered within the context of metaphysics and the philosophy of mind. There are, however, at least two related issues that have a direct bearing on ethics: the transition from "is" to "ought" and the relationship between determinism and responsibility.

The Transition from *Is* to *Ought*

Although having these two quite different perspectives is a significant problem in itself (and, as we shall see in the next chapter, the German philosopher Immanuel Kant had a lot to say about this), the greatest difficulties arise when the two standpoints are mixed. Whereas the spectator's viewpoint is *action explaining,* the actor's perspective is *action guiding.* A fallacy occurs when one tries to transfer information from one perspective to the other, taking a claim intended to explain behavior and using it to guide behavior. Recall the way in which this occurred in causal versions of ethical relativism. On a descriptive level, the causal ethical relativist claimed that people's behavior and values were causally determined by the culture in which they grew up. Yet the illicit move occurred when they attempted to shift from a descriptive level to a prescriptive one that says that we ought to follow the values of our culture.

Egoists often attempt to make a similar move. Although psychological egoism is in itself a purely descriptive position, it is often in fact advanced within the context of discussions about normative theories. The alleged truth of psychological egoism is then offered as support for ethical egoism—that is, for the normative claim that people ought to act in their own self-interest. Yet a moment's reflection reveals the peculiarity of such an argument. If strong psychological egoism were true, then what would be the point of telling people that they ought to act in their own self-interest? Strong psychological egoism states that people always in fact act in their own self-interest; and if this is true, there is little point in telling them that they ought to do so. (Of course, it might reduce the extent to which people condemn themselves and others for selfish behavior.) If strong psychological egoism were true, ethical egoism would be largely superfluous.

Over two hundred and fifty years ago, a Scottish philosopher by the name of David Hume pointed to a suspicious move in moral discourse from descriptive statements to prescriptive claims. No set of purely factual or descriptive premises, Hume contended, could entail a *normative* conclusion. The reason is clear. A normative conclusion contains the word *ought* or its equivalent. If all the premises are descriptive, however, none of them contains an *ought* statement. But since the conclusion of a valid deductive argument cannot contain anything that is not contained in the premises, the conclusion cannot contain an *ought* statement. Purely factual premises can yield only purely factual conclusions. According to Hume, one cannot derive an *ought* simply from an *is.*

Freedom and Responsibility

There is a second problem that relates to causal versions of psychological egoism and to other versions of determinism as well. If determinism is true, then our traditional notion of moral responsibility must either be jettisoned or at least severely restructured. Typically, we tend not to hold people responsible if they are not free. If, for example, someone slips LSD into another person's coffee without that person's knowledge and the other person then drives erratically, we would not hold that other person responsible for the erratic driving in the same way we would if the LSD had not been slipped into the coffee. The reasoning behind this is clear: We believe that the person is less free because of the influence of the drug and therefore less responsible. Of course, this judgment changes if the person chooses to take LSD rather than being tricked into taking it unknowingly, for then we consider the taking of the drug to be a free act.

If our traditional notion of moral responsibility is undermined by determinism, then our traditional notions of blame, praise, reward, and punishment are likewise radically changed. Traditionally, praise and blame presuppose that the person being praised or blamed is free. We praise people's heroic deeds, for example, when we think they could have done otherwise. If we thought their heroism was not a matter of choice but rather one of simple causal necessity, we would be much more reluctant to praise it or reward it. Similarly, we tend not to blame or punish those who could not have acted differently. If we do punish, it is for a different reason: to correct behavior rather than because the punishment is merited. We may punish a dog that has misbehaved, not because we think the dog "merits" punishment, but because punishment is necessary to correct the behavior in the future. Yet with human beings the situation is usually different. Although we may sometimes punish solely to change behavior, we usually believe that punishment is justified because the person knowingly and freely did something wrong. Thus, we punish even in situations where we have no reason to believe that the person will commit the crime again.

If we give up the notion of freedom, we also give up our traditional notions of responsibility, praise, blame, and punishment. If determinism is true, we lose much of our basic moral vocabulary.

The Task of Becoming Free

In concentrating on whether human behavior is free or causally determined, philosophers have tended to view the question of freedom in rather dichotomous terms: Either we are causally determined or else we are free. Scant attention is given to the possibility that we are partially free and partially unfree, yet there seems to be good reason for believing that this is in fact the case. Moreover, there is good reason for believing that progress in life consists, at least in part, in moving from a state of unfreedom to one of freedom.

Consider an example. A classic behaviorist experiment can be performed in the classroom. Imagine, for the sake of our example, an introductory college ethics course in which the students wanted the instructor to spend less time talking about Immanuel Kant and more time discussing John Stuart Mill. Whenever Kant is mentioned, members of the class, without the instructor's knowledge of its plan, engage in behavior that the instructor experiences as negative. Students may begin to look out the window, to appear bored, to shuffle their feet, to squirm around in their chairs, to look confused, to ask irrelevant questions, and generally to convey the impression that nothing in Kant's philosophy is of interest or value to them. When John Stuart Mill is mentioned, on the other hand, the reaction is quite different. Students perk up, look intently at the instructor, smile, ask intelligent and relevant questions, exhibit an interest in knowing more about Mill's philosophy, and even ask about supplementary reading. If the principles of behaviorism are correct, within a short period of time the instructor should be talking about Mill a lot and virtually ignoring Kant. This, so the behaviorist would argue, both illustrates and proves the behaviorist's claim that behavior is causally determined by environmental factors. Thus, determinism has once again been vindicated—or so it would appear.

Yet the story need not end here, with the hapless instructor abandoning Kant for Mill. Let's imagine that the instructor discovers what the students are doing. At this juncture, two interesting developments may take place. First, realizing what the class has done, the instructor may compensate for their unbalanced influence by making a special effort to spend time on Immanuel Kant, thereby consciously offsetting their impact. Yet there is a second, and even more important, step that the instructor can take. Realizing that any class's reactions to specific material may affect how much time an author is given in class, the instructor may ask whether he or she wants to be guided by such a principle. Once it is made explicit, it is unlikely that the instructor would adopt that principle of popularity as a sufficient criterion for determining which philosophers should be considered in an ethics course. The point here is that *once we realize that we are causally influenced in a particular way, we are often free to choose to accept or reject that influence.* Instead of making us less free, knowledge of deterministic influences may actually liberate us from their domination.

To be sure, such a change is not always possible, and the task of changing is often a difficult and slow one. But the basic insights remains: We begin largely in a state of unfreedom, and one of the measure's of progress in life is to become aware of the ways in which we have been determined in the past and freely choose to shape our lives in the future.

ETHICAL EGOISM

Ethical egoism purports to tell us how to live. It tells us that we should always act in our own self-interest. As such, it is a *consequentialist* theory—that is, it maintains that the rightness or wrongness of acts depends on their consequences. More specifically, it says that right actions are those that promote self-interest and wrong actions are those that detract from self-interest.

Is Ethical Egoism a *Moral* Theory at All?

The first striking thing about ethical egoism is that it doesn't seem to be an *ethical* theory at all. Whatever disagreements may exist among ethicians, one thing that most of them are agreed upon is that morality is about overcoming our selfishness and living our life with a positive concern for the well-being of other people for their own sake. Insofar as ethical egoism exhorts us to act in a purely self-interested way, it doesn't seem to be a moral theory at all—rather, it's what morality is attempting to overcome!

Ethical egoists have a number of replies to this charge, most of which consist in attempting to show that ethical egoism possesses enough of the formal characteristics—universalizability, consistency, and so on—of a moral theory to justify its inclusion in the domain of moral theories. We will not pursue this argument here but rather concede the point and turn to the more important question: Is ethical egoism a *good* moral theory—that is, an adequate or a sound one?

Types of Ethical Egoism

As usual, we need to draw some distinctions among various versions of the position we are discussing. Ethical egoism is no exception. At first glance, it appears straightforward enough: Ethical egoism is telling people that they ought to act in their own self-interest. As we look more closely, we see that this could be meant in several different ways.

The first point that needs to be clarified is whether the ethical egoists are saying (1) that they are going to act in their own self-interest and everything else is irrelevant, or (2) that each person ought to act in his or her own self interest, or (3) that everyone ought to act in my self-interest. This results in three distinct types of ethical egoism.

TYPES OF ETHICAL EGOISM

Type of Ethical Egoism	Main Thesis
Personal egoism	I am going to act in my own self-interest and everything else is irrelevant.
Individual ethical egoism	Everyone ought to act in my self-interest.
Universal ethical egoism	Each person ought to act in his or her own self-interest.

Let's look at each of these three positions.

Personal Egoism

Personal egoists maintain that they are going to act in their own self-interest and that anything else is irrelevant to them. They actually have no interest in telling other people how to act at all, and in this sense their position is hardly a moral theory at all. They are simply saying, "This is how *I* am going to act." There have been virtually no philosophical attempts to defend personal egoism since the mid-1950s, but this does not mean that no one lives according to this position. Personal egoists are simply the selfish, egotistical persons whose only concern in life is to further their own self-interest. Although the position has virtually no merit as a theory, it still has its adherents in practice.

Individual Ethical Egoism

The difference between personal egoism, which is hardly an ethical theory at all, and individual ethical egoism is that the latter does make a claim about how other people ought to act. If I were an individual ethical egoist, I would claim (1) that I ought to act in my own self-interest, and (2) that everyone else should also act in my self-interest. It is an ethical theory—even if ultimately it turns out not to be a good ethical theory—because it states how *everyone* ought to act.

Universal Ethical Egoism

Whereas individual ethical egoists think all people ought to act in their own self-interest, universal ethical egoists think that each individual ought to act in his or her own self-interest. Each person, universal ethical egoists maintain, ought to be out for himself or herself.

The relationship between individual ethical egoism and universal ethical egoism is an interesting one. At first glance, *individual ethical egoism* seems implausible. Why should everyone else act in my self-interest? That's absurd! Yet although universal ethical egoism initially seems to be the more reasonable position, we can see how one arrives at individual ethical egoism. Let's imagine that I am following the mandate of universal ethical egoism, looking out for my own self-interest and telling other people to look out for theirs. Is it then actually in my self-interest for you to act in your own self-interest? Wouldn't it in fact be more in my self-interest—and hence more consistent for me—if I could convince you (and everyone else, for that matter) to do things that will benefit me? In fact, if I were an ethical egoist, wouldn't I want everyone else to be altruists, especially to be altruistic toward me? Universal ethical egoism, in other words, seems to lead to individual ethical egoism.

In his defense of universal ethical egoism, Jesse Kalin has suggested an intriguing way out of this difficulty. There is, he points out, one type of situation in which we act solely out of our own self-interest but simultaneously want everyone else to act in his or her own self-interest as well: games. In sports or chess or any other type of competitive game, I will be trying as hard as I can to win, but I also expect my competitors to do the same. Indeed, I *want* them to do so. Competitive games provide a notable example of situations in which it is not inconsistent for me to try to maximize my self-interest but also to will that you try to maximize your self-interest at the same time.

The Concept of the "Self" in "Self-Interest"

When we discussed the concept of self-interest in psychological egoism, we saw that the notion of the "self" is open to several different interpretations. So, too, we find an ambiguity in the concept of the "self" in ethical egoism. The "self" of the ethical egoist's self-interest can be either the hedonistic self or the rational self. The hedonistic self is the pleasure-seeking self, while the rational self is the self that seeks long-term, reflective self-interest.

THE SELF OF SELF-INTEREST

Type of Self	Type of Egoism	Main Thesis
Pleasure seeking	Hedonistic	Act in such a way as to promote our own pleasure
Calculating	Rational	Act in such a way as to promote our long-term self-interest

Each of these types yields a very different picture of egoism.

Hedonistic Egoism. If we see the self purely as a pleasure seeker, then the injunction to promote self-interest will be a command to seek pleasure, to be a hedonist. This position suffers from all of the drawbacks of hedonism generally, including that there seems to be nothing morally admirable about it. Moreover, it is susceptible to what has been called the *hedonistic paradox:* Often we can best achieve pleasure by not directly aiming at it. Most contemporary ethical egoists are not hedonistic egoists.

Rational Egoism. When ethical egoists speak of self-interest, the majority of them mean rational self-interest. The rational egoist urges us to reflect on future alternatives and choose those that will be most beneficial to us in the long-run. The rational egoist places no restrictions on what can count as legitimate self-interest (pleasure, power, fame, success, etc.), except that presumably self-destructive, moral, and altruistic goals do not in principle qualify as being in one's self-interest.

Short-Term *versus* Long-Term Self-Interest

Egoists also draw a distinction between two concepts of self-interest that again depends on our conception of the self but this time centers around the *temporal* dimensions of the self. Self-interest can be either short term or long term, depending on whether we are considering what is immediately beneficial to the self or what is beneficial over the long run. Since pleasure tends to be immediate and calculation tends to look to the future, this distinction often parallels the distinction between hedonistic and rational egoism.

It makes a crucial difference whether we adopt a short-term or a long-term view of self-interest. Actions such as lying, cheating, and exploitation might be permitted in terms of short-term self-interest but prohibited if we considered them within the context of long-term self-interest. Consider a simple example from business. If a person has a small retail business in a local neighborhood and deals with the same clientele year after year, it may well be in the shopkeeper's long-term self-interest to be scrupulously honest with customers, even though in particular cases there might be a short-term advantage to cheating some customers. Of course, if the same person had a business on a major interstate highway and had very few repeat customers, it might be in his or her self-interest to gouge them whenever possible, since they are unlikely to return or to otherwise negatively affect subsequent business from other people.

In recent years, this distinction between short-term self-interest and long-term self-interest has become a crucial one for American corporations. In a time of swift corporate takeovers and of relatively short tenures for CEOs, short-term self-interest has increasingly overshadowed long-term self-interest with many corporations, often to the detriment of stockholders, employees, and the country as a whole.

Support for Ethical Egoism

Ethical egoism has been a topic of hot debate among philosophers for several decades, and it has generated dozens of refutations and replies to such refutations. Yet one finds a curious gap in the philosophical literature when one looks for strong statements of the *initial* reasons for accepting ethical egoism. There is no shortage of arguments against objections to it, but it is as if ethical egoists tend to believe that the initial commitment to ethical egoism is so obvious as not to need justification. A further contributing factor may be the fact that some form of egoism is a prevalent premise in areas such as economics, which begin with the assumption that all persons are self-interested actors. Let's examine those arguments that are available.

The Appeal to Psychological Egoism

Proponents of ethical egoism sometimes appeal to psychological egoism in order to gain support for their own position, but the relationship between the two positions is more complex than one of simple support. As we have seen earlier in this chapter, if psychological egoism were true, then ethical egoism would seem to be redundant. If people inevitably acted in their own self-interest, then there would be no need to urge them to do so. In fact, the very existence of ethical egoism seems to show that some ethical egoists believe psychological egoism is false. Otherwise there would be no need to urge people to act in this way.

The "Better World" Argument

Some ethical egoists advance an interesting argument in support of their position. They claim that if everyone behaved as ethical egoists, the world overall would be a better place. Many attempts to help other people, they suggest, are misguided and ineffective. Each person is best suited to promote his or her own self-interest, since no one else is more familiar with the agent's own desires and needs, and no one else is more directly in a position to act in the situation than the agent is.

Although this argument may be appealing, it has two serious flaws. First, it makes an empirical claim—namely, that everyone will benefit more if all people act solely in their own self-interest—that may well be false. It might well be true in a society composed solely of adults with roughly the same levels of skill and resources, but such a society has never existed. We live in a world with children and the elderly, with the infirm and disabled as well as the able bodied, with the developmentally delayed as well as the mentally gifted, with the poor and the starving as well as with the rich and well fed. We live, in other words, in a world of radical differences, many of which are beyond the individual's control.

Second, even if the argument were sound, it is not primarily an argument for ethical egoism; rather, it is a rule utilitarian argument—we will discuss utilitarianism in detail in Chapter 5—in which the justification for acting in a particular way is to be found in the way in which it benefits society as a whole. If the justification for acting as an ethical egoist is that it produces the greatest overall benefit for society as a whole, then presumably if it does *not* do so, we ought not to act in that manner.

The "Altruism Is Demeaning" Argument

The final argument that ethical egoists typically advance has its origins in the thinking of Friedrich Nietzsche, a nineteenth-century German philosopher, and in this century is most strongly developed by Ayn Rand in *The Virtue of Selfishness* (1964). Altruistic morality, Nietzsche argued, was demeaning because it was essentially a morality of the weak, a morality for slaves, for the herd, for those who were afraid to assert themselves. Altruism is for people who value themselves so little that they put other people ahead of their own selves. It is, moreover, a self-deceptive morality, for it takes a weakness (namely, failing to value oneself sufficiently) and turns it into a virtue (i.e., altruism). It is, finally, self-serving in a deceptive way. The weak, Nietzsche claims, preach the gospel of altruism in order to gain control over the strong, to try to convince the strong to take care of the weak, to give up their power. Genuine morality, Nietzsche maintains, is about self-assertion and self-transcendence, ideas he discussed under the headings of the superman (*Übermensch*) and the will to power. The morality of altruism is a morality of weakness and should be replaced by a morality of strength.

Ayn Rand, as we saw in the opening passage in this chapter, has developed a similar argument, claiming that altruism is about self-sacrifice. Altruistic morality maintains that one individual's interests—and sometimes even that person's life—ought to be sacrificed for another person. Such a morality does not value individuals and their full development. Ethical egoism, she argues, presents a far different picture of morality, one that affirms the absolute value of the individual and encourages all individuals to actively seek that which will promote their flourishing. It is the only moral position that genuinely values the individual.

The "It's Not So Different After All . . ." Argument

Finally, some ethical egoists advance an intriguing claim in support of their position. They argue that ethical egoism doesn't really result in such radically different behavior as its critics allege and that the egoist's perspective actually provides a unifying reason for meeting all the different obligations that we usually meet. For example, it is in our best interest, they argue, to tell the truth in the long run. People are more likely to trust us, and this to our advantage. We can gain more from a general policy of truthfulness than from one of deceit.

This argument depends on three crucial assumptions. First, it presupposes some weaker version of egoism. Strong egoists who consider only their own self-interest and leave no moral room for the interests of other people are far less likely to act in ways that coincide with common-sense morality or the requirements of other moral theories. Second, this argument takes for granted that we will consider the *long-term* consequences characteristic of rational egoism. Actions such as lying, cheating, or stealing may be justified in terms of short-term consequences but may not pass the test for long-term self-interest. Finally, this argument is much more compatible with rule egoism than act egoism. The act egoist might find a particular case of lying or cheating to be justified, but a *rule* permitting that as a general policy would hardly further the egoist's self-interest. Thus, the weaker, rational rule egoist would probably act in most—although not all—situations the same way that most moral people would act.

The intriguing part of this argument is that it suggests that there are frequently very good self-interested reasons for being moral, reasons that all too often are overlooked by advocates of altruistically oriented accounts of morality. Seen in this light, ethical egoism can be interpreted in two different ways. On one hand, ethical egoists will argue that this shows that ethical egoism can replace other, competing accounts of morality and introduce into the moral life a single principle—self-interest—on which all moral decisions can be based. On the other hand, critics of ethical egoism can look at the same situation and argue instead that ethical egoism simply provides a second line of defense, as it were, for being moral. When all other reasons fail to convince people, we can often point to considerations of self-interest. In order to help decide which of these two approaches we should assume, let's now consider some of the major criticisms of ethical egoism.

Criticisms of Ethical Egoism

Several main lines of criticism of ethical egoism have crystallized in recent years. They center around four questions that critics pose to the ethical egoist.

- Does ethical egoism yield consistent advice about how we should act?
- Is ethical egoism a morality that its adherents can proclaim publicly?
- Can ethical egoists be good friends?
- Are ethical egoists morally insensitive?

Let's consider each of these issues.

Consistency

A number of critics of ethical egoism have argued that it is essentially flawed because it yields contradictory commands about how we should act. Brian Medlin, for example, has argued that in any given situation ethical egoists must seek to promote their own self-interest and yet at the same time, if they are universal ethical egoists, they must will that everyone else also act to promote their own self-interest. We have already seen the difficulty with this position: Often it is in my self-interest for other people to act against their own self-interest. If I am a salesperson, for example, it is usually in my best interest to have other people pay full price for my products, even though it is not generally in their best interest to do so. If I am an ethical egoist, I seem committed to ensure both that they pay full price and that they not pay full price. Ethical egoism, in other words, seems *inconsistent*.

We have already seen Jesse Kalin's reply to this objection. There is no more inconsistency in ethical egoism, he argues, than there is in a hard-fought game of chess in which each opponent wants to win but also wants the other person to play as good a game as possible. This is an interesting reply, for it may let the ethical egoist off the hook on this charge, but it does so in a way that gives us a deeper insight into the egoist's world. Essentially, the world of the ethical egoist is a deeply competitive world in which each person is pitted against everyone else. It is hardly surprising that Kalin should appeal to examples from sports and other competitive activities. We will consider this issue further when we discuss friendship for the ethical egoist.

Public and Private Morality

We have already caught a glimpse of a second difficulty for ethical egoists. In order to promote their own self-interest, ethical egoists may well find it to their advantage to hide their moral beliefs, especially in a world that values altruism. If an egoistic politician were making a large donation to a hospital building fund because it was a good tax deduction and would look good in any subsequent political campaigns, it would hardly be to the egoist's advantage to *say* this. Rather, it would be better to claim that it was being done out of a spirit of kindness and concern for the community.

Although this might not be an ultimately decisive mark against ethical egoism, it does raise our level of moral suspicion. One of the hallmarks of moral theories since the Enlightenment is that they are essentially public in character. Indeed, some philosophers have even argued that it is precisely the public discussion of reasons that provides the most reliable procedure for guaranteeing their rationality. The reason for this is that genuine public discussion is the best way of ensuring that everyone's interests will receive full and equal representation. Consequently, when we encounter a moral theory that is resistant to public exposure, we are naturally suspicious about whether everyone's interests do receive full and equal representation. A moment's reflection tells us that this suspicion is well grounded. In fact, the egoist's own interests receive much more weight than everyone else's interests. James Rachels has argued that this is the major flaw of ethical egoism: It gives unwarranted weight to one's own interests at the expense of everyone else's without any morally relevant reason for doing so. This is akin, Rachels suggests, to racism, for racism assigns a higher value to the interests of some people than others and does so on the basis of a characteristic (skin color) that has no moral relevance.

There is a second, related issue about the private character of the ethical egoist's motivations. It is easy to imagine situations in which egoists must deceive other people about their motives, and such deception both raises serious moral issues in their own right and poses questions about how close the egoist can be to other people, especially nonegoists. Let's turn to the latter issue now.

Friendship

One of the more difficult issues for ethical egoism to handle is friendship. Clearly ethical egoists can have acquaintances, and at least in some sense they can and do have friends. Yet it is unclear whether they can have the type of deep friendships that most of us value highly. Even defenders of egoism such as Kalin admit that friendship poses a problem for ethical egoism. Deep friendships are grounded in a mutual concern for the welfare of the other person for his or her own sake, and it would seem that ethical egoism precludes having such concern. Certainly egoists can have friends and can help their friends, but only insofar as having and helping them promotes the egoists' own self-interest.

Consider the qualities many of us value in friends. Close friends are people we can trust—trust with our secrets, trust with our feelings, trust with those parts of ourselves that are most vulnerable. Conversely, we respect, protect, and cherish those same qualities in our friends. Moreover, we trust our friends to be loyal to us, just as we are loyal to them. Just as we stick by them, even when things get rough, so we expect that they will stick by us. Yet is it realistic to expect ethical egoists to do the same? Egoists ask whether respecting trust, remaining loyal, and other virtues are in their own self-interest or not. In those instances in which it is in their self-interest to respect trust, they will; in those cases when it is not, they will not. Moreover, since it may not be in their self-interest to tell you this, they may lie and tell you that you can trust them when you can't. This is not, of course, to say that they will always lie. They will lie only when it is in their self-interest to do so. Similarly, they will remain loyal to their friends as long as it is in their self-interest to remain loyal. But they will lie to their friends and betray their friends when it is in their self-interest to do so—and perhaps the most peculiar thing about ethical egoism is that they are *morally obligated* to do so when it is in their self-interest.

Is this picture of the ethical egoist as a friend too harsh? There are certainly mitigating factors. Truly enlightened rule egoists might realize that there is a big difference between short-term self-interest and long-term self-interest within the context of friendship. The behavior of such egoists might resemble the behavior of real friends, but even then there would be one crucial difference. Both might show concern for their friends, but the motives behind such concern would be quite different. Whereas genuine friends are concerned with their friends at least in part for their friends' own sake, genuine ethical egoists do not necessarily have any such reason to be concerned about their friends. The only motive that they must have is one of self-interest. They may be concerned about their friends, but only insofar as having such concern is in their own self-interest.

Moral Insensitivity

Although moral theories are generally evaluated on the basis of the *actions* that they specify, it is also possible to consider the *sensibility* that a moral theory encourages. Typically, an ethical egoist is sensitive to issues which many nonegoists overlook. For example, the ethical egoist is particularly sensitive to the self-deception that most of us engage in, especially when we are trying to think of ourselves as good people. Most of us, the egoist realizes, want to think of ourselves as good people; furthermore, we usually want others to think of us in the same way. This is an essentially self-deceptive desire, for we cannot admit it to ourselves without acknowledging a motivation that is inconsistent with our desire to think of ourselves as good people. A genuinely good person does not do good things in order to appear good, but rather because those things are the right thing to do.

Ethical egoists also tend to see individuals as largely, sometimes completely, responsible for their own lives, and this leads to a curious kind of moral insensitivity and unwillingness to help other people. There are at least two reasons for that unwillingness. First, ethical egoists are more likely than others to believe people are responsible for the misfortunes they encounter in life. Second, and this is in part a corollary of the first belief, they doubt that one person can really do anything effective to help another person. People have to help themselves, and in their eyes attempts at intervention usually create inappropriate dependency and cause more problems than they solve.

The issue, however, seems to go deeper than a simple unwillingness to help other people, although this is by itself no small matter. On a more basic level, there seems to be something that blocks the egoist's compassionate *perception* of the suffering of other persons. Egoists would seem to show little compassion for the suffering of others, for genuine compassion has nothing to do with self-interest. Compassion just is a concern for other people for their own sake, and it is precisely this concern that is beyond the ethical egoist's grasp. Yet to banish compassion from the ethical landscape is to impoverish our moral lives, to diminish ourselves and our humanity.

Consider three areas in which this issue of moral insensitivity manifests itself: world hunger, the suffering of animals, and our treatment of people with disabilities. World hunger certainly presents daunting problems on almost every level, but presumably the egoist's response is one of pure self-interest: starving people should be helped only when it is in our own self-interest to do so. Yet the egoist's assumptions hardly seem applicable in this situation. Certainly it is difficult to reasonably believe that all those starving people (in Bangladesh, sub-Saharan Africa, etc.) have brought their fate on themselves. It may be the case that a few government and military and business leaders have contributed to that fate, but it is a far cry from saying that the individual citizens are responsible for their plight. The egoist's other concerns about increasing dependency and the possible ineffectiveness of help are hardly conclusive, either. Certainly there is some danger of creating dependency, but some dependency in human life is appropriate. Furthermore, aid can be given in ways that minimize or control the extent to which it creates such dependency. Nor is the concern about the ineffectiveness of help really convincing. Such concern is legitimate, but the best way to deal with it is to find ways of helping effectively, not simply refusing to help. We are not limited to only two alternatives, ineffective help or no help at all.

The suffering of animals also presents problems for ethical egoists. Part of their view is that each person is responsible for presenting, pursuing, and protecting his or her own interests. It seems to follow from that that beings who cannot represent themselves have no standing. This has obvious implications for animals, who cannot represent their own interests to human beings because they cannot speak. Animals cannot take care of themselves in the same way that adult human beings can, and ethical egoism has no way of recognizing this except insofar as it fits into our own self-interest.

Finally, consider the issue of our treatment of persons with disabilities that prevent them from having, presenting, or pursuing their own interests. Some of these cases might be quite severe and present deep moral problems for any ethical theory: people with very advanced Alzheimer's disease, persons in possibly irreversible comas, individuals with profound mental retardation. Ethical egoists would attempt to help such persons only if it were in their self-interest to do so, and it is easy to imagine situations in which it would not be. Ethical egoism condones a moral callousness to the suffering of the disabled that conflicts with some of our deepest moral intuitions.

THE TRUTH IN ETHICAL EGOISM

Ethical egoism is a disquieting moral doctrine. There are good reasons for concluding that it is wrong, perhaps even profoundly wrong, in its exclusive focus on self-interest and in the curious way in which it simply seems to miss the point of the moral life. But even if it is wrong, we can learn from it. There are at least two areas in which the ethical egoist has much to teach us.

First, ethical egoism shows that there are often good self-interested reasons for being moral. All too often, we see self-interest as being in sharp conflict with morality. However, in many situations there are good long-term self-interested reasons for doing the morally right thing. Honesty, for example, is often the best policy for self-interested, prudential reasons as well as for moral reasons. Self-interest and morality, in other words, may often coincide, and one of the things that we can learn from ethical egoism is that there are often good self-interested reasons for acting morally.

Second, ethical egoism may well in part be a reaction to a relative neglect in some ethical traditions of the proper role of self-love in the moral life. Insofar as many ethical theories demand a strict impartiality toward one's own self-interest, they perhaps undervalue the importance of one's own special interests, projects, and attachments in life. As we shall see in Chapter 9, one of the strengths of Aristotle's virtue ethics is precisely its recognition of the fundamental importance of the virtue of self-love in the moral life. Yet Aristotle, in contrast to ethical egoists, was able to balance self-love with a genuine concern for the welfare of other people and a deep appreciation of the communal dimension of human existence.

Third, there is an important, if exaggerated, lesson we can learn from ethical egoism about personal responsibility. The ethical egoist sees each person as solely responsible for his or her own existence, as evidenced in the speech from *Atlas Shrugged* that opens this chapter. Once again, this is an extreme view, but it may serve as a helpful corrective to everyday moral attitudes that tend to see individuals purely as victims of forces beyond their own control. The truth, as usual, is somewhere in between these two extremes.

The moral life, we have suggested, is characterized by a plurality of values. Different moral traditions are like the three branches of the U.S. federal government, keeping each other in check, each balancing out the influence and power of the other two. We see at least three ways in which ethical egoist serves this function in regard to other moral traditions. It pushes us to reflect on the ways in which our moral motives often coincide with self-interest, to question whether our moral outlook gives sufficient weight to legitimate self-interest, and to probe the extent to which we may be more responsible for our lives than we thought. Ethical egoism helps to keep us honest with ourselves.

DISCUSSION QUESTIONS

1. Recall **statement 11** of the Ethical Inventory ("Everyone is just out for himself or herself").
   (a) What is the proper name for the theory that this statement exemplifies?
   (b) What is the evidence in support of statement 11? What evidence can be offered against it? How would the egoist try to refute such evidence?
   (c) Does the support for this argument ever rest on a tautology? Explain.
   (d) Has your rating of this item changed after reading this chapter? If so, in what way? If your rating has not changed, are your reasons for your rating any different now than they were when you first responded to this statement?
2. Recall **statement 12** of the Ethical Inventory ("Some people think that they are genuinely concerned about the welfare of others, but they are just deceiving themselves").
   (a) Why is it difficult, if not impossible, to refute this claim?
   (b) Has your rating of this item changed after reading this chapter? If so, in what way? If your rating has not changed, are your reasons for your rating any different now than they were when you first responded to this statement?
3. Recall your response to **statement 13** in the Ethical Inventory ("People are not really free. They are just products of their environment, upbringing, and other factors").
   (a) What theory does this statement exemplify?
   (b) Has your rating of this item changed after reading this chapter? If so, in what way? If your rating has not changed, are your reasons for your rating any different now than they were when you first responded to this statement?
4. Recall **statement 14** of the Ethical Inventory ("Everyone should watch out just for himself or herself").

    (a) What would the world be like if everyone followed this advice? Do you think the world would be a better place than it is now? Why or why not?

    (b) Has your rating of this item changed after reading this chapter? If so, in what way? If your rating has not changed, are your reasons for your rating any different now than they were when you first responded to this statement?

5. What is the most selfish act you can imagine? Why is it the most selfish one? If you found the act morally objectionable, what specifically was objectionable about it?

6. In his *Fable of the Bees,* Bernard Mandeville (1670–1733) argues, perhaps in jest, that "private vices" produce "publick benefits." Can you think of a situation in which this works? If so, is it exceptional, or can we make it the rule?

7. Is self-preservation a moral imperative or just a fact? Are there situations in which self-preservation is not the highest value? Is it selfish to prefer (saving) one's own life to that of others? From an evolutionary standpoint, is "survival of the fittest" selfish or selfless?

8. Is "enlightened self-interest" a contradiction in terms, or is it really the basis for all action?

9. Do you have any friends or acquaintances who act like ethical egoists? Does this present any special problems or issues in your relationship with them? Can an ethical egoist be a good friend? Why or why not?

10. Have you ever read any of the novels of Ayn Rand? If so, what was your reaction? What, if anything, appealed to you in her characters? What, if anything, did you dislike about her characters? How does her fiction fit in with the theory of ethical egoism?

11. `MOVIE` In the movie *Hollow Man* (2000), a scientist named Sebastian Caine (Kevin Bacon) discovers a formula to make people invisible. Caine becomes increasingly malevolent and tries to kill people. Compare this movie to Plato's Ring of Gyges discussed earlier in this chapter.

BIBLIOGRAPHICAL ESSAY

One of the **classic sources** for a statement of psychological egoism is **Thomas Hobbes**'s *Leviathan* (1651); it is available on the Web at gopher://gopher.vt. edu:10010/02/98/1. For a contemporary reinterpretation of Hobbes which partially challenges the belief that he was a psychological egoist, see Gregory S. Kavka, *Hobbesian Moral and Political Theory* (Princeton: Princeton University Press, 1986), especially Chapter 2. Bernard Gert's "Hobbes and Psychological Egoism," in *Hobbes' Leviathan: Interpretation and Criticism,* edited by Bernard Baumrin (Belmont, CA: Wadsworth, 1969), pp. 107–126, introduced the term "tautological egoism"; Gert argues against reading Hobbes solely as a psychological egoist. For a vigorous defense of Hobbes's place in English philosophy, see David Gauthier, "Thomas

Hobbes: Moral Theorist," in his *Moral Dealing. Contract, Ethics, and Reason* (Ithaca: Cornell University Press, 1990), pp. 11–23.

There are several **good, short introductions to egoism.** See Kurt Baier, "Egoism," *A Companion to Ethics*, edited by Peter Singer (Oxford: Blackwell, 1991), pp. 197–204; Richard Campbell, "Egoism," *Encyclopedia of Ethics*, edited by Lawrence C. Becker (New York: Garland, 1992) vol. 1, pp. 294–297; and Elliott Sober, "Psychological Egoism," in Hugh LaFollette, ed., *The Blackwell Guide to Ethical Theory* (Oxford: Blackwell, 2000).

There are several egoism resources on the **World Wide Web**: The most extensive set of resources is to be found at the Egoist Archive (http://www.nonserviam.com/egoistarchive/); the Max Stirner website (http://www.nonserviam.com/stirner/) also contains helpful resources on Max Stirner, one of the earliest German egoists; the Objectivism and Ayn Rand site (http://www.vix.com/objectivism/) contains information about Ayn Rand; LibertyOnline (http://libertyonline.hypermall.com/) is also an excellent resource. For a continually updated list of resources on ethical egoism, see the Ethical Egoism page (http://ethics.acusd.edu/theories/Egoism/index.html) of my *Ethics Updates* site. For an excellent assessment of the strengths and weaknesses of psychological egoism, see Hugh LaFollette, "The Truth in Psychological Egoism," (http://www.etsu.edu/philos/faculty/hugh/egoism.htm).

On **sociobiology and altruism,** see Edward O. Wilson's *On Human Nature* (Cambridge, MA: Harvard University Press, 1978), which is directed toward a nonscientific audience, and his *Sociobiology: A New Synthesis* (Cambridge, MA: Harvard University Press, 1975), which provides a more technical statement of the issues; more recently, Robert Wright's *The Moral Animal: Why We Are the Way We Are* (New York: Vintage Books, 1994) has furthered the case for evolutionary psychology. The literature generated by sociobiology is vast, but for three good anthologies of critical evaluations, see Arthur Caplan, ed., *The Sociobiology Debate* (New York: Harper & Row, 1978); Ashley Montagu, ed., *Sociobiology Examined* (New York: Oxford University Press, 1980); and my own article, "The Ambiguity and Limits of a Sociobiological Ethic," *International Philosophical Quarterly*, 23, no. 1 (March 1983): 79–89. For a discussion of the relevance of sociobiology to egoism, see Peter Singer, *The Expanding Circle* (New York: New American Library, 1982) and Kavka, *Hobbesian Moral and Political Theory*, pp. 56ff. For a short overview, see Alan Gibbard, "Sociobiology," in Robert E. Goodin and Philip Pettit, eds., *A Companion to Contemporary Political Philosophy* (Oxford: Blackwell, 1993), pp. 597–610.

For a defense of the possibility of **altruism,** see Thomas Nagel, *The Possibility of Altruism* (Princeton: Princeton University Press, 1970). On the rationality of altruism, see Kristen R. Monroe, Michael C. Barton, and Ute Klingemann, "Altruism and the Theory of Rational Action: Rescuers of Jews in Nazi Europe," *Ethics* 101 (October 1990): 103–122. For an overview of the psychological literature, see Dennis Krebs, "Psychological Approaches to Altruism: An Evaluation." *Ethics* 92 (1982): 447–458. For a further discussion of the villagers of Le Chambon, see Chapter 9 on virtue ethics and the bibliographical essay for that chapter. Also see the essays in the issue on altruism of *Social Philosophy & Policy* 10, no. 1 (Winter 1993) and the issue on self-interest, *Social Philosophy & Policy* 14, no. 1 (Winter 1997).

For a **review of the literature on ethical egoism,** see Tibor Machan, "Recent Work on Ethical Egoism," *American Philosophical Quarterly* 16, no. 1 (January 1979): 1–15. Alasdair MacIntyre's "Egoism and Altruism" in Paul Edwards, ed., *The Encyclopedia of Philosophy* (New York: Macmillan, 1967), vol. 2, pp. 462–466, contains a perceptive overview of work in this area. Also see Edward Regis, Jr., "What

Is Ethical Egoism?" *Ethics* 91 (October 1980): 50–62, for a careful consideration of the various meanings of ethical egoism. There are two excellent anthologies of articles on ethical egoism: David Gauthier, ed., *Morality and Rational Self-Interest* (Englewood Cliffs, NJ: Prentice-Hall, 1970); and Ronald. D. Milo's *Egoism and Altruism* (Belmont, CA: Wadsworth, 1973). For a review and analysis of attempts to reconcile egoism and traditional accounts of morality, see Gregory S. Kavka, "The Reconciliation Project," *Morality, Reason and Truth: New Essays on the Foundations of Ethics,* edited by David Copp and David Zimmerman (Totowa, NJ: Rowman and Allanheld, 1984), pp. 297–319.

Among the **major critiques of ethical egoism** are Christine Korsgaard, *The Myth of Egoism,* The Lindley Lectures (Lawrence: University of Kansas Press, 1999); C. D. Broad, "Egoism as a Theory of Human Motives," reprinted in Ronald Milo, ed., *Egoism and Altruism* (Belmont, CA: Wadsworth, 1973), pp. 88–100;. David Gauthier, "Morality and Advantage," *Philosophical Review* 76 (1967): 460–475, reprinted in his *Morality and Rational Self-Interest*; and his "The Impossibility of Rational Egoism," *The Journal of Philosophy* 71 (1974): 439–456 and his "The Incompleat Egoist," in his *Moral Dealing: Contract, Ethics, and Reason* (Ithaca, NY: Cornell University Press, 1990), pp. 234–273; James Rachels, "Two Arguments against Ethical Egoism," *Philosophia* 4 (1974): 297–314; Brian Medlin, "Ultimate Principles and Ethical Egoism," *Australasian Journal of Philosophy* 35 (1978): 111–118; Warren Quinn, "Egoism as an Ethical System," *Journal of Philosophy* 71 (1974): 456–472; Kurt Baier, *The Moral Point of View* (Ithaca: Cornell University Press, 1958), and his "Ethical Egoism and Interpersonal Compatibility," *Philosophical Studies* 24 (1973): 357–368; and Richard Brandt, "Rationality, Egoism, and Morality," *Journal of Philosophy* 69 (1972): 681–697. For an excellent collection of critical essays on self-interest from a wide range of disciplines, see Jane J. Mansbridge, ed., *Beyond Self-interest,* (Chicago: University of Chicago Press, 1990).

Jesse Kalin's articles provide a **tightly argued defense of the ethical egoist's position.** See his "On Ethical Egoism," *American Philosophical Quarterly Monograph* 1 (1969): 26–41;. "Two Kinds of Moral Reasoning," *Canadian Journal of Philosophy* 5 (1975): 323–356; and "In Defense of Egoism," in David Gauthier, ed., *Morality and Rational Self-interest* (Englewood Cliffs, NJ: Prentice Hall, 1970). The game metaphor in Kalin's argument is discussed in Sidney Trivus, "On Playing the Game," *The Personalist* 59 (1978): 82–84. Edward, Regis, Jr., "Ethical Egoism and Moral Responsibility," *American Philosophical Quarterly* 16 (1979): 45–52, defends a version of **nonmaximizing ethical egoism** that escapes some of the standard criticisms that ethical egoism permits behavior that commonsense morality would prohibit. More recently, see the defense of ethical egoism in John Van Ingen, *Why Be Moral? The Egoistic Challenge* (New York: Lang, 1994).

Much of the discussion of ethical egoism has appeared in a journal called *The Personalist* (which is now published under the name *Pacific Philosophical Quarterly*); see the articles by Emmons (1969); Brandon (1970); Emmons (1971); Skorpen (1969); Murphy (1971); Nozick (1971); Hospers (1973); Den Uyl (1975); Dwyer (1975); Carlson (1976); Burrill (1976); Sanders (1976); Benditt (1976); Sanders (1977).

On the issue of **ethical egoism and moral sensitivity,** see Anthony Duff, "Psychopathy and Moral Understanding," *American Philosophical Quarterly* 14 (1977): 189–200; Chong Kim Chong, "Ethical Egoism and the Moral Point of View," *Journal of Value Inquiry* 26 (1992): 23–36; and Daniel Putnam, "Egoism and Virtue," *ibid*. For general comments on the issue of moral sensitivity, see Larry May, "Insensitivity and Moral Responsibility," *Journal of Value Inquiry* 26 (1992): 7–22. For a consideration of **egoism and friendship,** see R. D. Ashmore, Jr., "Friendship and the Problem of Egoism," *The Thomist* 41 (1977): 105–130. On the role of **altruism in friendship,** see Lawrence A. Blum, *Friendship, Altruism, and Morality* (London: Routledge & Kegan Paul, 1980) and Jeffrey Blustein, *Care and Commitment* (New York: Oxford University Press, 1991). For an argument that the dichotomous categories of altruism and self-interest do not fit friendship, see John Hardwig, "In Search of an Ethic of Interpersonal Relations," George Graham and Hugh LaFollette, eds., *Person to Person* (Philadelphia: Temple University Press, 1989), pp. 63–81.

Much contemporary work about ethical egoism is inspired by **libertarianism.** Ayn Rand's novels, such as *Atlas Shrugged* and *The Fountainhead,* provide a powerful literary expression of the ethical egoist's standpoint; her explicit statement of the egoist's standpoint is to be found in her *The Virtue of Selfishness* (New York: Signet, 1964). For a libertarian approach that is particularly sensitive to the issue of **egoism and rights,** see Eric Mack, "How to Derive Ethical Egoism," *The Personalist* 52 (1971): 735–743; "Egoism and Rights," *The Personalist* 54 (1973): 5–33; and "Egoism and Rights Revisited," *The Personalist* 58 (1977): 282–288. Also see Tibor Machan, *Individuals and Their Rights* (LaSalle, IL: Open Court, 1989).

Citations. The quotation from Ayn Rand at the beginning of this chapter comes from her novel *Atlas Shrugged,* pp. 984, 993. The citation from Kavka is from his *Hobbesian Moral and Political Theory,* p. 66.

Further Information. For further information on the issues discussed in this chapter, see the Ethical Egoism page (http://ethics.acusd.edu/theories/egoism/) of my *Ethics Updates* site.

THE ETHICS OF CONSEQUENCES: UTILITARIANISM

In the 1970s, Americans became increasingly aware of the carcinogenic effects of asbestos. Becoming aware of its cancer-causing consequences was no easy matter, for asbestos often does not cause cancer until twenty or more years after exposure to the asbestos dust. During World War II, a number of American factory and dock workers handled large quantities of asbestos needed for the war effort. In the 1960s, a disproportionately large percentage of them were coming down with lung cancer—and researchers began to realize that this was the result of their earlier exposure to asbestos.

By the time the harmful effects of asbestos exposure were discovered, this substance was being widely used throughout the country for insulation and brake linings and pads. Asbestos was in office buildings, school buildings, nursing homes, and private residences. Because of its harmful nature, it was difficult and costly to remove. Workers had to have special training and wear special protective clothing and breathing apparatus before they could safely work with it. One of the questions we faced as a country was precisely what to do about this problem.

To answer this question, we had to look at the consequences of either leaving the asbestos in place (perhaps with an appropriate warning) or of removing it (at high cost). When we looked at the consequences, we had to add up the potential costs and benefits of the various courses of action in various types of situations. The clearest case was in elementary schools. Children exposed to asbestos might come down with lung cancer in their thirties; in addition, many of those who worked at those schools were comparatively young. Requiring the removal of asbestos from elementary schools was an easy decision: Whatever the costs of removing it, the potential damage was so great that few would disagree with regulations requiring its removal from schools. Should we also require its removal from all individual homes? Here the decision was more difficult, for the costs were higher proportionate to the benefits. For every elementary school in the country, there are probably hundreds of private residences insulated with asbestos. The work involved in removing asbestos from all those residences would be considerably more than the work required for the schools, and the enforcement task would be much greater as well. Moreover, the cost would presumably be borne by the individual residents or owners, who might be neither able nor willing to shoulder such a burden. Whereas a young couple with children would probably be willing to do whatever is necessary to remove the asbestos from their home, a retired couple in their eighties on a fixed income would presumably be more reluctant to spend a lot of money for this purpose. A utilitarian might well decide to leave this decision in each individual's hands. Finally, should we mandate the removal of asbestos from nursing homes and other such facilities, where the majority of people would not live an additional thirty years to be affected by asbestos? What about the welfare of those who were younger and worked in such facilities or visited them regularly? Utilitarians have to look closely at the consequences in each type of case.

Utilitarianism begins with one of the most important moral insights of modern times and couples it with a powerful metaphor which underlies our moral life. The insight is that *consequences count;* indeed, it goes one step further than this and claims that *only* consequences count. This puts it in sharp contrast to Kant's moral philosophy, which—as we shall see in the next chapter—places almost exclusive emphasis on the intentions behind an action. Utilitarianism goes to the other extreme, maintaining that **the morality of an action is to be determined solely through an assessment of its consequences.** It is for this reason that we call utilitarianism a *consequentialist* moral doctrine; morality, for the utilitarian, is solely a matter of consequences. (Utilitarianism is not the only consequentialist doctrine we have seen. Ethical egoism is also consequentialist but demands that we consider consequences only insofar as they affect our own individual well-being. Utilitarianism demands that we consider the impact of the consequences on *everyone* affected by the matter under consideration. The morally right action, the one that we ought to perform, is the one that produces the greatest overall positive consequences for everyone.

Once utilitarians have claimed that morality is solely a matter of consequences, they have to address themselves to several questions. First, they need to specify the *yardstick* or criterion in terms of which consequences are measured. Typically, utilitarians claim that we ought to do whatever produces the greatest amount of utility. But then *utility* must be defined. Pleasure, happiness, and preference satisfaction are the three most common candidates for the definition of utility. Second, utilitarians need to indicate *how the consequences can be measured.* They need, in other words, to provide an account of how the yardstick can be applied, how utility can be measured.

Third, utilitarians must address the question of how high their standards are, of *how much utility we must strive for.* How much, in other words, is enough utility? Although utilitarianism has often been stated in terms of maximizing utility, some have recently suggested that a less stringent and more attainable standard of expectations should be assumed. Fourth, utilitarians must indicate *what types of things are to be judged* in terms of their consequences. The three most common candidates here are acts, rules, and social policies. Finally, utilitarians must answer the question of *whom these are consequences for.* Clearly, they are not just the consequences for the individual agent—that would be ethical egoism. Do utilitarians take into account the consequences for all human beings or just for some subset, such as those in our own country? Do they take into account the consequences for future generations as well as the present one? Do they take into account the consequences for all sentient beings, animals as well as human beings; the natural environment as well as our constructed world; or just the human population?

Let's see how utilitarians have taken this basic insight about the moral significance of consequences and elaborated it into a formal theory of ethics.

DEFINING UTILITY

Utilitarians claim that the only thing that counts morally is whatever produces the greatest amount of *utility,* or the greatest overall positive consequences. Yet what is the proper yardstick of utility? Historically, utilitarians have taken pleasure and happiness as the measure of consequences. More recent versions of utilitarianism have turned either to higher ("ideal") goods or to preferences as the measure of consequences. Each of these four yardsticks has its strengths and its limitations.

Bentham and Pleasure

Originally, utilitarianism became influential with the work of Jeremy Bentham (1748–1832), who defined utility in terms of pleasure and pain. According to Bentham, we should act in such a way as to **maximize pleasure and minimize pain.** This position is known as **hedonistic utilitarianism.** Notice that it is very different from straightforward hedonism, which recommends maximizing one's own pleasure and minimizing one's own pain. Hedonistic utilitarianism recommends maximizing the overall amount of pleasure and minimizing the overall amount of pain.

Mill and Happiness

Bentham's philosophy quickly came under attack as the "pig's philosophy" because of what seemed to be its crude emphasis on sensual, bodily pleasures. John Stuart Mill (1806–1873), Bentham's godson, proposed a major reformulation of the utilitarian position by arguing that **utility should be defined in terms of happiness rather than pleasure.** Mill's standard seemed to be a definite advance over Bentham's, for it was based on a higher standard than mere pleasure. This is called **eudaimonistic utilitarianism.** (The word *eudaimonistic* comes from the Greek word for happiness, *eudaimonia*.) In order to see why this is the case, let's consider some of the differences between pleasure and happiness as the standard of utility.

Pleasure versus Happiness

The differences between pleasure and happiness are significant. We tend to think of pleasure as being primarily bodily or sensual in character. Eating, drinking, and having sex come immediately to mind as paradigm cases of pleasure. Happiness, on the other hand, is usually less immediately tied down to the body. We might initially characterize it as belonging more to the mind or spirit than the body.

Second, pleasure generally seems to be of shorter duration than happiness. This stems from the nature of pleasure itself. Pleasure, at least in the eyes of many psychologists and philosophers, is the enjoyable feeling we experience when a state of deprivation is replaced by a state of satiation or fulfillment. In other words, pleasure is what we feel when we drink a nice cool glass of water when we are thirsty. Yet this gives us an insight into the reason why pleasures are short lived. Once we are satiated, we no longer experience the object as pleasurable. Once we are no longer thirsty, drinking water becomes less pleasurable. Happiness, on the other hand, seems to lie in the realization of certain goals, hopes, or plans for one's life. Insofar as these goals are intrinsically rewarding ones, we do not tire of them in the same way that we may tire of certain pleasures.

Third, happiness may encompass both pleasure and pain. Indeed, we could easily imagine persons saying that their life is happy but still acknowledging painful moments. A good example of this is a woman giving birth to a long-hoped-for child. She may experience quite a bit of pain during and after the birth, but she may still feel happy. Conversely, we can imagine someone experiencing pleasure but not feeling happy. Think of someone smoking crack, which directly stimulates the brain's pleasure center. That person might take pleasure from it as he inhales deeply, but he could be feeling very unhappy with his life, career, marriage, and so on.

Finally, there is more of an evaluative element in our notion of happiness than there is in our idea of pleasure. In reading the preceding example, many nonsmokers might have been repulsed at the idea of taking pleasure in smoking cigarettes, especially in the morning. Yet this is not a reason for doubting that some smokers do find pleasure in it. We may want to distinguish between good and bad pleasures, between harmless and harmful ones, but we do not doubt that the bad pleasures are still pleasures. With happiness, on the other hand, we build in an evaluative component. We are likely to question whether someone is genuinely happy in a way that we do not question whether they are genuinely feeling pleasure.

The problem with weighing consequences is that it is much easier to weigh pleasure than happiness or ideal goods, yet pleasure is the least suitable standard. *The closer we move toward a suitable standard of utility, the less able we are to subject it to quantification.*

Other Accounts of Utility

Pleasure and utility are not the only possible standards of utility, and the twentieth century saw attempts to redefine the standard of utility in terms of ideal goods such as freedom and knowledge and justice (G. E. Moore) and individual preferences (Kenneth Arrow). These versions, *ideal utilitarianism* and *preference utilitarianism* respectively, provide variations on the utilitarian theme. We can summarize these various versions of utilitarianism in the following way.

THE MEASURES OF UTILITY

Type of Utilitarianism	Standard of Utility	Number of Intrinsic Goods	Main Proponent
Hedonistic	Pleasure	One	Bentham
Eudaimonistic	Happiness	One	Mill
Ideal	Justice, Freedom, etc.	Many	Moore
Preference	Preference	None	Arrow

No single candidate has emerged as the sole choice among philosophers for the standard of utility. The disagreement among philosophers over this issue seems to reflect a wider disagreement in our own society. If consequences count, we have still to decide upon what yardstick to use in measuring them. The attraction of preference theory in this context is that it permits this multiplicity of standards, all of which are expressed as preferences.

Indeed, there may be a distinct advantage to allowing a *multiplicity* of different types of factors underlying utility. This is a type of pluralism within a specific moral theory. Utilitarianism has sometimes been criticized for being too narrow, for reducing all our considerations in life to a single axis of utility, usually either pleasure or happiness. There is much to be said for a fuller, suppler theory that permits us to recognize that consequences need to be measured according to several yardsticks. The difficulty with such a move, however, is that it then makes utilitarianism a more complex doctrine, one that is more difficult to apply in practice. Furthermore, utilitarians who go in this direction then need to specify the relationship among the different kinds of yardsticks. When one alternative ranks high on the yardstick of happiness, for example, and another course of action is high on the scale of justice, which takes precedence? Finally, it threatens to rob utilitarianism of its chief advantage—namely, that it offers a clear method for calculating the morality of actions, rules, and social policies. Utilitarians who opt for a multiplicity of yardsticks must address themselves to questions such as these.

APPLYING THE MEASURE

Once we accept a standard of utility, we are still faced with the task of specifying how that standard is to apply to the world in which we live. This is a thorny but crucial issue for utilitarians because one of the major attractions of utilitarianism is that it promises precision in the moral life. If it can't deliver on this promise because it can't be applied precisely, then it loses its advantage over competing moral theories.

The Scale Metaphor

One of the things that makes utilitarianism attractive is the root metaphor that underlies much of its language about measuring consequences. Utilitarianism is grounded in a image with tremendous intuitive appeal to many of us: that of the scale. The very notion of weighing consequences presupposes that consequences are the kinds of things that can be placed on a scale. This metaphor pervades our everyday discourse about deciding among competing courses of action. Consider the types of things we often say.

- On *balance,* I'd rather go to the movies.
- When I *weigh* the alternatives, going to Hawaii looks best, even if it is hot at this time of year.
- Buying me an extra nice present *balanced* out the fact that they forgot to send it until a week after my birthday.
- Nothing can *outweigh* all the grief that the hit-and-run accident caused us.
- Only the death penalty can right the *scales* of justice.
- This is a *weighty* choice with *heavy* consequences.

Some of these scale metaphors have specifically monetary overtones, as though things were weighed in terms of their dollar value.

- I'm going to *pay him back* for all the grief he's given me over the years.
- How can I ever *repay* you for your kindness?
- That was a *costly* mistake.
- I'll be forever in your *debt.*

In these expressions, we see the way in which money metaphorically plays the role of the measure in terms of which consequences are assessed.

In order to weigh consequences, the utilitarian needs some kind of measure in terms of which utility is determined. We have examined various candidates for this yardstick: pleasure, happiness, ideals, and preferences. But we also need some way of marking off the units to be measured. Scales are often marked off in terms of ounces or grams. Yardsticks are usually marked off in terms of inches. How do we mark off units of utility? One of the ways of doing this is by assigning cardinal numbers (1, 2, 3, etc.) to pleasure or happiness, for example. In the following section, we will consider this approach by using the stipulative concepts of hedons and dolors. The other way is to assign ordinal (1st, 2nd, 3rd, etc.) or coordinal (comparative) rankings. This is the approach that preference utilitarianism takes. Let's look at both.

Hedons and Dolors

Once they agree upon the kind of yardstick, utilitarians must arrive at some consensus about the way in which the individual units on the measuring stick are to be marked off. Utilitarians sometimes refer to units of pleasure or happiness as **hedons** and units of displeasure or suffering or unhappiness as **dolors.** (The word *hedon* comes from the Greek word for *pleasure;* this is the same root that *hedonism* comes from. The word *dolor* comes from the Latin word *dolor,* which means "pain.") Particular things, at least in textbook examples, are then often assigned some number. A good corned beef sandwich may, for example, be 5 hedons, while a pleasant vacation to the Bahamas may be 6,000 hedons. A visit to the dentist could be 100 dolors, and the death of a close friend several thousand dolors.

Such a system may at first sound artificial, but utilitarians would argue that this apparent artificiality is not a serious problem. While there may be no absolute scale in which going to the dentist is a 100, it may be the case that having a close friend die is roughly twenty or thirty times worse than going to the dentist. It is this relationship of relative suffering (or pleasure) that the utilitarian seeks to capture in assigning numerical values to various consequences. This is, the utilitarian further argues, something that we do quite naturally in our everyday lives. The **utilitarian calculus** is but a refinement and formalization of that everyday activity of assigning relative values to various occurrences, of ranking them in relation to each other according to the amount of pleasure or pain they yield. But as soon as cardinal utilitarians admit this, they are on their way to becoming preference utilitarians.

The Decision Procedure

How do utilitarians go about deciding upon the moral worth of an action, granting that the consequences of an action can be specified in terms of hedons and dolors? They claim that in any given situation we must to the best of our ability (1) determine the consequences of the various courses of action open to us, (2) specify the hedons and dolors associated with each alternative, and then (3) perform that course of action that results in the greatest total amount of pleasure (i.e., of hedons minus dolors). Imagine, for example, that you are a utilitarian in the process of deciding between two pieces of proposed legislation about medical aid for the elderly. There are three possibilities open to you: to vote for a bill to reduce medical aid, to vote in favor of a bill that would increase such aid, or to vote against both and thus effectively vote in favor of keeping things the same. Reducing medical benefits for the elderly may result in 10 hedons apiece for 100 million people and 200 dolors for 20 million people, resulting in an overall utility of 3 billion dolors. Keeping benefits the same may result in 20 hedons apiece for 20 million people and 3 dolors for 100 million people, with a total overall utility of 2 billion, 600 million hedons. Finally, increasing benefits may result in 90 hedons apiece for 20 million people and 20 dolors for 100 million people, with a total overall utility of 200 million hedons. Thus, from a utilitarian point of view, we would be obligated to keep the benefits the same, since the other two possible courses of action both have a lesser overall utility.

HOW MUCH UTILITY IS ENOUGH?

One of the difficulties that utilitarians have faced centers around the question of how much utility we are obligated to produce. The usual answer has been that we ought to do whatever produces the greatest overall amount of utility. When we compare competing courses of action, we should choose the best one, the one that maximizes utility.

Maximizing Utility

It is easy to understand the initial plausibility of this answer. Imagine that we are considering whether to pass a particular piece of social legislation. We naturally consider how we can produce the greatest amount of good. If we are weighing the alternatives impartially, there is no attraction toward anything else, no pull toward doing less than the best. If some particular special interest group desired that we do less than the best, their wishes would be factored into the utilitarian equation along with everyone else's. There would, however, be no reason for giving them special weight. If we thought they deserved more weight, then presumably it would be for some reason that would be recognizable within the utilitarian framework. It is only when we have partial interests of our own that there is a desire to do less than the best.

Yet the picture changes rapidly when we consider what it would be like to be making decisions about our own personal lives in the same way. Here personal desires and wants have a much more prominent role. Yet traditional versions of utilitarianism seem to demand that we do the maximum, even in these more personal situations. The utilitarian always tries to produce the greatest overall amount of utility. This is in sharp contrast, for example, to Kantian ethics, which we will discuss in detail in the next chapter. Kant's position just states negatively that a particular action is morally forbidden, while the utilitarian tells us positively that we must choose the specific course of action which maximizes utility. Thus utilitarianism is an extremely demanding moral doctrine, since it demands that we sacrifice our own pleasure, happiness, or preference satisfaction for the greater good—that is, for social utility.

Supererogation

Philosophers have noted an interesting implication of the utilitarian view that we must always try to maximize utility. In many moral philosophies, it is often possible to act in a **supererogatory** fashion—that is, to go beyond the demands of duty and thus do something exceptionally meritorious. For the utilitarian, however, this is impossible. One is always obligated to do the thing that yields the greatest amount of utility, and it is precisely this obligation that constitutes duty. Thus, there is nothing above the call of duty. For the utilitarian, there is no room for supererogatory actions, for duty is so demanding that nothing above it is greater.

This is a cause for concern among some philosophers, for they believe that a moral theory that has no room for supererogation must be mistaken in some important way. Our everyday moral intuitions tell us that sometimes people do something that is above the call of duty. But if utilitarianism is correct, then this is impossible. Duty always calls for the maximum, so it is impossible to do anything above its call.

CONSEQUENCES OF WHAT?

The utilitarian maintains that we ought to prefer whatever produces the greatest overall utility, and this is determined by weighing the consequences. But the consequences *of what?* Utilitarians have given at least three different answers to this question, answers that are not necessarily mutually exclusive: acts, rules, and practices.

Act Utilitarianism

The first and most common version of utilitarianism says that **we should look at the consequences of each individual action in attempting to determine its moral worth.** This position, which is called **act utilitarianism,** maintains that we should always perform that *action* that will maximize utility, that will produce the greatest overall utility. Act utilitarianism is a tremendously powerful doctrine. One of its main attractions is that it seems to allow us to avoid rule worshipping, to deal with exceptions on the merits of the individual case.

John Scott–Railton

TALKING ABOUT ETHICS:
A CONVERSATION WITH
PETER RAILTON ABOUT
UTILITARIANISM

Peter Railton is a contemporary philosopher at the University of Michigan who has written extensively in moral philosophy from a utilitarian perspective. He is the author of numerous articles in utilitarian theory and a coeditor of *Moral Discourse and Practice: Some Philosophical Approaches* (Oxford, 1996).

Hinman: Throughout your work, you have continually come back to the utilitarian standpoint as the perspective that best illuminates the moral life. What first drew you to utilitarianism?

Railton: Strange to say, but looking back it seems I was in the right place at the right time. If I'd grown up in the fifties, morality for me would probably mean social convention and coercion—I'd have to rebel against it, a "rebel without a cause." Growing up in the sixties, morality for me was the very thing for challenging social convention and resisting coercion—I could rebel *with* it, a rebel with a cause. I was one of those shaggy student protesters you see in the black-and-white photos getting dragged by the hair by a helmeted policeman. This experience taught me a lot. It was my first real moral lesson, and it had two parts. First, morality isn't something that just happens—if it happens at all, it's something people make happen. Second, society can be way off base—on civil rights, foreign policy, social inequality—and the thanks you will get for protesting this can just as easily be a billy club and a threatening letter from the dean of students as a pat on the back for good moral alertness. Morality has a critical edge, it doesn't take the status quo or "what seems right" for granted, and it isn't always easy. Now my second lesson . . .

Hinman: Wait a minute. You just said morality has a critical edge, but it sounds as if you call this a moral *lesson* because it fits your preconvictions.

Railton: Fair point. That's why my second lesson was important. This
              time it was my turn to be taken by surprise by moral protest.
              I remember the first meetings when women students began
              to protest their unequal treatment, even *within* the activist
              movement, and when some people began to raise questions
              about the treatment of animals and the environment. I
              thought, "Come on, get serious. We've got to worry about
              people getting bombed in Southeast Asia or dying in coal
              mines, and you're talking about humane treatment for chick-
              ens, or equal treatment for middle-class college women."
              Well, people eventually got it through my head that I was
              wrong and was wrapping myself in righteousness to avoid fac-
              ing an uncomfortable truth: I had accepted gross inequalities
              in the treatment of women and had been pretty much com-
              pletely oblivious to the pain and suffering human societies
              inflict on animals. This taught me two more things. First, *I*
              could be as off base as anyone—so worrying about the moral-
              ity of an act or practice is quite different from asking, "What
              do I think of it?" or "How do I feel about it?" It's a lot more
              like belief: "Here's what I now think. But what are my
              grounds—and how would I get more evidence?" And sec-
              ond, that a key element in morality's critical force is overcom-
              ing the one-sidedness and partiality that come to us so
              naturally. We build mental and social barriers between "us"
              and "them"—other races, cultures, religions, species, and so
              on—which keep us from seeing or feeling what is really hap-
              pening to them.

Hinman: This sounds like an argument for moral objectivity, but why
              utilitarianism—why not objectivity about *rights?* These strug-
              gles you describe were movements for rights—civil rights for
              African Americans, equal rights for women, animal rights.

Railton: That's the way I tended to look at it, too. Something as im-
              portant as having basic needs met or equal treatment should
              be a guarantee, a right. But then rights also seemed to be bar-
              riers to responding to basic needs. Serious protests inevitably
              lead to innocent people being harmed; rebellions, like the
              American Revolution or slave rebellions, always involve vio-
              lence and violations of property rights that harm innocent
              people as well as oppressors. Could morality be saying that
              such protests or rebellions should never happen? Think where
              we'd be then! Or think about the way some people look at
              poverty: Do those people have a *right* to my help? That's an-
              other kind of barrier. It seemed to me that there had to be
              something more basic than rights, something that explains

where they come from and why they're so important but also helps us to see how to resolve conflicts of rights—and to see when rights aren't the whole story

So by then I was all set for utilitarianism, or *consequentialism,* as I prefer to call it. Consequentialism begins by asking what sorts of things matter for their own sake in life—happiness and overcoming of pain, sure, but also freedom, knowledge, accomplishment. The way these things matter does not depend upon any particular rights or moral views we might have—virtuous and wicked pleasure are both pleasant, deserved and undeserved freedom are both sought after. Consequentialism then says that, at the most basic level, our moral evaluations should reflect how fully these intrinsic values are realized, not giving anyone or any group special weight. You can't say, "Well, that person's happiness is coming from homosexual activity, which I despise, so it doesn't count" or "This calf—or for that matter, this fetus—would grow up and have certain good or bad experiences, but since it's not a person and doesn't have rights, that doesn't count." Should we permit homosexual marriages? Abortion? Eating the meat or eggs of free-range hens? The basic question for the consequentialist involves comparing the kinds of lives that would be enjoyed overall if we permitted these things, or if we prohibited them. This is a very hard question—we have to look at all kinds of evidence. "Moral intuitions," however strong, don't settle it. My strong hunch as of now is that we should permit all three, but I could be wrong. In any event, I can't tell whether I'm right or wrong without a lot of evidence about long-term consequences.

Hinman: But you've just said we should count everyone equally. Now, you're a middle-class parent in a prosperous society. Shouldn't you, as a serious consequentialist, really think that people in your position ought to spend a lot less of their time and resources on themselves and their own families, and a lot more on those in greater need? Don't you yourself deserve pretty severe moral criticism precisely for being so partial?

Railton: There's no question that I fall well short of doing the most possible to make the world a better place. But for the consequentialist it's a further question whether people like me are obliged to dramatically reduce their involvement in their own families or should be condemned and punished. We have to ask: What would things really be like if we all went around damning each other for things like giving special attention to one's own children? In some Quaker communities in colonial

North America people were shunned, investigated, and excluded for things like merrymaking when God's serious work
was to be done. In some really earnest Quaker communities,
a substantial fraction of the population might be under suspicion at a given time—and the rest were busy being self-
denying and feeling either self-righteous or nervous. This is
not an uplifting spectacle, and, as far as I can see, not a whole
lot of good came from it. Modern U.S. Quakers, by contrast,
run the American Friends Service Committee, which helps
people all over the world have decent medical care, civil rights,
self-sustaining agriculture, improve the status of women, etc.
Many Quakers regularly devote time to this activity, and some
even go off for several years to work for the AFSC overseas
after college. But these Quakers also have parties, hobbies,
active family lives, vacation homes. I see a lot of good coming
out of that, for them, the people around them, and people
around the world. I'm not a religious person, but I believe
we should take some lessons from the Quakers about how
much more can be accomplished when people work together
rather than engage in solo acts of charity; how long-term
moral activity—because it *does* often involve some sacrifice—
needs to be supported; and how one can easily distort one's
own moral understanding and risk losing the point of morality if one becomes too censorious and moralistic. The U.S.
has tremendously moralistic attitudes toward food and eating, and among the highest rates in the world of eating disor-
der and obesity to show for it.

Hinman: But if the motives from which one acts (say, personal motives within the family) are quite different from the justification one has in acting (say, that this is part of a morally good
life when viewed impersonally), isn't that schizophrenic, or
alienating?

Railton: There's no way to avoid differences between motives and justifications, unless we're going to say that motives are self-
justifying. A soldier may be motivated to fight bravely to the
death by love of his home country, but does this justify his
act? What if his country is engaged in a cruel and unjust war?
He may well believe that his country is just and worth fighting for. But if he's sane, he will also think that if he's wrong,
and his country is waging a terrible war of conquest, he
shouldn't be out there laying down his life for that.

Being intrinsically dedicated to something, or someone,
doesn't mean being unconditionally committed. Should my
wife really be unconditionally committed to me, regardless of

how rotten I turn out to be, how lousy I am as a father to our children or a companion to her? I'd think her emotion toward me was something more like obsession than love if that were the case. And I want her love, not her obsession. Is that alienating?

Hinman: You're beginning to sound pretty complacent to me: All consequentialism seems to ask of us is to be conditionally mindful of the larger world and to put in some volunteer time at the AFSC on the weekend, except when there's a big family picnic (with barbecued free-range chicken, of course!). That's a long way from your radical starting point.

Railton: It is. And in truth I cannot paint too "user friendly" a picture of any moral theory I'd really respect. A moral theory that lets us off the hook too easily can't be taking seriously the real, but avoidable, suffering that goes on in the world. I'm sure my current life falls short—I don't even put in the weekly hours at the AFSC, and I buy factory chicken when the free-range is sold out! I don't think of my complacent life as irrational, but I do think there are lots of good moral reasons for acting that I'm not attending to. I say to myself: I'll do more when the kids are more self-sufficient. But that's probably wrong—I'd be doing a better job of raising them if they saw in me a more regular commitment to broad social issues.

Hinman: Enough on your weaknesses. What about consequentialism's weaknesses?

Railton: Lots of the well-known criticisms of consequentialism don't seem to me to work very well—often they turn on consequentialist considerations ("Life would be miserable if . . ."). But there are many weaknesses. Maybe the biggest isn't talked about much. People tend to see consequentialism as too definite, too simple a theory to capture all the vague and multilayered phenomena of morality. There's something to this criticism, but I want to emphasize something else: Consequentialism may be too *indefinite* and too *complex*. We're used to hearing about act versus rule utilitarianism. But really there are dozens of kinds of consequentialism—cooperative utilitarianism, motive utilitarianism, conscience utilitarianism, total versus average utilitarianism, actual versus expected value utilitarianism, and on and on. It depends upon what you are evaluating. The motives with the best consequences, for example, may not be the ones that always lead to the acts with the best consequences (since motives have consequences other than the acts they produce—for example, they shape how we experience things). Robert Adams and

Donald Regan have done beautiful work showing the variety of consequentialism.

Morality is about how life goes, overall—not just about action and its consequences. The problem is that no one yet knows how to combine all these different evaluative focuses and criteria together into a unified picture. The underlying consequentialist intuition is that things should be arranged so as to bring about the best outcomes for all affected. But which things, and what kinds of outcomes? The result is a rather severe lack of determinacy at the very heart of the theory. All is not lost, though. We may be able to identify what matters most and to decide how much determinacy does—and doesn't—matter.

The Advantage of Focusing on Acts

One of the principal attractions of act utilitarianism is that it deals with individual decisions on a case-by-case basis. There is no such thing as an exception for the act utilitarian because every case is judged on its individual merits. This is in sharp contrast to a rule-oriented morality such as Kant's, which might well demand in some specific situation that we act in a way that would cause more harm than good. As we will see in Chapter 6, Kant held very strict views on lying. At times Kant seems to believe that we are *never* permitted to tell a lie, even if lying would result in saving innocent human life. The standard example is that of the Gestapo asking if you have seen any Jews who have escaped from their jails. If you know the location of any such Jews, and if you must follow a rule that prohibits ever telling a lie, then you must tell them the location of the fleeing Jews. The probable result of this action is that innocent people will be killed, people who might otherwise have escaped from their captors.

An act utilitarian, on the other hand, would have no difficulty lying in that particular situation if lying would produce the greatest overall amount of utility. It is simply a matter of doing the calculations, which is this case seems relatively straightforward. Moreover, such an approach accords with our basic moral intuitions. Common-sense morality tells us that it would at least be permissible to lie in such a situation—perhaps that it would even be required of us.

Despite its sensitivity to particular cases, or perhaps because of it, act utilitarianism is open to a number of objections. Let's briefly consider three of them: (1) the objection that it is too time-consuming to calculate the consequences of each individual actions; (2) a parallel objection that it is too difficult to predict the consequences of individual actions, especially the long-term consequences; and (3) the argument that act utilitarianism opens the door to abuses, especially to abuses of justice, because of its neglect of general moral rules.

Time to Calculate

Act utilitarians seem to be faced with quite a challenge. If they are going to weigh the consequences of each individual action they perform, they will probably spend a large and disproportionate portion of their lives just calculating consequences! That, critics charge, hardly seems like the best way to spend one's time. Furthermore, there may well be situations in which there simply is not time to calculate. When we see an out-of-control cement truck careering toward a pedestrian about to cross the street, we can hardly stop to calculate the hedons and dolors before trying to pull the passerby to safety!

Act utilitarians have an answer to such criticisms. We can, they maintain, live most of our lives on the basis of *rules of thumb,* rules that summarize past experience in such situations. Indeed, many of our general moral rules in society are precisely of this type. They express our collective social wisdom about what generally produces the best consequences for everyone. Act utilitarians have no difficulty with generally following such rules, but they insist that we be clear about the moral status of those rules. They are not absolute; rather, they are simply convenient summaries of past evaluations of individual acts. If, in some particular situation, we have reason to question whether the rule of thumb will produce the best consequences, then it is entirely appropriate to call that rule of thumb into question in that instance. So an act utilitarian who accepts the rule of thumb "Don't lie" may reconsider it in the Gestapo example.

Such an approach, act utilitarians maintain, gives them the best of both worlds: They are able to recognize the advantages of generally relying on rules in the moral life without being caught up in the rule worship that seems to characterize those who consider such rules to be absolute.

The Limits of Prediction

Act utilitarians face a second difficulty, one that they share with other versions of utilitarianism but that may be more acute for act utilitarians. How accurately can we predict consequences, especially long-term consequences of individual actions? Think, for example, of deciding which college to attend. It is often a difficult decision that involved endless comparisons. Yet for many of us, the most influential factors—such as the individuals we met, the friends we developed, the people we fell in love with—were ones we could never have predicted.

Most act utilitarians are willing to agree with critics about the limits of our predictive powers, but they reframe that insight in such a way that it no longer counts against act utilitarianism. Our predictive powers are limited, they concede, but this is a difficulty with life, not with act utilitarianism. The proper response to this limitation is not to reject act utilitarianism, but simply to recognize that this is part of the human condition. The best that we can do is try to increase our ability to foresee consequences. It is unrealistic, however, to hope that we can eliminate uncertainty completely. The moral life contains an ineluctable element of uncertainty, which can be reduced but never eliminated.

It is impossible to imagine that we could live without some basic belief in the general predictability of the human as well as the natural world. If we turn on the shower in the morning, we expect the water to come out and to be at the proper temperature—and it usually is. We don't expect that tomato juice will come out of the shower head, just as we do not expect that food will cook if we put it in the refrigerator. We would quickly go crazy if there were not a significant degree of predictability in the natural world. Similarly, in human affairs, we have general expectations about how people will behave. If we ask people questions, we generally expect that they will answer. If we give someone a million dollars, we generally expect that the person will be delighted about it. If a close friend dies, we expect to be sad. We could hardly act in the social world if we did not believe that there is a general predictability to human behavior. This predictability does not have to be complete. We can make mistakes in our predictions and be surprised, but the very idea of being surprised presupposes expectations. Predictability is necessary for living.

The Limits Imposed by Justice

Critics see a third difficulty with act utilitarianism, one that is potentially much more disturbing than the preceding two objections. Act utilitarianism, they charge, opens the door to potential abuse, to condoning—perhaps even requiring—acts that contradict our everyday moral intuitions, especially intuitions about justice.

Let us begin by considering a bizarre but real example. In Texas a few years ago, a woman had a clause in her will stipulating that she should be buried in her red Ferrari after she died. Apparently it costs quite a bit of money to bury someone in a Ferrari. What would be wrong with disregarding that provision of the will, giving her a regular burial, and using the money saved to do some good among the living? Clearly, one difficulty is that there are laws against such things, that one would be caught. But imagine what would happen if we embellished the example a little bit. Imagine that the woman told only you about her will, and imagine that you promised her that it would be carried out. Imagine, finally, that you know the location of her earlier will, which is exactly the same except that it contains no proviso about being buried in the Ferrari. What would be wrong with burning the most recent will and substituting the earlier one, a will that would leave all her money to a worthy charitable organization?

The obvious answer to this question is that you promised the woman to do what she asked. Yet promise keeping in itself has no value for act utilitarians; its value depends on the consequences of the particular promise. In this case, who would benefit from your keeping the promise? Clearly, the woman would not—she's already dead. Whatever benefit she might have derived from the thought of being buried occurred before her death. The institution of promising, including other people's confidence that their wishes will be honored after their deaths, would neither suffer nor benefit, since no one else knows her wishes in this matter. The numbers seem to come out clearly in favor of breaking the promise. Moreover, if the numbers do come out this way, then not only are we *permitted* to break the rules; if we are optimizing utilitarians, we are *obligated* to break them.

Consider a second, more difficult example. Imagine that you are the police chief in a small town that has been terrorized for months by a child rapist. Imagine that you discover through some unusual set of circumstances that the rapist has died in a freak accident, but there is no way that you could convince the public that the person was indeed the rapist. The threat is past, but the public still lives in fear, since you cannot convince them that the rapist is actually dead. Now imagine that you have arrested someone whom you could frame for the rapes, a hobo with tuberculosis who has only six months to live. What would be wrong with framing him for the rapes? There would be no danger that the real rapist would be free to continue his rapes; you are certain the rapist is dead. The public would be reassured, feeling that their town was once again safe. The man being punished would have died soon anyway, and he might actually receive better medical care in jail than on the street. The act utilitarian would seem to be justified in convicting the man, even though he had not committed these crimes, because his conviction would result in the greatest overall utility.

Rule Utilitarianism

Examples like these last two are disturbing to utilitarians, for they seem to suggest that act utilitarianism is too open to abuse, too likely to justify actions that conflict with justice or other values that intuitively are accepted by common sense morality. Yet many think that utilitarianism is still basically correct in its emphasis on consequences and in its standard of utility. The problem, they conclude, lies in the fact that utilitarianism is looking at the consequences of each individual act. Instead, we should look at the overall consequences of adopting a *rule* that everyone should act in a particular way under certain types of circumstances. This approach is known as **rule utilitarianism, which claims that we ought to act in accordance with those rules that will produce the greatest overall amount of utility for society as a whole.**

Clearly rule utilitarianism has a much better chance of dealing with the types of examples described here than act utilitarianism does. It would be much more difficult to imagine how one could justify a *rule* that supports breaking promises to the dead or convicting innocent people of crimes. Such rules simply do not maximize utility. By insisting that we justify rules instead of individual acts, the rule utilitarian seems to avoid certain injustices contained in act utilitarianism.

Act utilitarians disagree. They maintain that rule utilitarians are caught on the horns of a dilemma. They must maintain either that their rules are without exceptions or else that their rules do have exceptions. If their rules are without exceptions, then they are rule worshippers according to act utilitarians, for they say that we should follow the rule at any costs, even when it produces bad consequences. Act utilitarians would admit that we should generally keep our promises to the dead but that it would simply be rule worshipping to keep the promise about being buried in the Ferrari in the circumstances described. On the other hand, if rule utilitarians are willing to make exceptions in those cases when following the rule would produce bad consequences, then they are really covert act utilitarians. If, for example, they would be willing to break their promise to the dead in the Ferrari case, then they would really be thinking like an act utilitarian. They would be willing to admit that they can disregard the rule in any individual case when the overall utility clearly demands it. Thus, rule utilitarianism seems to collapse back into act utilitarianism.

Justice and Rule Utilitarianism

As we have seen, one of the principal concerns of critics of utilitarianism has centered around the possibility that act utilitarianism might require us to perform acts that clearly violate our common-sense moral expectations about justice. Yet it does not seem that rule utilitarianism is entirely immune to such criticisms, either. Imagine a society in which 10 percent of the population is enslaved but provided with many of the basic physical comforts of life such as good housing, nutritious food, and reasonable working hours. Imagine further that the slaves are given plenty of free entertainment (television, movies, music, etc.), much of which stresses the joys and rewards of being a good slave. As a result of this ongoing indoctrination and the tolerable physical conditions, the slaves do not feel a tremendous amount of discontent about their state in life. The masters, on the other hand, feel great that they have slaves, and it makes their lives significantly happier. Let's say that living in accord with this rule about slavery causes the slaves generally to feel about eight units of displeasure (8 dolors) apiece in their condition. Let's say that the masters experience two units of pleasure, 2 hedons, apiece as a result of being masters and having slaves. Recall that the slaves comprise only 10 percent of the population. Here's the picture we get.

	How much pleasure apiece?	How many people?	Total
Slaves	8 dolors	100	−800
Masters	2 hedons	900	+1800

Rule utilitarianism would seem to justify slavery under these conditions, but our clear moral belief is that slavery is unjust. There are two possible conclusions we could draw to resolve this dilemma. On one hand, we could argue that since utilitarianism leads to morally unacceptable conclusions (in this instance, the justification of slavery), it is unacceptable.

The other possible conclusion involves the modification, rather than the rejection, of utilitarianism. We could imagine that some people might agree to such a societal arrangement if they knew in advance that they would be among the masters rather than the slaves. However, would anyone agree to it if they did not know which of the two classes they would be in? Some philosophers—John Rawls in *The Theory of Justice* (1971) is the most influential of these—have argued that we need to set up limits on the range of possible rules that could be adopted, limits that would be determined by considerations of justice, by consensual agreements, by human rights, and the like. Within these limits, utilitarian justifications of particular rules would be permitted, but no justification would be allowed that violated those limits. It is, then, debatable whether proponents of such positions would still count, or count themselves, as utilitarians. Some contemporary theorists who accept this view, such as Samuel Scheffler, continue to insist that they are consequentialists.

Motives and the Domain of Applicability

There is another aspect to this continuing controversy between act and rule utilitarians, and it centers around the role of motives and intentions in the moral life. Although there has been some attempt recently (discussed later) to develop an account of motive utilitarianism, utilitarianism has long been open to the objection that it ignores intentions and motives. Typically, philosophers give hypothetical examples of this effect. Imagine that an assassin, motivated purely by resentment and envy, is trying to kill the president of a small Middle Eastern country during a public ceremony. The assassin's bullet misses the president but strikes a rock, causing oil to gush forth. The newly discovered oil proves to be a main source of revenue for the previously impoverished country, and soon the entire country prospers. Utilitarians would have to maintain that this act was good because the consequences were good. Yet this position seems to contradict our basic moral intuition that the assassin's motives of resentment and envy should count in our evaluation of the action.

Similar examples do not need to be far fetched. Consider the attempted military coup in Russia in 1991, in which old-guard communists tried to take over the government from Premier Mikhael Gorbochev. The coup failed, and in the end reformist leaders, especially Boris Yeltsin, emerged as far more powerful than they had been before. Presuming that this result will eventually bring more utility than any alternative, do we want to say that the hardliners' attempted coup was a good act? Clearly, it was not *intended* to strengthen Yeltsin's position. The fact that it had this consequence was purely accidental. Indeed, the coup was intended to produce exactly the opposite consequences. It seems as though our moral evaluation of that action should somehow take account of the intention behind the act.

It is here that the distinction between act and rule utilitarianism has a particular relevance. Although both act and rule utilitarianism ignore motives and intentions, this seems to be less of a problem for rule utilitarianism. When, for example, we want to assess the moral correctness of proposed governmental legislation, we may well wish to set aside any question of the intentions of the legislators. After all, good laws may be passed for the most venal of political motives, and bad legislation may be the outcome of quite good intentions. Instead, we can concentrate solely on the question of what *effects* the legislation may have on the people. When we make this shift, we are not necessarily denying that individual intentions are important on some level but are rather confining our attention to a level on which those intentions become largely irrelevant. This is particularly appropriate in the case of policy decisions by governments, corporations, or groups. In such cases there may be a diversity of different intentions that one may want to treat as essentially private matters when assessing the moral worth of the proposed law, policy, or action. Therefore, rule utilitarianism's neglect of intentions intuitively makes the most sense when we are assessing the moral worth of some large-scale policy proposed by an entity consisting of more than one individual.

Imagine again that the government is debating proposed legislation to change health care benefits for the elderly. We could examine the motives of the individual legislators and lobbyists who support or oppose the new bill, but doing this might be of little help in determining whether the bill itself was a good one or not. We might discover, for example, that a large percentage of the people who either support or oppose the legislation are motivated by a concern with political advancement or financial gain. Some may be acting out of principle, but the number may be roughly evenly split between the two camps. Looking at these individual motivations, we may simply decide that such motivations are just a matter of personal concern. They may tell us whether Senator X is morally well motivated in supporting this legislation, but they give us no insight into the question of whether the proposed law itself will prove to be a good or a bad one. Thus, we may decide simply to set aside the question of individual intentions and turn to the law itself. Once we do this, one of the ways in which we may assess its moral worth is by looking at what results or consequences would follow from adopting the proposed law. We then assess these consequences in terms of some yardstick—for example, in terms of the amount of pleasure and pain they may cause, or in terms of the amount of happiness and unhappiness which could result from their adoption. This is roughly what the rule utilitarian seeks to do: to assess the moral worth of a policy or rule in terms of the consequences that it will probably have.

Practices

Some philosophers have gone a step further than rule utilitarians by suggesting that utilitarian considerations have relevance in justifying the existence of certain types of practices, even though utilitarianism may not provide a proper basis for deciding particular acts within that practice. One can consider this position as a type of rule utilitarianism, but it is important to notice that there is a significant difference between rules and practices. Rules are more specific than practices, and a practice may encompass numerous rules. Stamp collecting, for example, is a practice, and it contains many specific action-guiding rules about what types of stamps to buy, when to sell, and the like. Practices include rules but contain more as well. They are often embodied in specific institutions (philatelic societies) and in patterns of social interaction (such as stamp collectors' conventions) that go beyond any specific set of rules.

John Rawls, a contemporary philosopher whose *A Theory of Justice* (1971) is one of the most influential works in recent ethics, has suggested that we may justify the *practice* of punishment as a whole through utilitarian arguments. A society without institutions and practices of punishment would produce less overall utility than one that contained such institutions and practices. Rawls avoids the problems raised by utilitarian justifications of specific acts of punishment by arguing that specific punishments be determined, not on utilitarian grounds, but rather on the basis of retributive considerations. The specific punishment would depend on the severity of the offense, not the utility of imposing the punishment. Specific individuals, in other words, would be punished because they deserved it, not because of the consequences produced by punishing them.

The merit of a suggestion like Rawls's is that it allows us to combine both utilitarian and Kantian insights. Utilitarian reasoning justifies the existence of the institution of punishment, whereas Kantian considerations of desert and retribution determine the nature and severity of specific acts of punishment.

Overview

When we summarize these various positions, we get the following chart.

CONSEQUENCES OF WHAT?

Type of Utilitarianism	Consequences of What?	Main Principle
Act	Each act	Perform the act that will produce the greatest overall amount of utility.
Rule	Rules	Follow the rule that will produce the greatest overall amount of utility.
Practice	Practices	Support those practices that produce the greatest amount of utility.

CONSEQUENCES FOR WHOM?

Utilitarianism is a type of **consequentialism.** It makes moral judgments on the basis of consequences. However, we need to ask: consequences for whom? Initially, that would seem to be a rather straightforward question with an equally straightforward answer: for people. Few things, though, are that easy. Let's examine three areas in which there is some controversy about who should count in determining consequences. The first of these relates to nonhumans. To what extent, if at all, should the suffering of animals count in our calculations of utility? Second, are all human beings included in our calculations of utility, or should subgroups (such as our nation or our family) be given special weight? Third, to what extent should we take into account the consequences for future generations? Let's look at each of these issues.

The Suffering of Animals

Utilitarianism, at least in some of its principal forms, is dedicated to the re-duction of suffering. Certainly human beings suffer, but suffering does not appear to be limited to human beings. Animals suffer, even if their suffering is not exactly the same type as ours. What, if any, weight should utilitarians give to animal suffering?

Pets

Clearly many of us, whether utilitarians or not, accord at least some value to the suffering of our pets. In fact, some of us will even go to great lengths, in terms of time as well as money, to preserve or restore the well-being of a pet. Although some of this may be a selfish concern for our own well-being if we were to lose the pet, in at least some of the cases there is no reason to doubt that it is also a concern for the animal itself. We *care* about our pets, and consequently their suffering counts. Yet the difficulty of saying this, for a utilitarian, is that this apparently violates the impartiality of the utilitarian outlook. From an impartial moral point of view, the suffering of one dog does not count any more than the same amount of suffering of any other dog. The only relevant difference is that in the case of pets, we need to add the suffering of their owners (and others who care about them) when the pets are in distress. There is a legitimate element in the utilitarian calculus, but it should be recognized that this element has nothing directly to do with the suffering of animals.

Painless Killing

It is also not clear that a utilitarian perspective prevents the killing of animals as long as this is done in a way that does not cause them suffering. Take rais-ing mink for their fur as an example. If the mink are bred and raised in con-ditions of comfort (a very large, enclosed area instead of individual cages) and if they are killed painlessly without feeling fear in advance, then it would seem that there is little a utilitarian could find objectionable in terms of suffering. We should realize, of course, that actual conditions rarely correspond to this example.

The Borders of Our Group

In theory, utilitarianism maintains that we be impartially concerned with overall utility. There is nothing in the theory to suggest that we draw a line at national borders or at some other point. Indeed, the history of utilitarian thought is quite interesting in this respect. It flourished in Britain precisely during its period of imperial expansion and was particularly influential in shaping—and being shaped by—Britain's rule of India. This reveals the potentially nondemocratic side of utilitarianism and suggests the importance of our answer to the question, "Who decides what the utility is?" The British were quite willing to rule India for the sake of the greatest utility—as long as they were the ones who decided what the utility was.

Today the situation is not quite the same. Many of us, especially those of us in affluent countries, often seem to draw the boundaries of utility at the customs booth. Yet there are few good arguments to justify this, except the claim that the citizens of a country are in the best position to decide what is best for that country. At the same time, however, we are faced with vast social and economic inequalities among countries, and there is little in utilitarianism to justify being concerned only with the welfare of one's own country.

Future Generations

The interests of future generations present a perplexing problem. On one hand, they do not yet exist—and, depending on our actions, they might never exist. On the other, they are affected by the consequences of our actions, just as we (although presumably to a lesser extent, given differences in technological effectiveness) have been affected by our ancestors' actions. When utilitarians compute consequences, should they take into account the consequences for future generations, people who are as yet unborn? If so, to what extent? These remain vexing questions not only for utilitarians, but for many other moral philosophers as well.

RACE, ETHNICITY, AND UTILITARIAN THEORY

What role, if any, do considerations of race and ethnicity have in utilitarian theory? Let's consider three related areas: (1) race, ethnicity, and impartiality; (2) the question of who weighs the consequences; and (3) the issue of group-specific consequences.

Race, Ethnicity, and Impartiality

As we have already seen, utilitarianism is, at heart, an impartial moral doctrine, and as such it does not give any *special* weight to the concerns of any particular group, whether racial, ethnic, or cultural. But its impartiality is, in many ways, also its potential strength for minority groups with little power, for utilitarianism *when properly applied* says that their suffering and unhappiness counts just as much as the suffering and unhappiness of those who do hold the power and influence in society.

Strict adherence to utilitarian impartiality alone could sometimes bring significant advantages to minority groups, but this is not always so. Consider a typical situation in which the interests of minority groups have not counted on a par with those of the majority group. Imagine the planning of a new highway for which private lands have to be appropriated. Often the lands appropriated for such projects are those that belong to poorer groups with less political influence. Does this state of affairs violate utilitarian principles? Utilitarianism states that everyone's suffering is of equal weight (presuming it is of equal intensity). That means that the suffering that a poor person of color experiences when uprooted is of equal value to the suffering that a rich white corporate executive experiences when uprooted, again presuming both have equally intense feelings about being relocated.

Group-Specific Consequences

One of the interesting issues in utilitarian theory is whether utilitarianism recognizes consequences that are harmful to groups racial, ethnic, or cultural groups as such, not just to the individual members of the group.

The Example of Hate Speech Legislation

Hate speech legislation provides an example of this type of consideration. One of the proposed justifications for banning hate speech has been that hate speech is typically demeaning and harmful to minority groups as groups, even in those instances where we cannot show that some specific individual was directly harmed by the speech. In at least some versions, such protection is explicitly restricted to minority groups. The majority group, in our society white males, is not offered the same protection.

For this type of argument to work, we need both empirical and normative premises. On the empirical side, we need premises that show that a given behavior–such as hate speech–is in fact harmful to a specific group. This is primarily the domain of the social sciences, and there is extensive data to support claims of this sort.

On the normative side, we need a premise to the effect that the continued existence of a particular group is of value to society. Alternatively, we might substitute some premise to the effect that all groups are of (equal?)

value to society, and that there is a value in encouraging diversity as such. The potential difficulty with this argument is that it promotes skinheads and neo-Nazis as much as any other groups. Supporters of such an argument would presumably want to claim that there is a value in diversity as such. They might well point to a similar issue in environmental ethics, where some would maintain that we ought to encourage biological diversity on utilitarian grounds. We can never predict, they maintain, what might ultimately become biologically valuable to our survival. Consequently, we should strive to preserve all species as biological "money in the bank" against some future disaster. Similarly, professing epistemic ignorance, some may maintain that we should encourage the continued existence of all groups in society, since they may ultimately preserve resources for society's preservation and flourishing that would otherwise be lost.

Given such premises, it seems possible in principle to develop sound utilitarian justifications for special treatment of racial, ethnic, or cultural groups.

Who Calculates the Consequences?

One of the attractions of utilitarianism is that it promises impartiality and objectivity grounded in quantification. If everything can be translated into units of utility, then there is an objective basis for deciding between competing courses of action. Ultimately, the numbers decide for us.

Yet as the inhabitants of India well knew when the British empire applied its utilitarian logic to them, it makes a difference who is doing the calculating. When one group in society does the calculations for another group, it is all too easy for those calculations to become miscalculations. What mattered to the native inhabitants of India was very different from what the British thought mattered to them, as Gandhi was to prove.

Similar considerations have certainly applied in the United States, where we have seen time and again that one group (usually white, upper middle class, and male) has made decisions for others group (including ethnic minorities). Even when the dominant group has done so with good will, it has often been wrong.

This is, at least in part, an epistemological point. Many would argue that those most directly affected by consequences are in the best position to estimate the importance of those consequences for themselves. There is also a moral and a psychological point here. The moral one is that those who will bear consequences should have a voice in determining those consequences. The psychological one is that people are more likely to bear onerous consequences when they themselves have had a voice in choosing them.

Thus, considerations of race, ethnicity, and culture have an important place in a utilitarian framework in regard to the calculator. All other things being equal, it is better that identifiable racial and ethnic groups be represented among the calculators of utility and that one group not assume the role of calculator for all other groups.

ISSUES IN UTILITARIANISM

We have developed a fairly comprehensive picture of utilitarian ethical theory in the preceding pages, but several key issues remain to be discussed if we are to round out our understanding of utilitarianism and evaluate its strengths and weaknesses. We will focus on four of those issues here: (1) the difficulties of reasoning about matters of life and death, (2) the role of emotions in the utilitarian view of the moral life, (3) the limits of personal responsibility, and (4) the place of personal integrity in the utilitarian's world.

Weighing Matters of Life and Death

We are sometimes hesitant about utilitarianism because it seems to weigh everything, even human life. Some things, many of us want to argue, cannot be put on the utilitarian scale. Kant, for example, clearly maintained that human beings were priceless; they could not be assigned a monetary value in the way that mere physical objects could be. Indeed, as we shall see in the next chapter, this was for Kant one of the principal differences between people and things: Things have a price tag, but people don't. Yet to put human life into the utilitarian balance seems to come perilously close to placing a price tag on it.

The Asbestos Example

At the beginning of this chapter, we discussed the example of removing asbestos from buildings. Some of you may have felt that human life is too precious to put into the balance, that any price is worth paying in order to save people's lives. Yet this is open to two rejoinders. First, sometimes we simply do not have an unlimited amount of funds; sometimes we have to make choices that result in letting some people die. But there is a second reply that is possible as well: Even though we say that human life is priceless, we don't really act that way. Let me give an example.

The Speed Limit Example

During the energy crisis of the 1970s, a national speed limit of 55 mph was instituted in order to conserve gasoline. One of the side effects of this change was that hundreds of lives a year were saved and thousands of traffic injuries were averted. Let's imagine that additional deaths and injuries could be avoided if we reduced the speed limit even further. At what point do we draw the line? At what point do we say that even if it means that a certain number of people will die or be injured in automobile accidents, we still want to keep the speed limit from being lowered?

My suspicion is that virtually all of us would draw the line at some point, even if it is considerably lower than the present limit. (Many would actually like the limit higher, and many drive as though it were.) My point here is not to argue in favor of any particular speed limit, but rather to illustrate that most of us in fact are willing at some point to put human lives into the equation. Notice, too, that these may be innocent lives; there is no guarantee that those killed or injured in traffic accidents are necessarily the ones at fault. We should not be too quick to judge utilitarians harshly solely because they are willing to put human lives into the equation. Most of us are willing to do the same, even if we are reluctant to admit it.

The Role of Emotions in the Utilitarian Moral Life

Recently, some philosophers have criticized utilitarianism because of the role—or lack of a role—that it gives to emotions in the moral life. There are two points that merit our attention here. The first is the question of whether we ought to accord more weight to some emotions than others; the second is the nature of our relationship to our own emotions in utilitarianism. The latter issue, as we shall see, leads directly into the question of personal integrity.

Which Emotions Are Given Weight?

Utilitarianism obviously gives moral weight to the emotions. If, for example, I am contemplating stealing some money from a friend, one of the things that I would have to take into account as a utilitarian is the suffering that my friend would undergo at the loss of the money and the possibility of even greater suffering if he discovered that it had been stolen by a friend. I would also, of course, have to take into account my own feelings, possibly quite positive ones with a high hedonic value, if I were to succeed in stealing the money. Let's assume that my friend would have only negligibly negative feelings at having the money stolen and only slightly more negative feelings if he discovered that I was the thief. Assume also that I would certainly get great pleasure and happiness from successfully taking the money. Under these conditions, it would appear—all other things being equal, which they never are in real life—that my feelings could tip the balance in favor of committing the theft. What the utilitarian seems unable to do is to distinguish between what we could call good and bad feelings—or, more precisely, morally justified and morally unjustified emotions.

Examples of this problem need not be far fetched, as the preceding one was. Consider the problem of racism in our own society. Certainly there are many courses of action—such as genuine integration of schools—that would at least initially bring about intensely negative feelings on the part of a large segment of the population. It is easy to imagine, if we were for the moment to grant the utilitarian premise that feelings can be placed on some hedonic scale, that integration would cause more negative feeling in the oppressors than it would cause positive feeling in the oppressed. Yet is this, again assuming other things to be equal, a sufficient reason for not seeking to eliminate racism from the society? (This, of course, does not even touch on the question of *who* weighs these feelings. One suspects that it would be much easier for a white to weigh sympathetically the amount of fear and displeasure that whites experience at the thought of integration, while presumably a black would be much more sensitive to the pain suffered by blacks. It is far from evident that there is a neutral standpoint here.)

The difficulty that the utilitarian faces is obvious: If all feelings are of equal value, and if all that distinguishes them is their valence (negative or positive), quantity (how many people experience the feeling), and intensity (how strong the feeling is for each), then morally good and justifiable feelings will have no greater weight than morally evil and unjustifiable feelings of the same sign, quantity, and intensity. Yet we want to say—or at least our everyday moral intuitions suggest—that some types of feelings should be given greater weight than others.

The utilitarian seems at first to have an answer to this, but it is just the appearance of an answer. It seems that one could differentiate among various emotions on the basis of their overall social utility. Altruistic feelings, for example, may have a greater social utility than discriminatory feelings. It may thus be beneficial from a utilitarian point of view to encourage courses of action that promote the development of altruistic feelings and reduce discriminatory feelings. Yet this position will hardly do, for it really just deals with the question of the feelings that result from particular courses of action, not the feelings that might provide reasons for such actions. We could imagine, in the integration case, for example, that the outcome might not bring about a greater amount of altruistic feelings. It could produce more bad feelings than good, but it might still be the right thing to do if we think that some of the negative feelings it produces are unjustified.

Thus, the first problem with the utilitarian account of the emotions is that it fails to provide any adequate way of discriminating between justified and unjustified feelings, between good and bad emotions, and is committed to giving both the same weight in its utilitarian calculations.

My Relation to My Own Emotions and Convictions

The second major problem with the utilitarian account of the relationship between morality and the emotions centers around the question of how I am related to my own emotions, deeply held beliefs, and reasoned commitments. Bernard Williams develops this objection in some detail, and here I shall only summarize the main elements of his argument.

Imagine the following kind of case, one of the type that Williams describes. A chemist—let's call him Harold—with a wife and children is out of work. He and his family are beginning to suffer significantly as a result of his unemployment. During the past few years, he has become increasingly convinced that all war, but especially chemical and biological warfare, is immoral. He is offered a job by an old friend as a chemist in a firm developing and producing chemical warfare weapons. Furthermore, he is told by his old friend that if he does not take the job, it will in all probability be given to a younger chemist he knows who is both a better chemist and quite committed to the development of such weapons. The moral quandary that he faces is this. He is morally opposed to war and does not want to participate in developing weapons of war. His deepest moral commitments tell him not to take the job. However, he knows that if he takes the job, he will fulfill his obligations to his family and, at the same time, he will not be doing anything that will result in chemical warfare being more advanced than if he refused the job. Indeed, if he turns the job down, then he will probably be helping the chemical warfare industry, since his position will be filled by someone better and more enthusiastic than he is. Thus the problem this example initially poses for us is this: What weight should Harold give to his own strong feelings against the morality of chemical warfare?

The standard utilitarian answer to this question certainly recognizes Harold's commitments, but only in a limited way. Clearly these deeply held feelings and beliefs are one of the factors that Harold must take into consideration, but no special consideration must be given to the fact that they are *his* emotions and beliefs. He must also take into consideration everyone else's emotions and beliefs, and these presumably must be given equal weight. Indeed, in this situation Harold might even be obliged to give less weight to his own feelings and convictions. After all, his own feelings are probably the ones over which he has greatest control, so he may be obliged to try to change them to positive feelings about warfare. One thing is clear: His emotions do not deserve special weight simply by virtue of the fact that they are *his* emotions. Indeed, the utilitarian might well want to argue that this is the very essence of morality: impartiality. In not giving special weight to his own feelings, Harold is simply assuming the moral point of view. To be moral is to be impartial.

Yet critics such as Williams have suggested that there is still a serious problem here, namely, that utilitarian morality sometimes demands that a person give up his or her most deeply held feelings and convictions. So, if it is precisely these kinds of things that make life worth living for an individual, then utilitarian morality may demand that the individual give up his or her very reason for existing. Something is seriously wrong, Williams argues, if morality makes this kind of demand on an individual.

The reason utilitarianism falls short of the mark here is that it fails to recognize any special relationship between the agent and his or her own feelings and deeply held beliefs, fails to recognize that these are my own in some unique way. When the utilitarian contemplates the consequences of an action (including the feelings it may create), there is nothing significant about the fact that some of the consequences may be *mine* in a special fashion. All feelings and commitments are taken into account simply as a group, summed up, and then the "bottom line" dictates the decision we should make.

The Limits of Personal Responsibility

In an intriguing example, Bernard Williams presents us with the following situation in which we must make a moral choice.

> Jim finds himself in the central square of a small South American town. Tied up against the wall are a row of twenty Indians, most terrified, a few defiant, in front of them several armed men in uniform. A heavy man in a sweat-stained khaki shirt turns out to be the captain in charge and, after a good deal of questioning of Jim which establishes that he got there by accident while on a botanical expedition, explains that the Indians are a random group of the inhabitants who, after recent acts of protest against the government, are just about to be killed to remind other possible protesters of the advantages of not protesting. However, since Jim is an honored visitor from another land, the captain is happy to offer him a guest's privilege of killing one of the Indians himself. If Jim accepts, then as a special mark of the occasion, the other Indians will be let off. Of course, if Jim refuses, then there is no special occasion, and Pedro here will do what he was about to do when Jim arrived, and kill them all. Jim, with some desperate recollection of schoolboy fiction, wonders whether if he got hold of a gun, he could hold the captain, Pedro, and the rest of the soldiers to threat, but it is quite clear from the set-up that nothing of that kind is going to work: any attempt at that sort of thing will mean that all the Indians will be killed, and himself. The men against the wall, and the other villagers, understand the situation, and are obviously begging him to accept. What should he do?

The utilitarian, Williams maintains, has a clear and easy answer to this question. Within the utilitarian perspective, there is no question that Jim should shoot the one prisoner so that the others could go free. It is not only the right thing to do, it is the *obviously* right thing to do. When we add up the hedons and dolors in even the most cursory way, we see clearly that the alternative that will produce the greatest overall amount of utility is for Jim to pull the trigger. Nineteen lives would be saved. Everyone wants him to do it.

The question that Williams raises here is an important one. He does not deny that shooting the one villager may be the best alternative, but he points out that in the utilitarian perspective Jim cannot attach any special weight to the fact that *he* is the one who pulls the trigger. Jim is equally responsible for the deeds that he does directly and the deeds performed by others that he could have prevented. Jim is responsible for Pedro's killing of the twenty prisoners because he could have prevented it himself by killing one of the prisoners. This, Williams contends, is a confused notion of personal responsibility. We bear a special relationship to, and responsibility for, our own actions that utilitarianism fails to capture.

The Siamese Twins

We see this same problem occurring in real life. In the summer of 2000, a couple in Malta had Siamese twins, Jodie and Mary. The family came to England for medical assistance. The doctors told the parents that if the twins were not surgically separated in the next few weeks, both would die. If the doctors operated to separate the twins, then the stronger twin had a good chance of surviving, although she would be severely handicapped and have to undergo multiple surgeries. The parents, devout Catholics, did not want the surgery, since they felt it would be killing one of the two twins. The British government, in a controversial decision, ordered the surgery against the parents' wishes; it also issues an order forbidding them from leaving England with the twins in order to avoid the surgery. The surgery was performed. This resulted in the death of the weaker twin; the stronger twin survived and is now doing better than expected.

From a utilitarian point of view, this decision should be an easy one: the possible life of one child versus the certain death of both. But for the parents it was an agonizing decision precisely because of the issue of responsibility: They refused to make a choice that would result in the death of one of their children in order to save the life of the other. This is precisely the issue of responsibility that Williams discussed. The issue is not simply that one child dies, but that one child dies as a result of the parents' decision.

Integrity and Impartiality

There are two final characteristics of utilitarianism that it is particularly important to note here. First, utilitarians are not allowed to give any special weight to the fact that certain consequences may affect them personally. The popular image of utilitarians is often of people who are just concerned with achieving their own selfish aims and who then view everything else simply as a means to the attainment of those ends. Yet the picture we get of utilitarians from an ethical standpoint is quite different. Utilitarians are not allowed to give any special weight to the fact that some negative consequences will affect them quite personally. If, for example, we have a utilitarian legislator who will personally suffer if there is not an increase in medical benefits for the aged, the utilitarian legislator will still be required to vote against such an increase if that increase would yield a lesser total utility than the alternatives. If, to take a second example, we have a utilitarian gourmet who is contemplating either having dinner at Chez Panisse, an expensive restaurant in Berkeley, or donating the money that would have been spent on the dinner to a charity devoted to relieving hunger in the world, it is clear from that utilitarian standpoint that there is only one morally right alternative: to give the money to help reduce hunger. Even though dinner at Chez Panisse may yield 100 hedons for the gourmet, the same amount of money may well bring 10 hedons for thirty people. Thus, utilitarians apparently cannot give special weight to the fact that certain pleasures or displeasures are their own; they must be weighed just like everyone else's hedons and dolors.

Peter Singer and World Hunger

An excellent example of how demanding utilitarianism can be in this area can be found in the work of Peter Singer. He sees the issue of world hunger from a utilitarian perspective, and doing so imposes strong obligations on those of us who live in more affluent countries. Singer begins with a simple question:

> If I am walking past a shallow pond and see a child drowning in it, I ought to wade in and pull the child out. That will mean getting my clothes muddy, but this is insignificant when the death of the child would presumably be a very bad thing.

Indeed, more generally we could say that if we can prevent something bad from happening without in the process giving up something of comparable importance, then we ought to do so. Singer then goes out to argue that we can eliminate some world hunger and absolute poverty without throwing ourselves into a state of equal deprivation; therefore we ought to do so.

Indeed, we spend money on many luxuries in our society that we could do without. Some could drive reliable, moderately priced automobiles instead of high-performance vehicles; others could have healthful but plain meals at home instead of expensive (and often unhealthful) meals at fancy restaurants; some could forgo having the latest gadget, and perhaps substitute talent and the hard work of practice for high priced equipment in sports and other areas. Indeed, if we think of this issue in purely impartial consequentialist terms, it seems clear that we should redirect our expenditures from luxury items to their more basic equivalents (a Toyota Camry instead of a BMW convertible) and then give the remainder to relief organizations. This raises interesting and important questions about how much a moral theory can demand of us.

Fundamental Projects

When we hear on the news that a concert pianist was involved in an auto accident in which his hands were crushed, or when we hear that a famous painter has gone blind, or that a well-known baseball pitcher has suffered irreparable damage to his pitching arm, we are especially moved. Our heart goes out to such people, because we realize the way in which such an accident strikes at the very heart of who they are as persons. Indeed, we want to say that certain projects, commitments, and desires are closer than others to people's sense of their own identity, their idea of who they are. Those closest to a person's sense of his or her own identity comprise what we shall call that person's *fundamental projects.*

The issue about fundamental projects becomes even more vivid if we recall Williams's example of Jim in the South American town. The way that Williams sets up the example, we are asked to imagine what Jim (a hypothetical character) would do. But let's change the example a bit. Imagine two different scenarios. First, instead of Jim, imagine a person whose whole life was devoted to peace and nonviolence. Mother Teresa or Martin Luther King, Jr., come to mind as obvious examples. What should *they* do? Second, imagine that a mercenary soldier, for whom killing is a casual activity, arrives in the village instead of Jim. What should the soldier do? Most of us would give quite different answers to these questions, depending on whether the visitor was someone like Mother Teresa or Dr. King or was someone like the mercenary. The reason for our different answers is precisely the issue of fundamental projects. To kill anyone would run counter to the whole sense of what Mother Teresa's or Dr. King's lives are about. It would not, however, contradict the mercenary's life at all (except perhaps in the fact that he isn't being paid for it). Utilitarianism seems to give insufficient recognition to this difference in fundamental projects.

LIVING THE UTILITARIAN LIFE

When we are considering so many arguments for and against utilitarianism and drawing so many distinctions between various types of utilitarianism, it is easy to lose sight of what it means to live life as a utilitarian. Yet utilitarianism is a moral theory that was meant to be lived, and a consideration of what it would look like in practice can provide us with a good way of drawing together some of our conclusions about utilitarianism.

Two insights guide the utilitarian's life. The first of these is that *consequences count*. Consequently, *utilitarians will always want to know what actual effects their choices will have for real people* (and perhaps other sentient beings as well). They continually direct their attention to the basic facts of the moral life, facts about who will be hurt and who will be made happy as a result of a particular decision. It may be very difficult at times to predict what the actual consequences of a particular decision will really be, but utilitarians are committed to trying to make such predictions as accurately as possible. To the extent that they are not able to make such predictions accurately, this indicates that there is an unavoidable element of luck in the moral life. The presence of luck is a problem with the moral life, but not an objection to utilitarianism as a moral theory.

Second, *utilitarians want the world to be a better place for everyone*. It is a benevolent moral doctrine; that is, it wishes people well and seeks to increase the amount of well-being in the world. Indeed, this is the whole point of morality for utilitarians: It produces a better, ultimately happier world. Ethical reflection is not something pursued in abstraction from the real pain and suffering of the world around us. The point of ethics is to help reduce that pain and suffering. Morality should make the world a better place for everyone.

Despite these strengths, many find that utilitarianism does not provide the whole story of the moral life. One of the dangers that many utilitarians—especially act utilitarians—face is that their principles might require actions that violate the rights of small groups of individuals. Act utilitarianism alone cannot provide sufficient guarantees against the possibility of such abuse. There are two ways to respond to this difficulty. On one hand, some philosophers have opted for some version of rule utilitarianism, which seems less susceptible to such difficulties. Other have suggested that *there must be a moral "floor" or minimum below which we cannot go,* even if utilitarian considerations seem to demand that we do so. To live only by utilitarian considerations, especially act-utilitarian ones, is to open the door to possible abuses of the minority when such injustices yield high benefits for the majority. Ethical theories that emphasize the importance of human rights seem to offer a standard of value in the moral life that escapes from these dangers. Chapter 7 of this book is devoted to rights-based moral theories.

Another difficulty plagues utilitarian accounts of ethics. *Utilitarians ignore the importance of intentions.* Although there are certainly plenty of circumstances in which intentions do not matter, there are times—especially in personal relationships—when they are of crucial importance. This dimension of the moral life has been almost completely ignored by utilitarians because of their exclusive focus on consequences. Three quite different approaches to morality help to understand this dimension of the moral life better than utilitarians alone have been able to do. First, Kantian accounts of morality, as we shall see in the next chapter, emphasize the importance of intentions in the moral life, especially the importance of acting out of a motive of duty. Kantians see something morally admirable about acting for the sake of duty that utilitarians are unable to recognize. Second, some critics of morality have argued that all major moral theories fail to provide an adequate account of our moral motivations. Such theories, critics like Michael Stocker argue, produce a kind of motivational schizophrenia, a deep and pervasive split between our actual motives and the legitimate reasons within any particular moral theory. Such criticisms can be answered, I will argue, only by a moral theory that focuses primarily on character. This, as we shall see in Chapter 9, is precisely the kind of theory that Aristotle offers.

DISCUSSION QUESTIONS

1. **Ethical Inventory.** Recall your response to **statement 16** ("When I am trying to decide what the right thing to do is, I look at the consequences of the various alternatives open to me") in the Ethical Inventory.

   (a) What moral theory does this statement illustrate?

   (b) Has your rating of this item changed after reading this chapter? If so, in what way? If your rating has not changed, are your reasons for your rating any different now than they were when you first responded to this statement?

2. **Ethical Inventory.** Recall **statement 17** in the Ethical Inventory ("The right thing to do is whatever is best for everyone") and your response to it.
   (a) In what types of cases, if any, are we not justified in doing what will produce the greatest overall amount of good? Be specific.
   (b) Has your rating of this item changed after reading this chapter? If so, in what way? If your rating has not changed, are your reasons for your rating any different now than they were when you first responded to this statement?

3. **Ethical Inventory.** Recall **statements 19** and **20** in the Ethical Inventory about whether pleasure or happiness is the most important thing in life.
   (a) If you agreed with statement 19, what arguments do you now see could be advanced against your position? How would you reply to these arguments?
   (b) Have your ratings of these items changed after reading this chapter? If so, in what way? If your ratings have not changed, are your reasons for your ratings any different now than they were when you first responded to this statement?
   (c) If you hold that neither pleasure nor happiness is of intrinsic value, what is? Explain.

4. **Scarce medical resources.** Take a contemporary social issue, such as kidney transplants, that involves the allocation of scarce resources and discuss the ways in which various types of utilitarians would recommend that we deal with it. How would their recommendations differ from the recommendations of ethical egoists? Which of these traditions do you find more convincing? Why? If you do not agree with either, what are your reasons for disagreement?

5. **Persons with disabilities.** In recent decades, Americans have been reconsidering their treatment of those with physical handicaps or disabilities in a number of different areas of life, including education and sports. The Americans with Disabilities Act (1990) has been a major factor in requiring equal access to public facilities for persons with disabilities. Imagine that a proposal has been put to your local school board to institute a limited sports program for physically impaired students. The projected cost of running such a program would be approximately four times as much per student as is spent on the regular sports programs, although the number of students is much lower. How would a sophisticated utilitarian deal with this proposal?

6. **Honesty.** Benjamin Franklin (1706–1790) said, "Honesty is the best policy." Is this true (as Franklin thought) only on utilitarian grounds? Or do we need some other justification for it? When, if ever, do you think honesty is *not* the best policy? Give an example.

7. **MOVIE** *Saving Private Ryan.* In the movie *Saving Private Ryan,* Captain John Miller (Tom Hanks) and seven other men are sent on a mission to find and bring to safety Private James Francis Ryan (Matt Damon), whose three other brothers have already been killed in combat. One member of the unit asks Capt. Miller, "Explain the math of this to me—risking the eight of us for one life." What would a utilitarian say about the mission to save Private Ryan? Do you agree with the utilitarian analysis in this instance?

8. **Is human life priceless?** Human life, the philosopher Immanuel Kant tells us, is priceless. However, we often seem to put a price tag on human life. Is this always wrong? Why or why not? If it is ever morally permissible to do so, when is this allowed? Why? If we don't put a price tag on human life, how do we deal with (a) the allocation of scarce medical resources in which we have the money to save only some of the people, and (b) jury awards in wrongful death suits?

9. **Utilitarianism and health care.** Imagine that you are a utilitarian who has $10 million to spend on health care for infants. Which would be better—spending it on extensive prenatal care or high-technology neonatal intensive care units? In order to answer this question, what further questions would you have to ask about each alternative? Would you agree with the utilitarian solution to this question?

10. **MOVIE** In Ridley Scott's movie *Black Hawk Down* (2001), is the story of an ill-fated mission by U.S. Rangers into the city of Mogadishu in Somalia. One of the concerns of the Rangers is never to "leave a fallen comrade to fall into the hands of the enemy." Discuss the pros and cons of this rule from a utilitarian standpoint in light of the movie.

BIBLIOGRAPHICAL ESSAY

The **classic texts** for utilitarianism are those of Jeremy Bentham, John Stuart Mill, and Henry Sidgwick. Among **Bentham**'s works, see, in particular, Bentham's *A Fragment on Government,* edited by J. H. Burns and H. L. A. Hart (London: Athline Press, 1977) and his *The Introduction to the Principles of Morals and Legislation,* edited by J. H. Burns and H. L. A. Hart (London: Athline Press, 1970). (These are also available in other, less expensive editions.) For excellent **introductions to Bentham's moral and political thought,** see John Dinwiddy, *Bentham* (Oxford: Oxford University Press, 1989) and Ross Harrison, *Bentham* (London: Routledge & Kegan Paul, 1984). Also see David Lyons, *In the Interest of the Governed* (Oxford: Clarendon Press, 1973) and H. L. A. Hart, *Essays on Bentham: Jurisprudence and Political Theory* (Oxford: Clarendon Press, 1982). Ross Harrison's "Bentham, Mill and Sidgwick," in Nicholas Bunnin and E. P. Tsui-James, eds., *The Blackwell Companion to Philosophy* (Oxford: Blackwell, 1996), pp. 627–642.

Many of **John Stuart Mill**'s works are relevant, especially his *Utilitarianism* and *On Liberty*. These are available on the World Wide Web and in various bound editions, including several that also contain critical essays. See John Stuart Mill, *Utilitarianism: Text with Critical Essays,* edited by Samuel Gorovitz (Indianapolis, IN: Bobbs Merrill, 1971); Mill's *Utilitarianism: Text and Criticism,* edited by James M. Smith and Ernest Sosa (Belmont, CA: Wadsworth, 1969); and *On Liberty: Annotated Text, Sources and Background,* edited by David Spitz (New York: Norton, 1975). For an excellent selection of Mill's writings on ethics, see J. B. Schneewind, ed., *Mill's Ethical Writings* (New York: Collier, 1965). Among the best books on Mill's philosophy is Fred Berger's *Happiness, Justice, and Freedom: The Moral and Political Philosophy of John Stuart Mill* (Berkeley: University of California Press, 1984). For a brief but comprehensive overview of Mill's thought, see Henry West, "Mill, John Stuart," *Encyclopedia of Ethics,* edited by Lawrence C. Becker and Charlotte B. Becker (New York: Garland, 1992), vol. 2, pp. 809–816.

Book IV of **Henry Sidgwick**'s *The Methods of Ethics,* 7th ed. (Indianapolis, IN: Hackett, 1981) is also a classic source of utilitarian thought. For a fine introduction to Sidgwick's thought and times, see J. B. Schneewind, *Sidgwick's Ethics and Victorian Moral Philosophy* (Oxford: Clarendon Press, 1977). For a brief introduction to Sidgwick's thought, see Marcus G. Singer, "Sidgwick," *Encyclopedia of Ethics,* edited by Lawrence C. Becker and Charlotte B. Becker (New York: Garland Publishing, Inc., 1992), vol. 2, pp. 1149–1152.

World Wide Web. Many of the classical works in utilitarianism are available on the World Wide Web. An up-to-date list of such works is available on the utilitarianism page of *Ethics Updates* at http://ethics.acusd.edu/theories/Utilitarianism/index.html. This also contains links to utilitarianism websites and other related resources.

Several of the editions of Mill's *Utilitarianism* and *On Liberty* contain excellent collections of **critical essays.** For an excellent collection of essays on Mill's *Utilitarianism,* see David Lyons, ed., *Mill's "Utilitarianism": Critical Essays* (Lanham, MD: Rowman & Littlefield, 1997). In addition, see *The Limits of Utilitarianism,* edited by Harlan B. Miller and William H. Williams (Minneapolis: University of Minnesota Press, 1982) as well as the collection of essays in the *Canadian Journal of Philosophy,* supplementary vol. 5 (1979). One of the more recent books that often provides a good starting point for studying utilitarianism is *Utilitarianism: For and Against* (Cambridge: Cambridge University Press, 1973), which contains an explication and defense of act utilitarianism by J. J. C. Smart and an interesting critique by Bernard Williams. The essay by Williams has been one of the most influential in raising the issue of moral alienation. One of the most nuanced and powerful replies to Williams and others on this issue is Peter Railton's "Alienation, Consequentialism, and the Demands of Morality," *Philosophy and Public Affairs* 13, no. 2 (Spring 1984): 134–171. This essay, along with a number of other important pieces, has been reprinted in an excellent anthology edited by Samuel Scheffler, *Consequentialism and Its Critics* (Oxford: Oxford University Press, 1988); also see David O. Brink, "Utilitarian Morality and the Personal Point of View," *Journal of Philosophy* 83 (1986): 417–438. The anthology that Bernard Williams and Amartya Sen edited, *Utilitarianism and Beyond* (Cambridge: Cambridge University Press, 1982) contains a number of perceptive articles. For a helpful anthology of essays on the place of rights in utilitarian moral theory, see R. G. Frey, ed., *Utility and Rights,* (Minneapolis:

University of Minnesota Press, 1984); Richard B. Brandt, *Morality, Utilitarianism, and Rights* (New York: Cambridge University Press, 1992); and Brad Hooker, ed., *Rationality, Rules, and Utility: New Essays on the Moral Philosophy of Richard B. Brandt* (Boulder, CO: Westview Press, 1993).

For very reliable, brief **overviews of utilitarian thought,** see David Lyons, "Utilitarianism," in Lawrence C. Becker and Charlotte B. Becker, eds., *Encyclopedia of Ethics,* (New York: Garland, 1992), vol. 2, pp. 1261–1268; Philip Pettit, "Consequentialism," in Peter Singer, ed., *A Companion to Ethics,* (Oxford: Blackwell, 1991), pp. 230–240. R. G. Frey's "Act-Utilitarianism" and Brad Hooker's "Rule-Consequentialism" can both be found in Hugh LaFollette, ed., *The Blackwell Guide to Ethical Theory* (Oxford: Blackwell, 2000), pp. 165–182 and 183–204, respectively. William H. Shaw's *Contemporary Ethics: Taking Account of Utilitarianism* (Oxford: Blackwell, 1999) is an excellent and highly readable introduction to both the theory and the application of utilitarianism. Anthony Quinton's *Utilitarian Ethics* (New York: St. Martin's Press, 1973) provides a helpful overview of classical utilitarian thought. Also see David Lyons, *Forms and Limits of Utilitarianism* (Oxford: Clarendon Press, 1965) and D. H. Hodgson's *Consequences of Utilitarianism* (Oxford: Clarendon Press, 1967). Russell Hardin's *Ethics within the Limits of Reason* (Chicago: University of Chicago Press, 1988) develops a defense of utilitarianism that relies heavily on game theory. Robert E. Goodin provides a strong defense of a utilitarian approach to public policy issues in *Utilitarianism as a Public Philosophy* (Cambridge: Cambridge University Press, 1995). For a very perceptive discussion of **well-being** in relationship to utilitarianism, see James Griffin, *Well-Being: Its Meaning, Measurement and Moral Importance* (Oxford: Clarendon, 1986). For an overview of utilitarian thought that includes other traditions (including the Chinese), see Geoffrey Scarre, *Utilitarianism* (New York: Routledge, 1996).

Richard Brandt introduced **the distinction between act and rule utilitarianism** in his *Ethical Theory* (Englewood Cliffs, NJ: Prentice-Hall, 1959). On this distinction, also see A. C. Ewing, "What Would Happen If Everyone Acted Like Me?" *Philosophy* 28 (1953): 16–29 and A. K. Stout's "But Suppose Everybody Did the Same?" *Australasian Journal of Philosophy* 32 (1954): 1–29. On the tendencies toward *rule* utilitarianism in Mill's work, see J. O. Urmson, "The Interpretation of the Philosophy of J. S. Mill," *Philosophical Quarterly* 3 (1953): 33–39 and Henry West, "Mill's Moral Conservatism," *Midwest Studies in Philosophy* 1 (1976): 71–80. For a defense of rule utilitarianism, see Brad Hooker, *Ideal Code, Real World: A Rule-Consequentialist Theory of Morality* (Clarendon: Oxford University Press, 2000).

The discussion of utilitarianism often takes place within the context of a contrast with Kantian and other deontological accounts of morality. John Rawls's "Two Concepts of Rules," *Philosophical Review* 64 (1955): 3–22 is an important attempt to reconcile partially these two traditions. Samuel Scheffler's *The Rejection of Consequentialism* (Oxford: Clarendon Press, 1982) provides a provocative rethinking of some of these issues, as does Michael Slote's *Common-Sense Morality and Consequentialism* (London: Routledge & Kegan Paul, 1985), which contains an extended discussion of satisficing consequentialism.

Citations. The example of Jim is found in Bernard Williams, "A Critique of Utilitarianism," in *Utilitarianism: For and Against* (Cambridge: Cambridge University Press, 1973), pp. 98–99. On the British, utilitarianism, and India, see Ragavan Iyer, *Utilitarianism and All That: The Political Theory of British Imperialism* (Santa

Barbara, CA: Concord Grove Press, 1983). The quotation from Singer is taken from Peter Singer, "Famine, Affluence, and Morality," *Philosophy and Public Affairs* 1(1972): 231.

Further Information. For further information on issues relating to utilitarianism, see the Utilitarianism page (http://ethics.acusd.edu/theories/Utilitarianism/index.html) of my *Ethics Updates* site.

THE ETHICS OF DUTY: IMMANUEL KANT

Duty in the Life of Edmund G. Ross

After Abraham Lincoln's assassination, Andrew Johnson succeeded to the American presidency, pursuing Lincoln's policy of reconciliation and re-building in the South. Radical Republicans, disliking Johnson personally and committed to pursuing a much more punitive policy toward southern states, barely had the two-thirds majority necessary to consistently override presi-dential vetoes. With the appointment of Edmund G. Ross, long an ardent opponent of Johnson and his policies, to finish out the Senate term of the deceased Jim Lane (a Johnson supporter), it looked as though the radical Republicans would at last have their solid two-thirds majority, enabling them not only to override vetoes but even to impeach the president.

The bill of impeachment was passed by the House early in 1868 and went quickly to the Senate for a vote on Johnson's removal from office. Public sentiment was strongly against Johnson, and especially strong in Kansas, Ross's home state. He knew well that he would probably lose his political career and any further opportunities for success in public life if he failed to vote against Johnson. He opposed Johnson's policies and disliked him per-sonally. Yet despite all of this and in the face of intense pressure and threats to his life and reputation, Ross took seriously his oath "to do impartial jus-tice." His was the deciding vote on the floor of the Senate, and his decision was clear: Andrew Johnson did not deserve to be removed from office. To remove him for what were essentially partisan political considerations would be equivalent to degrading the presidency itself and turning the United States *de facto* into a purely congressional government.

Ross was never elected to political office again. When he returned to his native Kansas, he was shunned by his former friends and sentenced to a life of isolation and relative poverty. Ross anticipated all of this, yet he voted the way in which he did because he believed it was the right thing to do. He did it despite the personal consequences, and he did it despite his personal feelings about Johnson and his policies. This is what Kant means by *acting for the sake of duty,* doing something because it is the right thing to do. If any moral philosopher is able to truly appreciate Edmund Ross's decision, it is Immanuel Kant.

In this chapter, we shall look closely at Kant's moral philosophy, beginning with a consideration of his understanding of the role of duty in the moral life. His ethical theory rests on three central insights. The first two of these insights state the conditions for a morally good act:

- An action has moral worth if it is done for the sake of duty.

- An action is morally correct if its maxim can be willed as a universal law.

Actions that have both moral worth and moral correctness are morally good actions. In addition to these two insights, Kant develops a third claim about the way in which we ought to act in order to respect both ourselves and other people:

- We should always treat humanity, whether in ourselves or other people, always as an end in itself and never merely as a means to an end.

These are the three pillars on which Kant's ethics rests: duty, universalizability, and respect. Let's consider each of these three insights in turn.

THE ETHICS OF DUTY

One of the morally admirable characteristics of Edmund Ross's decision is that he not only did the right thing, he did it for the right reason. Ross did not act for any self-centered motives. Indeed, if Ross had been an ethical egoist, he would have acted quite differently. There were plenty of factors pushing him in the other direction. He did not like Johnson, he disagreed with Johnson's policies, his political career would be ruined by a vote in Johnson's favor, and even his family's fortunes would be adversely affected. The only reason for voting against removing Johnson from office was that it was the right thing to do.

Contrast this actual case with a hypothetical variant. Imagine that the same events were unfolding today, but that Ross's motivation was somewhat different. Imagine that he was tired of politics, feeling that his political career had reached a dead end. Imagine, further, that he saw the crucial vote on Johnson as an excellent career possibility. By skillfully manipulating the media, he could focus attention on himself and the agony of his decision. Media coverage would increase dramatically. A bestselling book, talk shows, the lecture circuit, and perhaps even a miniseries beckon in the future. "Integrity," our hypothetical Ross says to himself, "is a big thing with the voters today. If I vote against removing Johnson from office, I might even have a good chance at the Presidency myself in a few years." Buoyed by these prospects, our imaginary Ross casts his vote against removing the President from office.

Acting for the Sake of Duty

Which action, Kant would ask, do we think is morally better? Both actions, in terms of their external characteristics and results (at least in regard to the U.S. president), are the same. Both are in conformity with duty in the sense that the external behavior conforms to the requirements of duty. Yet clearly, most of us would agree that the action in the real-life case is better than the one in our hypothetical example, because it was done for the right reason. This is one of Kant's key insights: An act's moral worth depends on the reason for which it is done. It is not enough that an act conform to duty; it must also be done for the sake of duty. It must be done out of a concern for what is morally right, not out of some self-serving motive. This is precisely what makes the real-life case better than the imaginary one. The act is done just because it is the right thing to do; in other words, it is done for the sake of duty.

Duty and Self-interest: The Grocer Example

In the *Groundwork of a Metaphysics of Morals,* a short work in which he presents the underpinnings of his moral philosophy, Kant himself offers examples of acting for the sake of duty. These give us some insight into why Kant attaches such moral importance to the motive of duty. Kant's first example is of a grocer dealing with inexperienced customers. While it is often in a merchant's self-interest to be honest, it is not always so. If we imagine a neighborhood grocery store in which the grocer knows almost all of the customers, and if those customers are long-term patrons and if they know one another, and if there is a competitive grocery store, then it is clearly in the grocer's self-interest to be honest. The grocer depends on repeat business, and if the grocer cheats even a few of the regular customers, they will probably tell others and the grocer's business will be seriously hurt. Self-interest and simple prudence dictate honesty as the best policy in such cases.

However, this is not always the case. Recall our example of someone who runs a gift shop in a toll plaza on an interstate highway. The customers rarely return, they virtually never know one another, and there is usually no immediate competition. In situations such as these, if there is little scrutiny by consumer groups or police, the shopkeeper has little reason to be honest out of self-interest. Indeed, self-interest may well dictate overpricing items and selling shoddy products that will not stand up to any extended use. There are, in other words, plenty of situations in which the motive of self-interest cannot be counted on to require the right action. In situations such as these, if we are not acting for the sake of duty, we will not perform the morally correct action.

Kant's example is intended to show that self-interest is not a sufficient motive to guarantee the moral rightness of our actions. It also serves to illuminate Kant's differences from the ethical egoist. Obviously, they disagree on what gives an action moral worth. Whereas the ethical egoist takes self-interest as the standard, Kant focuses on duty. However, Kant's example here challenges a second aspect of the egoist's position. Egoists often claim that the world will be a better place if everyone acts in terms of his or her own self-interest. Yet both the grocer and the gift shop examples show that there are common circumstances in which this is unlikely to be true.

Duty and Utility: The Suicide Example

The second example that Kant offers is of the person who refuses the temptation to commit suicide even though his life is wretched, filled with disappointments and misery. When such a refusal is motivated by duty, it has moral worth in Kant's eyes. It would not have moral worth, however, if the refusal were motivated by other considerations, such as a squeamishness about the actual act of killing oneself or a mere desire or inclination to live.

Kant's views on suicide provide an interesting contrast with the utilitarian perspective. Kant condemns all suicides, but contemporary Kantians are often less rigid in their reasoning about this issue. In a perceptive essay on "Self-Regarding Suicide," Thomas Hill, a contemporary Kantian philosopher as the University of North Carolina, develops a sensitive and insightful analysis of suicide that still manages to preserve a number of Kant's essential insights in a modified and more nuanced form. Hill does not suggest condemning suicide and does not even claim that suicide is always irrational. He recognizes that there is a range of cases in which suicide, although sad, is not necessarily morally objectionable. He does, however, argue that certain types of suicides show that the individual in question does not value life "as a rational, autonomous agent for its own sake." Those who commit suicide from motives of self-abasement, for example, sees themselves as unworthy of continued life, as not even meriting the punishment of continued existence. Except in the most extreme of cases, such judgments are unwarranted and are inconsistent with the fundamental self-respect that all human beings should have.

Utilitarian reasoning about suicide takes a quite different tack. Not surprisingly, it is a matter of weighing consequences. The motive is of virtually no importance. Good utilitarians must imagine what the course of the world would be like if they killed themselves and what the course of the world would be like if they continued to live. Which of these alternatives produces the greater utility? A sensitive utilitarian such as Richard Brandt, a contemporary utilitarian thinker whose work has long shown a deep awareness of the psychological complexity of the moral life, points out quite rightly that the people contemplating suicide must be wary of letting depression and other factors distort their judgment as they attempt to weigh such factors. Nonetheless, it is clear that the utilitarian might permit—indeed, even require—suicide under circumstances and for reasons that no Kantian would accept.

Duty and Inclination: The Sympathy Example

The final example that Kant offers is the most controversial. He is concerned with the moral worth of actions done in order to help another person when the motive is one of sympathy or some other feeling such as compassion. He contrasts two types of people who help others. On one hand, "there are spirits of so sympathetic a temper that, without any further motive of vanity or self-interest, they find an inner pleasure in spreading happiness around them and can take delight in the contentment of others as their own work." The actions of such people, Kant argues, have no moral worth, because they are done out of inclination or feeling instead of being done for the sake of duty. On the other hand, imagine a quite different case.

> Suppose then that the mind of this friend of man were overclouded by sorrows of his own which extinguished all sympathy with the fate of others, but that he still had power to help those in distress, though no longer stirred by the need of others because sufficiently occupied with his own; and suppose that, when no longer moved by any inclination, he tears himself out of this deadly insensibility and does the action without any inclination for the sake of duty alone; then for the first time his action has its genuine moral worth. Still further: if nature had implanted little sympathy in this or that man's heart; if (being in other respects an honest fellow) he were cold in temperament and indifferent to the sufferings of others—perhaps because, being endowed with the special gift of patience and robust endurance in his own sufferings, he assumed the like in others or even demanded it; if such a man (who would in truth not be the worst product of nature) were not exactly fashioned by her to be a philanthropist, would he not still find in himself a source from which he might draw a worth far higher than any that a good-natured temperament can have? Assuredly he would. It is precisely in this that the worth of character begins to show—a moral worth and beyond all comparison the highest—namely, that he does good, not from inclination, but from duty.

This is a strong, perhaps even startling claim. The person who helps other people out of a sense of duty without any feeling of care or compassion or sympathy is morally superior to the person who performs the same actions while motivated by altruistic feelings. Yet Kant's point here, whether we agree with it or not, is clear: There is something *morally* valuable in the actions of a person who, despite feelings to the contrary, does something because it is the right thing to do. We may like the person who does the same thing spontaneously out of a feeling of compassion or pity, but there is nothing morally praiseworthy in such a person's intentions.

Criticisms of an Ethics of Duty

It is hardly surprising that Kant has been criticized for his strong emphasis on the importance of duty. Let's consider three of the ways in which his position has been questioned.

Moral Minimalism

The first possible objection to Kant's emphasis on duty is that it seems to imply a kind of moral minimalism, that is, an undue emphasis on only doing what is morally required in a given situation. Genuinely altruistic acts, according to a critic such as Lawrence Blum in *Friendship, Altruism and Morality* (1980), go beyond the moral minimum. Yet such an objection, as Marcia Baron has pointed out, rests on a misunderstanding. Both morally required and morally *recommended* acts may be done for the sake of duty. Kant's emphasis on duty in this context focuses solely on duty as the motivation for actions; it is not restricted to acts necessitated by duty. Whether the act be morally required or merely morally recommended, the crucial thing is that it is performed for the sake of duty, done because it is the morally good thing to do.

Moral Alienation

A second, more serious and more complex charge has been leveled against Kant's emphasis on duty. Several critics of Kant's ethics have argued that his exclusive emphasis on duty as the sole motive of moral action leads to moral alienation. Although this objection is discussed in Chapter 8 in a more general form as an objection against all ethical theories, it will be helpful here to consider some aspects of the specifically Kantian version of the problem.

Recall the example of the man who had no "sympathy for the fate of others" but helped them solely out of a motivation of duty. Why is it wrong—or at least without moral worth—to help other people simply because you *care* about them? Indeed, as we shall see in Chapter 10, feminist approaches to ethics such as Carol Gilligan's often take care as the center of the moral life. One of Kant's answers clearly falls short of the mark. Emotions, he claims, are fickle and a moral life based on emotions would lack the reliability of one based on reason. Yet this position presupposes a questionable view of both emotions and reason. Some basic moral emotions such as caring, especially if strengthened though moral education, can be quite reliable. Indeed, they may often provide a stronger motivation than reason. Finally, reason may be less reliable than Kant thinks. There is no shortage of examples in which reasons have been offered for morally suspect actions, and certainly there are plenty of instances

There is, however, a deeper source for Kant's mistrust of the emotions. Essentially, Kant sees the moral agent as composed of reason and will—emotions are not part of the composition of the moral agent as such. There are complex reasons for this position that relate to Kant's views on freedom and causality, but we need not concern ourselves with those here. Suffice it to say that Kant saw the human person as deeply divided between reason and freedom and duty, on one hand, and irrationality and causality and emotion on the other. Emotions were a threat to the autonomy of the moral agent for Kant, not an enhancement of it.

Emotions need not be thought of in Kant's terms. They play an important role in our moral perceptions, usually have subtle cognitive structures, and are to some extent subject to choice. They play an especially important role in the ethics of personal relationships, an area that Kant neglected. Moreover, as we shall see in Chapter 9 when we discuss the ethics of character, there are other, more robust conceptions of the moral agent than Kant's. These fuller accounts of the moral agent recognize that our emotions are an essential part of who we are as moral agents.

Duty and "Just Following Orders"

The final objection to Kant's emphasis on duty does not come primarily from professional philosophers. Indeed, it rests on a deep misunderstanding of Kant's philosophy that is rarely found among professional philosophers. It is, however, a misconception that is sometimes found in popular ideas about Kant. Sometimes Kant's conception of duty is misinterpreted as implying that acting for the sake of duty is somehow equivalent to an unthinking obedience to authority, to just following orders. Indeed, Adolf Eichmann even appealed explicitly to Kant's notion of duty in his defense of his actions at Auschwitz, claiming that he was just "doing his duty." Indeed, when first arrested, Eichmann told his police interrogators that throughout his life he tried to follow Kant's philosophy, and especially to obey Kant's categorical imperative. When asked what he understood the categorical imperative to be, he replied that earlier in his life

> I had known the Categorical Imperative . . . but it was in a nutshell, in a summarized form. I suppose it could be summarized as, "Be loyal to the laws, be a disciplined person, live an orderly life, do not come into conflict with laws"—that more or less was the whole essence of that law for the use of the little man.

Yet it is clear from even the most cursory reading of Kant that his notion of duty is *not* equivalent to following orders, unthinkingly obeying the law, and the like. But if duty is not just following orders, how do we determine what our duty is? Let's now turn to Kant's answer to this question.

UNIVERSALIZABILITY
AND THE CATEGORICAL IMPERATIVE

The second principal insight of Kant's ethics centers on the universality of genuine morality. Before looking at some of the more technical ways in which Kant sought to formulate this claim of **universalizability**, let's see if we can grasp the basic intuition behind it. Then we can examine Kant's strictly philosophical formulations of this insight and see whether his formulations adequately capture the insight.

What's Fair for One Is Fair for All

One of our basic intuitions in the moral life centers around the belief that what is fair for one is fair for all. If I'm allowed to run traffic lights whenever I want to, then everyone else should be allowed to do so as well. There would be something wrong, something *unfair,* about allowing me to disobey traffic signals whenever I choose but demanding that everyone else treat them as binding. Part of Kant's insight into morality is that it is equally applicable to everyone.

But, you may want to say, don't we in fact sometimes allow people in our own society to disobey traffic signals? Ambulance drivers, police officers, and others in emergency situations are permitted to go through red lights, although they must do so with proper caution. Is Kant's ethics so rigid that it does not permit this kind of exception? No, of course not. But his commitment to moral fairness demands that we justify this exception in a particular way. Anyone driving an ambulance during a medical emergency is permitted to disobey traffic signals, although with proper caution. The exception depends on the person's role as an ambulance driver and is applicable to anyone who occupies that role. We will consider the issue of exceptions in more detail below.

Imperatives: Categorical and Hypothetical

Kant calls his basic moral principle the **categorical imperative.** It is an *imperative* because it tells us to do something, gives us a command; it is *categorical* because it is unconditional. The opposite of a categorical imperative would be a conditional or *hypothetical imperative,* such as, "If you want to get to UCLA, take the 405 freeway." The corresponding categorical imperative would be, "Take the 405 freeway." However, even though this command has the form of a categorical imperative, it is clear that it does not apply to everyone all the time. We would hardly want to tell everyone to take the 405 freeway all the time. Is there, in fact, any command or imperative that we would want to issue to everyone and tell them to follow it at all times?

Kant believes that there is such a **categorical imperative,** and one version of it that he gives is as follows:

- **Always act in such a way that you can will that the maxim behind your action be adopted as a universal law.**

A **maxim** for Kant is the subjective rule a person has in mind while performing an action. The test for a maxim, then, is whether people could consistently will that everyone adopt this maxim as a guide in their actions. Then it would pass the test of universalizability.

The Example of Lying

Kant gives several examples of how this categorical imperative might be applied, and the most powerful and defensible one relates to lying. A person who tells a lie is saying in effect that it is permissible to deceive another person for personal gain of some kind. This is the implicit maxim behind this action. Yet imagine what would happen if we willed that everyone adopt this as a maxim. Think of the things in our society that depend on believing what another person says. When we sign a check, we are giving our word that we have the funds to cover it; when we sign a contract, we are promising to abide by the terms of that agreement; when we make a date to meet a friend for dinner, we are saying that we will show up at the appointed time; when I write these pages, I am implicitly saying that what I write is true and worthy of your belief. But imagine if we were to adopt the maxim that people can lie whenever they think it is to their benefit to do so. If we will that everyone adopt such a maxim, then we undermine the very possibility of gaining an advantage from our own lying —for if this maxim were universally accepted, no one would believe what anyone else said or promised because they would know that it could easily be a lie. We cannot consistently will that everyone lie or make false promises whenever it is to their personal advantage to do so, for this would undermine the credibility of our own lies and thus negate their effectiveness. Thus this maxim cannot be willed as a universal law.

Consistency

Notice that this is not really an argument about consequences, although it may appear that way at first. Kant is not saying that if we start to tell lies, other people will follow suit and that that will be bad. (As we shall see in the next chapter, a utilitarian might make this argument.) Rather, he is saying that if we imagine the consequences, we cannot consistently will that everyone adopt this maxim. This distinction gives us an insight into what lies behind lying: When we tell a lie, we make an exception of ourselves. We say that the rules that apply to everyone else should not, at least in this case, apply to us. But, and here is the crucial part, we are not willing to admit this. For our lie to work, it depends on having other people believe us—and thus on their not knowing that we are lying. Thus, we have to affirm simultaneously two contradictory propositions: that people should tell the truth and that I should be allowed to lie. The first is necessary for my lie to be believed, the second necessary to permit me to tell it. Yet these two propositions are inconsistent and thus cannot be willed together.

Another way of making this same point is that, in lying, I have to will that other people not lie. If I were to will that everyone lie, then no one would believe anyone. In order for my lie to be believed, I have to will that people generally believe that we should tell the truth. My lying depends on a general expectation of truthfulness that would be undermined if I willed my maxim as a universal law.

Impartiality and Fairness

Behind Kant's argument is a further insight, one that we have already begun to consider: What's fair for one is fair for all. If a law applies to one person, it should apply equally to all. In this sense, we must treat everyone impartially. If it is wrong for other people to lie, it is also wrong for me to do so. I cannot give myself special treatment.

Indeed, our everyday morality often reflects Kant's insight here. We should be morally suspicious of ourselves when we find that we are making an exception of ourselves. If, for example, I say to myself that cheating on an exam is bad, but just this one time it's okay for me to cheat, then I am making an exception of myself. A good rule of thumb for the moral life is to be suspicious whenever we start making an exception of ourselves. We cannot be certain in advance that what we are doing is morally wrong, but we can be sure that it merits further moral scrutiny.

Thus, while there are tremendous difficulties surrounding the articulation and application of Kant's categorical imperative, I think he is correct in his basic insight that we cannot arbitrarily make an exception of ourselves. Yet this raises a further question: Can we ever make an exception?

Exceptions

Our last remark raises a more general question, one that has often been asked of Kant's ethics: Can it deal adequately with exceptions? The classic example involves lying to the Nazis. If you are sheltering Jews during World War II, and the Gestapo comes to your door and asks whether you are hiding any Jews, are you (if you are a Kantian) obligated to tell the Gestapo where the Jews are? Before answering this question, let's look at some easier examples.

The Speeding Car

Imagine that you are driving in the country with a friend who suddenly becomes gravely ill. You do not know for sure what has happened, but you suspect a heart attack. It is clear that he needs medical attention immediately, but the area is so deserted that there is not even a telephone between your location and the hospital. The hospital is ten miles away; seven minutes later you pull up to the Emergency entrance.

Were you justified in speeding? I think a Kantian could easily say, "Yes." True, you were making an exception of yourself, but presumably this is an exception that we would be willing to grant to anyone in the same emergency situation. Anyone with a critically ill passenger in the car and under the other requisite conditions is permitted to speed in order to bring the passenger to the hospital for medical attention. If we were to formulate the maxim behind this action, it might be something like this: A person is justified in breaking minor laws (such as traffic regulations) in order to save a person from death or grievous physical harm when there is no other feasible alternative and when proper concern for the safety of other persons is shown. This is a maxim that we could consistently will as a universal law. We in fact have countless such exceptions in our society, and no one finds them inconsistent. Despite what Kant thought, universalizability need not exclude exceptions.

The Gestapo Example

The more interesting and difficult case comes when we imagine the Gestapo example described earlier. Would you be justified in lying to the Gestapo, telling them that you did not know the location of any Jews? What would the maxim behind your action be? Initially, we might say that the maxim is something like this:

- A person is justified in lying to the Gestapo if it will result in preventing them from killing innocent people.

Yet we would hardly want to tie our maxim so closely to the Gestapo in particular. What makes us single them out? Presumably we would also find it justifiable to protect innocent people from, say, the death squads in Argentina, the Ton Ton Macoute in Haiti, Pol Pot's secret police in Cambodia, and perhaps even certain branches of the KGB in Russia or the CIA in the United States. Yet not all the groups in this list are the same. Some are official government agencies; others, such as the death squads, are not.

It is easier to develop a defensible maxim that applies to self-appointed groups such as the death squads in Argentina. It could be formulated as follows.

- It is permissible to lie to self-appointed vigilante groups in order to protect the life or well-being of an innocent person from those groups.

We could imagine willing such a maxim as a universal law without inconsistency, for we could say that such groups have no right to that information in the first place and that if they did receive the information, they would commit a serious evil. Yet it is more difficult to formulate a maxim that would cover the Gestapo example, because the Gestapo at that time was a legally sanctioned part of the German government. Here the maxim is more questionable.

- It is permissible to lie to legitimate government authorities in order to protect an innocent person's life or well-being from those authorities.

The difficulty with this maxim centers on the question of who decides whether someone is an innocent person. Generally, this is a decision that we accord to the judiciary; yet in this case, the individual is taking over a function that is usually reserved to governmental authorities. It seems that we open the door in abuse, and perhaps even anarchy, if we allow individuals to take such responsibility on their own shoulders at will. Yet it also seems to open the door to oppression and totalitarianism if we never allow individuals to assume such responsibility, for there will be cases (and the Gestapo example is surely one such case) in which this will be the morally right thing to do. Thus we see the issue coming into clearer focus. We must formulate a maxim that describes the conditions under which individuals are allowed to take this responsibility onto their own shoulders.

- It is permissible to lie to government authorities in order to protect an innocent person's life or well-being from those authorities when those authorities have clearly shown a pattern of abuse of their authority.

Even this maxim would need further refinement, but we can begin to see the way in which we would go about dealing with exceptions within the context of Kant's ethics.

One final point should be noted in regard to Kant's position on lying, even though this does not directly relate to the issue of maxims. Kant was deeply concerned with the question of moral responsibility, and the Gestapo example can help us to understand one of his concerns. If we lie, and something bad happens to the Jews we are sheltering anyway, we are partly responsible for those resulting bad occurrences in Kant's eyes. If, however, we tell the truth and something bad happens anyway, we do not bear some of the blame for those bad outcomes because we in fact acted according to duty. In Kant's moral universe, there is a kind of moral safety to be found in according for the sake of duty that insulates us from the vicissitudes of fate and **moral luck** in a way that is not possible in consequentialist doctrines.

Formulating Maxims

The preceding discussion of exceptions is important for two reasons. First, it shows that Kant's approach to ethics may be less rigid than it is sometimes portrayed as being. Second, it begins to focus our attention on the importance of maxims in the moral life. Let's turn to a closer consideration of this issue.

A **maxim is a subjective rule according to which we determine behavior.** There are all sorts of possible rules that we may have as maxims. Consider a few examples, most of which are stated in the form of imperatives.

- Never do anything that hurts other people's feelings if you can avoid it.
- Always be loyal to your friends.
- Never act in a way that would make your parents ashamed of you.
- Never do anything that you would be unwilling to acknowledge publicly in *The New York Times*.
- Always watch out for number one.
- Winning isn't the most important thing—it's the only thing!

These are all maxims that people in fact live by, subjective rules they have that help them to decide in particular instances how they ought to behave.

In stressing that we always have a maxim underlying our actions, Kant is emphasizing the way in which every action is tied into a subjective network of reasons that motivate us as well as to an objective system of moral rules. The maxim is the link that connects the subjective reasons behind our actions to the system of reasons that comprises an ethical standpoint. The test of universalizability determines whether those subjective reasons fit within the objective system of reasons.

Relevant Act Descriptions

In formulating a maxim, we must pay attention to the *way* in which we describe the act. "Exerting two pounds of pressure on a metal lever," "pulling a trigger," "shooting a person," and "killing a guard in order to rob a bank" may all describe the same act. We need to be sure that we choose the relevant act descriptions that are potentially morally suspect in order to test whether they pass the test of universalizability.

Sufficient Generality

In addition to choosing the relevant act descriptions, we should formulate maxims with a sufficient level of generality. "Shooting Bill Smith" is specific; "shooting armed robbers who are threatening to kill innocent bystanders" is more general because it refers to types of people rather than specific individuals.

From Maxims to Categorical Imperatives

For Kant, the measure of a maxim is whether it survives the test of being translated from a maxim into a categorical imperative, that is, into a maxim that would be universally binding on everyone. Thus the maxim has a three-fold relationship: (1) to the motivating reasons of the agent, (2) to the act itself, and (3) to a universal system of reasons. The test of universalizability, which we will now consider, determines whether the maxim is consistent with the universal demands of reason.

The Test of Universalizability

Recall Kant's formulation of the categorical imperative that we cited earlier:

> Always act in such a way that you can will that the maxim behind your action can be willed as a universal law.

We can now appreciate the way in which the test of universalizability measures the morality of our actions. Actions begin with motivating reasons that prompt us to act in a particular way. Latent in those motivating reasons is the maxim that guides our action. In order to make this implicit maxim clearer, we need to formulate the maxim, following certain guidelines about the relevant act description and sufficient generality. Then we need to determine whether this maxim is one that it would be possible for everyone to consistently and rationally accept. If it is, then the action is morally permissible.

This test of universalizability can appear mechanical and far removed from the concerns of everyday life, but it is not intended to be so. What Kant saw most powerfully was that morality consists in doing what *any* rational being would do in the situation. This involves setting aside our own personal preferences and potential gains in order to do the right thing. The test of universalizability, whatever its apparent artificiality may be, is intended to help us see which of our actions are ones that any rational being would willingly acknowledge as his or her own. One of the difficulties with Kant's imperative about universalizability is that the link between action and intention is weak at two crucial junctures. First, there is quite a bit of latitude about the *relevant act description* that a person can use in formulating a maxim. A murder can be described in various ways: exerting a certain amount of force on a piece of metal (a trigger), firing a gun, killing someone. Similarly, several possible maxims might fit the same act—and some maxims may be made universal, while other may not be. One maxim might be to kill your enemies, another might be to make the world safe for democracy. Maxims need to be tied more firmly to particular acts if Kant's categorical imperative is to be a strong moral force.

RESPECT AND USING PEOPLE

Imagine the following situation. A shy, unattractive guy named Harold is living in the college dorm. He has virtually no friends and seems too timid to seek them out. His roommates spend little time with him, and he spends most of his time studying, presumably because he has nothing better to do. Things remain unchanged for the first year and a half that Harold is at college. Then suddenly, within a single week, two things happen that greatly affect his popularity. First, he father gives him a new sports car for his birthday—probably the most impressive car on campus. Second, his sister, who is enrolled at a nearby women's college, comes to visit. There is general agreement that she is probably the most beautiful creature on the face of the earth. Suddenly Harold's popularity soars. He is invited to countless parties, although the invitations usually contain a request to bring his sister along. Invitations to go out to movies or bars abound, especially from guys with no transportation of their own. He quickly develops an extensive set of friends, a remarkably high percentage of whom lack either a car or a girlfriend or both.

At the risk of sounding cynical, we could reasonably assume that at least some of Harold's newfound friends are using him. They are not really interested in Harold as a person, or presumably they would have made overtures of friendship long ago. Rather, they are only interested in Harold insofar as he can loan them his car, give them rides, or introduce them to his sister. Many of us would want to say that there is something wrong with using people in this way. Certainly Kant would say so. Indeed, one of the most important contributions that he made to ethics was his discussion of respect for other persons and his injunction that we not use other persons as mere means to our own ends. Let's look more closely at what he meant by this statement and why there is something morally objectionable about behaving in this way.

Kant's Imperative about Respect

In *Groundwork of a Metaphysics of Morals,* Kant presents the following formulation of the categorical imperative.

- *Act in such a way that you always treat humanity, whether in your own person or in the person of any other, never simply as a means, but always at the same time as an end.*

Let's look more closely at what Kant says here. There are several things that we should note about Kant's exact language.

First, notice that Kant says that we should always treat humanity, whether in ourselves or in anyone else, as an end in itself and never merely as a means to an end. Kant's directive prescribes an attitude of respect toward ourselves as well as toward other people. We will consider the issue of self-respect later in this chapter.

Second, notice that Kant's imperative tells us how to act, not how to feel. This is particularly relevant in understanding respect, for we need to ask whether respect is just a way of acting or whether it also involves feeling a particular way.

Third, note that Kant says that we ought never to use humanity merely or only as a means, but that we should also at the same time treat people as ends in themselves. This seems to imply that some element of using people as a means to an end is permissible; what is prohibited is only using them as a means. We will consider this distinction in more detail below.

Thomas Hill

TALKING ABOUT ETHICS:
A CONVERSATION WITH
THOMAS HILL JR. ABOUT
KANTIAN ETHICS

Thomas Hill is one of the best-known scholars of Kantian ethics in the United States. In his work, he has applied Kantian insights to a wide range of moral issues, including suicide, the environment, affirmative action, and political violence. He is the Kenan Professor at the University of North Carolina at Chapel Hill.

Hinman: Throughout your work, you have seen the moral landscape from a Kantian perspective. What is it that initially drew you to Kant's moral philosophy?

Hill: I was brought up as a utilitarian. My father taught ethics at Macalester College in Minnesota. He believed in utilitarianism, at least the form of utilitarianism advocated by G. E. Moore. When I went to off college, I had already learned this and thought it was probably the truth about the moral life. And then I came to be dissatisfied with utilitarianism. It seemed to conflict with what justice requires, it seemed to give us reasons for breaking promises when we shouldn't, and so on. And also, Moore's particular kind of utilitarianism involved intuition, intuiting what's intrinsically valuable—and that didn't seem acceptable. Such intuition appeared to be a standard, but in actuality it provided no standard at all. Everybody has intuitions; appeals to intuition can't ever settle any dispute. It's open to anyone to claim as intuition what is really based on prejudice. And I couldn't go along with older-style (hedonistic) utilitarianism, which made the fundamental claim that we should only promote pleasure and avoid causing pain. These are two very important factors, but I think there's more to the moral life than pleasure and pain. So for those various reasons I was ready to find an alternative.

When I started studying Kant's *Groundwork* as a sophomore in college, I confess I didn't understand much of it at all, even though it seemed as though it must be rather profound and inspiring. In particular, I saw glimmers of the idea I still like the most, which is the idea of human dignity, that human beings, unlike things, have a kind of worth that should be respected: They should never be treated simply as means. So, one can't simply think that two people are worth twice as much as one. The idea of human dignity seemed to me just the kind of correction to utilitarianism that I was looking for, and this lead me into a more serious study of Kant.

Hinman: What other ideas of Kant do you find most attractive or inspiring?

Hill: The idea of the kingdom of ends had a twofold appeal. First, it is a useful device for thinking about the most basic moral questions. It invites us to ask whether our principles, or some modified version of them, would be principles that people, respecting each other, and setting aside their personal prejudices, could agree to as if they were all in a kind of political legislature making moral rules for their community, rules where they would be in a sense author of those rules and subject to those rules. Although this isn't a formula that allows you to reach quick and easy answers, it forms a way of thinking about moral questions that is morally appropriate and potentially helpful.

There's a second aspect of the kingdom of ends that I find attractive. When we think of the persistent, deep moral question, "What is morality?" we get many different views. Kant rejects the view that values are off in a platonic heaven or that they are something to be discovered through natural science. And he rejects the view that morality is a matter of determining how people feel. Instead, the fundamental idea is that moral constraints are just those rules reasonable, free people would agree upon if they would each set aside prejudices and special interests. On this view, there's nothing terribly mysterious about morality; it's simply a matter of what reasonable, thinking people would agree upon as the conditions for living together in some mutually beneficial and harmonious way—and I should add a mutually respectful way. It's not just a matter of promoting happiness, but also of respecting each other.

Hinman: You've suggested that Kant doesn't offer quick and easy answers. Can you expand on that?

Hill: Kant aimed to get to what he called the foundation or groundwork of morals, and most of the time in his writings he is probing very deep, abstract, basic issues. And there what we mostly get is a framework for thinking about moral issues, guidelines, fundamental principles, but not quick and easy answers. That's the best side of Kant.

But at the same time I have to admit that there's another side to Kant. He had a certain kind of overconfidence, I think, that prompted him to apply his formulas of the categorical imperative to a few sample cases in a way that was misleadingly simple. So I think when we read Kant, it's worthwhile to separate out his particular moral views from his basic moral theory, where he is a deep philosopher probing the very foundations of morality.

Hinman: The notion of respect has been one that runs throughout your work. Is it basic to Kant's philosophy?

Hill: Yes. Though it's only one of many of Kant's principles, it's a fundamental one that each human being should respect every other human being, regardless of that person's class, popularity, or utility to society. Kant held the view that we ought to respect even the worst human beings. Although Kant thought criminals must be punished for their crimes, he insisted that no human being ever forfeits the kind of respect owed to every human being.

Kant's principle of respect urges us to extend to every human being an attitude that, at least when reflecting rationally, we all have toward ourselves. We don't think that our own worth depends entirely on our class, popularity, or utility to society, but rather that we have worth simply as human beings.

Hinman: What other elements round out this picture of Kant's moral philosophy?

Hill: There is another main idea that is really quite simple, but it hasn't been enough emphasized in other philosophies, and that is the idea that moral duties are things that we have good reason to do, things that no reasonable person would fail to do—and not simply because it satisfies some desire or promotes self-interest. And this, of course, is the idea that there are categorical imperatives.

What Does It Mean to Use Other Persons Merely as Means?

In our opening example, we saw a relatively clear-cut case of a person being used as a means. It could be made even more indisputable if we imagined that Steve, one of Harold's roommates, constantly belittled and criticized Harold until he found out about the car and his sister. Then Steve pretended to be Harold's best friend while still continuing to belittle him behind his back. Finally, when Harold's car crashes and his sister decides to go to school in Australia, Steve drops his friendship with Harold. In a case such as this, most of us would say without hesitation that Steve was using Harold and that he was wrong to do so.

Yet many examples in life are not nearly as clear cut, and in order to decide on the more difficult cases, we need to have a clearer notion of what it means to use a person as a mere means—and then to understand what is wrong with doing so. Let's start with our initial example before considering some of the harder cases. Why would we be inclined to say that Harold's friends were using him? There are several possibilities. First, Harold's friends were deceiving him insofar as they pretended to have friendly feelings toward him when in actuality they did not have those feelings. Second, his friends might have profited at Harold's expense insofar as they gained use of his car and introductions to his sister that they might not otherwise have had. Moreover, Harold might have done favors for them that he would not have done if he had known their true feelings. Third, they undermined Harold's opportunity to make informed choices insofar as some of Harold's choices were based on inaccurate information about his apparent friends' feelings and intentions. Whereas Harold would, for example, be inclined to loan his car to someone he considered to be a genuine friend, he would not want to loan it to someone who disliked him. If someone was pretending to be his friend, Harold's choice would be skewed because of this false information. Fourth, we might object to this situation because it violates the rules of friendship. There are special obligations, one could argue, that pertain to being a friend, and Harold's so-called friends failed to live up to those obligations. Finally, we might object that, when Harold eventually discovered the truth (i.e., that his apparent friends were really only interested in his car and his sister, not him), he was hurt by it.

The Syphilis Experiments

Now let's consider some additional examples that at least on the surface appear to be examples of using other people and see if they exhibit the same characteristics that our first example did. In the 1930s, some U.S. doctors and government officials were interested in doing research on the long-term effects of syphilis on men. By this time, they knew that syphilis could generally be cured by administering penicillin. This knowledge meant that it was more difficult to do long-term studies, since once a case was found, it could usually be cured rather easily. It was decided to take a group of black men who were already diagnosed as having syphilis, not tell them that they had the disease, not treat them, and follow the development of the disease in them until they died. They became the unwitting subjects in a medical research project that cost them their lives. The project continued until 1972.

What do we find objectionable in this example? Certainly, we object to the fact that men were allowed to die when they could have been treated, easily and cheaply, in a way that would have prevented their death from that particular illness. In other words, we object to the easily avoidable pain and suffering and death that resulted from this course of action. Secondly, we object to the fact that the men were deceived. They should have been informed of their condition. Third, because they were not told what was actually going on, they were not given any choice about their participation in this experiment. Thus it is not simply the deception, but also the fact that the deception serves to undermine the conditions of a meaningful choice, that makes this so objectionable.

Moreover, we would probably object to this experiment even if it did not result in avoidable suffering and death for the participants. Imagine scientists doing a medical research project in which they were testing the efficacy of a drug that they already knew had no harmful side effects. Suppose, furthermore, that the condition it treats was not life threatening or painful. Most of us would still maintain that it would be wrong to administer this drug, without their knowledge or consent, to patients who were hospitalized for some other reason and then observe the effects of the drug. Our intuition here is that people have a right to know and to make up their own minds, and that we have an obligation to respect this right, even if no direct harmful consequences result from ignoring this right.

Lest the Tuskegee syphilis experiment seem to be something in the remote past, it is helpful (but sad) to note that such deeds still occur today. Medical researchers, seeking to trace the development of the HIV-1 virus, tracked its development in patients in rural villages in Uganda but made no attempt to notify the spouses of HIV patients in the trial groups. The researchers observed several hundred people with the HIV virus but made no attempt to treat them; nor did they treat other (often easily and inexpensively treatable) sexually transmitted diseases that the patients had. Once again, this incident raises important questions about treating people as ends in themselves and not just as a mere means to an end.

Factory Closings

Consider a less controversial and less clear-cut example: industrial plant closings. There has been a longstanding national debate over the issue of whether factory owners should be required to inform employees of a potential plant closing a given number of weeks or months before the plant is actually closed. Owners generally oppose such a requirement, because once workers know that their plant is going to close, absenteeism and quitting increase dramatically as workers look for steadier employment elsewhere. (Moreover, their competition immediately knows that the plant is closing, and this might put them at a further competitive disadvantage.) Consequently, efficiency and productivity decrease.

On the other hand, workers support such requirements about advance notification because, they argue, it allows them to look for alternative employment over a longer period of time and thus, increases the possibility of a smooth transition to another job. They further contend that when the owners know of a plant closing and do not notify the workers, they are using the workers to their own ends without regard for the welfare of the workers themselves. They keep the truth from the workers because it might otherwise adversely affect their profits.

Again, we see some common elements emerging here. The first relates to avoidable harm. By informing the employees in a timely manner, the company might reduce the amount of harm the employees experience. At the same time, this may increase the cost to the company. Second, we again find, if not deception, at least the withholding of important information. Third, we see why that information is important: It affects the choices that the workers may make. In many cases, they would have made different choices if they had known that the plant was closing very soon. Indeed, from the company's point of view, one of the reasons for not telling them is precisely to prevent them from making those choices. Finally, we see that the employees—or at least some of the employees—are hurt by them.

Firing Long-Time Employees

Consider another example that relates to employment. In a wide variety of areas of the American workforce, there has been a tremendous amount of change in recent decades, especially with the introduction of computers and other sophisticated equipment in the workplace. All too often, we find employees who have faithfully served a company for years, sometimes at great personal sacrifice, no longer able to keep up with changing times—or, in some cases, not even given the chance to do so. This situation raises the issue of using persons. Companies that fire such employees are often criticized for just using their employees and, when they are no longer useful to them, discarding them. While this may be an appropriate attitude to have toward tools (use them and discard them), it is not a proper way of treating persons.

Precisely what is objectionable in this practice? It may not involve deception, but it certainly seems to involve a change in messages. Employees might have been hired under one set of guidelines with the tacit assumption that those guidelines would continue to remain in effect indefinitely; yet, perhaps under new management, they might change significantly. Certainly one of the moral issues here is how far one is justified in making such changes, and whether employers who make those changes are also obligated to provide employees with the realistic opportunity to conform to the new standards. Our underlying intuition, whether valid or not, is that employers owe employees something, especially employees who have in the past met the employers' expectations.

The Elements of Respect

From the preceding examples, we begin to get a picture of what Kant means by *respect*. It is, first and foremost, an attitude that manifests itself in action. To respect someone is to act in particular ways toward that person (and to refrain from acting in particular ways). Although Kant occasionally refers to it as a feeling, the emotive aspect of respect is clearly of secondary importance. Respect is, first and foremost, a way of acting.

Action over Feeling

What kind of action does respect require of us? Kant is clearer on the kinds of action respect prohibits than what it requires. Most fundamentally, respect demands that we do not take away the conditions of moral agency or autonomy from other people. Central to Kant's understanding of autonomy is the ability to make up one's own mind on the basis of the relevant information. In several of our examples, using people involved (1) not allowing them access to information relevant to their own decisions, or (2) not allowing them to act on the basis of such information. Kant's views on punishment, which we have not discussed here, reflect this same view. For Kant, it would be insulting and a mark of disrespect if we did *not* punish a criminal. In punishing someone, we treat that person as responsible, as a full-fledged moral agent. To do less is to show a lack of respect.

Respect also involves recognizing the unique value of each individual and the fact that each person is priceless. In *Groundwork,* Kant makes an interesting remark about price. If something has a relative value, Kant says, then it has a price. If it has a price, it can be replaced by something else of equivalent value. If it has an absolute value, it has dignity and is not for sale. It is also irreplaceable. We can, I think, take this as a cue and say that what sets human beings apart from everything else on earth is that human beings do not have a price, are not for sale; rather, they have an absolute value, are unique, cannot be substituted one for the other.

What Is Worthy of Respect

Respect is directed only toward persons, and even then it is related to only one aspect of persons: their rationality. What we respect in other people, according to Kant, is their ability to reason and, on the basis of their reason, to choose to act in particular ways. Proper respect is always directed toward reason and will. Because there is a sense in which everyone possesses rationality to the same degree (although they may not exercise it to the same degree), respect is something that we owe everyone in equal measure simply because they are human beings. Respect of this type is not dependent on a person's unique accomplishments, but only on his or her rationality.

Respecting Animals

The dependence of respect on rationality has important implications both for how we treat other people and for how we treat animals. Precisely because it is reason and will that are the proper objects of respect, we cannot properly respect animals in themselves, for (at least according to Kant) animals have neither reason nor will. Animals have feelings, but in themselves those are not a proper object of respect for Kant. We have an indirect duty to respect animals, not because of the animal's feelings, but because of the effects that lack of respect toward animals would have on us and our behavior.

Respecting Feelings

Kant's attitude toward animals gives us an insight into the limits of his view of respect toward human beings. While we respect reason and will in human beings, we apparently have no direct duty to respect their feelings. Thus, Kant's notion of respect is curiously lacking in affective components in both subject and object. The subject, the person having the respect, is primarily the acting subject, not the feeling subject; the object of respect in the other person is primarily reason and will, not feeling.

Respecting Moral Voices

Carol Gilligan has suggested a different perspective on the issue of respect. Without explicitly directing herself to Kant's position, Gilligan has suggested that respect may be seen as the willingness to listen to another's voice. Respect for persons, she suggests, involves creating a space within which another person's voice may be heard; at the same time, this is a space that allows all participants in the situation to hear the resonance of their own voices.

It is easy to think of examples in which voices are not heard. Think of the classroom. All too often, there are persons in a class whose voices are literally never heard, individuals who never speak. There are also others whose voices may be heard occasionally but soon lapse into silence. Think of the students who say something very interesting in class, only to hear the response, "That's very interesting, but that's not what we're talking about here." Soon they stop speaking, for their words fall on deaf ears. Or consider an experience that many female graduate students of my generation have had: making an important point in class only to hear the professor later attribute it to a male student. Respect, Gilligan suggests, occurs when we allow voices to be heard, to resonate.

Within this context, it is also easy to see a Kantian inspiration—the spirit, not the letter, of Kantian ethics—underlying some versions of multiculturalism. Historically, certain voices have been left out of the moral conversation. In the United States, this is certainly true about the voices of women and people of color. The premise of genuine multiculturalism is precisely respect, respect for the voices of everyone, not just the privileged few. This is a tremendously powerful moral vision, one that beckons us toward a world in which everyone's voice is given a fair hearing.

Self-Respect

Kant's categorical imperative about respect not only enjoins us to respect other people, but also to "respect humanity" in ourselves as well. Thomas Hill, whose article on self-regarding suicide we discussed earlier in this chapter, has developed the most insightful and stimulating account of Kant's ideas on self-respect. In a 1973 article entitled "Servility and Self-Respect," Hill argues that it is sometimes a moral failing to fail to respect oneself. He develops three examples: the Uncle Tom, the self-deprecator, and the deferential wife. The third of these has, by far, generated the most interest and response. Let's look at his analysis of this type of case.

The Deferential Wife

Consider Hill's description of the deferential wife. As you read his account, ask yourself what—if anything—you find morally objectionable in the attitude of the deferential wife.

This is a woman who is utterly devoted to serving her husband. She buys the clothes he prefers, invites the guests he wants to entertain, and makes love whenever he is in the mood. She willingly moves to a new city in order for him to have a more attractive job, counting her own friendships and geographical preferences insignificant by comparison. She loves her husband, but her conduct is not simply an expression of love. She is happy, but she does not subordinate herself as a means to happiness. She does not simply defer to her husband in certain spheres as a trade-off for his deference in other spheres. On the contrary, she tends not to form her own interests, values, and ideals; and, when she does, she counts them as less important than her husband's. She readily responds to appeals from Women's Liberation that she agrees that women are mentally and physically equal, if not superior, to men. She just believes that the proper role for a woman is to serve her family. As a matter of fact, much of her happiness derives from her belief that she fulfills this role very well. No one is trampling on her rights, she says; for she is quite glad, and proud, to serve her husband as she does.

The deferential wife has not been coerced into this role, and she is not unaware of alternative ways of understanding the role of a wife. Nor is she unhappy. What, then, is morally objectionable about this type of case?

Hill argues that the deferential wife fails to understand and appreciate her own moral rights. Part of this failure of understanding is that she does not know when she is entitled to waive her rights and when she is not. The deferential wife seems to waive her rights—especially her right to being treated as an autonomous agent—in situations where such waivers are not justified. There is a close analogy here between how we treat ourselves and how we treat other people. For example, we do not have the right to kill another person, even if that person consents to being killed, because no one has the right to give up his or her life in this way. Similarly, we do not have the right to treat ourselves in certain fundamentally disrespectful ways, even if we consent to doing so. We do not have the moral right, for example, to sell ourselves into slavery, even though we voluntarily choose that course of action. To do so is to treat oneself in a fundamentally disrespectful way.

THE KANTIAN HERITAGE

We can see that Kant had a number of valuable insights into the moral life, insights that are not only still valid today, but that helped shape today's moral consciousness. Yet we can also see that Kant went too far with several of those insights, mistaking them for the entire story of the moral life when in fact they offer only part of the story. Let's briefly summarize what Kant got right, and then look at where he went wrong.

What Kant Helped Us to See Clearly

The Admirability of Acting from Duty

Despite many recent criticisms of Kant on this point, I think we have to agree with him that there is something morally admirable about people who do the right thing, even when they do not feel like doing it, because it is the right thing to do, because it is their duty. Morality is sometimes a struggle, and those with the courage to go beyond narrow self-interest and do what is right for its own sake are deserving of our admiration. Edmund Ross did the right thing, not because he would gain from it, not because he liked Andrew Johnson or his policies, but because it was the right thing to do. Even knowing that he would suffer as a result, he judged the case against Johnson fairly. That is admirable.

The Evenhandedness of Morality

The second element in the moral life which Kant undoubtedly got right is the evenhandedness of duty, his insight that from a moral standpoint we are all to be treated in the same way. This position is most powerfully stated as a negative injunction to ourselves: We are not permitted to make an exception of the laws of morality just in order to benefit ourselves or those we care about. The essence of this standard of morality is that it applies to everybody equally.

Respecting Other Persons

Without a doubt, one of Kant's key insights into the moral life was his insistence that we treat other people as ends in themselves, that we respect them as autonomous beings capable of reasoning and of making choices based on the results of that reasoning. This has been, I think, an absolutely central insight in ethics, and its impact on our understanding of the moral life has been profound. Largely because of Kant, we are able today to see the ways in which persons deserve respect for their right to think and act for themselves.

Where Kant Missed the Mark

The Neglect of Moral Integration

Kant was correct in emphasizing the admirability of acting for the sake of duty, but he emphasized this so strongly that he missed something more important and often more admirable: the quest for moral integration, for overcoming the split between duty and inclination. There is certainly something admirable about people who do the right thing even though they want to do something else, but I think our moral goal should be to move toward that state where morality and inclination coincide whenever possible. As we shall see in Chapter 9, Aristotle's distinction between the temperate person and the continent person offers a framework within which we can better understand this. At present, suffice it to say that our highest moral ideal should contain some idea of reconciling duty and inclination, healing the split between reason and emotion.

The Role of Emotions in the Moral Life

Closely connected with Kant's neglect of moral integration is his exclusion of the emotions from any positive role in the moral life. Emotions, for Kant, are like forces that sweep over us, threatening to overwhelm our commitment to the good and to distort our vision of what is right. Even when emotions push us in the right direction, they are still untrustworthy, for they are fickle as the wind, constantly changing direction. Indeed, even phrases like "push us in the right direction" give us a clear indication that emotions are not part of the self; they are external to who we are as persons. For Kant, our identity as persons—at least, as moral agents—is composed almost entirely of reason and will. Emotions are not seen as an essential part of who we are as persons.

This exclusion of emotions from a positive role in the moral life has serious and undesirable consequences. First, as suggested, it militates against the possibility of moral integration, against overcoming (or at least minimizing) the tension between reason and emotion, between duty and inclination. Second, it makes the moral life myopic, for often it is only through emotion that we can see suffering that would otherwise be hidden. Our emotions help us to perceive the world; they don't just block perception. Third, often in the moral life what is needed most is an emotional response, and it is precisely this which Kant seems least equipped to give. Often we cannot do anything to help a person in pain, but we can *care* and feel *compassion* for that person's suffering. Kant's ethics has little room for such emotive responses.

The Place of Consequences in the Moral Life

Kant wanted, for good reasons, to insulate the moral life from the vicissitudes of everyday life. If the moral worth of our actions depended on consequences, it would make morality a matter of chance, of luck. Yet in his attempt to insulate moral worth from chance, Kant seems to have gone too far. He provided us with part of the story, an important part for assessing the moral worth of the agent's intention, but he mistook part of the story for the entire story. As we saw in the previous chapter, consequences do count. It is to Kant's credit that he saw that they were not the only thing that counted, but he failed to provide an adequate account of their full role in the moral life.

DISCUSSION QUESTIONS

1. Recall your response in the Ethical Inventory to **statement 21** ("If someone tries to do the right thing but it works out badly, that person still deserves moral credit for trying") and your rating of **statement 22** ("It is important to do the right thing *for the right reason*.")
   (a) How important are intentions in the moral life? Should moral credit depend solely on intentions? Why or why not?
   (b) Have your ratings of these items changed after reading this chapter? If so, in what way? If your ratings have not changed, are your reasons for your ratings any different now than they were when you first responded to this statement?
2. Recall you response to **statement 23** in the Ethical Inventory ("What is fair for one is fair for all").

(a) Has your rating of this item changed after reading this chapter? If so, in what way? If your rating has not changed, are your reasons for your rating any different now than they were when you first responded to this statement?

(b) When, if ever, should exceptions be made to moral rules? How does your answer to this question compare with your rating of **statement 16**?

3. What was your initial response to **statement 24** ("People should always be treated with respect")?

(a) What does it mean to treat someone with respect? Does respecting people mean being nice to them? Explain. When, if ever, are you justified in not respecting someone? Explain.

(b) Has your rating of this item changed after reading this chapter? If so, in what way? If your rating has not changed, are your reasons for your rating any different now than they were when you first responded to this statement?

4. Recall your rating of **statement 25** ("We should never use other people merely as a means to our own goals").

(a) What does it mean to use someone merely as a means? Do you think this is a common attitude in our society?

(b) Has your rating of this item changed after reading this chapter? If so, in what way? If your rating has not changed, are your reasons for your rating any different now than they were when you first responded to this statement?

5. Join a discussion of the following question on the World Wide Web at http://ethics.acusd.edu. Kant says that it is never right to tell a lie, even to save a life. Is it always right to tell the truth, even if it hurts or destroys someone else? What matters more, the life of an individual or the majesty of the moral law?

6. Is a "conscientious Nazi" who does his duty for duty's sake obeying the categorical imperative? Or parodying it? Explain the reasons for your answer. Give an example of a contemporary equivalent of the "conscientious Nazi."

7. Use Kant's notion of a maxim to show what, if anything, is wrong with cheating on the final exam in a course that you do not like and feel you will not benefit from. How would Kant's approach to this kind of example differ from the approaches of the ethical egoist and the utilitarian? Which comes closest to your own position on the issue?

8. Drawing on your own experience, give a clear-cut example of a case in which one person is using another person merely as a means: Then give an equally clear-cut example of a case in which a person is respecting another person as an end in him/herself. Is it possible to live a life in which you do not use other people merely as a means? Why or why not?

9. MOVIE In both the book (1982) and movie (1985) *The Color Purple,* the issue of self-respect plays a central role. Indeed, one of the central themes of the movie is Celie's movement from servility to self-respect. How would you assess each of the major characters in terms of self-

respect? What role does fighting (and violence) play in the formation and destruction of self-respect? What role do loving relationships play in the strengthening of self-respect?

10. **MOVIE** In the movie *Quiz Show* (1994) we see an interesting portrait of the sticky web of deception. When a college professor is offered the possibility of fame and fortune in a rigged quiz show, he succumbs to temptation, thereby becoming enmeshed in a fabric of lies from which he cannot extricate himself. What does *Quiz Story* tell us about deception? Which moral framework offers the best perspective for understanding and appreciating the ethical issues raised by this movie?

BIBLIOGRAPHICAL ESSAY

Probably the most influential of **Kant's works in ethics** is his *Groundwork of a Metaphysics of Morals;* H. J. Paton did an excellent translation and commentary, published as *The Moral Law* (London: Hutchinson University Press, 1948); a more recent, fine translation is Mary J. Gregor, ed., *Kant: Groundwork of the Metaphysics of Morals,* introduction by Christine M. Korsgaard (Cambridge: Cambridge University Press, 1998). Robert Paul Wolff edited a helpful volume containing *Groundwork* and a number of classic critical essays in his *Kant: Foundations of the Metaphysics of Morals: Text and Critical Essays* (Indianapolis: Bobbs Merrill, 1969); also see Paul Guyer, ed., *Kant's "Groundwork of the Metaphysics of Morals* (Lanham, MD: Rowman & Littlefield, 1997) for an excellent collection of essays. Wolff's own commentary on *Groundwork* is published as *The Autonomy of Reason* (New York: Harper Torchbooks, 1973). W. D. Ross's *Kant's Ethical Theory* (Oxford: Clarendon Press, 1964) and most of Bruce Aune's *Kant's Theory of Morals* (Princeton: Princeton University Press, 1979) also provide excellent commentaries on *Groundwork*. More recently, Thomas E. Hill, Jr.'s *Dignity and Practical Reason in Kant's Moral Theory* (Ithaca, NY: Cornell University Press, 1992) offers an insightful analysis of many of the main themes in *Groundwork*.

Introductions to Kant's Ethics. H. B. Acton's *Kant's Moral Philosophy* (London: Macmillan, 1970) provides a good, short introduction to Kant's ethics. Roger J. Sullivan's *Immanuel Kant's Moral Theory* (Cambridge: Cambridge University Press, 1989) provides an excellent, comprehensive introduction to Kant's ethics. For short, insightful introductions to Kant's ethical thought, see Christine M. Korsgaard, "Kant, Immanuel," in Lawrence C. Becker and Charlotte B. Becker, eds., *Encyclopedia of Ethics* (New York: Garland, 1992), vol. 1, pp. 664–674 and Onora O'Neill, "Kantian Ethics," in Peter Singer, ed., *A Companion to Ethics* (Oxford: Blackwell, 1991), pp. 175–185.

Groundwork is just what its title implies: a groundwork or foundation for later work in ethics. Kant completed it with two works: his *Metaphysical Elements of Justice,* trans. John Ladd (Indianapolis: Bobbs Merrill, 1965) and his *Doctrine of Virtue,* trans. Mary Gregor (Philadelphia: University of Pennsylvania Press, 1964). The general place of ethics in Kant's large philosophy is developed in his *Critique of Practical Reason,* trans. Lewis White Beck (Indianapolis, IN: Bobbs Merrill, 1956). See Lewis White Beck's *A Commentary on Kant's "Critique of Practical Reason"* (Chicago: University of Chicago Press, 1960) for a thorough introduction to this important work of Kant's. His views on a number of ethical issues are also found in his *Lectures on Ethics,* trans. Louis Infield (New York: Harper & Row, 1961), the often neglected *Anthropology from a Pragmatic Point of View* (The Hague: Martinus Nijhoff, 1974) in an excellent translation by Mary Gregor. Kant's *Religion within the Limits of Reason Alone,* trans. Theodore M. Green and Hoyt H. Hudson (New York, Harper & Row, 1960), with a superb introductory essay on Kant's ethics and religion by John Silber; a far better translation, again with an excellent introductory essay, is available in Allen W. Wood and George Di Giovanni, eds., *Kant: Religion within the Boundaries of Mere Reason and Other Writings,* foreword by Robert Merrihew Adams (Cambridge: Cambridge University Press, 1998); also see Kant's *Religion and Rational Theology,* edited and translated by Allen W. Wood and George di Giovanni (Cambridge: Cambridge University Press, 2001), for additional writings on Kant on this topic. His moral philosophy is rounded out by his political writings, which have been translated and edited in a helpful anthology by Hans Reiss as *Kant's Political Writings* (Cambridge: Cambridge University Press, 1977).

Several of Kant's works are available on the **World Wide Web**: See the links given at the Kant page (http://ethics.acusd.edu/theories/Kant/) of my *Ethics Updates* site.

There are many **contemporary followers of Kant.** For a brief survey touching on Rawls, Donegan, and Gewirth, see John Marshall, "Kantian Ethics," in Lawrence C. Becker and Charlotte B. Becker, eds., *Encyclopedia of Ethics* (New York: Garland, 1992), vol. 1, pp. 674–677. Perhaps the most influential philosopher who works, broadly speaking, within the Kantian tradition is **John Rawls,** especially his *Theory of Justice* (Cambridge, MA: Harvard University Press, 1971). Further bibliography on Rawls will be available in Chapter 8 on justice. Some of the most interesting and sensitive work in the Kantian tradition includes **Thomas E. Hill, Jr.**'s essays, especially "Servility and Self-Respect," reprinted in his *Autonomy and Self Respect* (Cambridge: Cambridge University Press, 1991) and his *Dignity and Practical Reason in Kant's Moral Theory* (Ithaca, NY: Cornell, 1992), and his *Respect, Pluralism and Justice: Kantian Perspectives* (New York: Oxford University Press, 2000); **Onora O'Neill**'s numerous essays collected in her *Constructions of Reason* (Cambridge: Cambridge University Press, 1989); *Towards Justice and Virtue: A Constructive Account of Practical Reasoning* (Cambridge: Cambridge University Press, 1996); *Bounds of Justice* (Cambridge: Cambridge Univesity Press, 2000) as well as her earlier work, *Acting on Principle* (New York: Columbia University Press, 1975, published under the name Onora Nell), which addresses the question of how Kant's categorical imperative can actually be applied to specific actions; most recently, O'Neill has turned her attention to Kantian themes in bioethics in *Autonomy and Trust in Bioethics* (Cambridge: Cambridge University Press, 2002). **Barbara Herman**'s excellent essays are now collected in her *The Practice of Moral Judgment* (Cambridge: Harvard University Press, 1993). Also see the work of **Christine M. Korsgaard,** including her *Creating the Kingdom of Ends* (Cambridge: Cambridge University Press, 1996) and *The Sources of Normativity* (Cambridge: Cambridge University Press, 1996), as well as the symposium on her work that appeared in the journal *Ethics* 109, no. 1 (October 1998); and **Marcia W. Baron**'s excellent essays have been published in *Kantian Ethics Almost without Apology* (Ithaca: Cornell University Press, 1995) Also see the defense of Kant in **Stephen Darwall**'s *Impartial Reason* (Ithaca, NY: Cornell University Press, 1983) and in his "Kantian Practical Reason Defended," Ethics 96, no. 1 (October 1985): 89–99.

For a skilled defense of Kant's emphasis on **duty,** see both Barbara Herman's article "On the Value of Acting from the Motive of Duty," cited earlier, and Marcia

Baron, "On the Alleged Repugnance of Acting from Duty," *The Journal of Philosophy* 81 (1984): 179–219 and Onora O'Neill's "Kant after Virtue," in her *Constructions of Reason,* cited earlier. On Kant's interest in the **virtues,** see Robert Louden's "Kant's Virtue Ethics," *Philosophy* 61 (1986): 473–489 as well as the work of Onora O'Neill already mentioned. On Kant's notion of **respect,** see especially Steven Darwall, "Two Kinds of Respect," *Ethics* 88, no. 1 (October 1977): 36–49 and the essays of Thomas Hill already cited; also see the excellent collection of essays *Dignity, Character, and Self-Respect,* edited by Robin S. Dillon (New York: Routledge, 1995). On some of the difficulties surrounding the issue of **using persons as a mere means,** see especially Nancy (Ann) Davis's "Using Persons and Common Sense," *Ethics* 94, no. 3 (April 1984): 387–406.

The contrasting views of **suicide** are to be found in Thomas E. Hill, Jr., "Self-Regarding Suicide: A Modified Kantian View," in his *Autonomy and Self-Respect* (Cambridge: Cambridge University Press, 1991), pp. 85–103 and Richard B. Brandt, "The Morality and Rationality of Suicide," in his *Morality, Utilitarianism, and Rights* (Cambridge: Cambridge University Press, 1992), pp. 315–335. For an excellent collection of philosophical essays on the morality of suicide that includes Brandt's piece, see *Suicide: Right or Wrong?* edited by John Donnelly (Buffalo, New York: Prometheus Books, 1990).

On the **Tuskegee experiment,** see the website established by the Center for Disease Control: http://www.cdc.gov/nchstp/od/tuskegee/index.html. Also see James Howard Jones, *Bad Blood: Tuskegee Syphilis Experiment,* rev. ed. (New York: Free Press, 1993). Comments on the Uganda HIV-1 research can be found in M. Angell, "Investigations' Responsibility for Human Subjects in Developing Countries," *Journal of the American Medical Association* 342, no.13 (March 30, 2000): 967–969.

Citations. The example of Edmund Ross is drawn from Chapter 6 of John F. Kennedy's *Profiles in Courage* (New York: Harper & Row, 1955). Kant's example of the man "overclouded by sorrows" comes from Paton's translation of the *Groundwork, The Moral Law,* p. 64. The discussion of Eichmann's views on Kant comes from A. Zvie Bar-On, "Measuring Responsibility," *The Philosophical Forum* 16, nos. 1–2 (Fall-Winter 1984–1985): 95–109. For a description of the syphilis experiment, see James H. Jones, *Bad Blood: The Tuskegee Syphilis Experiment,* rev. ed. (New York: Free Press, 1992). The material from Carol Gilligan comes from an Ethics across the Curriculum workshop that she gave at the University of San Diego on January 27–28, 1996. Hill's description of the deferential wife is found in his "Servility and Self-Respect," *Autonomy and Self-Respect,* pp. 5–6.

Further Information. For additional information on Kantian ethics, see the resources listed on the Kant page (http://ethics.sandiego.edu/theories/Kant/) of my *Ethics Updates* site.

THE ETHICS OF RIGHTS: CONTEMPORARY THEORIES

When the founders of the United States stated in the Declaration of Independence that certain rights are inalienable, they were at the forefront of a moral movement that continues to exert a profound impact on our global society today. Indeed, at the same time that the Americans were implementing the notion of rights as one of the cornerstones of our democracy, the French were also developing their own equivalent to our Declaration of Independence, their Declaration of the Rights of Man and Citizen. Thus, two of the most influential political documents of the modern age take the notion of rights as the central concept upon which political organizations are built.

The interest in rights is not restricted to the seventeenth and eighteenth centuries. The second half of this century has witnessed a major resurgence of interest in the notion of **human rights.** In our own country, issues of rights play a central role in political life. The civil rights movement from the sixties onward has had an enduring impact on American society—and, as its name implies, it took *rights* as the cornerstone upon which the rebuilding of our society was to be based. More recently, issues about the rights of women and disadvantaged minorities, especially in the workplace, have been matters of national debate. The controversy over abortion has often been posed as a conflict of rights—the woman's right to privacy pitted against the fetus's right to life. With increasing medical advancement, we are now discussing whether persons have a right to die. Powerful groups in the United States still strongly champion the right to bear arms. Every year in many cities, there is a gay rights parade. Discussions about using animals in research and testing are often phrased in terms of animal rights. The language of rights has become the *lingua franca*, the common language, in terms of which we discuss our domestic political lives.

Talk about rights has not been confined to domestic issues. Human rights increasingly became a concern in American foreign policy in the last two decades. Our policy toward the Soviet Union, for example, was profoundly shaped by what we perceived as its neglect of human rights. In our dealings with Latin American countries, we have shown a steady, if selective, concern with human rights violations.

Appeals to rights are not limited solely to American foreign policy. The controversy in the Middle East is often framed as a conflict between Israel's right to secure borders and the Palestinians' right to a homeland. Ethnic communities talk of their right to self-determination. Shortly after its founding, the United Nations approved its Universal Declaration of Human Rights, encompassing and going beyond our own Bill of Rights. Interestingly, we have never ratified this broader declaration of human rights.

Nor, finally, is rights talk confined to the strictly political realm. We talk of fishing rights, of mineral exploration rights, of patent rights, of copyrights, and of many other rights that regulate our commercial interactions. This book is protected by a copyright.

Clearly, discourse about rights is pervasive in our society. We often see our relationships with one another in terms of rights, and occasionally see even animals and the natural environment in those terms. *The language of rights has proved to be the most powerful language for moral change in the twentieth century.* In this chapter, we shall look at a number of issues that lie at the heart of contemporary rights theory: theories about where rights come from, the various types of rights, how we determine what rights we have, and how we deal with conflicts of rights.

RIGHTS: SOME INITIAL DISTINCTIONS

Rights, Entitlements, Claims, Duties, and Responsibilities

Rights express a certain kind of relationship between two parties, the *rights holders* and the *rights observers*. Rights thus have two faces, depending on whether they are viewed from the perspective of the person who has the rights or from the perspective of the person who ought to respect those rights.

From the perspective of the rights holder, **a right is a permission to act** (Nozick), an *entitlement* "to act, to exist, to enjoy, to demand" (McCloskey). The rights-holder is entitled to *claim* whatever is covered or guaranteed by the right (Feinberg). When Rosa Parks refused to ride in the back of the bus in Montgomery in 1954, she was claiming that she had a right to sit wherever there was a vacant seat. She was entitled to choose where she wanted to sit without regard to the seat's designation for white passengers.

The work of John Locke (1632–1704) on human rights had a profound effect on the American Declaration of Independence.

From the perspective of the rights observer, **the right usually imposes a correlative duty or obligation** upon them. That duty may be either negative (to refrain from interfering with the rights holder's exercise of the right) or positive (to assist in the successful exercise of the right), depending on the nature and scope of the right.

Finally, and perhaps most controversially, to have a right may entail certain *responsibilities* on the part of the rights holder about how that right is to be exercised. I might, for example, have a right to drink alcohol at a party, but I will have certain corresponding responsibilities about arranging for a designated driver, not damaging my health, and so forth.

Let's examine some of the distinctions that this brief description of rights suggests, beginning with the difference between negative and positive rights.

Negative and Positive Rights

If a duty is simply negative, we need only refrain from interfering with the rights holder's exercise of the right. If the duty is a positive one, we are obligated to take positive steps to ensure that the right is respected. As such, a right (1) gives me a permission and (2) obligates others to respect that permission or entitlement.

For example, I have a right to free speech. That right gives me permission (within certain limits) to say whatever I want, and it obligates other people (within certain limits) to refrain from interfering with my speech. The right of free speech is one of a group of rights that we will call **negative rights** or **rights of noninterference.** Characteristically, these rights prevent other people from interfering with the actions (such as speech or religion) protected by those rights. Other rights enunciated at the beginning of our Constitution have a similar structure. The rights to life, liberty, property, and the pursuit of happiness all are construed largely as rights of noninterference. The right to life, for example, prevents other people from killing us. It does not, however, obligate them to do anything positive to assist us in living or to extend our lives.

Other rights, however, do more than prevent other people from interfering with us. Some rights impose an obligation on other people to do something positive for us. Contracts often embody such rights. If you have a rental agreement with your landlord for your apartment, your landlord is not only obligated to refrain from interfering with some of your actions (such as your right of free association), but is also positively obligated to do certain things for you (such as provide heat, adequate locks on doors, etc.). Our society is currently involved in a debate about whether, and to what extent, we have certain rights to basic health care. This health care right differs from rights of noninterference in an important way. If it were simply a right of noninterference, then we would say that no one is allowed to prevent us from obtaining basic health care. If, however, there is a positive right to basic health care, then someone—presumably the state—is obligated to provide us with such care, even if we are unable to pay for it. Following common usage, we shall call rights like these **positive rights** because they obligate others to do something positive for the rights holder.

The term *positive rights* may be misleading in two senses. First, note that sometimes the term *positive rights* is used in another way to designate those rights that a society in fact *posits* or recognizes. This usage will be discussed later, but unless specifically noted, we won't be using the term in that sense in this chapter. Second, although philosophers typically talk about negative and positive rights, it isn't really the rights that are positive or negative; rather, it is the *obligations* that the rights entail for rights observers. Negative rights (rights *from* x) entail only negative obligations of noninterference; positive rights (rights *to* y) entail positive obligations on the part of the rights observer to do something to assist in the rights holder's exercise of a right.

Who is obligated in the case of positive rights? In some instances, these rights obligate some specific individual, such as the landlord, to provide a particular good; in other cases such as the health care example, they obligate the state, or the employer or health care industry, to provide the service. The state must then decide how to apportion this obligation to particular individuals. In the health care example, the state would presumably contract

Negative and Positive Rights

	Examples	Obligations toward the Rights Holder
Negative	Life, liberty, property, pursuit of happiness	Avoid interfering with life, with expressions of liberty, with holding property, and with pursuing happiness
Positive	Basic subsistence, basic health care	Provide minimal subsistence needs of food, shelter, and clothing, provide basic health care

with some individuals to provide the service. The financial cost would be borne equitably by taxpayers. In other cases, the burden is distributed in a random fashion. We have a right to trial by a jury of our peers; the state then determines by lot which particular individuals are obligated to serve on juries at any specific time. The most controversial cases of rights in our society often involve instances in which the burden seems to be distributed in an inequitable way to certain individuals or groups. Affirmative action policies are sometimes seen as imposing an unfair burden on the individual majority job candidates who would otherwise have been selected if affirmative action policies were not in place.

We will be considering several of these specific rights later in this chapter, but it is worth noting here that there is at least one philosophical position—libertarianism—that maintains that there are *only* negative rights. Indeed, many libertarians claim that there is only one right, the negative *right to liberty,* which obligates other people to refrain from interfering with the exercise of a person's liberty.

Classifications of Strength

Absolute Rights

Rights can also be classified according to their strength. The strongest right is an **absolute right,** which cannot be overridden by any other *types* of considerations (such as utility or expediency) that do not involve rights. Ronald Dworkin captured this idea well when he said that rights are like "trump cards"; that is, they overrule any other types of considerations. The right to life, for example, may be an absolute right. It cannot be justifiably overridden by considerations of expediency or even utilitarian calculations. We are not justified in killing an innocent street person to gain body parts for transplants, even if doing so might yield greater social utility than not doing so.

Prima Facie Rights

Some philosophers have suggested that most, perhaps even all, rights are *prima facie* rights. The phrase *prima facie* is a Latin one that means "at first glance." To hold that a right is a *prima facie* right is to say that, at first glance, it appears to be applicable. However, upon closer scrutiny, we might decide that other considerations outweigh it. To call a right *prima facie* is not to say that it is merely apparent. The phrase acknowledges that the right is real but leaves open the questions of whether it is applicable and overriding in a particular situation. A *prima facie* right is a *presumptive* right, one that we initially presume to be relevant but must subject to further scrutiny. Gregory Vlastos, in his article "Justice and Equality," has argued that *all* rights are *prima facie* rights, subject in principle to being outweighed by other considerations.

The Justification of Natural Rights

In the last fifty years, we have seen several tragic situations in which the issue of human rights has arisen in a particularly perplexing and disturbing way. Think of the atrocities of the Third Reich against Jews, Gypsies, homosexuals, Poles, and others, all of whom the Germans attempted either to exterminate or to enslave—in large measure through actions that were first approved by German legislatures. Recall the situation of African Americans before the civil rights movement, when they were systematically and legally discriminated against. Think of the conditions under which blacks and people of mixed racial background recently lived in South Africa under the sanction of the laws that supported apartheid. All three of these situations share a common characteristic: They all involve *legally sanctioned* mistreatment of particular groups of people.

The fact that this mistreatment did not generally involve violating laws raises important questions for a philosophy of human rights. Do people have rights even when such rights are denied by their country's laws? Defenders of human rights have argued that the various persecuted groups just mentioned did have rights that their governments failed to recognize. Yet if this is the case, then rights must have some foundation that is independent of the particular governments and societies that recognize (or fail to recognize) them. Many theorists have tried to establish a foundation for human rights that is so secure that it justifies claiming that people have certain fundamental rights even if their government and society fail to acknowledge those rights. They see those rights as belonging to people simply by virtue of their nature. Such rights are **natural rights.** Theorists in this tradition offer different accounts of the foundation of natural rights. Some see their foundation as self-evident, some claim that they are grounded in God's will or the natural law, whereas others see rights as grounded in some characteristic of the person such as the ability to choose. However, they all agree that at least some rights belong to us by virtue of the fact that we are human beings and thus possess a human nature.

Broadly speaking, there have been four main approaches to establishing and justifying natural rights: (1) the appeal to self-evidence, (2) the appeal to a divine sanction or guarantee, (3) the appeal to a natural law, and (4) the appeal to human nature. These are not mutually exclusive and are sometimes combined to reinforce one another. Let's examine each of these approaches.

Self-Evidence

When Thomas Jefferson declared in the Declaration of Independence that it is "self-evident" that we possess certain inalienable rights such as the rights to life, liberty, and the pursuit of happiness, he was articulating an approach to rights that is still prevalent today. Even such a staunch defender of rights as Ronald Dworkin simply takes the *existence* of rights for granted in his *Taking Rights Seriously* (1977), dismissing those who question their existence as outside of "orthodox political theory" (p. 184). Similarly, Robert Nozick, whose *Anarchy, State, and Utopia* (1974) is one of the most influential defenses of rights theory among contemporary philosophers, takes the existence of rights to be self-evident. This *appeal to self-evidence* is an understandable one because some things appear so obvious to some of us that it is hard to see how anyone could question them. The United Nations Universal Declaration of Human Rights (1948) similarly offers no arguments in support of its long list of human rights but simply seems to take their existence for granted.

The difficulty with this claim to self-evidence is that even if it is true, it is usually unhelpful. The controversial cases about rights are the ones that we need help with, and it is these cases that are *not* self-evident to a significant number of people. Indeed, with the advantage of hindsight, we wonder how some of the founders of our country could have held the right to liberty to be self-evident and yet approved of slavery.

There is a further disadvantage of appeals to self-evidence. Most of the controversy about rights centers on the question of precisely *which* rights are justified. If we can begin with something more specific, more determinate than an appeal to self-evidence, then we are more likely to be able to shed light on the issue of which specific rights count as natural rights. As we shall see, the appeal to human nature offers a brighter prospect in this regard.

Divine Foundations

Some of the earliest formulators of strong doctrines of natural rights saw them as being founded in God—indeed, our Declaration states that it is self-evident that "all men . . . are endowed by their Creator with certain inalienable rights." Similarly, John Locke, whose *Two Treatises on Government* (1690) is among the major formative documents in modern political theory, referred to God as the ultimate source and foundation of human rights.

We have already alluded to one of the benefits of claiming a divine period at end of rights. Initially, appeals to rights were often advanced by citizens against the Crown, which claimed divine sanction for itself. In order to put some limitations on the rights of monarchs, justifications of the rights of citizens must have at least as strong a foundation—hence the need to justify rights as divinely sanctioned. Anything less would have failed to override the right of monarchs to do whatever they wanted to their subjects. A divine foundation for human rights offers the strongest imaginable basis for claims of natural rights insofar as there is (by definition) no stronger power imaginable than God to guarantee those rights.

One of the other attractive aspects of this tradition, in addition to the power associated with a divine foundation for human rights, is that it places rights firmly in the basic structure of the moral universe. Because rights come from God, they are part of the deep structure of the world rather than merely superficial phenomena posited by individuals or governments.

This foundation is quite powerful for many theists, but it suffers from drawbacks for believers and unbelievers alike. The issue for nontheists, whether they be atheists or agnostics, is obvious: Because they do not believe in God, they will not be convinced to take human rights more seriously because those rights are alleged to be founded in God's will. Yet theists have difficulties with the divine foundation for human rights as well. Many people believe in God without claiming to know God's mind. Even if rights come from God, how are we to know *which* rights God ordained? Indeed, it is not clear even that God, or the divine, speaks the language of rights in many traditions. One is hard pressed to find references to rights in the New Testament or in the work of Confucius or in many Native American religious traditions, to name but a few. It is not that these traditions are opposed to human rights; rather, it is simply that historically their message was not presented in terms of rights at all. One can deduce certain conclusions about rights from their original beliefs, but those implications are in a language foreign to the original.

Natural Law

It is a small step from claims about the divine foundation of human rights to attempts to base human rights in some notion of **natural law.** The natural order, at least insofar as it is uncorrupted by evil, was created by God. Consequently, there is an important (if limited) sense in which the natural is necessarily good. Anything that comes from an all-good source (i.e., God) must be good insofar as it is true to its origins. Furthermore, in many religious traditions, the natural order is oriented toward a final purpose or goal, union with the divine, which is necessarily good. After the goodness of the natural order is established in this way, it is a short step to claiming that people are entitled (that is, have a right) to whatever fulfills the natural order.

Appeals to natural law do not have to have a theistic foundation, but those that dispense with any theistic underpinnings encounter a difficulty not present for theistic theories of natural law and rights. The theistic approach to natural rights is based on a notion of the natural order as fundamentally good (because it comes from, and is oriented toward, the divine). Nontheistic approaches to natural law need some way of establishing that the natural order is fundamentally good. Without this, there is no basis for reaching a normative conclusion about rights without committing the naturalistic fallacy. (Recall that the **naturalistic fallacy** involves illicitly drawing a normative conclusion about what ought to be from a set of purely descriptive

NATURAL LAW ETHICS

Throughout history, the appeal to natural law was not limited to natural rights. Natural rights served to provide a powerful justification for other aspects of the moral code as well. Indeed, in certain traditions (such as Roman Catholicism) it continues today. The Catholic Church's prohibition of birth control, for example, is grounded in a view of the natural order that maintains that the sexual act is naturally oriented toward procreation and that anything that thwarts that purpose is immoral. Similar objections have been advanced against homosexuality.

Philosophically, one of the most interesting things about this tradition is that it bridges the fact/value dichotomy, the gap between *is* and *ought*. Because the natural order of things is created by God, it is fundamentally good. Thus to call something "natural" is to attach a normative as well as a descriptive label to it. It says that something is good, not simply that it is. ∎

premises about what is the case.) Certain versions of naturalism in ethics attempt to avoid this difficulty by adding a premise to such arguments, asserting that the natural order is in some fundamental way good.

Human Nature

In the last few decades, many arguments in support of rights as primary have not depended on appeals to self-evidence, God, or a notion of natural law with a theistic underpinning. Instead, drawing on the Lockean tradition, they have focused on the way in which some fundamental characteristic, or group of characteristics, of human nature (and perhaps of the nature of other types of beings as well) entails the recognition of their rights. Most of these characteristics, which we shall call **rights-conferring properties,** are ones that we think of as distinctively human: the ability to reason, the capability of making free choices, the ability to have interests and to make plans, and the capability of being autonomous. Some, such as the ability to have desires or the ability to suffer, are characteristics that humans share with other beings in the natural world. These arguments move from the existence of such a property to a conclusion about the existence of a corresponding right.

Arguments for *natural* rights that appeal to human nature usually involve the following steps:

- Establish that some characteristic of human nature, such as the ability to make free choices, is a *rights-conferring property,* that is, a property that is:
  - essential to human life
  - either morally good or morally neutral.

- Establish that certain *empirical conditions,* such as the absence of physical constraints, are necessary for the existence or the exercise of that characteristic.
- Conclude that people have a right to those empirical conditions.

This approach, however, is often only the first part of such arguments. As we have seen, to say that someone has a right is only half of the story; we also have to specify what obligations this establishes for other people. Here there is a significant difference between negative rights and positive rights. The final step in arguments for *negative* rights is to

- conclude that people have a *duty not to interfere* with the pursuit of those empirical conditions.

The final step in arguments for *positive* rights is to

- conclude that people (the state, society, or some other specified party) have a *duty to provide* those empirical conditions.

These are quite different.

Let's look more closely at each of these steps.

Determining Rights-Conferring Properties

Clearly, not all characteristics of human nature are rights-conferring properties. Two criteria are most frequently used together to determine which properties qualify as rights-conferring ones. The first criterion is this: *The more essential a property is to being human, the stronger it will be as a rights-conferring property.* Some things are just not important enough. Human beings possess the ability to spit, but few would want to argue that we therefore have a right to spit. Our humanity would not be diminished by restrictions on our freedom to spit. A good test of whether a property is essential to being human is to ask whether restricting it would diminish our humanity. Restricting expressions of religious belief is commonly accepted as something that diminishes our humanity, as are attempts to restrict freedom of expression.

Second, *rights-conferring properties are limited to those characteristics that are morally good or morally neutral.* One can present strong arguments that human beings are by nature aggressive and violent. Yet even if one grants the soundness of such arguments, few would want to conclude that we have a *right* to be aggressive and violent. It is this covertly normative criterion that explains how such arguments-seem to move from an essentially *descriptive* premise stating a characteristic of human beings to a fundamentally *normative* conclusion about a right that human beings have. The normative element is buried in the selection of characteristics that legitimately count as rights-conferring properties.

Several candidates have been advanced for rights-conferring properties. Among the most important of these are

- The fact of being born a human being
- Rationality, the ability to think
- Autonomy, the ability to make free choices
- Sentience, the ability to feel and suffer
- The ability to be a "self" or person
- The ability to have projects and plans

Some of these, such as rationality or the ability to be a self, are applicable only to human beings. Others, like the ability to suffer, are characteristics that human beings share with other kinds of beings, especially animals. These open the door to a notion of animal rights.

Rights-Conferring Properties and Indicators

There may be a difference between a rights-conferring property and the indicators that tell us that a being possesses that property. This is the case with a characteristic like brain wave activity, which is sometimes used as an indication of whether a being is able to think. If the ability to think is a rights-conferring property, then brain wave activity may be an indicator of its presence. We don't have rights because of brain wave activity. We have them because of the ability to think, and we determine whether a particular being has this ability or not by examining (among other things) brain wave activity.

One of the continuing controversies among rights theorists is trying to specify the rights-conferring properties and indicators in such a way that they are neither too broad nor too narrow. If they are too broad, they will include beings (e.g., animals) that some people may not consider to be proper rights holders; if they are too narrow, they will exclude beings (e.g., newborn infants or severely mentally retarded human beings) who should be rights holders. Some criteria, such as sentience, threaten to be too broad; some, such as the ability to make free choices, seem to be too narrow.

Determining the Conditions Necessary to the Exercise of Rights-Conferring Properties

After we agree upon a rights-conferring property, the next step in the argument is to determine the conditions necessary to the existence of that property. Typically, the rights-conferring property will be an *ability*, such as the ability to make informed choices or the ability to think. The next step in the argument is to show that certain conditions are necessary to the development or exercise of that ability. Consider our ability to make free choices. If we are to exercise this ability, certain conditions must be met. We must not, for example, be physically constrained. We cannot execute many free choices if we are physically tied up! It also requires information. We can hardly exercise our ability to be free if we do not have any information on which to base our choices.

An Example: Gewirth on Human Rights

All of this is rather abstract. Let's look at a particular example of this kind of argument, one advanced by Alan Gewirth in his book *Reason and Morality* (1978). It is one of the most tightly knit and sustained arguments for a notion of fundamental human rights that has been published in recent years.

Gewirth begins with a simple fact about human beings: They act voluntarily for purposes or ends. Human action is, in other words (at least sometimes), both free and purposive. Human well-being, according to Gewirth, consists of having the conditions necessary for performing purposive acts. Some of these conditions may be physical (absence of physical restraint), whereas others may be less tangible (education or self-esteem). Thus freedom and well-being are necessary to human existence. Because they are necessary, we have a right to them. Gewirth puts it this way:

> Since the agent regards as necessary goods the freedom and well-being that constitute the generic features of his successful action, he logically must also hold that he has rights to these generic features and he implicitly makes a corresponding rights-claim.

To deny that we have a right to freedom and well-being would, in Gewirth's eyes, be equivalent to denying that we must have freedom and well-being. But to deny that we must have freedom and well-being, Gewirth argues, is clearly mistaken. Whenever we claim to be doing anything for a freely chosen purpose, we are implicitly claiming that we must have the conditions necessary for free, purposive actions. Thus we are necessarily committed to believing that human beings must have freedom and well-being. If they must have freedom and well-being, then—according to Gewirth—they have a *right* to freedom and well-being.

The questionable part of Gewirth's argument is that he seems to move from a *fact* about human beings (namely, that they are purposive) to a claim about their *rights*. Critics, such as Alasdair MacIntyre in his book *After Virtue,* have argued that Gewirth's argument is doomed to fail. From the mere fact that human beings *need* some thing, nothing follows about their having a *right* to that thing. Rights, MacIntyre maintains, are simply "moral fictions" that claim an objectivity that they do not in fact possess. We cannot derive a right merely from a need.

There is, however, another way of reading Gewirth's argument that avoids MacIntyre's objection. Far from deriving a right from a need, Gewirth is advancing a **transcendental argument** in support of certain rights. Typically, transcendental arguments are arguments that claim to establish the conditions necessary to explain some undeniable fact. In our discussion of freedom and determinism, we encountered a typical transcendental argument: If we are to make sense out of making any choices at all, then we must posit freedom. Furthermore, we have to assume that we make *some* choices, even if it is only the choice about whether to accept this as a good argument or not. Thus a transcendental argument takes an undeniable fact and articulates the conditions necessary to it.

Gewirth's argument can be read as a transcendental argument of this type. The undeniable fact is that we are free and purposive beings. If someone tries to deny this, he or she is engaging in free and purposive activity. It would be deeply inconsistent and irrational to say that we are free and purposive beings and at the same time to deny that we have a right to be such. Implicitly claiming a right to be free and purposive is a condition of the possibility of being free and purposive. We are not dealing with some peripheral human need (such as the desire for a color TV set) or incidental characteristic (such as liking soccer), but rather with the core conditions of being human. Being free and purposive beings is at the very heart of being human, and it would be deeply irrational to deny that we have a right to be the kind of being that we most fundamentally are.

A Concluding Question

The value of MacIntyre's objection to Gewirth's position is that it focuses our attention on one of the central questions in the development of a theory of human rights: Which human characteristics—whether these be abilities, needs, or whatever—justify claims about human rights?

We can, of course, avoid—or at least postpone—MacIntyre's objection by introducing a premise claiming that we have a right to whatever we need, but such a premise is clearly not true as it stands. Drug addicts may need cocaine, but this fact hardly establishes that they have a right to it. I may need a new computer, but it's not clear that there is any interesting sense in which I have a *right* to one. If there is any defensible premise that links needs and rights in the desired way, it is clearly much more restricted in scope than a general claim that we have a right to whatever we need.

The central question that remains here is whether we have a right to anything simply by virtue of the fact that we are human beings—and if we do have such a right, to what, precisely, does it entitle us?

Who Has Rights?

As we have seen, there is considerable controversy about the criteria for judging whether a being possesses rights or not: sentience, rationality, free will, and the ability to have projects and interests were just a few of the candidates for the principal rights-conferring property. Our answer to this question has important implications for our position on what kinds of beings have rights. There is little controversy about acknowledging that adult human beings with normal capabilities possess rights; indeed, they are the paradigm case of rights-holders. If anyone is capable of possessing rights, it is such adult human beings. There are, however, borderline cases even in this area. Many of them are found at the beginning or end of life. Fetuses, babies born with only a brain stem but no higher functions, people in apparently irreversible comas, and the elderly who have lost a sense of personal identity all provide difficult cases that are often filled with moral anguish.

Let us briefly consider three areas in which the issue of rights emerges in provocative and puzzling ways: the rights of future generations, the rights of animals, and the rights of other living entities in the environment, such as trees.

The Rights of Future Generations

Generally, we think of rights as belonging only to *existing* individuals. Even in the controversy about the rights of the fetus, most opponents of abortion argue that the fetus is already a person, not just that it is a future, potential person. Yet future generations are more remote, more indeterminate than fetuses. Although we know that, barring some major disaster of global proportions, there will be future generations, we have absolutely no idea of who will comprise them. It seems odd, in light of most of our criteria, to think that nonexistent beings have rights. It is doubly odd if one further recognizes that if we treat the environment and one another sufficiently badly, there may be no future generations whose rights could be violated.

Despite these logical difficulties, there is a strong intuition in everyday morality that we owe something—at least a minimally habitable world environment—to future generations; and if we owe it to them, then they would seem to have a right to it. There is an underlying metaphor here that is quite powerful. Parents have duties to their children, and those children have rights vis-à-vis their parents. It is this metaphor that underlies our intuitions that unborn generations have rights, yet the logical constraints of the language of rights makes it extremely difficult, perhaps impossible, to give a coherent account of what it would mean to say that future generations have rights.

Animals and Rights

The case of animals presents an increasingly intriguing challenge for rights theorists. The arguments usually turn on two issues: (1) what properties are necessary for the possession of a right, and (2) do animals possess those necessary properties? The candidates for rights-conferring properties are precisely the ones that we would expect at this point: rationality, free will, interests and projects, and sentience. Because we have already surveyed the issues surrounding rights-conferring properties, we shall concentrate here on whether animals possess any or all of these properties.

Sentience, the ability to feel pleasure and pain, is the characteristic that almost everyone agrees that animals possess. Unfortunately for animal rights advocates, it is also the weakest candidate for being a rights-conferring characteristic. If the ability to feel pleasure and pain is a sufficient condition for having rights, then a number of different kinds of beings—presumably including fetuses—have rights. Some philosophers, such as Joel Feinberg, have maintained that animals do in fact have *interests,* and this is one of the characteristics that distinguishes them from mere things. One can act on behalf of an animal, for the sake of that animal, but it is impossible to act on behalf of a mere thing because there is no "behalf" or "sake" to act for. It is meaningful to talk about what is good for an animal in a way that would not make sense for rocks. One of the attractions of this view is that it would allow us to categorize the level of complexity of interests and perhaps work out a thesis about the proportionality of rights to interests.

Although there is relatively little prospect of showing that animals (with the possible exception of cats!) have *free will* in any interesting sense, proponents of animal rights point out that free will is too demanding a criterion for rights. Infants, adults in comas, and so forth would all fail the test. *Rationality* is a more promising candidate, but it suffers from some of the same drawbacks that the free will criterion possesses: It threatens to exclude certain classes of human beings to whom we would usually want to accord rights. If we take *language* as a typical rights indicator, then research into possible language use by dolphins, whales, and chimps becomes morally relevant.

If we were to acknowledge that animals have rights, then we would have the further question of what rights they have. Most proponents of animal rights argue that animals possess the right to live and the right to be free from unnecessary pain. Some maintain that these animal rights are as strong as human rights; others acknowledge that animals have rights but see those rights as less strong than the rights of human beings. The difficulty with this position, which seems to be a reasonable one, is that it raises the question of whether an animal's right can *ever* override a human being's right—and if it can't, then it seems pointless to attribute rights to animals.

Do Trees Have Standing?

The final question to be mentioned here is whether the environment has rights. This is the least plausible claim because the environment possesses none of the candidates for rights-conferring properties that we have discussed here. Yet our negative answer to this question does tell us something important about ourselves and the nature of the world in which we live.

Religious traditions have often been in the forefront of those who have attributed something like rights to the natural environment, although it is not clear that the language of rights provides the most appropriate idiom. Native Americans often have sacred places that they respect and that they treat as if those places had rights. Similarly, a number of religions have certain sacred animals that possess something like rights. There is a corresponding tradition in Christianity that sees human beings as stewards of creation, guardians of the natural world who are charged with preserving that world.

Our modern concept of the natural environment is largely shaped by the influence of natural science rather than by religious beliefs. We perceive nature differently because of science—in particular, we perceive it as oddly lifeless and lacking in integrity. Advances in science show all matter to be "in motion," and hence, far from "lifeless," but our common conception of the natural environment lags curiously behind. Imagine what it would be like if our only interaction with human beings were as medical doctors. Human beings would then be just biological systems showing certain disorders that need to be corrected. If we approached human beings solely as doctors (or biologists, for that matter), we would never arrive at the concept of a person and thus never come to an understanding that human beings have rights. Analogously, as we approach the natural world from a scientific or technological standpoint, we are unable even to see the ways in which the natural environment may have rights or an integrity of its own.

Finally, we should note two additional issues that are intertwined with the question of whether the environment can have rights. First, we may indeed have a moral relationship to our environment, but perhaps it is not best understood in terms of rights. The language of rights may simply be too confrontational, too individualistic, to capture the proper relationship of harmony between human beings and the natural world. Second, we should be aware that the rights of future generations are also intertwined with these issues insofar as future generations may have rights *to* the environment. When we abuse the environment, we may be violating the rights of future generations to its resources.

MORAL RIGHTS

Contemporary philosophers are divided over the issue of whether rights are primary and overriding of all other types of considerations (including other types of moral factors), or whether rights are secondary and other moral considerations can override them. Whereas advocates of a notion of natural rights usually fall into the former camp, defenders of a notion of rights as principally **moral rights** generally fall into the latter camp. They maintain that rights are secondary to, and derivative of, other moral considerations— and that, consequently, rights may be overridden by those other moral considerations. Within the Kantian tradition, philosophers often argue that rights are simply correlatives of duties. Within a utilitarian tradition, the existence and enforcement of rights are seen as dependent on considerations of utility. Within a contractarian tradition, rights emerge as dependent on a specific (although largely implicit) social contract and without justification outside of the community constituted by that contract. Rights do not come first in any of these traditions.

In the Western intellectual tradition, the notion of natural human rights has been subjected since Bentham to a sustained critique that has gradually made the notion of natural rights peripheral in our own day. The notion of rights has remained, but it has generally become a derivative or secondary ethical concept, dependent on something else (e.g., utility or duty) for its validity.

Utilitarian Arguments for Rights

Also since the time of Bentham, utilitarians have been suspicious of approaches to ethics that begin with rights as primary. This is not because they are against rights *per se,* but rather because they feel that rights—like everything else—are justified only to the extent that they maximize utility. Thus for most utilitarians, rights can be overridden if they conflict with other, stronger considerations of utility. This is in sharp contrast to the position of strong rights theorists like Ronald Dworkin, who maintains in *Taking Rights Seriously* that considerations of utility can never outweigh basic rights.

This issue has far-reaching practical implications. Consider the following example. Imagine a situation in which a very small tribe of Native Americans through a treaty owns an area of land that, although initially thought to be worthless, in fact contains valuable mineral resources essential to national security. Imagine, furthermore, that the land has a sacred meaning for the indigenous people and that the sacred character of the place precludes activities such as mining. A strong rights theorist would maintain that the Native Americans have a right to their own land and a right to use it as they see fit, no matter how much benefit would accrue to the larger society as a whole if mining were permitted on the land. Utilitarians, on the other hand, would weigh all the possible consequences of either allowing the land to remain a sacred place or using it for mining and then choose the alternative that maximized utility—and that alternative may well be the one that deprives the Native Americans of their rights.

This is not to deny, of course, that utilitarians can be defenders, even strong defenders, of human rights. It is merely to say that they defend such rights *only* insofar as defending such rights maximizes utility. A utilitarian might, for example, be a strong defender of the rights of the disabled but will do so only insofar as such rights maximize the benefits to society as a whole. A strong rights theorist, on the other hand, would defend such rights even if they failed to maximize utility for society overall.

Kant, Rights, and Duties

There have been two distinctively Kantian approaches to the issue of rights. The first, and more traditional, has been to see rights in terms of the obligations they impose on others. The other approach has been to explore the link between rights and respect. Let's briefly consider both of these approaches.

Rights and Obligations

In Kant and other **deontological** (duty-based) approaches to ethics, rights are simply the correlates of duties. It is duty or obligation that comes first, and rights follow from duties. I have a duty, for example, to keep my promises, and as a result of this duty those to whom I make a promise have a right to hold me to it. Duties ground rights, not vice versa. For deontological approaches to ethics, it is possible to reduce—and thus, in principle, to eliminate—all statements about rights to statements about duties. Yet duty is a broader category than rights because we may have some duties (including what Kant calls imperfect duties) that do not give any particular person a right in relation to us. We may have a duty to give to the poor, but that does not entitle any specific poor person to claim a right to some of our money. In addition to such imperfect duties, Kant sometimes claims that we have duties to ourselves—but it hardly makes sense to claim that we have a right that we can claim against ourselves.

The dispute between deontologists and strong rights theorists is in part a matter of emphasis. Whereas deontologists see the fundamental question of the moral life to be, "What ought I to do?" strong rights theorists focus principally on the question, "What do I have a right to do?" Whereas for the deontologists morality is about obligations to others, for the rights theorists it is about rights for oneself and others. Whereas one will concentrate on fulfilling duty, the other will be concerned primarily with defending claims about rights.

Rights and Respect

There is another aspect of Kant's moral philosophy that is tied more closely to the issue of rights. One version of the categorical imperative is to "respect humanity, whether in others or in oneself." To respect humanity, some contemporary Kantians have suggested, is to respect human beings' rights as autonomous, rational beings. The most fundamental right of human beings within this tradition is precisely to exercise their nature as autonomous, rational beings, that is, as beings able to freely give the law of reason to themselves.

Notice that Kantians hold that we have this duty to ourselves as well as to other people. In an influential article entitled "Servility and Self-Respect," Thomas Hill, Jr. has argued that failure to respect *one's own* rights is a moral failing. He discusses hypothetical examples of the self-deprecator, the Uncle Tom, and the deferential wife. "The moral defect in each case," Hill argues, "is a failure to understand and acknowledge one's own moral rights." We have a duty to respect our own rights as well as the rights of others.

A Pluralistic Approach to Rights

Although there is obviously disagreement among deontologists, utilitarians, and others about the proper justification of rights, there is also wide-ranging agreement that rights do play an important role in the moral life. *Rights establish minimum standards for our interactions with other people, a moral "floor" below which we do not want to sink in our interactions with one another.* We should not let the disagreements among these various traditions, important as they are, overshadow the significant extent to which they agree that rights do establish minimum requirements in our dealings with other people. Rights occupy a crucial place in the moral universe.

We can integrate the various approaches to the issue of rights that strong rights theorists and deontologists, utilitarians, and contractarians take. Strong rights theorists are saying that we have certain rights simply by virtue of the fact that we are human beings—all human beings have these rights and, at least initially, have them to the same degree. In addition to this, certain rights are recognized by those who accept a particular philosophical theory, such as utilitarianism or Kant's ethics. What we are finding is that, at least in regard to certain basic rights, there is widespread agreement among different traditions. Yet such agreement is of little help unless it can be translated into a consensus on specific rights. Let's turn to a specific consideration of what rights we have.

WHAT RIGHTS DO WE HAVE?

Our discussion of rights has been rather general until this point. Now we need to turn to an even more difficult question. Granting that we do have rights, *which* rights do we have? Perhaps the clearest way of approaching this issue is to refine and expand our earlier distinction between negative and positive rights.

Negative Rights: Rights to Noninterference

Negative rights, as we have already indicated, are misnamed: It is not really the rights that are negative, but rather the corresponding obligations imposed on the right observers. In the case of so-called negative rights, rights observers are obligated only to refrain from interfering with the rights holder's exercise of the right. Traditionally in American political thought, there have been three main rights to noninterference. Interestingly, the French Declaration of the Rights of Man and Citizen contains three rights as well, but only one is the same as that in the U.S. Declaration of Independence. For the French, the three main rights are liberty, fraternity, and equality.

The Right to Liberty

Virtually all philosophers believe that we have a *right to liberty,* that is, a right to pursue the projects and goals of our choice as long as doing so does not impinge on the rights of others. All people are obliged to observe our right to liberty by not interfering with our actions unless our actions interfere with their own rights to liberty. We all have a right, in other words, to the highest degree of liberty consistent with an equal degree of liberty for all.

Virtually all political movements in America are committed to the importance of the right to liberty, and it is one of the cornerstones of American democracy. However, there is at least one political philosophy and movement—libertarianism, at least in what James Sterba has called its "Spencerian" tradition—that takes my liberty as the *only* right we have. All other rights are derivative from, and thus cannot override or contradict, the right to liberty. Libertarians in this tradition are strongly opposed to any but the most unavoidable governmental restrictions. The strength and exclusivity of their commitment to liberty cut across traditional categories of liberal and conservative. They are as opposed to governmental regulation of big business as they are to governmental regulation of pornography. The sole value that they seek to preserve and enhance is the individual's right to liberty.

Joel Feinberg

TALKING ABOUT ETHICS: A CONVERSATION WITH JOEL FEINBERG ABOUT HUMAN RIGHTS

Joel Feinberg, a professor emeritus at the University of Arizona, is the author of numerous works on moral and legal philosophy, including *Rights, Justice and the Bounds of Liberty.*

Hinman: Throughout your work, you have continually come back to the concept of rights as fundamental to ethics. What is it about the rights perspective that you find so compelling?

Feinberg: I would like to place the answer to that question within the context of my life, but before doing so let me clarify a couple of things. First, we are talking here about moral rights, not only legal ones. These are rights that exist prior to, and independent of, legal enactment. Second, I understand a right to be a type of claim that is somewhere between the two extremes of force and begging.

I came into an awareness of the world at the end of World War II, and I have a number of examples of the kinds of horrors that shaped my awareness of rights:

- A world depression in the 1930s and inflation in the 1920s that left millions destitute
- World War II with 40 million dead and the Holocaust with 10 million dead
- Prohibitions in the United States against the use of contraceptives by married couples, eventually overturned in *Griswold v. Connecticut*
- The torture and murder of thousands of persons, mostly women, in Brazil and Argentina
- Women undergoing a ritual sexual mutilation, something that is done to millions of young girls every year, and usually done with an unsterilized razor blade
- Followers of the Ba'hai faith in Iran not being allowed to pursue their religious practices

What these examples have in common is the fact that in every one of them, people's moral rights have been egregiously violated. It is worth noting, too, that in several of these cases, the majority of the victims have been women. They have not been permitted to claim what is properly theirs.

Hinman: Does the rights perspective offer the best way of viewing these moral issues?

Feinberg: The best way is the way that fits the data at hand. Certainly there are other considerations in addition to rights.

Hinman: Criticisms of appeals to rights have a long history, beginning with Bentham's charge that rights are just "nonsense on stilts." What do you think of this criticism?

Feinberg: Let me rebut at least one version of this criticism simply by looking more closely at the criticism itself. One of the things that's said against my view and the view of other people who are called rights theorists is that this perspective promotes selfishness, that it is itself an expression of a kind of selfishness and divisiveness. Both left and right communitarians have held that view. Jeremy Waldron, after surveying some of these views in his book *Nonsense on Stilts,* concludes that Bentham, Burke, and Marx all see the rights of man as embodying "a demand for the immediate and unqualified gratification of purely selfish individual desires."

To come back from the examples of Gestapo and Nazis and rusty razor blades, and now to discover that the criticisms of those cases are invalidated because the rights perspective is selfish—I find this kind of criticism absurd and astonishing. Was the Indian woman in the nineteenth century who did not want to be burned alive on her husband's funeral pyre *(suttee)* being selfish when she objected? Are those who protested on her behalf being selfish? I find such a question morally absurd.

What does it mean, furthermore, to say that people are selfish? Does it mean that they pursue their own self-interest? Then we're all selfish. For this criticism to have any content, it must mean that selfish people are *excessively* concerned with their own welfare—and this simply seems false in the cases I've mentioned. Indeed, it borders on the grotesque to think that, for example, the victims of the terror in Argentina in the 1980s were being selfish because they tried to avoid being thrown alive out of airplanes.

Hinman: That raises an interesting limitation of these criticisms of rights: They seem to presuppose that all appeals to rights are made by the rights bearers themselves. Yet often assertions of rights are made on behalf of the powerless by others who do not themselves benefit directly from asserting those rights.

Feinberg: That's correct. Assertions of rights can be made in the first, second, or third person and in the singular or plural. And it's absolutely absurd and ridiculous to say of the girl who doesn't want to be circumcised with a rusty razor blade that she's being selfish.

Hinman: Some feminist critics have argued in a somewhat different way. The perspective of rights, they argue, will typically bring into prominence questions of individuality, separateness, etc., whereas a perspective of care or compassion might bring more clearly into focus the ways we are connected to each other.

Feinberg: It's not always clear what is being asserted here, but one interpretation is that rights are by their very nature a threat to the existence of genuine communities, including communities embodied in marriages, families, and friendships. The further implication is the appeals to rights in contexts of personal relations are strident and destructive of relationships.

Several points can be made about this type of claim. First, rights claims need not be made querulously or antagonistically; they can be made gently, regretfully, in a caring fashion, and in ways that may thus preserve important relationships. Second, rights occupy—or should occupy—an important place in love. Part of loving other people is recognizing and respecting their rights. We may very well want more for people we love than just what they have a right to, but certainly we want at least that much for them. Third, none of this should be construed as a suggestion that rights are the *only* good in the moral world or that they are sufficient for a good life. We may need many other things for a good life as well: affection, love, and physical safety. But none of this provides a good reason for devaluing rights.

The Right to Life

Talk about rights usually arises out of a context of political repression, and repressive regimes throughout history have threatened to kill those who challenge them. Minimally, the right to life asserts that other people are not entitled to kill us. Generally, this is a relatively uncontroversial right, but there are at least four areas in which contention still exists.

First, although there is widespread agreement throughout the world that the state does not have the right to kill people as a form of punishment, a few countries—the United States, some Middle Eastern countries—still claim that *capital punishment* is justified and continue to practice it. A very few countries, again including the United States, further maintain that the state has the right to kill adolescents or adults for their actions undertaken when they were adolescents.

Second, the right to life is most often invoked today in regard to the issue of *abortion*. The claim is simply that the fetus has a right to life and, consequently, no one is entitled to kill it except possibly under certain very narrowly circumscribed circumstances such as when the continuation of a pregnancy poses a direct threat to the pregnant woman's life. Usually there is little disagreement among the disputing parties about the validity of the right to life; rather, the disagreement centers on two other, related issues. First, does the fetus have a right to life in the same way that adults are generally recognized as having a right to life? This debate usually centers on whether the fetus is a person or not. However, for those (such as animal rights proponents) who hold that rights are not restricted to human beings, it would seem that even if the fetus were not a person, it could have rights to some degree. Second, if the fetus does have a right to life, can that right be overridden by the rights of the pregnant woman? Since *Roe v. Wade,* the primary *constitutional* ground for abortion has been the pregnant woman's right to privacy, which is seen as overriding any interest the state may have at least during the first trimester of pregnancy and, with qualifications, during the second trimester as well. Among the other arguments that have been advanced in support of a woman's right to choose to have an abortion is the claim that all people own their own bodies and thus have a right to control their own bodies. This will be discussed in more detail when we consider the right to property.

Third, some people—usually strong pacifists—maintain that the *right to life is absolute* and that consequently no one has the right to take the life of another human being. Some of the most influential moral leaders of our time, including Gandhi and Martin Luther King Jr., have espoused this belief and lived by it.

Fourth, animal rights activists and others claim that *the right to life is not restricted to human beings.* They argue that animals have a right to live and that we do not have the right either to kill them or to make them suffer.

There is a common thread running through all four of these cases, one that suggests a deep and pervasive respect for the right to life in all its forms. Insofar as this respect is based on a conviction that all living beings have a right to live and thrive, this suggests a powerful version of the right to life that cuts across traditional political boundaries. Except for the fact that it neglects the rights of animals, the doctrine of the "seamless garment" developed by the American Catholic bishops incorporates this deep respect for the right to life and forges a strong link between opposition to abortion and opposition to war. Respect for the right to life, they maintain, ought to be pervasive, not selectively applied only in certain types of cases.

Finally, there is a cluster of issues centering on the *end* of life that is a continuing area of moral discussion. Do people have the right to end their own

DO WE OWN OUR OWN BODIES?

One of the more interesting arguments advanced in support of a woman's right to choose an abortion has centered on property rights: A woman owns her own body and thus is entitled to do with it (including with the fetus, which is part of it) as she pleases.

This argument seems to involve two controversial principles. First, is ownership the best way of understanding our relationship to our own bodies? True, no one else owns them. But does the idea of ownership really capture the way in which we are related to our own bodies? If we own something, we can usually sell it—but that is hardly true about our bodies. Moreover, to own something implies a relationship of detachability, if not distance: What I own is separate from me. But it seems more accurate to think of my own body as part of me.

Second, even if we do own something, it is not clear—despite the tradition of Locke and Blackstone—that we can do whatever we want with what we own. Do we, for example, have a right to mutilate ourselves simply because our bodies are our own? If we own a priceless and irreplaceable work of art, do we have a right to do whatever we want with it—including scratching it up or destroying it—simply because we own it?

This is not, of course, to deny that we have a right to abortion, but simply to question whether the argument from ownership is a good one or not. ▪

lives voluntarily? Do others, especially physicians who have taken the Hippocratic oath, have the right to assist terminally ill people in voluntarily bringing about their own death? As contemporary medicine continues to improve its ability to keep people alive even when they cannot live a minimally satisfying life, this issue will become increasingly important. So, too, will the issue of how we define "life." Is life simply a matter of continued breathing, or is it more than that?

The Right to Property

The right to property lies at the heart of Western political thought since the time of John Locke. The English jurist William Blackstone exemplifies this tradition in his *Commentaries on the Laws of England,* one of the most influential documents in the development of American legal thought. He describes the right to property in the following terms:

> The third absolute right [after life and liberty], inherent in every Englishman, is that of property: which consists in the free use, enjoyment and disposal of all his acquisitions, without any control or diminution, save only by the laws of the land. . . . So great moreover is the regard of the law for private property that it will not authorize the least violation of it; no, not even for the general good of the whole community.

Clearly rejecting any utilitarian attempts to limit property rights on the basis of overall utility, Blackstone takes the right to property as absolute and unlimited. Indeed, there seem to be no constraints placed on people's use of their own property. The right to property became the paradigm or model on which all other rights are understood.

Those—including some libertarians in the Lockean tradition—who take the rights to life and property as basic are also deeply committed to the right to liberty, but for somewhat different reasons. For these Lockeans, the right to liberty is necessary in order to provide the necessary freedom to exercise the rights to life and property. In fact, the right to liberty may be redundant in this tradition because to say that we have rights to life and property is to claim the freedom necessary to pursue these rights. As Sterba has put it, for "Lockean libertarians, liberty is the ultimate political ideal because liberty just is the absence of constraints in the exercise of people's fundamental rights."

The Right to Equality

During recent decades in America, the right to equality has been a central consideration in our political and social life. From the civil rights movement of the 1960s through the movement for women's rights in the 1970s into the most recent legislation of the 1990s about the rights of Americans with disabilities, there has been a common theme of equal treatment and equal opportunity. It is a fundamental conviction of American society, even if we fail to live up to it in every instance, that we all have a right to be treated the same.

The right to equality has an unusual logical status because it is almost a "metaright," that is, a right that guarantees how we hold other rights. It guarantees that we all have the *same* rights, that some persons are not accorded an unfair or unjust advantage over others. For this reason, the right to equality is closely related to the idea of justice. To treat people justly is to treat them equally, not to give some an unfair advantage over others.

The right to equality has aspects of both negative rights and positive rights. It clearly imposes a negative obligation not to unjustly deprive certain people of opportunities on the basis of their race, sex, and so forth. In this way, the right to equality would prevent racial discrimination in regard to applicants for college or professional schools. However, it often goes further than this. If we need to provide people with equal *opportunity*, then this may require positive action on our part to ensure that such opportunity is present. At what point is equal opportunity provided? Consider the issue of minority admission to medical schools. Is equal opportunity guaranteed simply by not discriminating against minority applicants? What if societal conditions usually provide minorities with far fewer opportunities to compete equally earlier in life? Are we then providing genuinely equal opportunity to minority applicants to medical school merely by not discriminating against them at this relatively late point in the game? Considerations such as these have led some to conclude that the right to equal treatment entails positive obligations to provide opportunities to overcome previous discrimination.

Positive Rights: Rights to Well-Being

Do our rights end with negative rights? Are we entitled to claim only noninterference from other people, or do we have a right in some instances to expect something *positive* from them? If we do have positive rights, who is thereby obligated?

There have been two distinct approaches to the issue of positive rights, and these paint very different pictures of the place of positive rights in the moral landscape. On one hand, there are those who have maintained that, in addition to negative rights, we have certain other, positive rights. This suggests a twofold division of rights into negative and positive rights, a division embodied in the organization of this chapter. This approach has been reinforced by critics of positive rights. In denying the existence of positive rights, libertarians and others have accepted the twofold division of rights into negative and positive rights and simply argued that one of the two categories is empty. There is, however, a second approach to the issue of positive rights that suggests that *all* rights have both positive and negative aspects. The right to life, for example, would contain both a negative element that forbids others to kill us and a positive element that entitles us at least to the bare minimum necessary to life, such as food, clothing, shelter, and safety.

Rights to Well-Being

The second half of the twentieth century has witnessed a growing conviction that human beings have more than negative rights, that they have positive rights to the conditions necessary to their well-being. Not only, for example, do they have a right to life that entails that other people ought not to kill them, but also they have a right to life that entitles them to the kind of physical security necessary to human flourishing. The state is thereby obligated to provide such security. Similarly, the right to life entails a right to the basic conditions necessary to life: a right to employment and other goods necessary to subsist as a human being. This is the murkiest area of rights theory because it seems to open the door to an almost endless expansion of rights.

Positive Rights and Correlative Obligations

Rights theorists who both (1) support strong positive rights to well-being and (2) see rights as entailing correlative positive duties on the part of rights observers are faced with a significant challenge. These two beliefs together seem to create what Rodney Peffer in his "A Defense of Rights to Well-Being" (1998) has called "the problem of near innumerable positive obligations." The difficulty is clear. If we have extensive rights to well-being, and if people have positive duties to do things to fulfill those rights to well-being, then everyone will be saddled with countless duties to perform actions that will ensure that everyone else's rights to well-being are met.

When faced with a dilemma of this kind, we have three options: We can choose to deny either the first or the second horn of the dilemma, or we can try to go between the horns of the dilemma. Each of these first two options has been tried. Some philosophers (including most libertarians) have denied that we have positive rights, and this is certainly one way of eliminating the problem. Others, like McCloskey, have denied that rights entail corresponding duties. Peffer goes in this direction as well, denying that certain classes of positive rights entail corresponding positive obligations. So far, no one seems to have succeeded in going through the horns of the dilemma. Yet there does seem to be a way through the horns of the dilemma, namely, to admit that positive rights entail obligations, but that these obligations are shouldered by the group as a whole (usually, the nation), not by each individual separately.

Positive Rights: Social Contract Rights

The notion of *social contract rights* fills an important gap in our picture of rights. In discussing rights, it is important to distinguish between (1) rights to which *any* human being is entitled and (2) rights that belong to people who live in a particular society at a particular time. The former are natural rights that belong to people simply by virtue of their being human, whereas the latter belong to those who have them by virtue of their participation in a particular social contract. Whereas a right to freedom of the press may be part of the social contract in many contemporary Western societies, it would hardly be meaningful to speak of such a right as part of the social contract in societies that have no written language. Similarly, rights to health care presuppose a specific social contract, institutions, and practices that are not found in all societies.

One of the clearest examples of a social contract right in our own society is to be found in the rights of the disabled. During the past two decades, the rights of disabled students have become firmly established in our society with federal legislation requiring equality of educational opportunity. In 1990, the Americans with Disabilities Act extended this protection to disabled persons at all stages of life. It "bars discrimination against the physically and mentally disabled in public accommodations, private employment, and government services, and . . . also requires most businesses, transportation systems, public accommodations, and telecommunications systems to make changes in their plants and equipment to facilitate access for the handicapped" (Kavka, p. 262). The act raises important issues that bear on the controversy between utilitarian approaches to rights and the approaches of strong rights theorists. For a utilitarian, the rights of the disabled (or anyone else, for that matter) are to be guaranteed only to the extent that doing so maximizes overall utility. Yet the clear message of the Americans with Disabilities Act is that these rights are to be respected, even if doing so does not maximize utility in the narrow sense.

The strongest argument in support of establishing such a right as part of our social contract centers on the role of work in the creation and mainte-nance of self-respect. Beginning with a Rawlsian premise that self-respect is a vital primary good and the conviction that distributive justice prescribes "easing the plight of society's less fortunate members" (p. 272), Gregory Kavka has argued that in modern societies such as our own in which the work ethic is central, self-respect is achieved primarily through the recogni-tion that comes from workplace achievements. Given that those with disabil-ities are less likely to be able to achieve appropriate workplace recognition without enabling legislation, it is important to ensure equality of opportu-nity for them whenever possible.

THE LIMITS OF RIGHTS TALK

In recent years there has been a significant increase in criticism of rights-based approaches to morality. Let's consider three strains of that criticism: the claim, stemming from Bentham, that talk about rights is just "nonsense on stilts"; the claim that rights talk places too great an emphasis on individ-ualism and is therefore inimical to the building of genuine community; and the claim that appeals to rights have no place in intimate relationships such as families or close friendships.

Nonsense on Stilts

When Jeremy Bentham argued that talk about human rights is just "non-sense on stilts," he was articulating an attitude toward rights that is still held today. In *After Virtue* (1981), Alasdair MacIntyre pursues the same line of argument, claiming—as we saw in our discussion of MacIntyre's critique of Gewirth—that rights are "moral fictions which . . . purport to provide us with an objective and impersonal criterion, but they do not." MacIntyre does not deny that a given society may *decide* to establish certain rights for members of that society, but his point is that rights do not *exist* prior to, or independently of, such decisions. Moreover, the very notion of rights is a social one, embedded in the fabric of particular societies and invented to further the ideal of autonomy. It is far from universal. There is not even a word for "rights" in any classical European language until the fourteenth century; in Asian languages, it was not until several centuries later that a word for a "right" was introduced. Rights, MacIntyre is suggesting, are so-cial inventions that claim an objectivity and independence that they do not in fact possess. One of the most flagrant examples of such covert inventive-ness is the United Nations Declaration on Human Rights, which contains such rights as the right to "periodic holidays with pay" and the right "to enjoy the arts." Such statements of rights, MacIntyre implies, lack any justification and contain a spurious claim to objectivity.

There is certainly some truth in criticisms such as these, but it is not the whole truth about rights. If there is such a thing as a right to "periodic holidays with pay," it is hardly a universal right of all human beings that has existed throughout all time. It may be a good idea to institute such a right in industrial and postindustrial societies, but it is "nonsense on stilts" to think that such a right has always *existed* in some sense. But critics such as MacIntyre go too far, mistaking sound criticisms of certain rights for good reasons to reject all rights. There is a much stronger case for maintaining that people have a right to life, even when their society fails to recognize it, than there is for maintaining that they have a right to paid holidays. There are a few rights that are truly basic in the sense that it is impossible for us to imagine how a society could flagrantly disregard them and still be a humane and moral society. There are other rights—basic human rights—that are more appropriately understood as being the result of decisions, and these we have described as social contract rights. MacIntyre's criticisms are sound insofar as they are limited to social contract rights that claim to be basic human rights.

Rights, Community, and Individualism

To see the world in terms of rights, it is often argued, is to see human beings as isolated, autonomous individuals who interact with one another essentially as strangers. Although there are certainly circumstances when that way of seeing the world is appropriate, to see the world exclusively in terms of rights stresses individualism at the expense of community. Let's consider some of the reasons in support of this criticism.

The Autonomous Rights Holder

Consider, first of all, the image of the rights holder that underlies much of modern thinking about rights. Essentially, rights holders are isolated individuals who are making claims against other individuals or groups. The basic claim of the rights holder is, "*I* have a right. . . ." Indeed, one finds very little talk in the literature of rights about the rights of groups or any association above the individual level. This is hardly surprising in that the classic texts about human rights, including Hobbes and Locke and Rousseau, all tend to depict the original state of nature as composed of separate individuals, often in a relationship of conflict with one another. Although occasional mention is made of, for example, the family, there is no real notion of the rights of a family as distinct from the rights of the individuals comprising it. Rights are essentially individualistic.

The Right to Liberty

The heavy emphasis on the right to liberty as one of the most important of human rights further emphasizes the individualism characteristic of modern approaches to rights. The right to liberty generally depicts each individual as being entitled to pursue projects and plans as he or she sees fit as long as they do not interfere with other people's right to liberty. Each person is seen as an island, and the purpose of the right to liberty is to ensure that no one imposes any undue expectations or restrictions on the goals that he or she wishes to pursue.

The Right to Privacy

In the Anglo-American tradition, the right to privacy has come to assume an importance not found in other countries, and this has intensified the emphasis on the isolated individual. Interestingly, the right to privacy is not explicitly mentioned in the U.S. Constitution, and it initially found its way—as Mary Ann Glendon tells us in *Rights Talk* (1991)—into constitutional law as a *family* right to privacy that protected a married couple's right to choose to use contraceptives. In *Eisenstadt v. Baird* in 1972, the Supreme Court ruled that decisions about bearing or conceiving children are a matter of individual rights and thus not subject to governmental intrusions. This decision paved the way for *Roe v. Wade* a year later, which grounded a woman's right to choose an abortion in her right to privacy. At this point, the right was firmly established as an exclusively individual right that does not necessitate consent from, or even consultation with, anyone else in the family. The individualism characteristic of this approach emerged most clearly in 1992, when the California State Supreme Court ruled in favor of a minor's right to have an abortion without notifying her parents. The right to privacy became almost an absolute moral right that eclipsed other morally relevant concerns in a situation.

The point of these criticisms is not to suggest that these rights ought to be abolished, nor is it to suggest that individualism is a bad thing. Rather, it is to suggest that an *exclusive* emphasis on rights has a distorting effect on our vision of the moral life. We certainly have rights to liberty, to privacy, and the like; but if those are the only things that we find salient in the moral landscape, we will have a distorted and incomplete picture of the moral life. It will be distorted, seeing people as isolated individuals when they are more than that; it will be incomplete because it fails to see the bonds that hold us together, the relationships of caring, concern, and love that give richness to our personal lives.

Rights and Close Relationships

Recall the California State Supreme Court decision guaranteeing a minor's right to obtain an abortion without parental notification or consent. Without disagreeing with the decision itself, we can certainly ask whether the establishment of such a right addresses the most morally relevant aspects of the situation. Think of the questions that one might want to ask about such a situation. What is the relationship between the pregnant girl and her parents like? Would her parents oppose the abortion if they knew? Why? Would they support her choice, even if they disagreed with it? What impact will her choice have on the relationship between her and her parents? Will the secrecy of the choice estrange her from her parents? Was she already estranged from them? What would it take for this choice to be a genuinely positive one? These are questions that are largely neglected as long as we focus solely on the question of whether the girl has the *right* to make the decision without informing her parents.

There is something odd, critics of rights-based moralities argue, about seeing close relationships primarily in terms of rights. In close family relationships, friendships, and relationships of love, rights are usually irrelevant unless something has gone seriously wrong. In the parental notification case, for example, it is difficult to imagine that the plaintiff finds herself in a family characterized by good communication and a mutual respect for differences. It is necessary to appeal to the right to privacy only when all else has failed.

It is easy to understand why appeals to rights seem out of place in close relationships. Rights, as we have seen, establish the moral *minimum* appropriate to our interactions with other people, and yet intimate relationships are precisely those that are characterized by a concern for the other person that makes the moral minimum either irrelevant or at least much less morally relevant than other considerations such as compassion, care, or love. There is simply more to such relationships than rights, and to see close relationships exclusively in terms of rights is to either miss or to distort much of what is morally significant in them. When someone genuinely cares for another's welfare for the sake of that other person, then questions about moral minimums are usually not in the forefront. Rather, the morally relevant questions are about what is best for the other person and what is best for the relationship. Usually, it is only when relationships begin to break down that appeals to rights come to the fore.

Some of the most interesting work on the connection between rights and relationships has come out of the research of Carol Gilligan. She has argued that the rights orientation is a typically male approach to the moral life that is in sharp contrast to the relationship-oriented approach that usually characterizes females' understanding of the moral life. This controversy is discussed in detail in the chapter on the ethics of diversity, and we shall postpone an extended discussion of this issue until then. Suffice it to note here that feminists have been split on the value of rights talk. On one hand, there is a tradition of feminist thought—exemplified by Gilligan's work—that sees rights talk as a typically male approach to the moral life. Those who work in this tradition have been critical of approaches to the moral life that take rights as central because they feel that such a focus obscures the importance of caring and compassion in the moral life. On the other hand, some feminists have been wary of such a line of reasoning. They have advanced at least two points. First, even within traditional contexts such as the family, it is important to have a strong notion of rights. To ignore rights is to open the door to various kinds of abuse—abuse that they feel is often found in the family. Even the most conservative statistics on the prevalence of child abuse and spousal rape within the family attest to the fact that abuses of rights occur far too frequently within families. Second, they argue that many of the advances that women have gained in this century have been based precisely on appeals to rights. To eschew appeals to rights would be to give up valuable moral and political ground, to retreat from genuine equality.

THE ROLE OF RIGHTS IN THE MORAL LIFE

Rights play a crucial role in the moral life because they define the moral minimum below which we cannot sink in our relations with other people. Basic human rights establish the "floor" for our relations with any other human being whatsoever, the minimal requirements for our treatment of any person at all. It is crucial to the flourishing of the moral life that we have and respect such a set of basic requirements for our interactions with other human beings. Far from being a threat to moral community, rights in fact establish the minimal conditions for the flourishing of a moral community.

We can understand the role of rights in the moral life in terms of some of our earlier metaphors. If we return to our "checks and balances" metaphor, we can see that rights provide a constant check against possible abuses of human dignity, against any attempts to treat people with less respect than they deserve as human beings and as members of a particular moral community. If we were to recast this insight in terms of the nutritional metaphor introduced in chapter 1, we could say that rights are like the minimum daily requirements given for various vitamins and minerals. Health agencies attempt to specify how much of particular nutrients we must minimally have in order to have a healthy life, but this hardly tells us what a wonderful dinner would taste like. Similarly, rights tell us what the minimum daily requirements are for living together—but they hardly tell us what a happy and flourishing community would be like.

Finally, if we were to place this discussion of rights theories within the context of our pluralistic approach in this book, we would see that the appeal to rights is but one among several standards of value. Recall the baseball analogy. Being a good hitter is one of the standards we generally employ in judging who the best baseball player is. It is not, however, the only standard. In some instances (such as pitchers), it may not even be the most important standard. Similarly, rights provide us with an important standard in the moral life, but not the only standard. They are not the whole story of the moral life, and in some instances they are not even the most important part of that story. Rights are about what we minimally owe one another, but often—especially in relationships with people we care about on a personal level—rights are not the morally most salient aspect of the situation because the relationship involves much more than the minimum. The moral life is often about doing more than the minimum, and we must turn to other moral theories—especially virtue ethics—to shed light on those additional elements.

DISCUSSION QUESTIONS

1. Recall your response to **statement 26** ("Morality is basically a matter of respecting people's rights").
   (a) In light of your study of other moral theories, has your rating of this item changed after reading this chapter? If so, in what way? If your rating has not changed, are your reasons for your rating any different now than they were when you first responded to this statement?
   (b) Are there any moral situations in which rights are not of primary importance? If so, describe one such situation. What moral factor in the situation is more important than rights?
2. Recall your rating of **statement 27** ("Some rights are absolute").
   (a) If you agreed with this statement, which rights do you think are absolute? Why?
   (b) Has your rating of this item changed after reading this chapter? If so, in what way? If your rating has not changed, are your reasons for your rating any different now than they were when you first responded to this statement?
3. Recall your rating of **statement 28** ("I have a right to do whatever I want as long as it does not impinge on other people's rights").
   (a) What philosophical/political position does this statement best represent?
4. Recall your response to **statement 29** "People have a right to health care, even if they can't afford to pay for it."
   (a) Do people have any positive rights to welfare? If so, who is obligated to see that these rights are met? How are such rights determined?
   (b) Has your rating of this statement changed after reading this chapter? If so, in what way? If your rating has not changed, are your reasons for your rating any different now than they were when you first responded to this statement?
5. Recall your response to **statement 30** "Animals have rights."
   (a) Do animals have rights? If so, what are those rights? Do all animals have them? How are such rights determined?
   (b) Does the environment have rights? If so, what are those rights? How are they justified?
   (c) Has your rating of this statement changed after reading this chapter? If so, in what way? If your rating has not changed, are your reasons for your rating any different now than they were when you first responded to this statement?

6. In his book *If I Were a Rich Man Could I Buy a Pancreas?* (Blooming-ton: Indiana University Press, 1992), Arthur L. Caplan has discussed a troubling new problem. In recent years in countries where it is not ille-gal, poor people have begun to sell some of their own body parts such as eyes or kidneys to rich people in need of a transplant. Do people own their own bodies? If they do, are they entitled to sell parts of them if they wish to do so? Why or why not?

7. **MOVIE** In the movie *John Q* (2002), Denzel Washington stars as a dis-traught father whose medical insurance won't cover a heart transplant for his son. In desperation, he takes over the hospital's emergency room to force them to do the transplant. This storyline raises interesting ques-tions. Do people have a right to health care? How far does that right extend? Does it just include basic coverage, or does it extend to more cutting-edge procedures such as heart transplants?

8. An NBC television series, *Reasonable Doubt*, contained an unusual char-acter: a female assistant district attorney who is deaf (presumably since early childhood) and has severe difficulty speaking. She has an inter-preter, presumably paid for by the state, to translate what other people say into sign language and to translate her sign language into the spo-ken word. To what extent are governments obligated to provide equal access to all people, including those who are physically impaired? What limits, if any, should apply to the government's obligation to provide equal access? Do private employers have the same obligations?

   Talk with people who have some type of physical handicap. How do they view this issue? What are their reactions to your views?

9. **Smoking and Rights.** Do I have a right to smoke cigarettes in public? Why or why not? In arriving at an answer to this question, what kinds of factors is it legitimate to consider on each side of the question? Do differ-ent philosophical traditions typically present different answers to this ques-tion? Explain. (For further information, see Robert E. Goodin, *No Smoking: The Ethical Issues* [Chicago: University of Chicago Press, 1989].)

10. The U.S. Constitution does not mention (let alone guarantee) U.S. cit-izens the right to privacy. Nevertheless, Americans consider privacy to be a basic human right. How would you defend this concept? (Examine Supreme Court cases on the subject, such as *Griswold v. Connecticut* [1965], or the writings of the late Justice William O. Douglas. The clas-sic article is by Warren and Brandeis, in *Harvard Law Review* [1890]). What rights override the right to privacy? When?

11. **MOVIE** The movie *Gandhi* (1982) presents interesting issues about the relationship between rights and ethical relativism. Are rights relative to whatever the majority—or, in the case of the British in India, the mi-nority who held the majority of political power—believes, or are there basic human rights that no political regime can legitimately override? Why or why not? Do laws such as these requiring that people of one na-tionality carry special identification violate those people's rights? Again, why or why not?

12. **MOVIE** In an old but not dated movie, *The Battle of Algiers* (1965), we see a clear depiction of the French use of torture in Algeria and the Algerian use of terrorist bombs. Discuss the issues of torture and terrorism in time of war. How would human rights advocates view these practices? How would utilitarians view them? What are the strengths and weaknesses of each position?

BIBLIOGRAPHICAL ESSAY

The **classic source** for discussions of rights is John Locke's *Two Treatises on Government* (New York: New American Library, 1965). For a collection of critical essays on the *Treatises*, see Edward J. Harpham, ed., *John Locke's Two Treatises of Government: New Interpretations* (Lawrence, KS: University Press of Kansas, 1992); for critical essays on various aspects of Locke's political philosophy, see Richard Ashcraft, ed., *John Locke: Critical Assessments* (London: Routledge, 1991) and Vere Chappell, ed., *The Cambridge Companion to Locke* (Cambridge: Cambridge University Press, 1994). Also see A. John Simmons, *The Lockean Theory of Rights* (Princeton: Princeton University Press, 1992). For a communitarian critique of Locke, see Thomas L. Pangle, *The Spirit of Modern Republicanism: The Moral Vision of the American Founders and the Philosophy of Locke* (Chicago: University of Chicago Press, 1988). For a nuanced history of the **Universal Declaration of Human Rights**, see Mary Ann Glendon's *A World Made New: Eleanor Roosevelt and the Universal Declaration of Human Rights* (New York: Random House, 2002); despite its title, this work includes a detailed consideration of the contributions of Peng-chun Chang, René Cassin, and Charles Malik as well as Eleanor Roosevelt to the drafting of the Universal Declaration of Human Rights. For a philosophically sophisticated discussion of the U.N. declaraton, see James W. Nickel, *Making Sense of Human Rights* (Berkeley: University of California Press, 1987).

Several excellent **anthologies** contain a number of the most influential philosophical articles on rights in recent years. A. I. Melden's *Human Rights* (Belmont, CA: Wadsworth, 1970) contains excerpts from the Virginia Declaration of Rights, the Declaration of Independence, the Declaration of the Rights of Man and Citizen, and the U.N. Universal Declaration of Rights as well as standard articles by MacDonald, Hart, Vlastos, Wasserstrom, and Morris. David Lyons's *Rights* (Belmont, CA: Wadsworth, 1979) contains the Hart and Wasserstrom articles and pieces by Rawls, Dworkin, Hill, Nozick, Feinberg, and Lyons himself. Jeremy Waldron's *Theories of Rights* (New York: Oxford University Press, 1984) contains papers by MacDonald, Vlastos, Hart, Gewirth, Lyons, Scanlon, Dworkin, Mackie and Raz. Also see Ellen Paul, Fred Miller, and Jeffrey Paul, eds., *Human Rights,* (Oxford: Blackwell, 1984), which was originally published as vol. 1, no. 2 of *Social Philosophy & Policy*; other issues of this journal dealing with rights include *Reassessing Civil Rights* (vol. 8, no. 2); and *Economic Rights* (vol. 9, no. 1); also see Ellen Paul, Fred Miller, and Jeffrey Paul, *Property Rights* (New York: Cambridge University Press, 1994) and *The Right to Privacy* (Cambridge: Cambridge University Press, 2000). Also see the special issue of *Ethics* 92, no. 1 (October, 1981) devoted to rights. More recently, see Harry J. Steiner and Philip Alston, eds., *International Human Rights in Context : Law, Politics, Morals*, 2nd ed. (Oxford: Oxford University Press, 2000).

Two of the most influential **libertarian approaches to rights** are Robert Nozick, *Anarchy, State, and Utopia* (New York: Basic Books, 1974) and Ronald Dworkin, *Taking Rights Seriously* (Cambridge, MA: Harvard University Press, 1977). Tibor Machan's *Individuals and Their Rights* (LaSalle, IL: Open Court, 1989) contains a detailed libertarian defense of the primacy of human rights.

The treatment of rights in **John Rawls's** *A Theory of Justice* (Cambridge, MA: Harvard University Press, 1971) has also been quite influential and will be discussed in the next chapter. Some of the most important work in this area has been done by **Joel Feinberg**, whose essays on this topic are collected in his *Rights, Justice, and the Bounds of Liberty* (Princeton: Princeton University Press, 1980). **Alan Gewirth** first fully presented his account of human rights in his *Reason and Morality* and elaborated them further in *Human Rights: Essays on Justification and Applications* (Chicago: University of Chicago Press, 1982). For a careful overview of the conceptual distinctions involved in thinking about rights, see **Alan White**, *Rights* (Oxford: Clarendon Press, 1984) and Jeremy Waldron, *Liberal Rights: Collected Papers 1981–1991* (New York: Cambridge University Press, 1993). **Judith Jarvis Thomson** has developed a comprehensive account of rights in her *Rights, Restitution, and Risk: Essays in Moral Theory*, edited by William Parent (Cambridge, MA: Harvard University Press, 1986) and *The Realm of Rights* (Cambridge, MA: Harvard University Press, 1990). Carlos Santiago Nino's *The Ethics of Human Rights* (Oxford: Clarendon Press, 1991) is a strong defense of human rights by someone who has lived through many abuses of rights in Argentina as well as the trials that followed them. Carl Wellman's *Real Rights* (New York: Oxford University Press, 1995) offers a strong defense of rights. The Oxford Amnesty Lectures 1993, *On Human Rights*, edited by Stephen Shute and Susan Hurley (New York: Basic Books, 1993), contains excellent lectures by Stephen Lukes, John Rawls, Catharine MacKinnon, Jean-François Lyotard, Agnes Heller, and Jon Elster.

There have been several extended **surveys of the philosophical literature on rights:** Rex Martin and James W. Nickel, "Bibliography on the Nature and Foundations of Rights, 1947–1977," *Political Theory* 6 (1978): 395–413; Martin and Nickel, "Recent Work on the Concept of Rights," *American Philosophical Quarterly* 17 (1980): 165–180; Tibor R. Machan, "Some Recent Work in Human Rights Theory," *American Philosophical Quarterly* 17 (1980): 103–116.

Important discussions of the relationship between **rights and utilitarianism** are to be found in David Lyons's "Utility and Rights," *Nomos XXIV: Ethics, Economics and the Law* (New York: New York University Press, 1982), and Alan Gewirth's response to Lyons, "Can Utilitarianism Justify Any Moral Rights?" in *Human Rights* (Chicago: University of Chicago Press, 1982). For Gewirth's more recent position, see *The Community of Rights* (Chicago: University of Chicago Press, 1996) More recently, Russell Hardin's "The Utilitarian Logic of Liberalism," *Ethics* 97, no. 1 (October 1986): 47–74, presents a utilitarian justification of rights; Arthur Kuflik's "The Utilitarian Logic of Inalienable Rights," *ibid.*, 75–87, criticizes Hardin and pursues an alternative consequentialist path to the justification of inalienable rights. Hardin's position is further developed in his *Morality within the Limits of Reason* (Chicago: University of Chicago Press, 1988), especially chapters 3 and 4. Richard B. Brandt's *Morality, Utilitarianism, and Rights* (Cambridge: Cambridge University Press, 1992) contains two of his most important essays on the place of rights in utilitarianism, "The Concept of a Moral Right and Its Function," and "Utilitarianism and Moral Rights." Also on Mill and rights, see David Lyons, *Rights, Welfare, and Mill's Moral Theory* (New York: Oxford University Press, 1994).

For a provocative contemporary **critique of the appeals to rights**, see Mary Ann Glendon's *Rights Talk: The Impoverishment of Political Discourse* (New York: The Free Press, 1991); Chapter 3 contains a fascinating history of the development of the right to privacy that forms the basis for my treatment of that topic here. The connection between appeals to rights and individualism is discussed in critical detail in C.B. MacPherson's *The Political Theory of Possessive Individualism* (1962). More recently, Joseph Raz has pursued this line of criticism in his "Against Rights-Based Morality," reprinted in Waldron's *Theories of Rights*. Robert Louden's "Rights Infatuation and the Impoverishment of Moral Theory," *Journal of Value Inquiry* 17, no. 2 (1983): 87–102 argues strongly against the tendency to see the moral life solely in terms of rights. For a much more positive evaluation of this connection, see George Kateb's "Democratic Individuality and the Meaning of Rights," in Nancy L. Rosenblum, eds., *Liberalism and the Moral Life*, (Cambridge, MA: Harvard University Press, 1989), 183–206.

For a consideration of the issue of **animal rights,** see the anthology edited by Tom Regan and Peter Singer, *Animal Rights and Human Obligations* (Englewood Cliffs, NJ: Prentice-Hall, 1976). Also see Regan's *All That Dwell Therein: Essays on Animal Rights and Environmental Ethics* (Berkeley: University of California Press, 1982), his classic *The Case for Animal Rights* (Berkeley: University of California Press, 1985), his recent *Defending Animal Rights* (Champaign: University of Illinois Press, 2001), and Singer's *Animal Liberation* (London: Cape, 1976). For a strong critique of this tradition, see Peter Carruthers, *The Animals Issue: Moral Theory in Practice* (Cambridge: Cambridge University Press, 1992.)

For the case in favor of **economic welfare rights**, see especially Henry Shue's *Basic Rights. Subsistence, Affluence, and U.S. Foreign Policy.* For a strong defense of welfare rights, see Rodney Peffer, "A Defense to Rights to Well-Being," *Philosophy and Public Affairs* 8, no. 1 (Fall 1978): 65–87. Also see, most recently, the issue of *Social Philosophy & Policy* 9, no. 1 (Winter 1992), devoted to economic rights. Included in this volume is Gregory S. Kavka's "Disability and the Right to Work," one of the early philosophical pieces on the **rights of persons with disabilities.** More recently, see Anita Silvers, David Wasserman, and Mary Mahowald, eds., *Disability, Difference, Discrimination* (Lanham, MO: Rowman & Littlefield, 1998) and Leslie Francis and Anita Silvers, eds., *Americans with Disabilities*, (New York: Routledge, 2000).

The link between **rights and respect** is developed most forcefully in Joel Feinberg's "The Nature and Value of Rights," reprinted in his *Rights, Justice, and the Bounds of Liberty*, pp. 143–158. It also plays a key role in Thomas Hill's "Servility and Self-Respect;" that essay and his later reflections on it, "Self-Respect Reconsidered," are reprinted in his *Autonomy and Self-Respect* (Cambridge: Cambridge University Press, 1991), pp. 4–18, 19–24.

A. I. Melden's *Rights and Persons* (Berkeley: University of California Press, 1980) contains a sensitive and nuanced discussion of the issue of **rights and the family.** His more recent *Rights in Moral Lives* (Berkeley: University of California Press, 1988) provides a perceptive historical overview of rights theory, including a very illuminating chapter on Mill and human rights and a provocative discussion of animal rights. Loren E. Lomasky's *Persons, Rights, and the Moral Community* (New York: Oxford University Press, 1987) develops a libertarian concept of rights that attempts to be sensitive to issues of community and individual projects. For a perceptive Kantian approach to this issue, see Onora O'Neill "Children's Rights and Children's

Lives," *Ethics* 98 (1988), reprinted in her *Constructions of Reason* (Cambridge: Cambridge University Press, 1989), pp. 187–205. Also see Susan Moller Okin, *Justice, Gender, and the Family* (New York: Basic Books, 1989) and John Hardwig, "Should Women Think in Terms of Rights?" *Ethics* 94 (1984): 441–455.

For a thorough **history of the concept of natural rights,** see Richard Tuck, *Natural Rights Theories: Their Origin and Development* (Cambridge: Cambridge University Press, 1979). On the specifically **American tradition of rights,** see the essays in Michael J. Meyer and W. A. Parent, eds., *The Constitution of Rights: Human Dignity and American Values* (Ithaca, NY: Cornell University Press, 1992).

Citations. The quotation from Alan Gewirth comes from his *Reason and Morality*, p. 63. Feinberg's description of the value of rights is found in "The Nature and Value of Rights," reprinted in Lyons, *Rights*, p. 87. The quotation from Blackstone is found in Mary Ann Glendon's *Rights Talk*, p. 18. Sterba's comment on Lockean libertarians is found in his *How to Make People Just*, p. 11. The quotes from Kavka on rights of the disabled are from his "Disability and the Right to Work," *Social Philosophy & Policy* 9, no. 1 (Winter, 1992): 262, 272.

Further Information. See the page on Rights Theory (http://ethics.sandiego. edu/theories/rights/) in my *Ethics Updates* site for numerous links to resources on the World Wide Web relating to human rights.

JUSTICE: FROM PLATO TO RAWLS

If the concept of human rights is of relatively recent origin, just the opposite could be said about the concept of justice: It is a moral concept with a rich and long history, stretching back before the time of Plato and Aristotle and running as a constant thread from ancient thought to the twenty-first century. No one in the twentieth century stated the importance of justice more eloquently than John Rawls in the famous opening paragraphs of his 1971 classic, *A Theory of Justice:*

> Justice is the first virtue of social institutions, as truth is of systems of thought. A theory however elegant and economical must be rejected or revised if it is untrue; likewise laws and institutions no matter how efficient and well-arranged must be reformed or abolished if they are unjust. Each person possesses an inviolability founded on justice that even the welfare of society as a whole cannot override. For this reason justice denies that the loss of freedom for some is made right by a greater good shared by others. It does not allow that the sacrifices imposed on a few are outweighed by the larger sum of advantages enjoyed by many. Therefore in a just society the liberties of equal citizenship are taken as settled; the rights secured by justice are not subject to political bargaining or to the calculus of social interests. The only thing that permits us to acquiesce in an erroneous theory is the lack of a better one; analogously, an injustice is tolerable only when it is necessary to avoid an even greater injustice. Being first virtues of human activities, truth and justice are uncompromising.
>
> These propositions seem to express our intuitive conviction of the primacy of justice.

Justice, Rawls is telling us, is fundamental to social institutions and the laws that govern institutions and people.

But what, exactly, is justice? This is a long-debated question by philosophers and jurists and political leaders, and our consideration of justice will begin with a brief consideration of one of the earliest philosophical texts about justice: Plato's *Republic*. After that we will look at one of the most recent theories of justice, but one that is extraordinarily powerful: John Rawls's account in *A Theory of Justice* (1972). Then we will turn to a consideration of types of justice, especially distributive justice and conclude with a discussion of just war theory.

PLATO'S ACCOUNT OF JUSTICE

Plato's *Republic* is one of the classics of Western philosophy, and it constitutes a long meditation on the nature of justice. Indeed, after Plato's death *The Republic* was often referred to by its secondary title, "On Justice." Over the course of its ten books, it describes the ideal state, and that itself is the embodiment of justice. For Plato, justice is an unavoidably social and political

Plato's account of justice set the stage for many subsequent discussions of justice.

concept, so a meditation on the nature of justice naturally becomes a meditation on the ideal society and state.

The Athenian Conception of Justice: Justice as Honesty in Word and Deed

In Book 1 of *The Republic*, we see Plato survey several different and conflicting conceptions of justice. It is helpful to look at these, because they provide a set of models for everyday conceptions of justice in our own times. The conversation begins with Cephalus, an elder statesman in Athens and widely recognized as a just man, talking with Socrates, who has asked him what the greatest benefit of his wealth has been. Cephalus replies that as he gets older, he thinks more about what will happen after death and gains hope from the knowledge that he has lived in justice and piety. This prompts Socrates to ask Cephalus what justice is. Cephalus replies that justice comes down to being truthful and paying your debts.

As will occur throughout *The Republic*, Socrates poses objections to the definition of justice. Imagine, Socrates says, that someone has stored his weapons with you. Later, the friend comes back "not in his right mind" and asks you to return the weapons to him. No one would fault us, Socrates says, from refusing to give the weapons back. But if this is so, "then speaking the truth and paying your debts is not a correct definition of justice."

The Conventional View of Justice: Helping Friends and Harming Enemies

Cephalus gives up on defining justice and turns the conversation over to Polemarchus, his son. Polemarchus states the conventional view of justice, namely, that justice consists in helping your friends and harming your enemies. In dealing with your enemies, you should return evil for evil, according to Polemarchus. This definition, Socrates suggests, might be useful in war, but it offers us little guidance in times of peace. Socrates then proceeds to twist Polemarchus' ideas around to the point that Polemarchus seems to be saying that the just person is best at being unjust.

The Cynical View of Justice: Might Makes Right

The next definition of justice that Socrates considers is advanced by Thrasymachus, who maintains that "justice is nothing else than the interest of the stronger." This is a definition that continued to have adherents throughout the twentieth century, most notably in the school of *Realpolitik*. The only thing that makes any difference, this view of justice asserts, is power, and justice is whatever the powerful declare it to be.

There is obviously a certain amount of realism in this view: Justice is rarely achieved without the support of the power structure, but only the cynic agrees with Thrasymachus that justice is *only* the interest of the stronger. If that were the case, there never would be justification for criticizing the state for acting unjustly.

Plato's View of Justice

It would be simple if Socrates then went on to tell us what justice really is, but this is not the way Socrates (and Plato) taught. Rather, we have to look at the entirety of *The Republic* to see what Plato really meant by justice, and even that is the source of much disagreement among scholars. Here I will offer simply one view of what Plato may have meant by justice.

Justice in *The Republic* is harmony, both internal and external. Internal harmony is a proper balance in the soul, and external harmony manifests itself in the state. The virtuous individual possesses inner harmony, a balance among the faculties of the soul. In order to live a good life, the virtuous individual must live in a just society. Thus, inner and outer justice need one another: Without just individuals, a just society is impossible; without a just society, the life of the just individual may not be a happy one.

DISTRIBUTIVE JUSTICE: JOHN RAWLS

John Rawls has had a profound impact on contemporary moral and political philosophy. His most important work, *A Theory of Justice,* was first published in 1971, but parts of it had already been in circulation in preliminary drafts and in journal articles for several years earlier. After publication, it established the conceptual landscape within which discussions of justice were to occur, at least in the English-speaking literature. You could agree with Rawls or you could disagree with him, but you couldn't ignore him.

Rawls's Moral Concerns

There is almost no trace of Rawls's personal life and concerns in his published writings. Aside for thanking individuals for their comments and support, he says nothing personal. But in a helpful review essay devoted to several recent books by Rawls, the philosopher Thomas Nagel gives us some insight into the motivations underlying Rawls's work.

According to Nagel, Rawls was always deeply concerned about the "injustices associated with race, class, religion, and war." Slavery was the model of injustice for Rawls, and a good moral theory would not only condemn slavery but would do so for the right reasons. He was an infantryman in World War II and was familiar with the horrors of war, horrors perpetrated by friends as well as foes. And he was deeply aware of how lucky he had been in many ways, not the least of which was not to have fallen in combat. And he was acutely aware of the extent to which that luck was not deserved— it was simply luck. Throughout his work, Rawls remains highly sensitive to this issue of luck, and his goal is to create a society in which luck plays a minimal role in the rules that govern that society. Out of this comes Rawls's deep egalitarianism, his desire to see everyone treated as fairly as possible. *A Theory of Justice* provides an account of what is involved in such fair treatment.

The Original Position: A Thought Experiment

Imagine you are put in the following situation. You are one of a group of people who have been assigned the task of devising the basic rules that will govern society and the interactions of individuals in society. Your job is to work with the other people in the group to devise this set of principles. Furthermore, you are representing someone else in doing this, as are all the other delegates. You are to act rationally, and all of you are to act in the best interests of the people you represent. There is just one catch: You are behind what Rawls calls the "veil of ignorance."

The Social Contract

Until Rawls introduces the notion of the veil of ignorance, his account forms a standard hypothetical *contractarian approach*—that is, he sees the foundation of morality in some kind of social contract, usually implicit rather than an actual contract agreed upon at some historical time. Perhaps the most well-known representative of this approach to social theory was Jean-Jacques Rousseau, whose work *The Social Contract* (1762) continues to be studied today.

The Veil of Ignorance

Rawls's distinctive addition to the concept of the social contract was to ask the participants to imagine that they do not know any particulars about the person each of them was to represent. Thus, as a representative in the original position, I would be committed to acting rationally on behalf of the person I represent and to seeking to devise the best possible rules for that position. But since I am behind the veil of ignorance, I do not know anything in particular about the person I am representing. Is the person male or female, young or old, rich or poor. In what areas is the person talented: the arts, science, sports, human relations? In what country does the person live?

   Imagining ourselves behind the veil of ignorance is a powerful psychological and conceptual tool for helping us to overcome the prejudices of everyday life. Think about gender. If we imagine ourselves to be acting in a rationally self-interested way but not knowing whether we were representing a male or a female, we might well find ourselves revising some of the basic sex-based roles in our own society. Indeed, as we shall see in Chapter 10 when we discuss gender and moral theory, the political philosopher Susan Moller Okin uses precisely this line of reasoning to suggest that the benefits and burdens of family life fall differently and unfairly on the shoulders of men and women. Imagine being behind the veil of ignorance and asking what the basic principles regulating family life should be. It is highly likely that we, not knowing whether we represented a male or a female, would argue in favor of a much more equitable division of labor than presently exists in our society.

Imagine that you are behind the veil of ignorance and do not know what country your principal lives in. How would this affect your views of international economic justice? Remember that you do not know whether you are representing someone from an affluent and comfortable country or someone from a famine-ridden, debt-plagued country. The challenge would be to devise principles of international economic justice that would be fairest to all, no matter what their economic situation. Our views on world poverty might change significantly not knowing whether we would have to explain our decision to a poor person or a wealthy one, to a resident of an impoverished country or an economic giant.

It is easy to see the Kantian dimension present in this notion of the veil of ignorance. Kant asks us to set aside our moral individuality and ask what any rational agent ought to do in a given situation. (This is the force of Kant's imperative that we ought to be able to will the maxim of our actions for all rational beings.) By denying us knowledge of the specifics of our situation and by asking us to represent in a rational and prudential way the best interests of that person concealed behind the veil of ignorance, Rawls forces us into a kind of neutrality that has a clearly Kantian flavor. Although we are self-interested in this context, we don't have any specific knowledge of the particular self that would allow us to be partisan in standard ways. Deliberation in the original position behind the veil of ignorance should ensure that no one's interests are short-changed.

We can also see the way in which Rawls's veil of ignorance helps to even out some of the effects, both positive and negative, of mere luck. We do not know whether or not we have been lucky enough to be very intelligent, to be very athletic, to be very gregarious, to be very rich, to be part of the ruling elite. The veil of ignorance flattens out some of those quirks of fate and in so doing provides a more level playing field for the moral life.

Rawls's Principles

Deliberating behind the veil of ignorance in the original position, what principles will we adopt for our society, according to Rawls? He maintains that we would reach agreement on two basic principles, one on basic rights and liberties and the other on the distribution of social and economic inequalities.

The Basic Rights Principle

In *A Theory of Justice,* Rawls maintains: "Each person has an equal claim to a fully adequate scheme of equal basic rights and liberties, which scheme is compatible with the same scheme for all; and in this scheme the equal political liberties, and only those liberties, are to be guaranteed their fair value."

The Difference Principle

"Social and economic inequalities are to satisfy two conditions:

(a) they are to be attached to positions and offices open to all under conditions of fair equality of opportunity; and
(b) they are to be to the greatest benefit of the least advantaged members of society." (Rawls, pp. 5–6; formatting added)

These two principles of basic rights and difference form the core of Rawls's position, and both can be seen as principles of distributive justice. The first principle, the basic rights principle, establishes how we should distribute liberties. Part (a) of the difference principle establishes how we should distribute opportunities. These two principles are also indexical, that is, if there is a conflict, principle 1 overrides principle 2, and (a) overrides (b). Let's look at some examples to see what Rawls means by these principles.

Consider the difference principle, part (a). (This example will be more concrete than Rawls would give, but it illustrates the point quite well.) We have driving laws regulating speeding, stoplights, and the like. If two people were speeding and the police let one go because the speeder was the child of the chief of police, we would consider that action unjust. If, however, the police did not stop a speeding ambulance because it was rushing someone to the hospital, that would not offend our Rawlsian sense of justice. The exception would be based on the position or office (ambulance driver), which is open to all, whereas this is not the case with the child of the chief of police.

The difference principle, part (b) might be used to justify attempts to level the playing field after inequalities because of racial discrimination. We might, for example, treat people differently because they had been severely deprived because of racial bigotry. Such differential treatment might involve additional tutoring, more active recruitment, and the like. The underlying justification, in Rawls' eyes, is that these are the least advantaged members of society and differential treatment is justified in order to narrow the gap between the least advantaged and the majority of society.

Similar considerations might be used to justify the Americans with Disabilities Act. It is reasonable, within the light of the difference principle (b), to provide access ramps in public places for people with disabilities who require such ramps, to provide elevators in multistoried buildings, and the like. Again, the key insight here is that differential treatment is justified precisely in the case of the least advantaged.

On the other hand, this principle would not justify large tax exemptions for the wealthy, precisely because this action would not benefit the least advantaged but rather the most advantaged.

DISTRIBUTIVE JUSTICE: NON-RAWLSIAN THEORIES

Much of the work done in the last fifty years has centered on the question of **distributive justice,** and Rawls's *A Theory of Justice* is one answer. It is not, however, the only one. Let's first look at two of the problems these theories of distributive justice are intended to address: the distribution of scarce goods and the distribution of inequalities. Then we will look at three additional theories—egalitarian, welfare, and libertarian or market-based approaches—that will round out our account of distributive theories of justice.

The Distribution of Scarce Goods

Many things in society are in comparatively short supply, where the need (or demand) exceeds the supply. Take, for example, the need for kidney transplants. The demand for kidneys far exceeds the supply. How can we best deal with this situation? Consider several possible approaches.

First, we could say that the kidneys should go to the medically most needy (i.e., those closest to death from kidney failure), perhaps further determined by the likelihood that the transplant will be successful. This is the *Rawlsian approach*. Second, we could say that everyone has an equal right to these resources and, where they are scarce, simply have a lottery. This would be an *egalitarian approach*. Third, we could say that the kidneys should go to those whose continued functioning would be most beneficial to society as a whole. This is the *utilitarian or welfare approach*. Thus religious or financial leaders, creative scientists and industrialists, and the like would be more likely to receive transplants than, say, vagrants or dishwashers or clerks in stores. Fourth, we could simply say that kidneys go to the highest bidders. After all, that's what we do with many other commodities in our society. We can call this the *market-based approach*.

Presumably, when we ask questions such as these, we have in mind some principle of justice for apportioning those scarce goods. If might be a market principle, a principle of need, a principle of desert or merit, a consequentialist principle of benefit, or yet some other principle. The point here is simply that theories of distributive justice arise, at least in part, precisely out of the need to provide answers to questions such as these.

The Distribution of Inequalities

Inequalities abound in life. Some people are rich, some poor. Some are musically gifted, others are tone deaf. Some have photographic memories, others must work very hard to remember even a small portion of what they read. Some are held hostage by terrorists, others move about freely. Some people are physically attractive to many others, some are not. Some people come from homes in which they have every advantage, while others come from homes characterized by neglect and abuse. Some children are born into families of affluence in wealthy countries like the United States, whereas other children are born into conditions of starvation in Bangladesh and often do not survive to reach adulthood. Some people are genetically predisposed toward good health, whereas others suffer early attacks of cancer and other disorders despite living cautious lives.

Clearly we respond to some of these inequalities differently than others, and a theory of distributive justice is intended to help us distinguish among different kinds of inequalities and decide how to respond to each kind. There are some kinds of inequalities, such as musical ability or physical attractiveness, which do not call for any special response from us. Other types of inequalities, however, may place some moral demands on us.

Consider the response to the families of victims of the 9-11 attacks in the United States. A fund was established to compensate families of victims, and it soon raised fundamental issues about compensatory justice. Should each family, whether rich or poor, be given the same amount of money for each family member lost in the attacks? Should families who lost family members who were the principal earners of income be compensated more than those families who lost nonworking members of the family? (This is sometimes done in lawsuits for damages due to wrongful death.) Even more fundamentally, should these families be compensated when, for example, a family that had lost its breadwinner the day before in a mugging receives no compensation? What makes some families more deserving than others when they have had an equal loss?

Egalitarian Conceptions of Justice

Egalitarian conceptions of distributive justice maintain that everyone ought to be treated equally. An egalitarian distribution of income, for example, would require that all persons (or at least all workers) receive the same income. Sometimes this is justified on the basis of a claim that everyone deserves equal respect.

Obviously, an egalitarian conception of distributive justice would demand an economic structure much different from our own. Capitalism distributes income according to a market model, and typically in liberal democracies the government attempts to rectify the grossest injustices through taxation and consequent redistribution of some of the income through social welfare programs. However, the basic wage structure remains market driven. For an egalitarian approach to distributive justice to be implemented, a very different and much more centralized economic system would have to be in place. Theoretically egalitarian systems of distributive justice exist in some state-controlled economies such as Cuba, but the reality often falls far short of the ideal. In the Soviet Union, allegedly egalitarian distribution schemes were marred by flagrant patterns of exceptions for state and Communist party officials. The result was egalitarianism for the poor and luxury for the powerful.

Welfare Conceptions of Distributive Justice

Utilitarian conceptions of justice stress the way in which the just distribution of resources is the one that produces the greatest overall amount of welfare or utility. Although there is extensive debate about the precise definition of welfare or utility, as we have seen in Chapter 5 on utilitarianism, the basic insight here is simple and easy to state: A just distribution of goods and opportunities and liberties is the one that produces the greatest overall amount of welfare.

Welfare-based conceptions of distributive justice are open to some of the same difficulties we discussed in regard to utilitarianism in general. It seems, for example, to open the door to what we would usually consider unjust treatment of individuals in certain circumstances. It might justify racist or sexist treatment of minorities as just under certain empirical conditions. Rawls rejected the utilitarian account of justice because of cases such as these. Moreover, Rawls argued that even when the welfare or utilitarian conception of justice arrived at the right answer, it did so for the wrong reasons. Racial discrimination, for example, is not unjust because it is inefficient; it is unjust because it is inherently unfair and deprives some individuals of their basic rights unjustly.

Libertarian Conceptions of Distributive Justice

One of the most powerful challenges to Rawls's account of distributive justice comes from libertarians, who advance a market-based theory of distributive justice. Perhaps the best known of these challenges was Robert Nozick's *Anarchy, State and Utopia,* which appeared in 1974, three years after Rawls first published *A Theory of Justice.*

For libertarians, ownership of property plays a central role. Inspired by the work of British philosophy John Locke (1632–1704), libertarians see ownership as the central right of human beings, beginning with ownership of one's own body. The natural world is originally not owned by anyone, but by transforming it through work, individuals can make it their own. Is there any limit on how much of the natural world any one individual can acquire? Obviously, libertarians do not want to justify a world in which a few people could lay claim to vast portions of the world to the exclusion of everyone else, but it is also clear that they want to leave as much room as possible for people to approach this limit. Nozick argues that there is such a limit: individuals cannot lay claim to so much of the natural world that other people are thereby put in a worse position than when the land was un-owned.

Consider the days in which the United States had vast tracts of land, usually taken from the indigenous Americas who had been living there, that it offered to settlers. In these cases, the U.S. government chose a broadly egal-itarian conception of distributive justice, distributing the land in limited parcels to all who staked a claim. If it had adopted a libertarian strategy, it would have permitted a few individuals to claim vast amounts of land up until the point at which doing so would put others in a worse condition.

Interestingly, this example raises another problem for libertarian accounts of distributive justice. What does the libertarian say about property that may at some earlier time have been acquired unjustly? Nozick admits that he needs some kind of principle of rectification of past injustices, but that prin-ciple has yet to be adequately formulated.

Because libertarians take ownership to be the fundamental right, they often see attempts by the state to deprive individuals of their ownership to be unjust. The most obvious example is taxation. Welfare theorists will often see a high rate of taxation as just so long as it serves to promote the welfare of all citizens, including those who are most disadvantaged. Libertarians, on the other hand, see much taxation as unjust, because the government taking something that rightfully belongs to one individual and giving it to some-one else. Unless there is an extraordinarily serious justification for that kind of action, it is tantamount to theft. For libertarians, government should be minimal and taxes should be kept as low as possible. The principal role of government should be the protection of property rights. Not the taking of property.

So, too, libertarians see government regulation on the use of private prop-erty to be equally unacceptable. If I own a piece of property, I ought to be able to do what I want with it as long as I do not directly harm someone else. An interesting example of this occurred in the area of Lake Tahoe. Well-known for the color and clarity of its water, Lake Tahoe started to feel the effects of pollution in the 1980s. Regulators decided that certain parcels of land could not be sold or built upon until an adequate solution to the pollu-tion problem was reached. This did not apply to all pieces of land in the area, only those regulators earmarked as having a runoff to the lake. As a result, some individuals were unable to sell or use their land while their neighbors could do both—and despite not being able to sell or use their land, these in-dividuals had to pay taxes on that property. This is precisely the kind of situ-ation that libertarians find outrageous and unjust.

Justice and the Politics of Difference

Numerous critiques of standard accounts of distributive justice have appeared in recent years, and one of the most interesting and well-articulated of those critiques is Iris Marion Young's *Justice and the Politics of Difference* (1990).

In contrast to the many theorists we have seen who take justice to be pri-marily about the distribution of goods and burdens in society, Young sees justice primarily in terms of the overcoming of oppression and domination, which are seen principally in terms of groups. In her analysis, Young distinguishes five faces of oppression: exploitation, marginalization, powerlessness, cultural imperialism and violence. When Young talks about justice, she is talking about the justice of social movements such as the civil rights movement, feminism, and other political movements of the sixties and beyond. Ideally, the just society would be one where there is no oppression or domination. This is more than, and different from, the proper distribution of goods and burdens in society, and Young pays particular attention to the ways in which decisions are made in society, to the societal division of labor, and to the way in which the culture perpetuates oppression. Her analysis of oppression is much more concrete, picking up the details and nuances of the lived experiences of oppression rather than the general theory. She wants us to see the specific ways in which people are oppressed because of their race, their gender, their sexual orientation. Understanding the concrete faces of oppression is an important step toward overcoming such oppression.

Young draws a key distinction between "theoretical claims" about justice and "situated claims." Traditionally, discussions about justice have assumed a theoretical standpoint that promised objectivity and neutrality. Recall, for example, Rawls's account of the original position and the veil of ignorance. By stripping the moral agent of all individuality by putting actual identity behind the veil of ignorance, Rawls's theory lays claim to an impartiality that, in Young's eyes, is misleading. She criticizes Rawls and others in this tradition, maintaining that it is, first, an impossibility and, second, a "fiction." Impartiality cannot really be achieved. What happens instead is that individuals claiming such impartiality exclude all those characteristics that are different from their own and unwittingly treat their own limited viewpoint as the impartial standpoint from which all of morality can be judged. In this way, so-called impartial theories often perpetuate the hierarchical power structure of society. Thus, the apparently neutral standpoint is really a particular standpoint dressed up in the clothing of impartiality. What Young proposes instead is that our discussion of justice be grounded in an awareness of the specific social, political, and economic conditions of our society.

Young does not offer an alternative theory of justice, to be ranked alongside those of Rawls and others; rather, she offers particular studies of injustice and points to directions in specific cases for improving justice. (Indeed, she even characterizes her work as an antitheory.) Consider the issue of affirmative action. Both defenders and critics of affirmative action see the issue primarily in terms of whether discrimination is ever justified. Young, on the other hand, argues that the primary issue is not discrimination but oppression. The fundamental question of justice, then, is what we can do to overcome oppression. Once the question has been posed in this way, affirmative action in Young's eyes ceases to be objectionable. Indeed, we can discriminate among groups and treat them differently if the goal is to overcome oppression.

CRIMINAL JUSTICE

We have been examining competing approaches to justice in the preceding sections, but there is another issue of justice that those discussions often neglect: the justice that we seek when someone has broken the law, has committed a crime. Let's briefly consider this issue and the competing accounts of justice that have been advanced in response to wrongdoing.

Retributive Justice

The dominant justification of punishment in the United States appears to be the appeal to retributive justice. At its core, the notion of **retributive justice** usually depends on some version of the **lex talionis, the law of "an eye for an eye, a tooth for a tooth."** This is retributive justice: If someone has hurt me, that person will be hurt in return in the same way. Often, this notion of retributive justice is used to justify the death penalty: an eye for an eye, a death for a death.

Despite the fact that the *lex talionis* has some initial plausibility in a small range of cases, we in fact can see that there are many cases where this literal interpretation of the *lex talionis* makes no sense at all. How, for example, are we to punish those who hijack airplanes? We can't very well hijack their planes, since they do not have any. What about arsonists? Do we set their homes on fire? Or rapists? Do we rape them in return? Or burglars? Do we steal their money and possessions when they are asleep?

While some would probably advocate those extreme responses, most of us would admit that the literal interpretation of the *lex talionis* is insufficient for two reasons. First, there are many types of crimes for which it makes no sense to do the same thing to the perpetrator. The more plausible interpretation of this principle is a metaphorical one that says something like this: The more serious the crime, the more serious the punishment.

But even this will not suffice. We need to recognize that in the most serious of cases, we may restrain ourselves from extreme punishment because the act of punishing diminishes us. Take rape as an example. To rape a rapist as punishment would be to demean ourselves, the punishers. So, too, we do not torture the sadistic murderer, even though on the basis of some principle of proportionality we believe the murderer deserves to suffer as much as his victims. Again, we restrain ourselves because we would be debasing ourselves to carry out the punishment.

Interestingly, recognizing these two limitations of the *lex talionis* helps us to find a middle ground in regard to the death penalty. Proponents of the death penalty, if one accepts this principle, are justified in claming that certain criminals have done such horrendous things that they deserve to die. Opponents of the death penalty can admit this while arguing at the same time that even if some criminals deserve to die, we do not deserve to kill them. The issue is the effect of the punishment on the punishers.

Those who hold a strictly retributivist account of justice are open to some objections. How should we treat the person who has done something horrible in his youth, subsequently led an exemplary life, and then in old age is apprehended for that crime committed long ago? Retributivists are committed to saying that the magnitude of the crime remains the same, whether committed yesterday or fifty years ago. Other, more forward-looking accounts of punishment would be less likely to punish to the full measure of the law.

Compensatory Justice

When American citizens of Japanese ancestry were sent to detention camps in California during World War II simply because of their ancestry, and when they were deprived of their property as part of this process, they were treated unjustly. It was an injustice because they were deprived of their constitutional rights, rights that are at the very core of our constitution and guaranteed to all citizens. When the treatment of Americans of Japanese descent was done by the government (in contrast to acts of injustice done by individuals), it was an injustice done in our name. As a result, it is argued, we as a country owe them something to compensate for the injustice committed against them.

The notion of **compensatory justice** provides an interesting alternative to retributive justice. In both accounts, the injured party (or family or descendents) has a claim against the wrongdoer. In retributive justice, the injured party "cashes in" this claim by asking for the wrongdoer to suffer in some way proportional to the offense. In compensatory justice, on the other hand, the injured party cashes in the claim by asking the wrongdoer to make up for the injury.

The notion of compensation, however, depends on a principle of equivalency—that money, for example, can compensate for suffering. It works well in those instances where people have suffered monetary damage, but in other cases it is less appropriate.

Restorative Justice

Although retributive justice has occupied central stage in the Anglo-American legal system, it is not the only conception of justice possible. Indeed, critics of retributivism often point to its potential harshness, especially to those cases in which retributive punishment seems to do more harm than good.

A number of countries, just emerging from harsh and oppressive regimes, have struggled with the limits of retributive justice and, in the process, have fashioned a conception of restorative justice that serves as an important counterbalance to traditional retributivist theory. This was certainly true in a number of Latin American countries such as Chile, which emerged from a long period of harsh rule by Augusto Pinochet and his government. A similar situation existed in South Africa, where decades of apartheid and oppression by the white minority government had resulted in countless injustices against black and mixed-race South Africans.

Countries with such a history face a difficult choice when they finally throw off their oppressive regimes. Once the oppressors have been removed from power, the new government can try to bring past offenders to justice for their past wrongdoings. Retributive justice certainly would support such a course of action, but there are distinct costs associated with pursuing retributive justice in such contexts. First, the extent and intensity of trials for past injustices could easily create deep divisions in society, intensifying the level of hatred between past and present regimes. Such trials, far from healing a society, may actually make it more divided. Such animosity and division, many feel, is a moral evil to be avoided if possible. Second, there are often pragmatic considerations that come into play as well. It is not unusual for the new government to need the expertise of the previous regime in the day-to-day business of running the country. If a large number of those who occupied key positions in that earlier government are in jail, then the possibility that they could participate in the rebuilding of the country is eliminated. Despite such moral and pragmatic considerations, most people feel that horrible injustices have been perpetrated and they are convinced that it would be wrong simply to let people go unpunished. The idea that the guilty should not only go unpunished, but could go simply go about their lives as though they had not done those terrible deeds deeply offends our sense of justice. Thus it would seem that such countries face an insurmountable dilemma.

South Africa and several Latin American countries have explored a third possibility that lies somewhere between retribution and amnesia. Truth and justice commissions have been established in a number of countries whose aim is not to punish, but to set the record straight about what happened during the years of oppression. Thus, these commissions aim at justice as reconciliation, but they are clear that reconciliation cannot be founded on lies. Thus, the truth about those days must be established before reconciliation is possible.

These commissions do not require repentance on the part of those who come forward, nor do they impose punishments. The principal reason for restricting the commissions in this fashion is that otherwise perpetrators would simply not come forward. But critics of these courts of reconciliation have argued that this is simply not enough. They argue that justice has not been done as long as there is no punishment, and especially if there is neither punishment nor retribution.

Justice as *Hozho*

The theme of balance and harmony has run throughout a number of our discussions of justice, beginning with Plato's *Republic* and the harmony of the soul. Restorative justice often seeks to reestablish a harmony in society, and at times counties forgo harsher paths to justice for the goal of harmony.

The notion of justice as harmony also lies at the heart of the Navajo conception of justice, as we indicated in Chapter 3. The Honorable Robert Yazzie, chief justice of the Navajo Nation, describes the traditional Navajo conception of justice and the ceremonies that accompany it: "Our traditional Navajo justice ceremony is called *Hozhooji Naat'aanii*. Many Navajo words have no corresponding term in English, so I will say that it is a term which refers to talking and planning to restore damaged relationships, guided by a person with wisdom who helps plan things to regain K'e (respect)."

This is a forward-looking notion of justice, far from the strict retributivism of a philosopher such as Immanuel Kant. Moreover, in sharp contrast to standard Western approaches to justice, it involves healing ceremonies and the spiritual rehabilitation of the offender. Finally, this is a highly participatory process, involving all affected parties.

GLOBAL JUSTICE

Considerations of justice have traditionally been situated within a community, whether this be a local community, a state, or a nation. There is, however, an increasing awareness of global justice, an awareness that may well characterize the twenty-first century.

The term *global justice* is ambiguous. It may, on one hand, refer to seeking just solutions to problems that are global in nature. On the other hand, it may refer to a global conception of justice, that is, a theory of justice that cuts across national and regional and cultural boundaries. These two senses of justice are related, with global problems serving as the driving force for the development of a global conception of justice. Here we shall examine several areas in which issues of global justice arise. First, we will consider the issue of justice in war, which typically involves transnational considerations of justice. Second, we will turn to a consideration of the environment as an example of a *global problem* that in turn gave rise to the field of environmental justice. We will conclude with a discussion on the prospects for a *global theory* of justice.

Justice, War, and Peace

Medieval Christian theologians and philosophers (there often wasn't a clear division in those days) were quite concerned with the application of the concept of justice to conflicts. The most influential of these thinkers was Thomas Aquinas, whose account of just war set the stage for most subsequent discussions of this issue. Much more recently, Michael Walzer's *Just and Unjust Wars* (1977) has become the definitive work on this issue. These issues have been a matter of deep concern not just to political philosophers, but also to the military and political leaders who must sometimes make decisions about whether to commit their nation to war or not. The premise on which this entire discussion rests is a simple one: War is a terrible, terrible evil, and there must be much in its favor before it becomes justified.

Aquinas and many others distinguish two distinct areas where the concept of justice can be applied to issues of war: (1) the *just conditions for entering into a war* (called **jus ad bellum,** "justice toward war"), including the question of just cause of war; and (2) the *just conditions for conducting a war* (**jus in bello,** "justice in war"). Let's look at each of these.

Jus ad bellum: When is it just to enter into a war?

Just war theorists from Aquinas to Walzer list a number of conditions. Let's look briefly at each one.

The first is that there must be a *just cause,* and this usually means that you have been attacked. Typically, starting a war is never just.

Second, you must have the *right intention.* This condition excludes such actions as going to war to expand your territories or influence; it does permit going to war to stop aggression. It is very important for a country to have a clear idea of what it is trying to accomplish by going to war. Is it simply to stop the aggression?

Third, the war must be *publicly declared by a lawful authority* such as a head of state. Part of the rationale for this requirement is to prevent segments of a country (such as the military) from committing the nation to conflict without an adequate decision-making process. It also prevents pursuing wars in secret without the consent of the whole nation.

Fourth, war must be the *last resort.* If it is possible to achieve your just ends of other means such as blockades or diplomatic pressures, then it is unjust to resort to war.

Fifth, there must be some *probability of success* before you are justified in going to war. Here the rationale is simple: War is such an evil that it ought not to be undertaken if there is not some chance of bringing about a significant good.

Sixth and finally, there must be *proportionality* between the possible benefits of war and the amount of pain and suffering and death that the war will cause.

If all of these conditions are met, then entering into a war is just.

Jus in bello: The Just Conduct of War

Once a country has entered into a war justly, there still remain important moral considerations about how the war may be conducted. Let's look at the three conditions typically outlined as those necessary for the just conduct of war.

First, we must always conduct war in such a way that we *discriminate between combatants and civilians.* This is one of the most basic rules for conducting a war properly. Civilians cannot be targeted for attack, nor can they be used as human shields to deter enemy attacks. Most just war theorists interpret this condition in such a way as to permit unavoidable collateral civilian casualties, although exactly where the line is to be drawn here becomes an contentious issue.

Consider an example. In attacking an enemy, there is the least chance of civilian casualties if the attack is conducted by ground soldiers. If low-level air attacks are used, the chances of civilian casualties increases but casualties to one's own forces go down. If high-level air power is used, the chances of civilian casualties become even greater and the safety of one's own forces increases greatly. The question that then arises is this: In the conduct of war, to what extent is a country justified in trading off increased civilian casualties for increased safety of its own military personnel?

Second, there must be a *principle of proportionality* in the conduct of war. Countries should only use as much force as is necessary for the achievement of their just goals. This excludes massive attacks when the legitimate goals of the conflict are minor. Often, when this condition is ignored, we see local conflicts grow into much larger wars simply by their own momentum.

Third and finally, just wars must be conducted in a way that *uses no means that are evil in themselves*. In recent decades, there has been a consensus developing among most nations that biological warfare agents such as smallpox and anthrax are forbidden because they are means that are evil in themselves. In the Balkans, we saw rape used as a means of war, intended to destroy family and civic structures and thereby destroy the enemy, and such means clearly fall into the category of means that are evil in themselves: There are no circumstances in which their use is permissible. Many would include torture among those means that are evil in themselves.

These conditions of a just war have been shaped over the years to fit the traditional model of large nation states. In the late twentieth and the beginning of the twenty-first century, we have seen situations arise which this doctrine of just war was not originally designed to cover. Let's briefly consider two of those here.

Humanitarian interventions

It's clear that just war theory specifies the conditions under which a nation can respond to an attack. But what do powerful nations do when they see grave injustices, such as genocide, occurring in other countries? It seems to violate our basic sense of justice and decency simply to stand by and allow such things to happen, despite the fact that the attacks are not against our own nation. Typically, diplomatic and economic pressure are the first lines of offense here, but in some situations they have relatively little impact on the situation. Nonmilitary interventions may sometimes make a difference, but at least in some cases nothing short of military intervention offers the hope of protecting the innocent in such situations.

Are nations who are not directly attacked ever justified in intervening militarily for humanitarian reasons to prevent the loss of civilian lives? Does this count as a "just cause" for entering an armed conflict? The answer that has emerged in the West is an affirmative one: Sometimes third-party military intervention for humanitarian intervention may be justified in order to save the lives of innocent people. Typically, this is done under the sanction of some multinational organization such as the UN or NATO, in part to prevent it from degenerating into some kind of nationalistic campaign. Within this context, all the conditions for just war will continue to apply.

Terrorist threats

Traditionally, war has taken place between nation states. What happens when a nation is attacked by an entity that is not a state? Consider the Taliban attacks against the United States. No nation declared war against the United States, and many would say that if the United States were to declare war on the Taliban, this would in effect raise the Taliban's level of status to that of a nation state.

So, too, terrorists typically do not distinguish between military and civilian targets. Indeed, they often prefer to attack civilian targets. They are easier to attack with fewer casualties, and attacks against civilian targets can often bring terror to the entire population. One of the principal objections to terrorism, from the standpoint of just war theory, is that it often ignores the crucial distinction between combatants and civilians. Not only does it target civilians, but terrorists often themselves hide out among civilian populations; because they do not fight in uniform, the line between civilians and terrorists is often blurred.

Jus post bellum: A Just Peace

Although typically the discussion of justice and war has been limited to *jus ad bellum* and *jus in bellum,* the classic sources also contain a discussion of a third type of justice: **justice in peace,** or *jus post bellum.* According to Brian Orend, there are five conditions for a just peace: just cause for termination; right intention; public declaration and legitimate authority; discrimination; and proportionality. A just cause for peace exists when the rights that were originally violated are now restored. The right intention excludes motives of revenge against the defeated, and both victors and vanquished must be subjected to the same laws. This precludes, for example, holding the defeated accountable for war crimes but not doing the same thing for yourself and your allies. Whatever punishment is exacted must discriminate appropriately between general citizens and military personnel and, within the military, between those responsible for prosecuting the war and those not in leadership positions. Finally, a just peace is marked by proportionality, where punishments exacted are proportional to the severity of the offense.

One of the most intriguing aspects of the notion of a just peace is that it can guide the conduct of a war. Faced with difficult decisions, national leaders can ask themselves which alternative will increase the possibility of just peace at the end of the conflict. In the American Civil War, we saw the way in which certain actions, such as Sherman's march through South Carolina, left a bitter legacy that endangered the prospects of a just peace. On the other hand, the leadership that Abraham Lincoln showed, including his generous terms of surrender, promoted the possibility of a just peace. Wise leaders are able to conduct war in a way that maximizes the possibility of creating a just and lasting peace.

War is not the only problem that crosses national borders and raises issues about justice beyond borders. Let's turn to a consideration of other global problems and issues of global justice.

Global Problems

One of the principal factors contributing to the emergence of a global conception of justice is the emergence of ethical issues with a global dimension as well as an increasing awareness of the global nature of many existing ethical problems.

The Environment

Consider the emerging field of *environmental justice*, a field well grounded in an awareness of the global nature of both ethical problems and their solutions. Increasingly, philosophers and others working in this area have pointed to the way in which problems such as famine and atmospheric and water pollution transcend national boundaries in several ways. We can see this clearly in many cases of environmental pollution. Small developing countries may feel the effects of large, highly industrialized countries in at least two ways. First, they may experience the effects of such pollution directly through, for example, reduced air and water quality that is directly traceable back to developed countries as its point of origin. Second, and more frequently, they may experience the polluting effects of foreign-owned industry in their own country, since highly industrialized countries often locate factories in developing nations in order to avoid the more stringent labor and environmental regulations they encounter at home.

Just as there is a growing awareness that many problems are global, so too there is a growing consensus that the solution to those problems is global as well. No single country can solve, for example, the problem of atmospheric pollution, *even for itself,* because no one owns or controls the atmosphere. Individual countries can, of course, reduce atmospheric pollution that originates within their own borders, and doing this may make a significant difference in their air quality. However, they are still subject to the effects of pollution emitted into the atmosphere by other countries, and there is simply no way that they can solve this problem in isolation.

Nor is the effect of atmospheric conditions limited to the quality of the air we breathe. Atmospheric conditions can have profound effects on farming, and this in turn can have a major impact of food production. If severe climate changes (such as holes in the ozone layer) result in global warming, this can have very negative effects on crop production, which can precipitate famines in certain regions of the globe. Once again, we note that a country may well act responsibly within its own borders and nonetheless suffer the impact of environmentally irresponsible actions taken by those outside its borders. In cases such as these, no solution is possible as long as one stays within the national borders. The question of justice as fairness then emerges quite clearly: is it just, is it fair, for some nations (and their populations) to suffer the harmful consequences of actions taken by other nations, especially when those actions are performed with knowing disregard of their negative consequences on other countries?

Economic Exploitation

Many products today are manufactured in a way that crosses national boundaries. A car advertised as "made in America" might have been assembled here, but many of the parts of the car could have been manufactured around the world. Moreover, many of the consumer goods sold in the United States are made outside the country. In some cases, U.S.-based manufacturers have moved their factories to other countries, where labor is cheaper, environmental and safety restrictions are more lax, and natural resources are more easily and cheaply available.

To what extent do considerations of economic justice extend beyond national boundaries? It is clear that some large international companies use labor and resources from developing countries in ways that many social theorists label as exploitation. Take the example of Nike. They have been accused by critics of exploiting labor in China, Vietnam, and other countries; they are accused of low salaries (20 cents an hour in Indonesia, according to a *CBS News* story), poor working conditions, and (at least in the past) employing very young workers. At the same time, critics point out, Nike shoes sell at very high prices and its president has become the fifth wealthiest person in the United States. Nike counters that its wage structure matches local wages, and this fact raises precisely the question at the heart of this section: How can we achieve economic justice in a world marked by radical economic disparities? These are truly global problems, not confined to a single country or region. To deal with them, we need a global account of justice.

Global Theory

Retributive Justice

One of the earliest attempts to develop and implement a global notion of retributive justice occurred after World War II with the Nuremberg trials. During World War II, Germans under the leadership of Adolph Hitler set about to systematically eradicate Jews, Gypsies, and homosexuals, as well as to enslave other groups (such as the Poles) as less than human. The staggering atrocities committed by the Germans at concentration and death camps such as Auschwitz and Dachau were on a scale seldom seen before.

The Nuremberg trials asserted a global conception of justice, at least in the very minimal sense of declaring that certain kinds of flagrantly egregious behavior violated even the minimum standards of justice. Yet Nuremberg and other such trials have often been plagued by the fact that they have only been established *after* the crimes have taken place, and in the eyes of some this fact has been a mark against their legitimacy. Laws, critics argue, cannot be passed retroactively, and they argue that it is unjust to hold someone accountable to laws that were not on the books when the alleged offenses occurred.

The International Criminal Court, which was established by the Rome Statute in 2002 and scheduled to become operational in 2003, has been ratified by over sixty nations and promises "to prosecute people accused of genocide, crimes against humanity and war crimes." This is a restricted jurisdiction, since many crimes do not fall under these three headings, but it is precisely the jurisdiction that Nuremberg and other war crimes tribunals lacked. It remains to be seen whether countries (including the United States) will be willing to give up some claims of national sovereignty in order to support such a world court of criminal justice.

Distributive Justice

Environmental theorists are leading the way in the development of a theory of global distributive justice. This is an extraordinarily important area, but one in which much work remains to be done. Typically, discussions of distributive justice have tended to occur within the context of nations, for there is rarely any transnational apparatus for controlling the distribution of resources and opportunities. Individual countries, for example, may redistribute wealth through taxes and other means, but there is no international organization with comparable worldwide authority.

Economists and others are actively engaged in the process of developing a global theory of distributive justice. One of the foremost figures in this area has been Amartya Sen, the Nobel Prize–winning Indian economist who has devoted his life to understanding and articulating the demands of justice and equality within a global economic context.

Issues of global distributive justice emerge in many contexts. Perhaps the most notable of these has been in regard to world hunger. The vast disparity that exists between the affluence of highly industrialized nations and the poverty and hunger of many developing nations raises fundamental issues of justice. Is it fair that so few would have so much, while so many exist in abject poverty?

Consider a second example of this issue: the rise of HIV and AIDS and the price of medicine to combat them. In July 2002, a United Nations report predicted that AIDS would claim 65 million lives by the year 2020, triple the number who have already died. By then, the death toll from AIDS will rival the death toll from all the wars of the twentieth century combined. Political leaders in affected countries have argued against traditional patent regulations that prevent them from producing anti-AIDS medications, and they argue that it is unjust for such companies to charge such high prices that countries often cannot afford to provide medicines to much of their population.

Two of the most prominent attempts to articulate global theories of justice come from rights-based theories and from utilitarianism. Henry Shue, for example, has argued in *Basic Rights* (1996), 2nd ed. that everyone has certain positive rights, including the right to subsistence. Peter Singer, on the other hand, has forcefully articulated the utilitarian case for a global theory of economic justice, especially in regard to the issue of world hunger.

CONCLUSION

Justice is one of the most fundamental concepts in the moral life. Little children appeal to it ("It's not fair that she gets two pieces of cake") just as critics of multinational corporations make use of it ("Paying workers 20 cents an hour is unjust!"). We find ourselves facing two distinct kinds of questions. The first concerns precisely what we mean by justice, and here philosophers and social scientists can cooperate in articulating the precise meaning of justice. The second concerns the implementation of justice, how we make the world a just place to live. This is an issue that concerns everyone: politicians, religious leaders, and everyday citizens. As we shall see in our concluding chapter, the implementation of just social, economic, and political structures is the foundation of a lasting world peace.

DISCUSSION QUESTIONS

1. Review the just conditions for entering into a war. Which of those have been met in the United States' war on terrorism? Which have not been met? To what extent is this a just war?
2. Imagine that you are the CEO of a major U.S. company with manufacturing plants around the world. You have been accused of employing people in other countries at wages below the subsistence level. What would you do?
3. Consider your response to **statement 33** in our initial survey ("Justice consists of treating everybody exactly the same"). In what kinds of situations, if any, would justice demand treating people differently?
4. Recall your response to **statement 34** ("A just society is one in which everyone has the maximal amount of liberty"). When is the government justified in restricting liberty? What is the justification for such restrictions? How would a libertarian and a liberal differ on this issue?
5. Our world today is characterized by vast economic differences between rich countries and poor countries. Are these differences injustices? Why or why not? How should we respond to them?

6. When, if ever, are we justified in intervening to prevent injustices beyond our national borders? If, for example, genocide is occurring in another country, to what extent do other nations have an obligation to intervene in such situations?

7. **MOVIE** In the movie *Twelve Angry Men* (1957), we see a nuanced portrait of different conceptions of justice. Drawing on the ideas in this chapter, describe the different conceptions of justice that various jurors exemplify.

8. **MOVIE** In the movie *Long Night's Journey into Day* (2000), directed by Frances Reid and Deborah Hoffmann, we see a portrait of justice in South Africa. What does the film tell us about restorative justice? How does it affect your understanding of this concept?

BIBLIOGRAPHICAL ESSAY

The literature on justice is vast, stretching back to Plato's dialogues to the latest postmodernist critiques of justice. Here are some of the highlights.

Anthologies include Carol C. Gould et al., eds., *Morality and Social Justice: Point—Counterpoint* (Lanham, MD: Rowman & Littlefield, 1994); Robert C. Solomon and Mark C. Murphy, *What Is Justice?*, 2nd ed. (New York: Oxford University Press, 1999); Jonathan Westphal, ed., *Justice* (Indianapolis, IN: Hackett, 1996); Ellen Frankel Paul, Fred Miller, Jr., and Jeffrey Paul, eds., *The Just Society*, (Needham Heights, MA: Cambridge University Press, 1995); Milton Fisk, *Justice* (Atlantic Highlands, NJ: Humanities Press, 1993); Will Kymlicka, ed., *Local Justice: How Institutions Allocate Scarce Goods and Necessary Burdens* (Newbury Park, CA: Sage, 1992); Klaus R. Scherer, ed., *Justice: Interdisciplinary Perspectives* (New York: Cambridge University Press, 1992); James P. Sterba, ed., *Justice: Alternative Political Perspectives*, 3rd ed. (Belmont, CA: Wadsworth, 1998). For an excellent overview of theories of justice (to which I am indebted in this presentation), see Julian Lamont, "Distributive Justice," *Stanford Encyclopedia of Philosophy:* http://plato.stanford. edu/entries/justice-distributive/.

John Rawls's conception of justice dominates the literature. See his *A Theory of Justice,* rev. ed. (Cambridge, MA: Harvard University Press, 1999), originally published in 1973; *Political Liberalism* (New York: Columbia University Press, 1996); *The Law of People* (Cambridge: Harvard University Press, 2001); Samuel R. Freeman, ed., *Collected Papers* (Cambridge, MA: Harvard University Press, 1999); Barbara Herman, ed., *Lectures on the History of Moral Philosophy* (Cambridge, MA: Harvard University Press, 2000). John Rawls, Erin Kelly, ed., *Justice as Fairness: A Restatement* (Cambridge, MA: Harvard University Press, 2001). For critiques, see Samuel R. Freeman, ed., *The Cambridge Companion to Rawls* (Cambridge: Cambridge University Press, 2002); Norman Daniels, ed., *Reading Rawls: Critical Studies on Rawls' "A Theory of Justice"* (Palo Alto, CA: Stanford University Press, 1990); Tomas Pögge, *Realizing Rawls* (Ithaca, NY: Cornell University Press, 1990); Robert B. Talisse, *On Rawls* (Pacific Grove, CA: Duxbury, 2000); Andrews Reath, Christine M. Korsgaard, and Barbara Herman, eds., *Reclaiming the History of Ethics: Essays for John Rawls* (Cambridge: Cambridge University Press, 1997); Chandran Kukathas and Philip Petit, *Rawls: A Theory of Justice and Its Critics* (Stanford: Stanford University

Press, 1990); Robert Paul Wolff, *Understanding Rawls: A Reconstruction and Critique of a Theory of Justice* (Princeton: Princeton University Press, 1971); and Thomas Nagel, "The rigorous compassion of John Rawls: Justice, Justice, Shalt Thou Pursue," *The New Republic* (1999), available online at http://www.tnr.com/archive/1099/102599/nagel102599.html.

Among the many other excellent books on justice, see Onora O'Neill, *Bounds of Justice* (Cambridge: Cambridge University Press, 2000) for a tightly argued case for seeing justice in cosmopolitan terms, and especially for her discussion of transnational economic justice; Brian Barry, *Justice as Impartiality* (New York: Oxford University Press, 1996) and his *Culture and Equality: An Egalitarian Critique of Multiculturalism* (Cambridge, MA: Harvard University Press, 2001); James P. Sterba, *Justice for Here and Now* (Cambridge: Cambridge University Press, 1998) for both applications of the concept and an attempt to reconcile apparently conflicting accounts of justice; Robert C. Solomon, *A Passion for Justice* (Lanham, MD: Rowman & Littlefield, 1995) for a nuanced treatment of the affective dimension of justice; Patrick Riley, *Leibniz' Universal Jurisprudence: Justice as the Charity of the Wise* (Cambridge, MA: Harvard University Press, 1996), for a notion of justice based on wisdom and love instead of the standard contractarian account; Geoffrey Cupit's *Justice as Fittingness* (New York: Oxford, 1996) argues that injustice is a form of unfitting treatment; James S. Fishkin, *The Dialogue of Justice: Toward a Self-Reflective Society* (New Haven: Yale University Press, 1993); Jeffrey Reiman, *Justice and Modern Moral Philosophy* (New Haven: Yale University Press, 1990); John E. Roemer, *Theories of Distributive Justice* (Cambridge, MA: Harvard University Press, 1996.)

On **Kant and justice,** see Thomas E. Hill, Jr., *Respect, Pluralism and Justice: Kantian Perspectives* (New York: Oxford University Press, 2000); Allen D. Rosen, *Kant's Theory of Justice* (Ithaca, NY: Cornell University Press, 1993), as well as the work of Onora O'Neill cited earlier.

On the **libertarian conception of justice,** see especially Robert Nozick, *Anarchy, State, and Utopia* (New York: Basic Books, 1977); Loren E. Lomasky, *Persons, Rights, and the Moral Community* (New York: Oxford University Press, 1987); and G. A. Cohen, *Self-Ownership, Freedom, and Equality* (New York: Cambridge University Press, 1995).

On **pluralist conceptions of justice,** see Jon Elster, *Local Justice: How Institutions Allocate Scarce Goods and Necessary Burdens* (Newbury Park, CA: Sage, 1992); Georgia Warnke, *Justice and Interpretation* (Cambridge, MA: MIT Press, 1993) discusses the hermeneutical turn in theories of justice; Michael Walzer, *Spheres of Justice: A Defense of Pluralism and Equality* (New York: Basic Books, 1990); David Miller and Michael Walzer, *Pluralism, Justice, and Equality* (New York: Oxford University Press, 1995); Michael J. Sandel, *Liberalism and the Limits of Justice*, 2nd ed. (Cambridge: Cambridge University Press, 1996); William A. Galston, *Liberal Pluralism: The Implications of Value Pluralism for Political Theory and Practice* (Cambridge: Cambridge University Press, 2002).

The literature on **race and justice** is extensive. See especially Bernard Boxill, *Blacks and Social Justice,* Revised Edition (Lanham, MD: Rowman & Littlefield, 1992); Gertrude Ezorsky, *Racism and Justice: The Case for Affirmative Action* (Ithaca, NY: Cornell University Press, 1991). On reparations, see *When Sorry Isn't Enough: The Controversy over Apologies and Reparations for Human Injustice* (New York:: New York University Press, 1998).

On **just war theory,** see the excellent overview by Brian D. Orend, "War," in the *Stanford Encyclopedia of Philosophy* (http://plato.stanford.edu/entries/war/). Michael Walzer's *Just and Unjust Wars: A Moral Argument with Historical Illustrations,* 3rd ed. (New York: Basic Books, 1979) remains the classic text, and Jean B. Elstain's *Just War Theory* (New York: New York University Press, 1994) is an excellent anthology. On Walzer, see Brian Orend, *Michael Walzer on War and Justice* (Montreal: McGill-Queens University Press, 2001); also see his *War and International Justice): A Kantian Perspective* (Waterloo, ON: Wilfrid Laurier University Press, 2001). My presentation here of just war theory is based on Orend's account.

On **retributive justice,** see Robert M. Baird and Stuart E. Rosenbaum, *Punishment and the Death Penalty: The Current Debate* (Buffalo, NY: Prometheus Books, 1995); Michael Davis, *To Make the Punishment Fit the Crime: Essays in the Theory of Criminal Justice* (Boulder, CO: Westview Press, 1992); Jeffrey Reiman, *The Rich Get Richer and the Poor Get Prison,* 6th ed. (Boston: Allyn & Bacon, 2000).

On **environmental justice,** see K. S. Shrader-Frechette. *Environmental Justice: Creating Equity, Reclaiming Democracy* (New York: Oxford University Press, 2002); Luke W. Cole and Sheila Foster, *From the Ground Up: Environmental Racism and the Rise of the Environmental Justice Movement* (New York: New York University Press, 2000); David Schlosberg, *Environmental Justice and the New Pluralism: The Challenge of Difference for Environmentalism* (New York: Oxford University Press, 1999); Andrew Dobson, *Justice and the Environment: Conceptions of Environmental Sustainability and Dimensions of Social Justice* (New York: Oxford University Press, 1999); Peter S. Wenz, *Environmental Justice* (Albany: State University of New York Press, 1998); Benjamin J. Richardson, ed., *Environmental Justice* (New York: Kluwer Academic Publishers, 1999);

On **international justice,** see Robin Attfield and Barry Wilkins, eds., *International Justice and the Third World* (New York: Routledge, 1992); On international economic justice, see Amartya Sen, *On Ethics and Economics* (Oxford: Blackwell Publishers, 1989) and *Inequality Reexamined* (Cambridge: Harvard University Press, 1995) and, most recently, *Development as Freedom* (Garden City, NY: Anchor Books, 2000).

Further Information. For web-based resources on justice, see the Justice page on my *Ethics Updates:* site. http://ethics.sandiego.edu/theories/justice/. This page includes original texts, articles, and videos of contemporary philosophers discussing the issue of justice.

THE ETHICS OF CHARACTER: ARISTOTLE AND OUR CONTEMPORARIES

The Village of Le Chambon

The first big Nazi raid on the village of Le Chambon came in the summer of 1942. The villagers had already been warned about what would happen to them if they tried to hide Jews from the Nazis, and it was no surprise when squads of police descended on the village looking for the hundreds of Jews who were in fact hidden in the village and the surrounding countryside. The police vans were followed by a group of buses, ready to cart away the prisoners.

The villagers had prepared well. None of the Jews who had been hidden was found for several days. Philip Hallie tells us what happened next.

> Later in the week they captured an Austrian Jew named Steckler—he had made the mistake of going to a pharmacy without all of his papers. The police put him— their only prisoner—in one of the big buses. As he sat there, the villagers started gathering around the periphery of the square. The son of Andre Trocmé [the village pastor], Jean-Pierre, walked up to the window of the bus at which Steckler sat and gave him his last piece of rationed (imitation) chocolate. This started the closing of the circle of villagers. They brought their most precious foodstuffs and put them through the window into Steckler's arms. Soon the quiet little man had a pile of gifts around him about as high as he sat in the seat.
>
> When the buses left with their one Jew the villagers sang a song of affection and farewell to him. A few days later he came back—he was only half-Jewish, and at this time he was legally classified as non-Jewish. He was pulling a cart with the presents on it as he came into the square. When the villagers gathered happily around him, smiling and nodding in their restrained Huguenot way, he wanted to give them back their gifts. They would not take them, precious as those food-

stuffs were to them. Steckler wept. This is the story of the first big *rafle* or raid upon Le Chambon-sur-Lignon.

From then until the end of the war, the villagers of Le Chambon were responsible for saving the lives of thousands of innocent Jews, especially children.

When we look at the villagers of Le Chambon, we are struck not only by what they *did*, but also by who they *were*. We are struck by what *good people* they were. Their goodness did not seem to stem from any Kantian test of universality or utilitarian calculus of consequences. It came from the heart, from who they were as persons. They did not follow some elaborate set of rules, but rather responded spontaneously to the suffering of those around them. It is, first and foremost, a goodness of *character*. As we shall now see, there is an entire tradition in ethics that takes this, character, as the central focus of ethics. Let's look at that tradition more closely.

FROM THE ETHICS OF ACTION TO THE ETHICS OF CHARACTER

Asking a Different Question

In our discussions of Kant and of utilitarianism, we looked at two different answers to the question of how we should *act*. Kant and the utilitarians answer this question in quite different ways. For Kant, the answer depends largely on our *intention:* Always act for the sake of duty, that is, because it is the right thing to do. Moreover, act in such a way that the maxim behind your act can be willed as a universal law. The utilitarians give a very different answer to this question. For them, the rightness or wrongness of actions depends on *consequences* instead of intentions. The right action is the action that produces the greatest overall amount of happiness or pleasure. Yet what both the Kantians and the utilitarians have in common is that they see ethics as being an answer to the question, "What ought I to *do?*"

Aristotle approaches ethics in quite a different way. For him, ethics is primarily concerned with answering the question, "What kind of *person* should I be?" Ethics concentrates on *character* rather than on action. Thus it is that Aristotle is principally interested in *virtues* and *vices,* that is, in those strengths and weaknesses of character that either promote or impede human flourishing.

The contrast between act-oriented approaches to morality (including both utilitarianism and Kantianism) and character-oriented approaches (especially Aristotle) raises some important philosophical questions about how these two approaches relate to one another and whether one of them is preferable to the other. Before pursuing these questions, consider an analogy between this controversy and our American criminal justice system.

A Judicial Analogy

In order to ensure justice, we as a country established a criminal justice system that has two distinct dimensions to it. First, it is a system of *laws,* of rules for acceptable behavior. Indeed, our system of laws has become increasingly well articulated, detailed, and complex. As we discover loopholes in the present laws, we add new laws in the hope of closing the loopholes. Yet at the same time there is a second dimension that we have built into this process: *people.* We leave the application of these rules to the good judgment of various people, especially the judge and jury. Both judge and jury have to use their own judgment in determining how these rules are to be applied. They temper the laws, applying them (as least in the best cases) with fairness, compassion, insight, and wisdom. The application is not automatic; human judgment has to enter into the process. Indeed, in order to ensure that that judgment will be as unbiased as possible, we have a number of people on the jury, not just one. In order to ensure that the judge is unbiased, we try to remove the selection process as much as possible from partisan politics and not make judges dependent on politics for their continued tenure. In order to ensure that the rules are paid sufficient attention, we expect that the judge will be very well versed in the law. The appeals process helps to guarantee that the rulings of those judges who ignore the relevant law will be overturned.

What can we learn from this example? Well, we see that as a country we have decided to rely on both laws and people, both principles and persons. We have built that dual reliance into our system of justice. We put our money on laws, on our ability to develop a system of rules to determine what is acceptable or unacceptable behavior—but only up to a point. We also put our money on people, on individuals who will have the good judgment to know how to apply the laws. Neither can exist without the other. Without laws, judges and juries would be free to decide arbitrarily about cases, and no one would have firm guidelines for his or her behavior. Yet without judges and juries, the laws could never be applied fairly. Their judgment, their insight, their wisdom are necessary to interpret and apply those rules. As a country, we have shown the good judgment to depend on both laws and people.

Persons and Principles

Ethics is similar to the law in this respect: It needs both principles and persons. Both the Kantians and the utilitarians articulate principles that shed vital light on the moral life, and they are not to be ignored. Yet the application of those principles depends on people of good judgment and character, and it is precisely this that virtue ethics hopes to provide. It is in this sense that virtue ethics offers the context within which both deontological and consequentialist moral considerations can be embraced. This is not to say that virtue ethics reconciles these two approaches within a single unified theory, but rather that it offers a way of understanding how we as moral persons can contain the creative tension that comes from the conflict between these two approaches.

Moreover, we are obviously not suggesting that there is no correlation between character and actions. Particular character traits lead to specific kinds of actions. A courageous person manifests his or her courage in courageous acts. Indeed, the acts often are our best clues to what the person's character is really like.

Nevertheless, there is good reason for giving virtue ethics a limited kind of priority over act-oriented approaches. We have already seen one sense in which virtue ethics has that priority: It embraces both Kantian and utilitarian approaches. Yet there is another way in which virtue ethics seems to me to be, if not prior, at least more desirable than deontological or utilitarian approaches. In order to show this, let's go back to Kant.

The Temperate Person and the Continent Person

In Kant's moral philosophy, when there is a conflict between duty and inclination, between what you ought to do and what you feel like doing, duty is always supposed to conquer inclination. However, there is relatively little concern on Kant's part to heal the rift between duty and inclination, between reason and emotion. Rather, he simply urges us to follow the path of duty and reason, eschewing inclination and emotion. The alternative is to suggest that we try to overcome this dichotomy, that we attempt to reconcile what we ought to do and what we feel like doing.

Here Aristotle is particularly insightful. He draws a distinction between two different types of persons, the temperate "and the continent" person (*Nichomachean Ethics,* Book VII). Temperate people are individuals who do what is right *because they want to.* The continent person also does what is right, but does not really *want* to do so. Let me offer an example in regard to eating. My wife is a temperate person: She eats in moderation and naturally chooses healthful foods as the mainstays of her diet. She actually seems to enjoy celery and carrot sticks. Her eyes light up at the thought of raw broccoli. I, on the other hand, am at best a continent person in this regard. I may eat salads, fish, and whole grains, but there is not a day that passes that I don't *want* rich Brie cheese, red meat, and cheesecake. I may not always eat these things, but I certainly want them. I think that, at least in regard to food, my wife has the better life.

As we have seen in the previous chapter, the Kantian moral person seems in greater danger of being the continent rather than the temperate person, and I think this is a serious drawback in Kant's ethics. For Kant, moral actions do not have to come from the heart, only from the head. Yet I think our moral ideal should be one of *striving* to have our actions come from both head and heart, from both reason and feeling. Moreover, part of that process of reconciling reason and emotion will involve educating the emotions, something that has been all too often ignored in the past.

A similar problem arises with utilitarianism. Motives count for relatively little among most utilitarians, and emotions occupy a strange place in the utilitarian calculus. Although emotions certainly count for the utilitarian, the difficulty is that everyone's emotions count equally. Indeed, if any emotions are to be given less weight, it is the agent's own feelings, because these are at least somewhat under his or her control. Thus, utilitarianism also tends to promote this split between the reasoning part of the self and the emotional part.

All other things being equal, an ethics that seeks to heal this split is preferable to one that perpetuates it. This was one of the most striking characteristics of the villagers of Le Chambon: They risked their own lives to save the Jews, not from any externally imposed sense of duty, but because they wanted to do so. They responded from the heart. However, we are not always able to do this. Temperate people have rightly ordered appetites, and for them act-oriented moralities that emphasize the importance of rules will usually be of secondary importance. Intemperate people, on the other hand, do not have rightly ordered desires, at least in the areas in which they are intemperate. For them, it is important to have rules that govern and control their actions. Thus act-oriented moralities that provide rules of behavior will properly have a more prominent place in the lives of intemperate persons.

CHARACTER AND HUMAN FLOURISHING

One of the principal attractions of Aristotle's ethics is the way in which it encourages human flourishing. Indeed, Aristotle's ethics is largely concerned with the question of what promotes human happiness or flourishing, about what leads to a fuller and happier human life. (The Greek word for "happiness" that Aristotle uses, *eudaimonia,* can also be translated as **flourishing** or "well-being.") Virtues and vices are understood precisely within this context. **Virtues** are those strengths or excellences of character that promote human flourishing, whereas **vices** are those weaknesses of character that impede human flourishing. Courage, for example, is a virtue because we have to be able to face and overcome our fears if we are to achieve our goals in life. Yet what, exactly, is human flourishing?

Aristotle on Human Flourishing

Flourishing and Function

The notion of human flourishing or happiness is a notoriously slippery one, but Aristotle's approach is helpful, even if ultimately incomplete. Two lines of argument run through his approach to determining what counts as human flourishing. On the one hand, flourishing is understood in a *functional* context. A hammer, for example, is a good hammer if it does what it was designed to do well—if it hammers nails well. A guitar is a good guitar if it is

Aristotle (384–322 B.C.E.), who is shown here with his pupil Alexander the Great, emphasized the strong connection between ethics and politics.

capable of making good music. Aristotle expresses it this way in Book II of *Nichomachean Ethics,* which is abbreviated *EN.*

> Every virtue causes its possessors to be in a good state [or disposition] and to perform their functions well; the virtue of eyes, e.g., makes the eyes and their functioning excellent, because it makes us see well; and similarly, the virtue of a horse makes the horse excellent, and thereby good at galloping, at carrying its rider and at standing steady in the face of the enemy. If this is true in every case, then the virtue of a human being will likewise be the state [or habit or disposition] that makes a human being good and makes him perform his function well.

Notice, however, that these are objects designed to meet a particular human purpose, such as hammering nails or making music. Human beings do not have an obvious function in the same unproblematic way that hammers and guitars have functions.

(Of course, within certain religious contexts, human beings do have an obvious function or purpose, and this purpose is ordained by God. Within such a worldview, virtues have a much more obvious justification: They are those strengths of character necessary for us to fulfill God's plan for us. But such a view presupposes that we have been given a purpose by a divine being and that we can know what that purpose is.)

Flourishing and Uniqueness

On the other hand, Aristotle sometimes understands flourishing in terms of the exercise of *unique properties*. Consider a plum tree. Its unique characteristic is that it bears fruit (plums). Consequently, a good plum tree will be one that does this well. In a similar way, there is a unique characteristic that sets human beings apart from other kinds of beings: the ability to reason or think. Consequently, a good human being will be one who reasons well. Human flourishing is thus defined in terms of reasoning or thinking—for Aristotle, ultimately in terms of the contemplative life.

Two Conceptions of Flourishing

When flourishing is approached through an analysis of function, Aristotle tends to emphasize the way in which happiness is related to practical wisdom. People of practical wisdom, Aristotle tells us in *Nichomachean Ethics,* are persons who can deliberate well about what is good for their life as a whole, not just what is good for some part of it or what is expedient. Such individuals often find that flourishing has deeply social and political elements to it. According to this conception of flourishing, human beings are profoundly social by nature, and participation in the common life of the city-state, the *polis,* is an essential part of any happy life. Happiness or flourishing would be impossible without community. We can call this the *political conception of happiness,* but it is important to recognize that the word *political* does not carry negative connotations for the Greeks of Aristotle's time. For the Greeks, the political realm encompasses virtually everything that is concerned with forging a common life together.

There is a second conception of flourishing in Aristotle's thought that exists in uneasy tension with the first. This is the theory of flourishing that derives from the uniqueness argument. According to this theory, flourishing essentially consists in contemplation of the good. Leisure is a necessary presupposition of such a view because there must be some way of creating the time necessary for contemplation. This is the *contemplative conception of happiness.* Whereas the political conception of happiness sees happiness as residing at least partially in activity, the contemplative conception of happiness stresses the way in which happiness is found through a withdrawal from the world of everyday affairs.

A Pluralistic Approach to Happiness

Aristotle's own writings suggest that he vacillates between these two accounts of happiness, and scholars have been divided about which represents his true view or whether the two accounts can be reconciled. If we were to extend our pluralistic approach to this issue in Aristotle's philosophy, we could say that happiness itself can be understood pluralistically. Happiness in general may be seen as the satisfaction that comes with achieving one's most important goals in life, but we can recognize that there is a wide range of acceptable goals. Some of those goals may be located firmly within the social realm, whereas others may be principally contemplative. Yet we can also recognize that there are some minimal restraints imposed on these goals by both our social and our intellectual natures. Just as we cannot find happiness in complete isolation from other people, so we could hardly find it without some significant reflection on the goals we choose to strive for. Both elements are necessary to some minimal extent, but there is a wide range in the relative weight we give to one over the other.

Assessing Aristotle's Account of Flourishing

Antireductionism

There is much to be said in favor of Aristotle's account of human flourishing, not the least of which is that it is antireductionistic. Aristotle does not try to reduce human existence to a single common lowest denominator. This is in stark contrast to theories that reduce human beings to some single factor, such as genetics (as sociobiology does) or economics (as both some Marxists and some capitalists try to do) or environment (as strict behaviorism does), that human beings have in common with other types of living beings. Aristotle sees human beings as unique among other living beings and does not try to downplay or ignore that aspect of human beings that makes them unique.

Holism

However, Aristotle does at times seem to go almost to the other extreme, apparently looking only for the *highest* common denominator. Because thinking is what makes human beings unique, he treats it as the *only* thing that does so. As a result, at times he has a more intellectualistic and contemplative notion of human nature and of virtue than is warranted. His mistake in reasoning is a simple one, as we can see from another example. My computer has a number of fancy gadgets, including a CD-ROM drive that holds six disks. The CD-ROM drive makes it unique, yet its excellence lies in the *totality* of its functions, not just in the CD-ROM drive. Similarly with human beings: Their excellence lies in the totality of their functions and powers (including the ability to feel), not just in their ability to think. Aristotle, by sometimes overemphasizing the role of thinking in his conception of human flourishing, was not sufficiently *holistic* in his approach. I stress this because all too often the positive role of emotions and feelings in the moral life is denied or neglected. This is a danger to which Aristotle sometimes, but not always, succumbs.

Ethics for the Nobility

There is yet another drawback to Aristotle's account of the virtues, one that it shares with most other ancient and, to a lesser extent, medieval and modern accounts. It is an ethics for the ruling class, for privileged, free, adult Greek males whose main interests were domestic politics, war, and leisure. Such an ethics completely excluded women and most foreigners, many of whom were treated as slaves or as less than full moral persons. Yet the life that this privileged class enjoyed depended in large measure on the support of these excluded groups. Greek leisure, which Aristotle saw as the presupposition of philosophy, is based on these inequalities.

What are we to say about all this? Clearly, in important respects, Aristotle was on the right track. Just as clearly, we see that his vision at times was clouded or distorted, in part because of the era in which he lived. We can learn from Aristotle's account of flourishing, but we can hardly take it as the final word.

Contemporary Accounts of Flourishing

Contemporary thinkers—psychologists, economists, and other social scientists as well as philosophers—have continued Aristotle's task of understanding human flourishing. Broadly speaking, their approaches fall into two categories, depending on where they locate the primary barriers to human flourishing. For those who see the main barriers to human flourishing as being *external* to the individual, their account of a flourishing life will usually stress external, *social* factors. For those who see the main barriers to human flourishing as *internal* to the individual, flourishing is usually depicted primarily in internal, *psychological* terms.

External Approaches

The external or social approach to human flourishing covers a wide range of kinds of factors that affect human well-being. Some are obvious: Many people feel that economic factors, for example, play a significant role in determining human flourishing. Here flourishing or well-being can be described in terms of such objective factors as standard of living. Those who achieve a certain level of economic well-being are said to be flourishing, whereas those who fall below the minimum level are not seen as flourishing. Economists and social scientists are deeply concerned about this issue and seek to develop indices of well-being in a society. One of the more intriguing concepts, championed by Robert Putnam in his book *Bowling Alone,* (2000), is the idea that societies have a certain amount of *social capital* that functions to make communities stronger and permit individual character to flourish more fully.

Other types of external factors may be less immediately obvious to most of us. Think, for example, of the relationship between architecture and human flourishing. The ways in which we structure our living and working environments both reflect and affect our interactions with other people.

Workplaces with no common areas for employees encourage an isolation and separation from coworkers not found as readily in working environments that stress interaction. Homes in which all the chairs face the television reflect a different conception of happiness than do homes in which the chairs all face one another.

Historically, utopian thinkers have often provided us with possible models of a social life that encourages human flourishing. Many such models presuppose that people will be happy (i.e., will flourish) if certain material and social conditions can be met. Many versions of both Marxist and capitalist social theories share this presupposition.

After flourishing is specified in terms of external conditions, we have a clear path to increasing the amount or degree of flourishing in society. We merely have to increase the external conditions necessary to flourishing, whether these be specified in terms of income, health care, or some other objective factor.

Internal Approaches

Many theorists have linked human flourishing primarily with some *internal* state. Virtually all spiritual approaches to human well-being, for example, see flourishing primarily as a state of the soul that is largely (perhaps even entirely) independent of external conditions. Similarly, many psychological accounts of flourishing emphasize the internal factors within the individual's psyche that affect well-being. Some psychological approaches like Freud's or Jung's see the path to flourishing as an *intra*-psychic one, where the crucial question is about the balance among competing psychological factors. Other psychological approaches have looked even more directly at the question of human flourishing, especially at factors that affect peak experiences. The work of Abraham Maslow has been particularly influential in this area.

What is common to most of these internal approaches is the presupposition that we are often our own worst enemy, preventing ourselves from having the very satisfactions we value so highly. We sabotage ourselves without even realizing what we are doing. The road to happiness primarily involves overcoming internal barriers to flourishing, and this is often a matter of spiritual discipline or psychological health. In this tradition, flourishing is primarily a state of mind rather than a state of matter.

THE STRUCTURE OF VIRTUES

We have already talked a lot about virtues without really defining what we, or Aristotle, mean by the term. Let's remedy that situation.

The Definition of Virtue

Virtue, Aristotle tells us, is **(1) a habit or disposition of the soul, (2) involving both feeling and action, (3) to seek the mean in all things**

relative to us, (4) where the mean is defined through reason as the prudent man would define it (*EN*, II, 6). Virtue leads, as we have already seen,
to happiness or human flourishing. Each of these parts in Aristotle's definition is important, so let's pause to examine each.

Habits of the Soul

Aristotle tells us that virtue is a *hexis,* a disposition or habit. We are not born
with virtues. They are not natural or inborn; rather they are acquired, often
through practice. Moral education for Aristotle thus focuses on the development of a person's fundamental character, what Aristotle calls "soul."

Feeling and Action

Virtue, for Aristotle, is not simply a matter of *acting* in a certain way; it is
also a matter of *feeling* certain ways. Virtue includes emotion as well as action. The compassionate person not only acts in certain ways that help alleviate the suffering of others, but also has certain kinds of feelings toward
their suffering.

   The inclusion of feeling in the definition of virtue is important to our
concerns here because as we saw in the previous chapter, the exclusion of
emotions from the moral life (or at least their devaluation) leads to significant problems for Kantian, utilitarian, and egoistic moral theories. Aristotle's account of the moral life in terms of virtue, with its emphasis on the
emotive or affective character of virtue, allows us to set aside this objection.

Seeking the Mean Relative to Ourselves

A virtue, Aristotle tells us, involves finding the mean between the two extremes of excess and deficiency. Courage, for example, is that middle ground
between cowardice (too little) and foolhardiness (too much).

   In virtues that contain several elements, there might be several associated
vices, depending on which of the elements are in excess and which are defi-
cient. Courage, when we examine it more closely, has at least two components: fear and confidence. We can err in regard to either factor: We may
have too much or too little fear, or we may have too much or too little confidence in ourselves.

   Aristotle himself suggests that this tripartite framework may not always
be applicable. The example he gives is murder. There is, he tells us, no mean
in regard to murder. It is just an extreme. Yet I think Aristotle is confused
on this matter because murder is neither a virtue nor a vice. It is an *action,*
not a quality of character. Indeed, the relevant quality of character would be
something like respect for life, which is a virtue that can have extremes. On
one hand, there are those with too little respect for life. They kill and injure
others with no regard for the pain and suffering they are inflicting. On the
other hand, there are those who would never knowingly even step on an ant.

One could argue that they have an excessive respect for life. Unfortunately, our society is plagued much more by the former than the latter.

Defining the Mean through Reason and the Prudent Person

Interestingly, Aristotle gives two ways for determining what the mean is: through reason and through observing the prudent person. This duality reflects precisely the point made earlier in this chapter through the judicial analogy: We need both principles and persons for the moral life. Rather than choosing one or the other, Aristotle chooses both, seeing them as complementary.

Virtues and Spheres of Existence

One of the common criticisms of Aristotle's list of the virtues is that it is arbitrary. Certainly it is culturally bound, shaped by the values of ancient Athens. Yet there are some universal elements, and Aristotle provides a good hint about how these can be established. There are, he suggests, certain spheres of existence that all of us have to encounter. We all have to develop an attitude toward the accomplishments and successes of other people: envy, admiration, or belittling are some of the possible attitudes. We all have to develop an attitude toward the offenses and hurts that others inflict on us. Some people will be resentful and revengeful, others forgiving, still others will just be doormats. Correlatively, we have to develop an attitude toward *our own* offenses to other people. Again, there is a wide range of possibilities, from being indifferent to being overly guilty. Somewhere in the middle is the proper attitude of remorse and reparation.

Notice, too, that the emphasis here is not on individual actions, but rather on character, which manifests itself in habits of perception and behavior. Take courage as an example. Aristotle's question is not whether this or that particular action is courageous. Rather, he asks what a life without courage, or without courage in a particular range of situations, would be like. The focus is not on specific acts, but rather on the patterns that reveal a person's character.

There are a variety of ways in which we might summarize these various spheres of existence. The next page shows a table that I have developed, amending a similar outline by Martha Nussbaum.

Thus, Aristotle tells us that virtue is the disposition of the soul through reasoning to find the mean in all things relative to us. The mean is that middle ground between two extremes, the extremes of excess (having too much of something) and deficiency (having too little of something). The mean is described differently, depending on the particular sphere of existence in which we are seeking the mean. Certain spheres of existence are found in almost all cultures.

Sphere of Existence	Deficiency	Mean	Excess
Attitude toward self	Servility Self-depreciation	Proper self-love Proper pride Self-respect	Arrogance Conceit Egoism Narcissism Vanity
Attitude toward offenses of others	Ignoring them Being a doormat	Anger Forgiveness Understanding	Revenge Grudge Resentment
Attitude toward good deeds of others	Suspicion Envy Ignoring them	Gratitude Admiration	Over-indebtedness
Attitude toward our own offenses	Indifference Remorselessness Downplaying	Agent regret Remorse Making amends Learning from them Self-forgiveness	Toxic guilt Scrupulosity Shame
Attitude toward our own good deeds	Belittling Disappointment	Sense of accomplishment Humility	Self-righteousness
Attitude toward the suffering of others	Callousness	Compassion	Pity "Bleeding heart"
Attitude toward the achievements of others	Self-satisfaction Complacency Competition	Admiration Emulation	Envy
Attitude toward death and danger	Cowardice	Courage	Foolhardiness
Attitude toward our own desires	Anhedonia	Temperance Moderation	Lust Gluttony
Attitude toward our friends	Indifference	Loyalty	Obsequiousness
Attitude toward other people	Exploitation	Respect	Deference

Executive and Substantive Virtues

Virtues, Aristotle tells us, are those strengths of character that promote human flourishing. Some of those strengths, later commentators have suggested, are strengths of the will. *Perseverance* in the face of a difficult and lengthy task is a virtue of the will, what some have called an **executive virtue**. So, too, is *courage*, the ability to act in the face of one's fears. These virtues of the will are largely independent of moral goodness. One can just as easily persevere in a life of crime as a life of goodness; the bank robber may exhibit as much courage as the FBI agent who tries to capture him. Other virtues are more closely related to moral goodness, and we will call these **substantive virtues**. *Compassion* is clearly a substantive virtue because it is directly tied to a concern for moral goodness in a way that perseverance and courage are not.

Let's turn now to consider some specific virtues and their associated vices.

COURAGE

The Everyday Need for Courage

Think about the people you know who are afraid of something. Do you know anyone who is afraid to ask someone out on a date for fear of rejection? Do you know anyone who is afraid of saying something dumb and looking stupid—and consequently doesn't ask questions in class? Or is afraid to disagree with friends and consequently says whatever the friends want to hear? Do you know anyone who got into trouble but was afraid to ask for help from family or friends? Do you know anyone who is afraid to end a bad relationship because he's afraid of being alone? Do you know anyone who was afraid to "just say 'no'" to something she didn't want to do because her friends would think less of her?

Think about those people. All of them are faced with something they fear, and the challenge is for them to overcome that fear. When Aristotle suggests that virtues are necessary to human flourishing, it is easy to see that this is the case with courage, especially if we think of courage as facing and overcoming our fears. *If we are unable to overcome those fears, we will often be unable to obtain or accomplish some of the most important things in life.* Take, for example, the person who is afraid to ask anyone out on a date. He will probably be lonely and feel unfulfilled. Or consider the person who is afraid to speak out in front of other people and especially to disagree with others. He will be unable to hold certain kinds of jobs that require leadership, and he probably will not be able to be a loyal friend. He certainly would not be able to defend his friends against the criticisms of others because he is afraid to speak out in disagreement. Moreover, it would be difficult for such a person to have close friends because others would find it hard to get to know him. If he lacks the courage to disagree, then he will always present a pleasant and compliant face to others, and thus they will never know his true feelings. He has to have the courage to stand up for himself, or else he will never be able to be a good friend.

Courage, in other words, is a virtue of everyday life that involves facing and overcoming our fears.

The Elements of Courage

Fear and Danger

You may have been surprised by the preceding examples of courage because we most often think of courage in a military context or in situations of great objective danger.

Let's begin by considering what courage is a response to, what sphere of experience it belongs to. At least two candidates immediately present themselves. Courage can be seen as a response either to *danger* or to *fear*. It's important to distinguish between danger and fear because one is objective and the other is subjective. *Danger* refers to *objectively* specifiable characteristics of a situation or object that threaten our safety or security in some way. A burning building is dangerous because, if we are trapped in it, we will be incinerated by the fire or killed indirectly through asphyxiation. Similarly, driving a car at high speeds on icy pavement is dangerous because the car could easily go out of control, resulting in possible injuries or death. *Fear*, on the other hand, is a *subjective* reaction that we have to certain objects or events. Certainly some of the things I fear may be objectively dangerous. I may, for example, be afraid of driving very fast on icy roads. However, there are also lots of people who are afraid of things or events that are not in fact dangerous. Many people are afraid of snakes, even when they know that they are harmless. Some people are afraid of flying on airplanes, even when they know that the flight is probably safer than the drive to the airport. Other people are afraid of things that most of us never even notice. One friend of mine, for example, is very afraid of birds, even though in fact the birds she encounters (sparrows, robins, etc.) are not actually dangerous at all.

This distinction becomes useful in understanding courage because we get two different conceptions of courage, depending on whether we see courage as a response to fear or to danger. If courage is a response to danger, then those who overcome their fears of things that are not actually dangerous will not count as courageous. Moreover, if courage is a response to objectively specifiable dangers, then a response to such things as psychological dangers will not count as courage. Finally, if courage is a response to danger, then those who do not have the good sense to be afraid of dangerous things will be counted as courageous. On the other hand, if courage is seen as overcoming fear rather than danger, this opens the door to admitting these three types of cases as legitimate instances of courage.

The underlying issue here is interesting because what is really at issue is the question of *rightly ordered fears*. People who have the courage to go on picnics despite a deathly fear of squirrels may be courageous, but their courage does not exist within a context of rightly ordered fears. Their fears are not proportionate to the actual risk present in the situation. Similarly, the person who does not feel fear when thrown into a pit full of poisonous snakes does not have rightly ordered fears, either, because that is a genuinely dangerous situation in which fear is an appropriate response. Paradigmatic or model cases of courage occur within a context of rightly ordered fears.

Confidence and Risk

We must have not only rightly ordered fears to be fully courageous, but also an appropriate level of confidence in our own ability. Self-confidence is grounded in our perception of risk, our own measure of our ability to deal with a specific type of challenge or task. The assessment of risk is based on two factors: the objective danger and our own level of ability to deal with that kind of danger. Thus the level of risk depends in part on our level of ability. It is much riskier for me to drive in a Grand Prix auto race than it would be for a professional driver because the professional would presumably have a much higher level of ability. The lower one's level of ability, all other things being equal, the riskier the task becomes.

Courage, in its fullest sense, rests on (1) *rightly ordered fears* and (2) an *accurate assessment of risk,* of one's ability to meet the specific kind of challenge being presented. Differing levels of ability may make one person's action courageous, whereas another person's identical action would simply be an everyday noncourageous action. Imagine flying on an airplane when the pilot suddenly has a heart attack. I have no idea of how to fly a plane, and for me to take over the controls and follow radio instructions on how to land the plane would be courageous. For my friend Norm, who can fly virtually anything with a semblance of two wings, to land the plane would be "a piece of cake" and require no courage on his part.

The Extremes

Aristotle suggests that courage is the mean between two extremes. One of these extremes is initially quite clear: *cowardice.* The cowardly person is the person with a deficiency of courage, with too little courage. There are two ways of being cowardly: A person may have (1) too much fear or (2) too little self-confidence. We might call having too much fear *timidity* because the word *timidity* comes from the Latin word *timere,* which means "to fear." On the other hand, one can have too much courage, and this is the other extreme. Aristotle suggests that there are two ways in which this can happen. First, an individual may have too much confidence in his own ability, and such a person Aristotle calls *rash* or *foolhardy.* Second, a person can have too little fear. (Aristotle says that we lack a name for such a person, just as we lack names for many other virtues and vices.) In a sense, this is the opposite of the example about the person who is afraid of harmless birds. Such people aren't afraid of things of which they *should* be afraid.

Proper Ends

Thus courage involves at least two elements: *proper confidence* and *rightly ordered fears.* Yet proper confidence and proper fear are not the only two elements necessary to courage. We can imagine a scene in which someone is standing outside of a burning building, wailing, "My baby is trapped inside." A passerby realizes what is happening and courageously rushes into the building and saves the infant. We would, without hesitation, call this brave or courageous. But what if the person had been standing outside the building, wailing, "I left my hamburger inside." If a passerby were to rush inside to rescue the hamburger, we—or at least I—would be inclined to say that he was a fool. The hamburger was not worth the risk, and it would have been easy to buy another one for a few dollars. This suggests another element to courage: *good judgment.* We need to balance the risk against the possible gains and be sure that the possible gains are worth those risks. In the case of the trapped baby, they clearly are; in the case of the hamburger, they are not. Thus courage involves three elements: rightly ordered fears, proper confidence, and good value judgments about ends.

Some Difficult Cases

If courage involves rightly ordered fears, proper self-confidence, and good value judgments about ends, we are left with some perplexing cases that do not quite fit into the standard model. I will briefly describe two.

The Mountain Climber

In his book *Into Thin Air,* (1998), Jon Krakauer chronicles a disastrous attempt to reach the summit of Mount Everest. Eight people died in the attempt, several with spouses and children. What do we want to say about the mountain climber who has both rightly ordered fears and proper self-confidence? Is it the climber's judgment about ends that seems suspect? A climber who completes a challenging climb in order to save someone's life is clearly courageous. Our problem is with the one who does the same climb simply in order to get to the top. Does this show good value judgments about the ends being sought?

Clearly, if the point of mountain climbing is to get to the top, it's silly. Why not just take a helicopter? (Even better, why not just stay home?) Yet it seems that, for people who regularly climb, the point is to continually reconquer their own fear. They need to climb for the self-knowledge it gives them. Yet I would still hesitate to see climbing as a full-fledged case of courage because it does not seem to be in the service of particularly high ends.

It is also important to ask what kind of character a person develops when courage is that individual's central virtue. The world then is seen in terms of potential challenges, occasions to prove one's courage. Such opportunities are sought out, perhaps even created. Other virtues, such as compromise or compassion, may well recede into the background to the extent that they conflict with proving one's courage.

The Terminally Ill

Another set of difficult cases centers on those people with terminal illnesses. What about their courage? What is their goal? The thing about their courage is not *that* they face death and the possibility of dying painfully, but *how* they do so. It is not that they do so fearlessly. Indeed, fear seems quite appropriate in such a situation. Rather, it is how they manage to impress a meaning on their suffering that is most significant for our understanding of courage.

Courage and Gender

Aristotle is unabashed about it: Women can't be courageous in the fullest sense. Aristotle's model of courage is the warrior who intrepidly faces the possibility of death in war. Because women are not allowed to fight in wars, they cannot be courageous. If they do succeed in performing courageous acts, they will usually be acts that have traditionally been confined to male roles.

Nor is this view restricted to Aristotle or ancient Greece. Consider our own society—where, incidentally, women still had not been allowed in active combat roles as of 1997. On rare occasions, women's courage in traditional male roles is recognized and valued. For example, Major Rhonda Cornum's courage as an Iraqi prisoner of war during the Gulf War was certainly given wide publicity and praise. A flight surgeon, pilot, paratrooper, and biochemistry Ph.D., Cornum was captured when her helicopter was shot down in the Iraqi desert. With two broken arms, a badly injured knee, a shoulder shattered from a bullet wound, and a bad infection, Cornum's only regret was that she wasn't able to swallow her wedding ring before her captors got it. Yet this is the exception. In general, two points stand out. First, the courage of women is usually under-recognized and undervalued in our society. Second, courage is seen as much more integral to male identity than it is to female identity in our society. Let's briefly examine both of these issues.

The Under-recognition of Women's Courage

Women are no less courageous than men, but on the whole the ways in which they exhibit their courage are less likely to be recognized and valued as courageous than are the ways in which men exhibit their courage.

Sometimes women exhibit a degree of physical courage in the face of physical dangers that is comparable to that of their male counterparts, but it often goes unnoticed. Consider the courage of both the Native Americans and the European pioneers in North America. The courage of the Native American men and the pioneer men who fought each other is generally accepted and valued—even though many of us have profound doubts about the morality of the goal of colonization. Yet the courage of both Native American and pioneer *women* is largely unrecognized and undervalued, despite the great dangers and hardships that they faced.

Women also faced dangers unique to them, most notably childbirth. Prior to the development of modern antiseptic procedures and childbirth techniques, the danger of death was high, the chances of great suffering even higher. Yet women facing such danger intrepidly were rarely recognized for their bravery.

Not all dangers are purely physical. Consider those who have been sexually abused as children and confront their pain—and often their abusers—in order to heal. Most of the victims of such abuse are women. (We are, however, discovering that a greater percentage of men were sexually abused than we had previously realized.) The courage they show in facing their greatest fears and overcoming them is remarkable, but we are more likely to recognize the courage of soldiers as the genuine article than we are to recognize the courage of individuals who overcome this type of fear.

Finally, consider the courage that some girls show in the passage from adolescence to adulthood. In *Meeting at the Crossroads: Women's Psychology and Girls' Development* (1992), Lyn Mikel Brown and Carol Gilligan have suggested that girls face a developmental challenge requiring great courage as they begin to move into womanhood. Brown and Gilligan found that the transition from girlhood to womanhood was one in which girls typically found themselves increasingly interpersonally isolated, emotionally disconnected, and intellectually uncertain about the truth of their own experience. It took great courage for them to refuse to give up the sense of connectedness that they had developed in girlhood, for them to insist—often against prevailing social expectations—on retaining and enhancing their relationships with other people. So, too, did it take great courage—what Annie Rogers refers to as "ordinary courage"—to remain true to their own experience and to speak out on behalf of that experience.

Courage and Gender Roles

Courage is tied to the issue of gender in a second way as well in our society. Our society, whether rightly or wrongly, tends to see courage as much more integral to a masculine identity than to a feminine identity. If a man is not courageous, he is much more open to the charge of being less of a man than a woman is open to the corresponding charge if she is not courageous. Failing to be courageous is not usually seen as detracting from her femininity (except possibly in the area of defending her children) to the same extent that it is seen as detracting from a man's masculinity.

Most of us, myself included, would be highly skeptical about this restriction of courage to men. But it raises important philosophical questions about the role of gender in ethics and the ideals toward which we are striving. We shall return to this issue in Chapter 10 in our discussion of the ethics of diversity.

COMPASSION

Responding to the Suffering of Others

One of the striking things about the villagers of Le Chambon was their ability and willingness to respond spontaneously and wholeheartedly to the plight of the Jews who came to their doors. It is precisely this responsiveness to suffering that is at the heart of compassion. Even the etymology of the word *compassion* highlights this element of compassion. It comes from the Latin words for *with* and *feel* or *suffer* or *endure*. To experience compassion for people is, at least to a limited extent or in some metaphorical fashion, to share their suffering with them. Yet the etymology takes us only part of the way because compassion is more than simply "feeling with"; it also involves a disposition to respond to others' suffering in a caring way that seeks to alleviate that suffering or to comfort those who are experiencing it. Let's look at both aspects of compassion: feeling and acting.

Compassion and Emotion

Compassion begins in *feeling,* in our affective relationship to the world. The compassionate person is not some type of utilitarian computer that infers or deduces the suffering that another person is experiencing; rather, the compassionate person suffers with the other person to some extent. This is the heart-wrenching dimension of compassion. I remember watching my father in a hospital room fighting for his life after major surgery, and my heart poured out to him. Similarly, the villagers of Le Chambon responded to the Jews who came to their doors by opening their hearts as well as their homes. At other times, we may experience compassion less intensely, but the basic affective response to the suffering of another person is the same.

There are at least two reasons why this affective dimension of compassion is so important. First, without compassion we will often fail to *recognize* the suffering of others as suffering. The compassionate person has, as it were, the emotional radar to detect suffering that would otherwise not be noticed as suffering. The Nazis did not perceive the suffering of the Jews as suffering, but rather simply as what they deserved. Often, precisely in order to be able to treat other people inhumanely or to prevent our own lives from being disturbed by the suffering of others, we shut ourselves off emotionally from perceiving the suffering of other people as suffering. Think, for example, of how many of us shut out the suffering of the homeless or the aged or those with AIDS. We don't let ourselves *feel* anything for these people because such feelings may disturb our lives.

Second, those who are suffering often need precisely this affective dimension of compassion, need the *feeling* of being cared about. A woman who had been saved through the village of Le Chambon commented on the difference between the experience of those who were saved through Le Chambon and those who were saved by fleeing to another country. "If today we are not bitter people like most survivors," she wrote, "it can only be due to the fact that we met people like the people of Le Chambon, who showed to us simply that life can be different, that there are people who care, that people can live together, and even risk their own lives for their fellow man."

Compassion, Moral Imagination, and Action

The relationship between compassionate feelings and compassionate action is a complex one. Compassion that *never* resulted in action would hardly be compassion. Yet we can imagine situations in which the compassion is genuine and yet, due to unusual circumstances, action is not possible. Compassion always involves the *desire* to do something about the situation, but it does not guarantee the opportunity to do so.

Even when the opportunity to act is present, compassionate feelings do not always tell us what the right course of action is. In order for compassionate feelings to be translated into actions, we need good judgment and often moral imagination as well. Recall the example of Le Chambon. For Jean-Pierre to bring a gift to Steckler on the bus, for the village to sing a song of affection and farewell to him—these were compassionate actions that showed an impressive amount of moral imagination as well.

It is precisely this element of moral imagination that traditional moral theories such as Kant's or Bentham's neglect. They seek to provide us with a set of *rules* for living the moral life, but moral imagination and creativity are precisely what take us beyond the rules. We might liken this to the difference between painting by the numbers and painting one's own composition. When I was a kid, we used to get these "paint-by-number" kits that contained a picture that was already outlined, and in each space was the number of the color to be painted in there. Some hope that the moral life is this way: Your moral principles will tell you exactly what to do. My own view is that the moral life is more like painting your own picture: Ultimately you have to sketch out your own picture and, based on your best knowledge and training, choose your own colors.

Compassion and Pity

One final element in our definition of compassion is worth noting here: the difference between pity and compassion. The difference centers on the issue of equality. When we pity people, we look down on them, we see them as less than we are. Pity is essentially a response that promotes *inequality,* establishing the superiority of the persons feeling pity over those they pity. This is part of the moral ambiguity of pity: In the act of pitying people, we both pull them up (by trying to help them) and put them down (by treating them as less than we are). It is little wonder that few people want to be pitied. When they are the object of pity, they pay a high price for the help they receive.

Compassion, on the other hand, presupposes a certain kind of *moral equality.* The villagers of Le Chambon did not look down on those they helped, but rather realized that "there, but for the grace of God, go I." This is why it is so much better to be the object of compassion rather than of pity. If people feel compassion toward you, they see you as an equal who happens to be suffering. Their emotive response joins with you rather than separates itself from you. You feel affirmed and supported rather than put down.

The Moral Extremes

If you recall Aristotle's strategy for analyzing the virtues, you will remember that he suggests that they can be bracketed between the two extremes of excess and deficiency. Aristotle doesn't discuss compassion, probably because he does not see it as a virtue. (He does discuss well wishing in Book IX of

Nichomachean Ethics, but that is the closest he comes to something like compassion.) Yet compassion offers an interesting challenge to the general claim that there can be both an excess and a deficiency in regard to any particular virtue. Let's look at this issue more closely.

Moral Callousness

There is relatively little difficulty with discussing what a deficiency of compassion would be like. It is a type of moral insensitivity or callousness, a state in which we fail to respond, either in feeling or action, to the suffering of other people.

In extreme cases, this lack of responsiveness may reach pathological dimensions. Sociopaths are individuals who seem to lack all feeling about the suffering of others, including that suffering that they may directly or indirectly inflict.

Other cases are less extreme, either in their intensity or their range. Some individuals may find that their level of compassion for anyone is low. Kant, in the passage cited in Chapter 6, talks of the man in whose heart "nature had implanted little sympathy." Such people have a generally low level of responsiveness to the suffering of anyone around them. At other times our lack of compassion is selective: Certain individuals, groups, genders, or races fall outside of the domain of those whom we are willing to perceive compassionately. In either type of case, we want to count this as a moral failing.

Moral Education

The degree of compassion that we are capable of feeling is not fixed and immutable, although it cannot be changed instantaneously by a sheer act of the will. We have, I think, a natural disposition toward compassion, but whether that compassion grows or atrophies depends on many factors, especially on childhood experience and education. Barriers to the growth of compassion may be mild or severe. A person's capacity for compassion is often dependent on childhood role models, usually parents. If our parents showed little or no compassion for the suffering of others, or if their compassion systematically eliminated certain individuals or groups as undeserving of compassion, we will probably have a tendency to be like them. In extreme cases when a child has been brutalized throughout childhood, whether physically or sexually or emotionally, the capacity for compassion may be all but extinguished.

There are various ways in which our capacity for compassion may be educated. The word *education* goes back to the Latin word *educere,* which means "to lead out of." Usually, moral education is a matter of leading us out of our narrowness and provinciality. Literature and the other arts are especially powerful in accomplishing this task because they develop both our understanding and our emotions at the same time. They help us to see the world through other people's eyes and to understand the richness of their perceptions.

Sometimes the barriers to compassion are much stronger. Individuals who have been brutalized as children, for example, have often erected amazingly high and thick walls that prevent them from recognizing the suffering of others. In such cases, intensive psychotherapy is often the only way of dismantling those walls. Such therapy, when successful, liberates people from the walls that imprison them and cut them off from their own capacity for compassion. As such, it, too, is a form of moral education.

Can We Have Too Much Compassion?

The question of whether it is possible to have too much compassion may seem a strange one that only philosophers would ask. After all, an overabundance of compassion is hardly our major social problem. If anything, our society needs to find ways of increasing compassion; it does not have to worry about having too much of it. Yet there is a value in asking this question because it rounds out our discussion of compassion by drawing our attention to two final points about compassion.

Indeed, we find that the charge of "too much compassion" is made in our society when we claim that someone is a "bleeding heart." Those who make such a charge rarely explain what they mean, but we can outline two interpretations of the "bleeding heart" criticism that will help us understand compassion better.

First, to call people "bleeding hearts" may imply that they do not know how to *act* properly on their compassion. At times, our compassion for others' suffering may lead us to act in ways that decrease those other people's responsibility for their own lives. If, for example, we see an older man with shaky hands trying to pour a glass of milk, we may take the pitcher and pour it for him as an act of compassion. In the process, however, we may rob him of a sense of his own autonomy and dignity. This, then, gives us one interpretation of the "bleeding heart" charge: Bleeding hearts may be individuals who feel a proper amount of compassion but act on it in inappropriate, albeit understandable, ways. From this we learn that it is not enough to feel compassion; we must also have the good judgment to know how best to act on it.

There is a second interpretation of the "bleeding heart" charge that gives us another insight into the nature of compassion. The charge might imply that the virtue of compassion has been given disproportionately great weight in either of two ways. First, our compassion for another's suffering may outweigh our perception of other characteristics of the individual. Our compassion for the suffering of a prisoner facing execution may overshadow our perception of the atrocious character of the prisoner's crimes. Second, and this is often a corollary of the first point, our compassion may outweigh other appropriate virtues, such as anger or justice. This suggests that we do not have to worry about having too much compassion as long as we are sure that it is balanced by other virtues. The answer is not to decrease the amount of compassion we have, but rather to increase the strength of the other virtues that balance compassion.

Gender and Compassion

In recent years extensive work has been done on the relationship between gender and ethics, and much of it has centered on the role of compassion in women's moral lives. We will be examining this issue in more depth in the next chapter, but several comments are in order here.

Compassion, Courage, and Gender

There is an interesting symmetry in the relationship between courage and masculinity and the relationship between compassion and femininity in our society. Just as an absence of courage counts against a man's masculinity, so an absence of compassion often counts against a woman's femininity.

There is another interesting barrier to the expression of compassion, a barrier that may be encountered more frequently by men than women. Often we encounter situations in which we want to show compassion, but we don't know what to *do*. We see someone crying in grief, we see a homeless, lost soul on the street, or we might even see someone dealing with the frustrations of aging. Because we don't know what to do, and because we are uncomfortable with our own impotence, we often push away these feelings of compassion. We do this because we can't stand the feelings of impotence and frustration that we experience when we cannot act on our compassionate feelings. This is more likely to be a problem for individuals who have been socialized into believing that they must always respond to situations through action. Insofar as men in our society are more likely to be socialized in this way, they are more likely to encounter this barrier than women are.

SELF-LOVE

Until she met Shug, Celie—the central character in Alice Walker's *The Color Purple* (1982)—was terrified. She never thought that she deserved much, if anything at all, in life. So her treatment at her husband's hands hardly came as a surprise. But the terror remained because she feared that each moment could be worse than the preceding one. From her earliest days, she felt that what she wanted just didn't count. Indeed, she hardly knew what she wanted. And then she met Shug.

Shug—short for "Sugar"—taught Celie what it means to love yourself. Sometimes she taught Celie by telling her—telling her how to act, telling her that it is OK to feel certain things. But her most powerful teaching came through her life: She taught Celie how to love herself by the way she lived her entire life. *The Color Purple* tells the story of Celie's journey toward self-love—and of her courage in persisting in this journey. And it is precisely this self-love or proper pride that Aristotle claims in *Nichomachean Ethics* is the central virtue upon which all the other virtues rest.

The Definition of Self-Love

Self-love, like other virtues we have discussed, has both an emotive and a behavioral component. It involves having certain *feelings* as well as *acting* and *knowing* in certain ways. We can understand it initially by comparing it with love for other people.

Loving Others

My wife and I love each other, and certain kinds of feelings and actions are typical of that love. We feel a real tenderness for each other, a sense of deep joy that we are in the world and that we are in each other's lives. I cherish her, and I want her to be happy; she feels the same about me. We both want what is best for the other person. *Love wants to see the other person flourish.* These feelings come out in the way we act as well. Besides lots of hugs and other displays of affection, we do many things to take care of each other. If we're overworking, one of us may plan a vacation for us to get away and just relax—or just go out for a nice long, relaxing dinner or even prepare a nice hot bubble bath for the other one at night.

Of course, none of this is perfect. We have our disagreements and arguments about things. We don't simply agree with one another: Love contains plenty of room for disagreement and criticism and even disapproval. When I want to order thick-sliced bacon for breakfast, my wife doesn't hesitate to remind me about cholesterol and calories. When she volunteers for one more committee, I don't hesitate to remind her about leaving some time to have a personal life. We find a real peace and harmony in our love for one another, but we still have plenty of room for disagreement, criticism, and growth.

Nor does our love for each other eliminate our love and concern for the rest of the world. For example, we both love our own families in which we grew up, and our love for each other certainly does not eliminate our love for them. We love each other first and foremost, but certainly not solely. Indeed, the other person whom we love is not an isolated being, but someone in a network of varying relationships. The other person, at least to some extent, is these relationships, and thus loving the other person is also indirectly loving the relationships that comprise that person's world.

Finally, it should be noted that love rests on a foundation of knowledge. One fundamental difference between love and infatuation is to be found here: Infatuation is the feeling of love but the illusion of knowledge. Just think of the question we ask most frequently after the infatuation has passed: How could I have been so blind? Infatuation is the feeling of love without the substance. Genuine love, on the other hand, knows the other, and indeed love itself illuminates the other. Conversely, being loved involves being known. Only those who can let themselves be known are able to participate in deep and reciprocal love.

Loving Ourselves

We can understand the meaning of self-love by first looking at its similarities to love of another person. First, it involves having certain kinds of *feelings* toward ourselves, feelings of positive regard, respect, and concern. Notice that this does not preclude self-criticism. *Self-love is not unconditionally positive self-approval.* It may include rigorous self-examination, but it does so within the context of a deep concern for the genuine welfare of the self.

Similarly, self-love involves *acting* in certain ways toward ourselves. People who genuinely love themselves act in ways that promote their flourishing, even when that is difficult. Alcoholics who are clean and sober are acting in ways that show a genuine self-love, even though it might be extremely difficult for them to do so. *Self-love does not mean doing whatever you want to do.* Rather, it means doing whatever promotes your genuine flourishing.

Just as in loving another person we also love that person as situated in the world, as connected to others in a wide range of relationships, so, too, loving ourselves involves loving our larger social relationships and commitments. The "self" in self-love is not just some inner core, but a self engaged in the world.

Finally, self-love demands self-knowledge. This is no easy task, and certainly one that is never complete. From the Delphic oracle's admonition "Know thyself" to Freudian psychoanalysis, the path to self-knowledge has always been an arduous one, but there is little doubt that this quest for self-knowledge is fundamental to self-love.

The Vices of Deficiency

Recall the story of *The Color Purple*. Celie provides us with a striking example of someone who has too little self-love.

A deficiency of self-love manifests itself in various ways. Some people are *self-deprecating,* putting themselves and their accomplishments down whenever possible. Others are *self-effacing,* hiding themselves and their achievements from notice by others. Some are *servile,* making their own needs and desires subservient to the needs and desires of others. When they do this by trying to please the people around them, they are *obsequious.* Some are simply *unaware of themselves* because they have never come to know themselves well enough to be certain of their own likes and dislikes, their own hopes and fears, their own beliefs and doubts.

Usually the behavior associated with these attitudes toward the self is easy to recognize. Yet sometimes it manifests itself in opposite ways. People with very low self-esteem may behave in straightforwardly self-effacing or self-deprecating ways. However, they may compensate for their feelings of inadequacy by going to the other extreme, acting in arrogant or conceited ways.

What, if anything, is wrong with these traits? Within Aristotle's perspective, the answer is clear: They detract from flourishing. People who always put themselves down, who hide their own accomplishments, and who put their needs behind everyone else's are less likely to flourish. They suffer from a kind of *anorexia of the spirit* in which they starve themselves from the nourishment of relationships of equality with other people.

The Vices of Excess

Excesses of self-love take many forms: Arrogance, conceit, egoism, vanity, and narcissism are but a few of the ways in which we can err in this direction. (The richness of our vocabulary here suggests that this type of vice is either more common than the vices of deficiency, or else we focus more carefully on this type when it occurs.) In some cases there is an excess of attention to the self, an absorption in the self *(narcissism);* other cases involve valuing the self too highly *(conceit);* some involve patterns of behavior that show little regard for the welfare of others *(arrogance);* still others involve too great an attention to some aspect of one's appearance *(vanity).*

Self-Love and Friendship

One area in which the need for proper self-love emerges most clearly is friendship. Aristotle suggested that it is difficult, if not impossible, to have good friendships without proper self-love. There is good evidence to suggest that he is right in this regard. Reciprocity and mutual concern are at the heart of friendship, and either too much or too little self-love throw these factors out of balance.

The Obsequious Friend

We all have seen people who are so desperate to have friends that they will do anything for the other person. They give up themselves in order to be accepted by the other person as a friend. Such friendships are usually doomed. The obsequious friend is constantly vulnerable to abuse because the friendship is often valued at all costs. Moreover, who would want that person for a friend after the person's true character is evident? One of the things that we depend on our friends for is to help us to see things in our lives that we may be missing or misinterpreting. But the obsequious friend is unwilling to stand up to a friend, to articulate a different vision of reality. Obsequious friends simply mirror back what they think we want them to see and say.

The Narcissistic Friend

The situation is hardly any better when friends are narcissists because this, too, upsets the reciprocity and mutual concern that are so central to friendship. Narcissists are so self-absorbed that they cannot be genuinely concerned for the welfare of their friends. An essential part of being a good friend is being concerned about one's friends for their own sake. This does not mean that friends are purely altruistic, but it does mean that they are not solely concerned about themselves.

Both too little self-love and too much self-love destroy the balance between self-love and love for the other person that is the foundation of genuine friendships.

Self-Love and Moral Traditions

Ethical Egoism

As we saw in Chapter 4, ethical egoism has a very important moral insight: We ought to value ourselves. It falls short of the mark, however, on two counts. First, it fails to provide an adequate account of how we ought to act in order to value ourselves. Second, it mistakes part of the story (valuing oneself) for the whole story. Aristotle, in stressing the centrality of the virtue of self-love, manages to capture the insights of ethical egoism without repeating its mistakes.

There are several prominent differences between the Aristotelian concept of self-love and the egoist's concept of selfishness or self-interest. First, typically, egoism understands the self in much narrower terms than the Aristotelian tradition does, and very often it fails to recognize the importance of the self's various engagements in the world. Second, most versions of egoism fail to include any affective dimension in this relationship to the self. There is no element of self-*love;* at best, it is a matter of self-interest. Third, although some conceptions of egoism refer to the self's interest, none of them contains a critical notion of flourishing like the one we find in Aristotle. Flourishing is not a matter of satisfying preferences or fulfilling our every whim, but a much fuller, richer, and also more critical notion. Finally, the egoist's self-interest is rarely understood to require self-knowledge in the way that Aristotelian flourishing does.

Self-Love, Self-Respect, and Kant

Kant's categorical imperative emphasized the importance of respect for oneself as well as for other people. That notion of self-respect, which contemporary Kantian philosophers like Thomas Hill have explored in fascinating detail, has important similarities to Aristotle's notion of self-love. Yet there are important differences that center in part on the more general differences between love and respect. Love contains a broader and richer affective component than respect does. We can respect a stranger we do not even care about personally; we can hardly love such a stranger without knowing him better or without caring about him. There is an intimacy to love that is not necessarily present in respect. Also, love and respect result in different actions because love is much more active and concerned about the other person than respect is.

The Place of Self-Love in the Utilitarian Calculus

One of Bernard Williams's principal criticisms of utilitarianism centers on the way in which it fails to give adequate weight to the individual agent's fundamental projects. An ethics of virtue that makes self-love the cornerstone of the moral life avoids this trap. Self-love involves giving a privileged place to one's own fundamental projects, to those hopes and dreams and values that are central to one's identity as a person because these are usually crucial to flourishing.

Pride, Humility, and the Christian Tradition

Initially, one of the startling contrasts between the Aristotelian and Christian traditions centers on the question of what counts as proper self-love or pride. On the surface, the contrast is stark: Aristotle calls pride a central virtue, whereas Aquinas condemns it as a cardinal vice, the root of all other vices.

When we look below the surface, however, the disagreement is less clear-cut, more nuanced. In fact, Aristotle (and Greek society in general) has something akin to what Aquinas calls "pride." For the Greeks, *hubris* is the overstepping of the bounds established by the gods. It is their equivalent of the Christian sin of pride. On the other side of the fence, Aquinas stresses the importance of the virtue of proper self-love. Part of the disagreement between Aristotle and Aquinas thus proves to be verbal. The same words (actually, the Greek and Latin equivalents of those words) mean different things. What Aquinas condemns as pride may be closer to what Aristotle calls *hubris* than what he calls "pride." Indeed, Lucifer's pride is quite close to Oedipus's *hubris*.

But this is only part of the story. For Aquinas, *humility* is clearly a central virtue, whereas this is not true for Aristotle. This reflects a larger difference in worldviews. Humility essentially consists in knowing one's place and in not overvaluing one's self and one's achievements. One's "place" is more clearly and firmly articulated in a Christian worldview than it was for the Greeks, and there has been a more elaborate institutional structure in Christianity to remind people of exactly what their place is. To encourage humility as a virtue is to promote a stable and placid social and political order.

PRACTICAL WISDOM, ETHICAL PLURALISM, AND THE GOOD LIFE

At the very heart of Aristotle's understanding of the moral life is his notion of *phronēsis,* which is variously translated as wisdom, practical wisdom, prudence, and even intelligence. Practical wisdom, although it has a paradoxical ring to it because wisdom is usually thought to be contemplative rather than active, is the most accurate translation. In discussing *phronēsis,* Aristotle is stressing two elements in this faculty of judgment. First, he is emphasizing the *practical* dimension of such judgments, which are essentially concerned with applying something general—a conception of the good life, of human flourishing—to very specific cases. Second, by calling this "wisdom," he is emphasizing the fact that it goes beyond the mere mechanical application of rules. In this way, Aristotelian moral judgments are certainly distinguished from mere calculations of the type that we find in utilitarianism. Indeed, *phronēsis* is closer to art than it is to science. Let's look at this more closely.

Practical Wisdom

Practical wisdom has several elements. It involves the reflective and affective application of a general disposition to right action of some kind (i.e., a virtue such as courage) to a particular situation (e.g., a threat by a mugger) in light of an overall conception of human flourishing. Thus there are three principal elements: a virtue, a particular situation, and a conception of the good life or human flourishing.

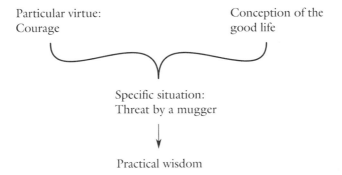

Particular virtue:
Courage

Conception of the good life

Specific situation:
Threat by a mugger

Practical wisdom

Thus, practical wisdom consists in the application of a specific excellence of character to a particular situation in light of an overall conception of the good life. This application has both an intellectual and an affective dimension. It is a thinking process, an act of reflection in which we take a general concept and apply it to a specific case. Yet it is accompanied by an affective process by which the individual has rightly ordered desires as well.

Wisdom and Cleverness

Part of wisdom is knowing the best way to achieve a particular end, and for this there is no exhaustive set of rules detailing how to determine in any particular case what the best means are. Rather, it is a matter of what Aristotle calls *cleverness*. In discussing this issue, Aristotle makes an interesting and important point about the difference between wisdom and mere cleverness. The simply clever person, Aristotle maintains, knows the best means to any particular end, but does not know which ends are worth pursuing. The wise person, in contrast, not only knows how best to achieve a particular end, but also understands which ends are worth striving to achieve.

The Reciprocity of the Virtues

Aristotle makes what appears to be a startling claim in his discussion of the virtues: You can't have one virtue without having the others. Yet given Aristotle's conception of practical wisdom, this makes good sense. Virtues don't exist in isolation; they are connected both to particular situations and to a general conception of human flourishing. If this is the case, then to fully have any one specific virtue is to see how it fits into the more general schema of a good life. And in order to do that, one must have the other virtues that are necessary to pursuing the good life as well.

This insight into the relationship between specific virtues and an overall conception of human flourishing allows us to resolve some of the difficult cases we saw earlier. Take courage as an example. Foolhardy and reckless individuals are those who face great dangers for things of little value; they have failed to integrate their ability to face fear into a larger conception of human flourishing and as a result do not possess the full virtue of courage. A similar issue exists with compassion. The person we have called a "bleeding heart" is one who responds by giving help (or money) in an unreflective way and without a sufficient overall conception of the good life. The genuinely compassionate person will respond to the suffering of others in both a thoughtful and an emotional way and will do so within the context of a conception of the good life for both the compassionate person and the person in distress.

The Elusiveness of Practical Wisdom

It is sometimes difficult to know how to respond to moral problems in a way that shows practical wisdom. Think, for example, of the problem of poverty in our society today. The challenge that we face as a nation is how to respond to the great economic inequalities found in our midst, especially those inequalities that have little to do with ability or perseverance. Welfare and other programs for the poor were certainly intended to respond in this fashion, and they were partially successful in doing so. However, programs were often developed and administered without a clear conception of human flourishing, the good life that we are seeking to realize. As a result, steps were motivated by compassion but were not sufficiently guided by a conception of the good life. Think, for example, of Aid to Families with Dependent Children. A well-meaning program, it inadvertently created financial disincentives for fathers to remain with their families—hardly a model of clear thinking or of human flourishing. Or take the example of public housing projects. They were well intentioned in most cases but rarely successful in their goals. They created more alienated and isolated communities increasingly troubled by violence and a sense of hopelessness and were rarely guided by a realistic vision of the good life.

Learning to be compassionate well, which is what virtue is all about, is difficult. So, too, is learning to be an accomplished artist or a skilled physician or a good parent. But the difficulty is no reason to abandon the attempt. If anything, it is a motive to try even harder.

Ethical Pluralism and Practical Wisdom

Aristotle's account of practical wisdom also provides a useful insight into ethical pluralism. The virtuous person always acts in light of a general conception of human flourishing. Each of the moral theories we have studied in this book contributes to our understanding of human flourishing, and the virtuous person of practical wisdom is the one who is able to balance these competing theories in particular situations, discerning which is most morally significant in a specific case.

Consider the example of telling the truth. The Kantian tells us that we must never lie because to do so is an act of profound disrespect for the autonomy of the other person. The rule utilitarian looks to the consequences of everyone's following a particular rule about lying, whereas the act utilitarian urges us to look at the consequences in each and every case before deciding whether a lie is justified or not. Ethical egoists simply urge us to act in a way that maximizes self-interest, and there is nothing intrinsically objectionable to lying as such. All of these considerations are morally illuminating, and the challenge faced by virtuous people is to balance them in particular situations. The point is not to prove one set of considerations right and all the others wrong; rather, it is to admit that all are relevant at least to some degree and then to seek the course of action that best balances these competing considerations. Moreover, in the Aristotelian view, it is not simply a question of telling the truth or lying; it is also a matter of how the truth is told (with care and consideration about its impact or crassly), when it is told, and to whom it is told. The virtuous individual uses moral theories to illuminate the moral landscape and to serve as a guide in navigating a path toward the good life.

CONCLUSION: THE ETHICS OF CHARACTER AND THE ETHICS OF ACTION

We can now see how this account of practical wisdom allows us to reply to some of Aristotle's critics. One of the principal criticisms leveled against Aristotle's approach to ethics is that it fails to tell us how to act. Despite all the illuminating things that Aristotle has to say about good character, we are still left without answers to the pressing moral questions of the day such as abortion, euthanasia, the death penalty, and the allocation of scarce medical resources.

There is much merit in this criticism, and this is a good reason for saying that virtue ethics is seriously incomplete without the moral traditions we have considered earlier in this book. An ethics of character must be completed by an ethics of action, of this there is no doubt. We can cultivate the virtue of compassion, for example, but when we act compassionately, we must still be aware of the moral concerns raised by other traditions. When we act compassionately toward other people, we must also be aware of their rights, take into account the consequences of our compassionate actions, and treat other persons as ends in themselves. Good character, in other words, does not obviate the need for other types of moral consideration.

However, an ethics of action is equally in need of an ethics of character for at least two reasons. First, one of the single greatest difficulties that act-oriented moral philosophies face is in applying a moral theory to a particular case. A morally sensitive character is more likely to ensure that we apply a principle with insight and creativity. Without good character, we will often be able to apply moral principles in only a mechanical manner, largely insensitive to the nuances of the situation. Second, as we have seen throughout this book, there are several moral traditions that are relevant to our considerations of how to act. The virtue of practical wisdom consists, in part, of being able to balance such potentially competing concerns about rights, duty, and consequences. The wise person is the individual who is able to know when the concerns of one tradition take precedence over the concerns of the other traditions.

DISCUSSION QUESTIONS

1. Recall your rating of **statement 36** in the Ethical Inventory ("Morality is mainly a matter of what kind of person you are").
   (a) After having studied several other approaches to ethics in addition to Aristotle's, what do you think the main arguments against this statement are?
   (b) Has your rating of this statement changed after reading this chapter? If so, in what way? If your rating has not changed, are your reasons for your rating any different now than they were when you first responded to this statement?
2. Recall your response to **statement 37** ("Sometimes courage seems to go too far").
   (a) Is courage a simple virtue, or does it have several components? If it is complex, what are its components?
   (b) If you agreed with this statement, give an example of when courage goes too far.
   (c) Has your rating of this statement changed after reading this chapter? If so, in what way? If your rating has not changed, are your reasons for your rating any different now than they were when you first responded to this statement?
3. Recall your rating of **statement 38** ("Compassion for the suffering of others is an important character trait").
   (a) In your view, can a person ever have too much compassion? Explain.

(b) Has your rating of this statement changed after reading this chapter? If so, in what way? If your rating has not changed, are your reasons for your rating any different now than they were when you first responded to this statement?

4. Your rating of **statement 39** ("It is important to care about yourself") gives an indication of your views on the importance of self-love as a virtue.

(a) Explain what it means to care about yourself. Give an example of doing so and an example of failing to do so. How important a virtue is this?

(b) Has your rating of this statement changed after reading this chapter? If so, in what way? If your rating has not changed, are your reasons for your rating any different now than they were when you first responded to this statement?

5. For Aristotle, virtues are those strengths of character that promote human flourishing. But exactly what is human flourishing? Address yourself to both the substantive and the epistemological issues that this question raises. Can you give any examples of someone who is clearly not flourishing? Are there any difficulties in *knowing* whether someone is flourishing? Are there many different legitimate conceptions of human flourishing? If so, how do you deal with these difficulties?

6. I have suggested that there are typically some gender differences in our society in regard to virtues such as courage and compassion. Based on your own experience, do you think this is true? Are there any other virtues in our society that exhibit gender differences? Are there any vices that are valued differently in men and women? Are there reasons why virtues and vices *should* be different for women and for men?

7. One of the virtues not discussed in this chapter is forgiveness. Think about the place of forgiveness in a person's character. Is it ever possible to be too forgiving? Not forgiving enough? Does *not* forgiving sometimes play a positive role in our lives? How does too little forgiveness detract from human flourishing? Why is it sometimes hard not to forgive another? If it is possible to be too forgiving, how could this detract from human flourishing? Why is it sometimes hard to forgive? How does forgiving—and not forgiving—yourself relate to human flourishing? How does self-forgiveness differ from forgiveness of other people? Explain.

8. Aristotle said to "count no man happy until he is dead." What does this mean? Is it true? Why must virtue (and human flourishing) wait that long?

9. **MOVIE** The movies *Glory* (1989) and *The Color Purple* (1986) present quite different views of courage. Compare these two movies in regard to the relationship between courage and gender. What does such a comparison suggest about this relationship?

10. **MOVIE** Was Gandhi courageous? If so, what does that suggest about the relationship between courage and violence? How does this contrast

with the picture of the relationship between courage and violence in *Glory?* Is the willingness to fight necessarily a sign of courage?

11. **MOVIE** In the movie *Amélie* (2001), the main character, a young waitress in Paris named Amélie, begins to practice random acts of kindness, which bring happiness to her as well as others. Analyze this movie within the context of virtue ethics, especially in regard to the virtues of love and compassion.

BIBLIOGRAPHICAL ESSAY

The classic source for discussions of the virtues is Aristotle's *Nicomachean Ethics* (abbreviated EN). It is available in a number of translations. For a list of Aristotle's works available on the Web, see the Reference Room page of my *Ethics Updates* (http://ethics.acusd.edu/books/); this includes links to the Perseus Project (http://www.perseus.tufts.edu/) at Tufts University, a superb site that includes both Greek text and English translations of Aristotle's works as well as extensive critical apparatus. Helpful **student commentaries/introductions** to EN include Gerard J. Hughes, *Aristotle on Ethics* (New York: Routledge, 2001); Christopher Biffle's *A Guided Tour of Selections from Aristotle's "Nicomachean Ethics"* (Mountain View, CA: Mayfield, 1991) and Roger Sullivan's *Morality and the Good Life* (Memphis, TN: Memphis State University, 1977). The account of the virtues in EN is supplemented, and occasionally contradicted, in Aristotle's other major work in ethics, the *Eudemian Ethics* (EE). For a translation and commentary on books I, II, and VIII of EE, see Michael Woods, *Aristotle's "Eudemian Ethics"* (Oxford: Clarendon Press, 1982). In addition to EN and EE, Aristotle's *Politics* and his *Rhetoric* contain important sections relating to the virtues.

   General works on Aristotle include Sir David Ross's *Aristotle* and W. K. C. Guthrie's section on Aristotle in his *A History of Greek Philosophy* (Cambridge: Cambridge University Press). **Works specifically on his ethics** include Nancy Sherman, *The Fabric of Character: Aristotle's Theory of Virtue* (Oxford: Clarendon Press, 1989) and her *Making a Necessity of Virtue* (Cambridge: Cambridge University Press, 1997); John Cooper, *Reason and Human Good in Aristotle* (Cambridge, MA: Harvard University Press, 1975) and his *Reason and Emotion: Essays on Ancient Moral Psychology and Ethical Theory* (Princeton: Princeton University Press, 1999); W. F. R. Hardie, *Aristotle's Ethical Theory* (Oxford: Clarendon Press, 1980); Richard Kraut's *Aristotle on the Human Good* (Princeton: Princeton University Press, 1989); Sarah Broadie, *Ethics with Aristotle* (New York: Oxford University Press, 1991); Julia Annas, *The Morality of Happiness* (New York: Oxford University Press, 1993); C. D. C. Reeve, *Practices of Reason: Aristotle's Nicomachean Ethics* (Oxford: Clarendon Press, 1995); and Gerasimos Santas, *Goodness and Justice: Plato, Aristotle, and the Moderns* (Cambridge: Blackwell, 2001). Two excellent anthologies of articles on Aristotle's ethics are Amélie Rorty's *Essays on Aristotle's Ethics* (Berkeley: University of California Press, 1980); Jonathan Barnes, Malcolm Schofield, and Richard Sorabji, *Articles on Aristotle: 2; Ethics and Politics* (New York: St. Martin's, 1977), which contains an excellent bibliography; and Steven Engstrom and Jennifer Whiting, *Aristotle, Kant, and the Stoics: Rethinking Happiness and Duty* (Cambridge: Cambridge University Press, 1998). One of the most fascinating treatments of Aristotle's ethics is to be found in part 3 of Martha Nussbaum's *The Fragility of Goodness: Luck and Ethics in*

Greek Tragedy and Philosophy (Cambridge, MA: Harvard University Press, 1986); also see her *The Therapy of Desire: Theory and Practice in Hellenistic Ethics* (Princeton: Princeton University Press, 1994). For a perceptive discussion and evaluation of Aristotle's ethics in light of current work in feminist ethics, see Cynthia A. Freeland, ed., *Feminist Interpretations of Aristotle* (University Park: Pennsylvania University Press, 1998) and Marcia Homiak, "Feminism and Aristotle's Rational Ideal," in *A Mind of One's Own: Feminist Essays on Reason and Objectivity* (Boulder, CO: Westview Press, 1993), pp. 1–18.

The **contemporary resurgence of interest in the virtues** begins with Philippa Foot's "Virtues and Vices" in her *Virtues and Vices and Other Essays In Moral Philosophy* (Berkeley: University of California Press, 1978), pp. 1–18 and Alasdair MacIntyre's *After Virtue,* 2nd ed. (Notre Dame, IN: University of Notre Dame Press, 1984). Several **reviews of the literature** are noteworthy: Arthur Fleming, "Reviewing the Virtues," *Ethics* 90 (1980): 587–595; Gregory Pence, "Recent Work on the Virtues," *American Philosophical Quarterly* 21, no. 4 (October 1984): 281–297 and his "Virtue Theory," in Peter Singer, ed., *A Companion to Ethics* (Oxford: Blackwell, 1991), pp. 249–258; Marcia Baron, "Varieties of Ethics of Virtue," *American Philosophical Quarterly* 22 (January 1985): 47–53; Gregory Trianosky, "What Is Virtue Ethics All About?" *American Philosophical Quarterly* 27, no. 4 (October 1990): 335–344; and Phillip Montague, "Virtue Ethics: A Qualified Success Story," *American Philosophical Quarterly* 29, no. 1 (January 1992): 53–61. Also see Alasdair MacIntyre's "Virtue Ethics," in Lawrence C. Becker, ed., *Encyclopedia of Ethics,* 2nd ed. (New York: Garland, 1992), pp. 1276–1282. For an insightful analysis into **historical views of virtue,** see Richard White, "Historical Perspectives on the Morality of Virtue," *Journal of Value Inquiry* 25 (1991): 217–231. Also see the excellent bibliography in Robert B. Kruschwitz and Robert C. Roberts, eds., *The Virtues* (Belmont, CA: Wadsworth, 1987). Other collections of contemporary articles on virtues and vices include Michael Slote and Roger Crisp, *Virtue Ethics* (New York: Oxford University Press, 1997); Amélie Oksenberg Rorty, *The Many Faces of Evil* (New York: Routledge, 2001); Christina Hoff Sommers and Fred Sommers, *Vice and Virtue in Everyday Life,* 5th ed. (Belmont, CA: Wadsworth, 2000); vol. 13 of *Midwest Studies in Philosophy* (1988) on virtue theory; the special double issue on the virtues in *Philosophia,* 20 (1990); Owen Flanagan and Amélie Rorty's *Identity, Character, and Morality* (Cambridge, MA: MIT Press, 1990); Halberstam's *Virtues and Values* (Englewood Cliffs, NJ: Prentice-Hall, 1988); John W. Chapman and William A. Galston, eds., *Virtue* (New York: New York University Press, 1992) and John Deigh's *Ethics and Personality: Essays in Moral Psychology* (Chicago: University of Chicago Press, 1992). On the more popular front, see William Bennett, *The Book of Virtues* (New York: Simon & Schuster, 1993). Joel Kupperman's *Character* (New York: Oxford University Press, 1991) presents a character-based ethical theory that places the discussion of particular virtues and vices within the context of the individual's character; Lester Hunt's *Character and Culture* (Lanham, NJ: Rowman and Littlefield, 1997) explores the interaction of character and culture. For a utilitarian approach to virtue, see John Kilcullen, "Utilitarianism and Virtue," *Ethics* 93, no. 3 (April 1983) 451–466.

Aristotle's discussion of **courage** appears primarily in his *Nichomachean Ethics,* book III, chapters 6–9. See Antony Duff, "Aristotelian Courage," *Ratio* 29 (1987): 2–15; David Pears's "Courage as a Mean" in Amélie Rorty's *Essays on Aristotle's Ethics* (Berkeley: University of California Press, 1980) is an insightful, detailed consideration of Aristotle's views on this virtue; for a critique of Pears's position, see

Michael Stocker's "Courage, the Doctrine of the Mean, and the Possibility of Evaluative and Emotional Coherence" in his *Plural and Conflicting Values* (Oxford: Clarendon Press, 1990), pp. 129–164. Douglas Walton's *Courage* (Berkeley: University of California Press, 1986) provides a standard account of courage that focuses on courageous actions rather than character, while Lee Yearley's *Mencius and Aquinas: Theories of Virtue and Conceptions of Courage* (Albany: State University of New York Press, 1990) offers an interesting cross-cultural comparison between the thought of an early Confucian and a medieval Christian. For a provocative picture of courage that also recognizes its negative side, see Amélie Rorty's "Two Faces of Courage" in her *Mind in Action* (Boston: Beacon Press, 1988). Also see chapter 2, "Courage," in John Casey's *Pagan Virtue* (Oxford: Clarendon Press, 1990); Lester Hunt, "Courage and Principle," *Canadian Journal of Philosophy* 10 (1980): 281–293 and Daniel A. Putnam, "The Emotions of Courage," *Journal of Social Philosophy* 32 (2001): 463–470. On ordinary courage in adolescent girls, see Lyn Mikel Brown and Carol Gilligan, *Meeting at the Crossroads: Women's Psychology and Girl's Development* (Cambridge, MA: Harvard University Press, 1992) and Annie Rogers's paper, "The Development of Courage in Girls and Women," *Harvard Educational Review* (1993). For an account of Rhonda Cornum's experiences as a prisoner of war, see, *She Went to War* by Rhonda Cornum as told to Peter Copeland (Novato, CA: Presidio Press, 1992). For an insightful discussion of gender and virtue in Aristotle, see "Gendered Virtue: Plato and Aristotle on the Politics of Virility," chapter 4 of Stephen G. Salkever's *Finding the Mean* (Princeton: Princeton University Press, 1990), pp. 165–204.

The explicitly philosophical literature on **compassion** is relatively limited. The best pieces are Lawrence Blum's "Compassion," in A. O. Rorty, ed., *Explaining Emotions,* (Berkeley: University of California Press, 1980), pp. 507–518; Martha Nussbaum, "Compassion: The Basic Social Emotion," *Social Philosophy and Policy* 13 (1996): 27–58; Brian Carr, "Pity and Compassion as Social Virtues," *Philosophy* 74 (1999): 411–428; Nancy Snow's "Compassion," *American Philosophical Quarterly* 28, no. 3 (July 1991): 195–205; and Adrian M. S. Piper, "Impartiality, Compassion, and Modal Imagination," *Ethics* 101, no. 4 (July 1991): 726–757; also see the section on compassion in Richard Taylor's *Good and Evil* (New York: Macmillan, 1970). For a perceptive and intriguing discussion of the place of compassion in contemporary American life, see Robert Wuthnow's *Acts of Compassion* (Princeton: Princeton University Press, 1991). The story of the village of Le Chambon is recounted in Philip Hallie's *Lest Innocent Blood Be Shed* (New York: Harper Colophon, 1979) and his articles, "Skepticism, Narrative, and Holocaust Ethics," *Philosophical Forum* and "From Cruelty to Goodness," in Christina Sommers and Fred Sommers, eds., *Vice and Virtue, in Everyday Life,* 3rd ed. (San Diego, CA: Harcourt, Brace and Jovanovich, 1992).

There is an extensive literature on the issue of **self-love and self-respect.** For insightful discussions of Aristotle's position on this issue, see David O. Brink, "Eudaimonism, Love and Friendship, and Political Community," *Social Philosophy and Policy* 16 (1999): 252–289 and Marcia Homiak "Virtue and Self-Love in Aristotle's Ethics," *Canadian Journal of Philosophy* 11, no. 4 (December 1981): 633–651. On the relationship between self-love and friendship in Aristotle, see especially Richard Kraut's *Aristotle on Human Good* (Princeton: Princeton University Press, 1989). One of the most influential contemporary philosophical articles on self-respect is

Thomas Hill's "Servility and Self-Respect," reprinted in his *Autonomy and Self-Respect* (Cambridge: Cambridge University Press, 1991). Interesting responses to Hill's article include Larry Blum, Marcia Homiak, Judy Housman, and Naomi Scheman, "Altruism and Women's Oppression;" *Philosophical Forum* 5 (1975): 222–247; George Sher, "Our Preferences, Ourselves;" and Marilyn Friedman's "Moral Integrity and the Deferential Wife," *Philosophical Studies* 47, no. 1 (1985): 141–150. On the relationship between self-respect and race, see Michelle M. Moody-Adams, "Race, Class, and the Social Construction of Self-Respect," *Philosophical Forum* 24 nos. 1–3 (Fall-Spring 1992–93): 251–266. For a superb discussion of self-interest and related concepts that challenges the traditional dichotomy between self and other, see Kelly Rogers, "Beyond Self and Other," *Social Philosophy & Policy* 14, no. 1 (Winter 1997): 1–20.

For a brief but excellent overview of issues about **pride,** see Lawrence Becker's "Pride," in Lawrence C. Becker and Charlotte B. Becker, eds., *Encyclopedia of Ethics,* (New York: Garland, 1992), vol. 2, pp. 1013–1015. For a defense of pride, see Richard Taylor, *Restoring Pride: The Lost Virtue of the Age* (Amherst, MA: Prometheus, 1996) and Tata Smith, "The Practice of Pride," *Social Philosophy and Policy* 15 (1998): 71–90. Also see Gabriele Taylor, *Pride, Shame and Guilt: Emotions of Self-Assessment* (Oxford: Oxford University Press, 1985) and Norvin Richards, *Humility* (Philadelphia: Temple University Press, 1992).

Citations. Philip Hallie's description of Le Chambon is drawn from "Scepticism, Narrative, and Holocaust Ethics," p. 40. The quotation from Aristotle's Nichomachean Ethics is from book II, chapter 6, 1106a16–24 in Irwin's translation, with minor changes. Martha Nussbaum's chart of the virtues is found in her "Nonrelative Virtues," *Midwest Studies in Philosophy* 13 (1988): 35. The woman's comments about Le Chambon are quoted in Hallie, ibid., p. 44. The story of Shug is found in Alice Walker, *The Color Purple* (New York: Harcourt, Brace and Jovanovich, 1982).

Further Information. For additional information about the issues raised in this chapter, see the page on Aristotle and virtue theory (http://ethics.acusd.edu/theories/aristotle/) on my *Ethics Updates* site.

THE ETHICS OF DIVERSITY: GENDER

Introduction

Even a cursory glance at the history of moral philosophy reveals that this is a discipline that was written *by* men. Just look back over the major moral theorists discussed in this book: Aristotle, Kant, and Mill. All men. There are some rare exceptions such as Mary Wollstonecraft, but they are decidedly exceptions and seldom acknowledged in the histories of moral philosophy written by men. Moreover, closer inspection reveals that it is also a discipline almost exclusively *about* men's moral experiences. The moral life of women was largely ignored or, when discussed at all, often misunderstood. Until recently, moral philosophy was by men and for men.

This has changed radically in recent years. Women's moral voices have come to play a major role in the development of moral theory in a way that had never occurred in the past. Indeed, those voices have reshaped our understanding of the history of moral philosophy, introduced new and fundamental concepts into moral theory, and have drawn the attention of both men and women to previously neglected moral issues. Let's consider each of these three areas, beginning with the ways in which women's moral voices have helped us to see the distortions of traditional moral theory. Then we will turn to a consideration of the ways in which women's voices have introduced new moral concepts into ethical theory, concentrating on the example of Carol Gilligan's work on an ethics of care. Finally, we shall look at the moral issues that emerge as significant after women's moral voices are allowed into the discussion.

RETHINKING THE HISTORY OF ETHICS

The Canon

It is difficult to appreciate the enormity of the exclusion of women from the history of ethics. To think that century after century, men and women exist side by side, confronting and reflecting on life's moral dilemmas—and yet, if one looks at the history of moral thought, it would seem as though women hardly existed. The canon of ethical theory—Plato, Aristotle, Augustine, Aquinas, Hobbes, Locke, Hume, Mill, Kant, Hegel, Nietzsche, Kierkegaard, Marx, Ayer, Moore, Wittgenstein—is notable for the absence of women.

What are we to make of this absence? Certainly part of what we want to say is that there were female moral philosophers such as Mary Wollstonecraft and Harriet Taylor and that they were often omitted from histories of ethics, despite the quality of their work. And of course, after they were excluded, they could no longer influence subsequent generations of thinkers, including other women. Part of the philosophical effort of rethinking the history of ethics centers on recovering the work of excluded authors like Wollstonecraft and Taylor.

We cannot, I think, conclude from the exclusion of women from the history of ethical theory that no one ever spoke on behalf of women's moral experience. John Stuart Mill's "The Subjection of Women" (1869) argues eloquently and forcefully against any attempt to relegate women to secondary moral status. Yet this is an exception, and the vast majority of moral philosophers simply ignored women's moral experiences or interpreted them solely from a man's standpoint.

The absence of women's moral voices, coupled with the exclusion or distortion of women's moral experiences, had serious implications for moral theory. Many contemporary feminist ethical theorists have argued that traditional moral theory is marked by several distortions. Let's examine several of these. As we shall see, these feminist criticisms parallel some of the criticisms of ethical theory that we have already seen earlier.

Autonomous Man

The starting point of modern moral theory—and this includes Hobbes, Locke, Mill, and Kant—is the isolated individual, separate from everyone else and seemingly independent. The central task of moral philosophy then becomes one of constructing an account of how such individuals ought to treat one another, how they can be brought together into some kind of harmonious coexistence. It is, essentially, an ethics of strangers, a set of rules for governing the interactions of people who neither know nor care about one another. Human beings, traditional theories tell us, begin in a state of nature where everyone is at war with one another. The challenge of morality is to provide both a motivation and a blueprint for peaceful coexistence.

Feminist moral philosophers have pointed out that this is a very odd picture of the human world and a picture that is in fact very much removed from reality. When we discuss the work of Carol Gilligan, we will see the ways in which she emphasizes the connectedness among human beings—a connectedness that women are more likely to recognize than are men. Indeed, many feminist moral philosophers have pointed out that the basic state of human beings in the world is one of connectedness and relationship. Caroline Whitbeck, for example, argues that people come to know and understand themselves through one another and that the basic unit is not the isolated individual but rather the mother-child combination. After the primacy of relationships is recognized, the nature of morality looks quite different. Whereas in traditional moral theories morality is designed to govern the interactions of autonomous strangers, feminist accounts of moral theory suggest that the focus of the moral life is primarily one of preserving relationships.

Social Contract Theory

When moral philosophers asked how autonomous man entered into moral relationships, they often replied by outlining some kind of contract theory. Individuals freely chose to subject themselves to certain rules from which everyone would presumably derive long-term benefit. Indeed, one of the powerful moral metaphors in social philosophy since the time of Rousseau (1712–1778) has been the social contract: Society is seen as a voluntary association of independent agents. John Rawls's account of the original position in his *Theory of Justice* (1971) and *Political Liberalism* (1993) continues this long tradition, and we find other versions of social contract approaches to morality in works such as David Gauthier's *Moral by Agreement* (1987), Russell Hardin's *Morality within the Limits of Reason* (1990), and Bernard Gert's *Morality: A New Justification for the Rules* (1989). Morality within this tradition is seen as the coming together of strangers who are guided largely by self-interest.

There are at least three ways in which this picture of morality as a social contract can be misleading. If we look at an early account of social contract such as Rousseau's, we see an account of the social contract that recognizes gender differences, but it does so in a way that clearly places women at a disadvantage. Rousseau's account of the social contract is certainly one of the most influential in history, but when we look at his picture of the education of those who would enter into that contract, we see how deeply gender bias affected his account of the world. In *Émile* (1762), Rousseau describes the virtues to be cultivated in this education of this autonomous man (Émile): fortitude, temperance, justice, and so forth. But when he turns to a discussion of Sophie, Émile's mate, Rousseau encourages quite different virtues such as patience, subservience, and flexibility—virtues that, not accidentally, make Sophie an ideal supporting character in Émile's life.

The dominant form of contract theory today avoids these kinds of distortions, but it does so at a high cost. Rawls, for example, urges us to consider what fundamental rules ought to govern society. We are to do this by imagining that we do not know what our specific position in life will be. We place ourselves behind a "veil of ignorance" about such matters and then ask what the basic rules ought to be—and from this we can deduce the fundamentals of justice. However, there is something odd here. The need for such a contract is created by imagining oneself stripped of all individual identity. The social contract is, in effect, an answer to a problem that it created itself. (Not all feminists reject social contract theory, as we shall see later in our discussion of Susan Moller Okin's work on the family.)

In contrast to this notion of a social contract among strangers of equal power, the moral philosopher Annette Baier has argued that the fundamental moral glue that holds society together is not contractual at all. Trust, she argues, antedates contracts. The basic moral fabric of society is woven from threads of trust, and trust is essentially grounded in relationships. Again, we begin to see the importance of the family because it is in the relationship between infant and parents that trust is first established. We do not come into the world as rational economic actors, but rather as helpless infants totally dependent on others for our survival.

Impartiality and Universality

The third way in which traditional ethical theory has been distorted is in its emphasis on impartiality and universality. The ideal moral agent is a being who has been stripped of personal identity (including gender, race, ethnicity, and personal relations). In the Kantian tradition, this is the ideal rational agent, who acts on the basis of maxims that can be willed as universal laws of humanity. In utilitarianism, the ideal moral agent is an impartial calculator, one who adds up the hedons and dolors associated with various courses of action and then chooses the alternative that produces the greatest amount of utility. Again, there is no room for individuality or what philosophers now call *moral particularity*. The ideal utilitarian is an impartial moral agent who acts the same way any other moral agent would act.

In its search for universality, traditional ethical theory often demands that we strip ourselves precisely of those things that, in the eyes of many feminist philosophers, constitute our humanness. We are our relationships, they say, yet it is precisely these relationships to which the traditional demand for impartiality denies moral legitimacy. Traditional moral theory delights in posing dilemmas like Godwin's, where we must choose between saving the life of our mother or the life of some famous individual who clearly contributes greatly to the good of humanity. Presuming that our identity as children and perhaps also as parents is central to who we are as persons, choosing the famous individual over our mother would be tantamount to denying the moral validity of that central relationship.

Moral theory, many feminist moral philosophers maintain, must concern itself much more directly with the details of everyday moral experience and abandon its refuge in its illusory universality and impartiality. As we shall see in part 3 of this chapter, the demand for universality and impartiality also has a distorting effect insofar as it takes attention away from the actual conditions of oppression under which many women live.

Transition

Thus, contemporary feminist moral philosophers, looking back on the history of ethics, see the ways in which ethical theory needs to be revised. For some, these revisions involve the development of new moral concepts. We will be examining an example of this when we look at Carol Gilligan's development of an ethic of care. For others, it involves attending much more closely to the ways in which women's moral issues have been hidden or misunderstood. Let's first look at Gilligan's work and then turn to a consideration of the new moral issues that contemporary feminist moral philosophers are examining.

NEW MORAL CONCEPTS: THE ETHICS OF CARE

Carol Gilligan's work on moral voices has had a profound impact on our understanding of both women's moral experience and moral theory. It is particularly interesting to see how her ideas developed because she did not set out to develop a feminist theory at all. Let's begin by looking briefly at the background against which Gilligan's ideas developed and then turn to a consideration of her own position on women's moral voices and the ethics of care.

The Kohlbergian Background

Kohlberg's Question

Lawrence Kohlberg's work in the psychology of moral development set the stage for discussions of moral development in the second half of the twentieth century in America. As a young man, Kohlberg was profoundly affected by World War II and its aftermath, including the events leading to the founding of the state of Israel. When Israel was still struggling for statehood, it was under a strict embargo that was intended to prevent the importation of food and medicine and armaments as well as the immigration of people. Some people defied this embargo, thereby breaking the law, in order to participate in the founding of the state of Israel. Kohlberg, deeply moved by their actions, wondered why some people would break the written law for the sake of what they held to be a higher good, a higher law. Clearly, many of them were not doing this for their own gain; indeed, breaking the law often actually cost them money and sometimes even their freedom or their lives. How was it, Kohlberg wondered, that some people obeyed this higher law whereas others refused to deviate from the letter of the law?

The Six Stages

Kohlberg would spend his life working out an answer to this question. What he found is that people pass through *stages* of moral development, some progressing further than others, most never getting beyond the fourth of six stages. The first two stages, which Kohlberg labels *preconventional morality*, are usually seen early in childhood. Stage 1 is dominated by the desire to avoid punishment, whereas stage 2 embodies an attitude of "You scratch my back, I'll scratch yours." Stages 3 and 4, which comprise *conventional morality*, usually are found in adolescence and adulthood. The third stage is what Kohlberg calls "the 'good boy/nice girl' orientation" in which the principal motivation is the desire to be a good person in one's own eyes as well as in the eyes of others. Stage 4 is characterized by following the rules of duly constituted authorities—a "law and order" mentality. The final two stages, comprising the level of *postconventional morality*, are usually never reached by most of the population. Kohlberg describes stage 5 as a social contract orientation, in which individual rights are given reasoned acceptance and revised in the light of well-reasoned critical discussions. The sixth and highest stage, which only a few persons like Mother Teresa, Gandhi, and Martin Luther King, Jr. have reached, is characterized by an orientation toward universal ethical principles of justice, reciprocity, equality, and respect. These principles are arrived at through reason and are freely accepted.

Characteristics of the Stages

Kohlberg sees these stages as universal, sequential, and irreversible. His initial research covered a Malaysian aboriginal village, villages in Turkey and the Yucatan, and urban populations in Mexico and the United States. He found that the boys and young men in these cultures all went through the same sequence of stages, regardless of such factors as ethnicity, religion, or class. He found, further, that one could not skip over a stage, moving, say, from stage three to stage five without going through stage four. Nor, Kohlberg claimed, could one go back a stage; movement could be only forward. Finally, we should note an ambiguity in Kohlberg's scale, one that has a significant impact on how we understand his work. On one hand, his stage theory is *descriptive* in character. That is, it simply claims to present the facts about how individuals change morally. On the other hand, his theory is also *normative* in character insofar as it claims that later stages are better than earlier ones. Indeed, this very notion of *development*—as opposed to mere *change*—suggests that later stages are preferable to earlier ones.

The Stages and Traditional Moral Theories

Obviously, Kohlberg's later stages bear striking resemblances to some traditional moral theories. Stage 5 clearly reflects social contract theories and rule utilitarianism, whereas stage 6 stresses Kantian themes of universalizability and rationality. (I suspect that Kohlberg was influenced by John Rawls, whose *Theory of Justice* circulated in manuscript form for many years before its publication in 1971; in that work, Rawls notes some of his differences with Kohlberg.) Clearly, the more impartial and the more universal one's moral reasoning is, the better it is for Kohlberg.

Gilligan's Starting Point

When Carol Gilligan began her research into moral development, she had no particular interest in gender issues. She was, however, interested in Kohlberg's work, and in the early seventies she began to study the moral reasoning of draft resisters. What attracted her to this study was that it presented precisely the same problem that Kohlberg had originally grappled with: How is it that some people come to obey a higher law than the written law of the land? Then something happened to Gilligan's study that social scientists have nightmares about. President Nixon canceled the draft. Although this change was politically welcome, it obviously undermined Gilligan's research project because there was no longer any draft to resist! Fortunately, she was still at an early stage of her research, and she shifted to study another difficult moral choice in our society: abortion.

Now, the interesting thing about this story is that Gilligan did not set out to study women's moral voices; indeed, if the draft had not been canceled, her subject pool—just like Kohlberg's—would have been composed entirely of men. (It is an interesting sign of the times that twenty-five years ago research could be confined solely to males and virtually no one would object—or even notice.) It was initially only a quirk of political fate that directed her attention toward an exclusively female group of subjects for her research. Yet it was Gilligan's sensitivity to what she then heard from her subjects that led to her tremendously influential work. When she began her research with women who faced the decision about abortion, she realized that what she was hearing did not fit into the framework that Kohlberg had established. We began to realize that women speak about their moral lives in a distinctive voice, one that Kohlberg's theory is unable to appreciate.

Women's Moral Voices

The Metaphor of Voice

In 1982, Carol Gilligan published a collection of her articles as a book entitled *In a Different Voice: Psychological Theory and Women's Development*. Its impact has been profound, not just in Gilligan's own field of developmental psychology, but also in a wide variety of other areas. Philosophy, religious studies, clinical psychology, communication studies, history, political science, literature, and art criticism are but a few of the traditional disciplines influenced by her work. The metaphor of "voice" became a particularly powerful one, and women in a number of fields concentrated on the challenge of "finding their own voice" in their specific fields.

The metaphor of voice struck a chord, as it were, with many women, and it is worth pausing for a moment to consider its power. By talking about women's voices instead of their theories or perspectives, Gilligan chose a focus that is more concrete and potentially more capable of integrating differences harmoniously than are other, more common metaphors for moral diversity. Throughout this book, we have seen how the language of theories leads quickly to competitive and combative accounts of morality in which ultimately only one theory can be correct. Appealing to perspectives instead of theories offers more room for diversity, but there is virtually no trace of individuality in the perspectives themselves. To speak of voices, however, is immediately to conjure up something concrete, something with tone, texture, and cadence. Think, for example, of the distinctive voice of a singer like Whitney Houston, of a politician like Barbara Jordan or Margaret Thatcher, of a poet like Maya Angelou, or of actresses like Meryl Streep, Dolly Parton, and Whoopi Goldberg. Their voices are rich, nuanced, evocative, and utterly distinctive. The finely textured specificity found in the appeal to voices is not found in talk about theories or perspectives.

Three other characteristics of voices are particularly noteworthy. First, voices combine both emotion and content. *How* something is said is closely tied to *what* is said. Voices are *embodied* in a way that theories are not. Second, voices are described and assessed in a wide range of terms, most of which have little to do with "true" and "false" or "right" and "wrong." Voices may be strong or weak, full-bodied or hollow, lilting or deep, strident or sweet, excited or dull, trembling and hesitant, or clear and confident. Third, voices may be different without excluding one another. Think of the ways in which people sing together. They may blend their voices in a choir. They may sing harmony, one voice in distinctive counterpoint to another. They may toss a melody back and forth from one person to another, taking turns singing. One may be the lead singer, others may sing background. There are, in other words, numerous ways in which voices may interact with one another.

Think about this in regard to yourself. If you were asked to describe your moral *theory,* it would probably be in impersonal language that gives little clue to who you are as an individual. On the other hand, if you were asked to describe your moral *voice,* it would be much more specific, much more indicative of who you are as a person, much more recognizable to your friends as *you.* It might be quiet or loud, questioning or obedient, strident or cajoling, authoritative or confused, stiff or supple, humorous or serious, fearful or reckless. Although we can certainly describe different types of voices, even the types have a concreteness and specificity about them that theories lack.

In her novels, poetry, and essays, Alice Walker (1944–   ) gives voice to the experiences of African-American women.

Let's now hear what Gilligan found out about women's moral voices. We will begin by contrasting women's voices to men's voices and then look more specifically at the voices that characterize the stages of women's moral development.

Differences between Men's Voices and Women's Voices

When Gilligan began doing her research with female subjects, she noticed that their responses didn't seem to fit neatly into Kohlberg's framework. It's not that the responses couldn't be squeezed into that framework, but rather that something essential and distinctive was lost in the process and other things were misinterpreted or misvalued. Gilligan's study showed, first of all, that women tended much more often than the men of Kohlberg's studies to see the moral life in terms of *care* rather than *justice*, in terms of *responsibility* rather than *rights*. Whereas men see problems as moral issues when they involve competing claims about *rights,* women see problems as moral issues when they involve the *suffering* of other people. Whereas men see the primary moral imperative as centering on *treating everyone fairly,* women see that moral imperative as centering on *caring* about others and about themselves. Men typically make moral decisions by *applying rules fairly and impartially,* whereas women are more likely to seek resolutions that *preserve emotional connectedness* for everyone. Similarly, men tend to look back and to judge whether a moral decision was correct or not by asking whether the rules were properly applied, whereas women tend to ask whether relationships were preserved and whether people were hurt. The quality of the relationships, rather than the impartiality of the decisions, is the standard for evaluating decisions for women. The meaning of responsibility also changes. For men, responsibility is primarily a matter of being *answerable* for actions, for having followed (or failed to follow) the relevant rules. For women, responsibility is primarily a matter of taking care of the other person, including (and sometimes especially emphasizing) that person's feelings. Moreover, it is directed toward what the other person actually feels and suffers, not what "anyone" (i.e., an abstract moral agent) would experience. Responsibility is directed toward real individuals, not toward abstract codes of conduct.

These differences tend to reflect deeper differences between men and women, differences in the ways in which they conceive of the self. Men are much more likely to see the self in terms of autonomy, freedom, independence, separateness, and hierarchy. Rules guide the interactions among people, and roles establish each individual's place in the hierarchy. In contrast, women tend to see the self in terms of relatedness, interdependence, emotional connectedness, and responsiveness to the needs of others. Instead of depending on rules as men do, women are much more likely to show an immediate response to the plight of the other person. They experience themselves, first and foremost, as *connected;* the self is its network of relationships.

These differences also affect what men and women will tend to experience as comfortable or threatening. Typically, men will experience the top of a social or professional hierarchy as appealing, as attractive to their sense of autonomy, as compatible with their sense of separateness. Women are more likely to experience it as isolated and detached, as threatening to their sense of connectedness. Conversely, men are more likely to feel at risk in situations that threaten their sense of autonomy and separateness—especially in situations of dependency and intimacy. Women are more likely to feel at risk in situations that threaten their sense of responsiveness and connectedness— and these are typically situations of independence and hierarchy.

The Stages of Women's Moral Development

Gilligan sees women as developing through stages of moral growth, just as men do, but the stages are different in important respects. She divides her schema into three levels, just as Kohlberg did. However, instead of having two stages under each level, Gilligan has three full stages and a transitional period between each stage. Thus, there are three full stages and two transitional stages.

Moral development for females begins, according to Gilligan, with the concern for *individual survival* as paramount. This is level 1 of moral development, corresponding to Kohlberg's preconventional level. It is followed by the *transition from selfishness to responsibility,* in which women start to become aware of morality as requiring that they be responsible for the well-being of others. Level 2, which corresponds to Kohlberg's level of conventional morality, is one in which *goodness comes to be equated with self-sacrifice.* Many of us have probably had mothers or grandmothers who saw their lives in precisely these terms: To be a good person is to take care of other people (husband, children, family) at the expense of herself. For them, it wasn't a struggle to motivate themselves to take care of other people—the struggle came when they tried to give themselves permission to take care of *themselves.* It is precisely this struggle to include the self that constitutes the second transitional stage. It is often a difficult struggle because initially it feels more like moral regression than moral progress because morality is equated with self-sacrifice. Gradually, however, this experience gives way to a third level, one in which moral goodness is seen as *caring for both self and others.* This highest level is one that takes inclusiveness and nonviolence as ideals and that condemns exploitation and hurt.

The Voice of Care

A clear theme emerges throughout these stages: Women's moral voices are voices of care. Whether it be a narrowly defined care for one's own survival, an altruistic care for other people, or an inclusive care for both self and others, *morality is primarily about caring.* It is not about rules, universalizability, the impartial computation of consequences, or anything like that. It is about a direct relationship of emotional responsiveness to the suffering of persons, both self and other.

Gilligan's Traditionalism

One of the striking things about Gilligan's work, especially in light of its strong impact on feminist thinking, is the traditional, almost stereotypical picture of women that it seems to promote. Women emerge as more concerned about relationships, emotional connectedness, and care-giving than are men, who seem more independent, rule-oriented, and emotionally detached. Gilligan herself states that her findings are only generalizations and that it is certainly possible that some individuals do not fit into the pattern that she associates with their biological sex. It seems that the danger here is that this moral theory may perpetuate traditional sex-based stereotypes. Yet I think there is a way of retaining many of Gilligan's insights about *masculinity* and *femininity* without necessarily tying those as closely to *males* and *females* as she does. Let's look at the issues raised by this gender-based morality.

Integrating Diverse Voices

A deep ambiguity runs through Gilligan's work. Clearly, her work is *descriptive*. It articulates women's moral voices and the differences between their voices and men's without necessarily making any value judgments about which are better. However, at times her work also seems to have *normative* implications, suggesting that one voice may be as good as, perhaps even better than, another. Some of Gilligan's statements suggest that she thinks both men's voices and women's voices are of equal value in morality; other statements suggest that she may see women's voices as superior. In this context, we can set aside the question of what Gilligan herself says about this question and look at the various possible positions on this issue and consider them on their own merits.

The Separate but Equal Thesis

Assuming that, in general, men and women have different moral voices, one of the ways in which we could deal with the differences is to keep the two separate but equal. Men and women have different moral voices. Men's voices are right for men, women's voices right for women. Neither is superior to the other; they are just different.

The problem with this thesis is fourfold. First, it is very difficult to retain the "but equal" part of such a position. After the two voices have been separated, it is all too easy to dismiss the second voice as less important. Second, such a position tends to perpetuate gender-based stereotyping because only males are given male voices and only females are given female voices. Third, it suggests that men and women have nothing to learn from one another because each sex has its own moral voice. Fourth, males who have a "female voice" and females who have a "male voice" are looked down upon. The separate but equal approach is, as it were, a form of sex-based isolationism.

The Superiority Thesis

The second possible position is to maintain that one of these two voices is superior to the other. Historically, this has been the dominant position, most often with men maintaining (usually implicitly, occasionally explicitly) that men's voices are superior to women's voices in morality. In recent times, the roles have sometimes been reversed, with women claiming the superiority of women's voices.

There are two problems with this position. First, to say that one voice is completely true for everyone in all situations is interesting but obviously false. To say that one voice is partially true for some people in some situations is accurate, but it is so vague as to be unhelpful without further elaboration of the particular conditions under which one voice takes precedence over the other. Such further elaboration then yields a position that is significantly different than the original thesis.

The second problem with this position is that it is exclusionary. It excludes whichever position is seen as not true—and that usually means that we cannot learn from that other, excluded voice. If, on the other hand, we admit that we can learn from the other voice, then we find ourselves defending a version of one of the next two positions.

The Integrationist Thesis

The integrationist maintains that there is ultimately *only one moral voice,* a voice that may be the integration of many different voices. The integrationist need not claim to know precisely what this voice is but must be committed to the claim that ultimately there is only one voice.

The principal difficulty with the integrationist thesis is that it is susceptible to losing the richness that comes from diversity. The integrationist position tends to be assimilationist, blurring the distinctive identities of the sources of its components. It celebrates a moral androgyny as a replacement for the sex-based voices.

The Diversity Thesis

The final thesis claims that we have diverse moral voices and that this diversity is a principal source of richness and growth in the moral life. We can learn from one another's differences as well as from similarities. The diversity thesis in the area of gender most closely embodies the pluralistic approach characteristic of this book.

The diversity thesis has two complementary sides. First, there is the *external diversity thesis,* which suggests that different individuals have different (gender-based) moral voices and that here is a fruitful difference from which we can learn. Men can learn from women, just as women can learn from men. What makes this an *external* diversity thesis is that it sees diversity as something that exists among separate individuals.

The *internal diversity thesis* sees diversity as also existing *within* each individual. Each of us, in other words, has both masculine and feminine moral voices within us, and this diversity of internal voices is considered a positive thing. One of the attractions of this position is that it minimizes gender stereotyping because it denies that only men can have a masculine dimension or that only women can have a feminine dimension. Men can have both masculine and feminine dimensions to their moral voices, just as women can have both.

Nor is it necessary to think that an increase in one type of voice necessarily leads to a decrease in another. Sandra Bem has suggested that masculine and feminine traits in general may be mapped along two different axes, such that an individual may be high in both (androgynous), low in both (undifferentiated), high in femininity but low in masculinity (traditional feminine), or high in masculinity but low in femininity (traditional masculine). This leads to the following schema.

The Bem Scale

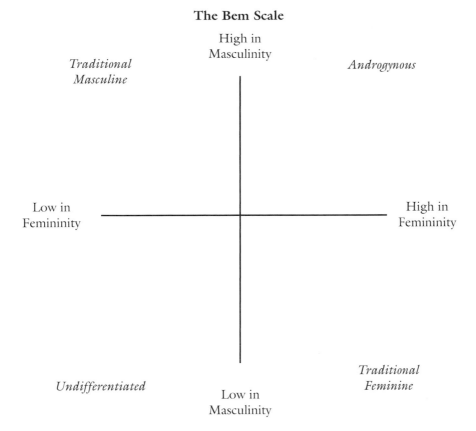

High in
Masculinity

Traditional
Masculine

Androgynous

Low in
Femininity

High in
Femininity

Undifferentiated

Traditional
Feminine

Low in
Masculinity

The principal strength of this scale is that it does not make masculinity and femininity mutually exclusive traits. This is in sharp contrast to models that plot masculinity and femininity on a single axis with "strongly feminine" and "strongly masculine" at the opposing ends of the axis. On Bem's scale, one can be high in both, or low in both, as well as high in just one or the other. More often than not, males identify with a masculine gender and females with a feminine gender. We are probably most familiar with individuals who are high on only one of these scales, but we have occasional examples of individuals who are high on both scales.

TALKING ABOUT ETHICS:
A CONVERSATION WITH
CAROL GILLIGAN ABOUT
VOICE AND ETHICAL
THEORY

Carol Gilligan, a professor at the Harvard Graduate School of Education, is the author of *In a Different Voice* (1982) as well as numerous other works on girls' and women's moral development.

Hinman:	The concept of voice plays a central role in your thought. What do you mean by "voice"?
Gilligan:	I use the word "voice" coming out of a background in literature and also in music, so I'm very aware of the physical, even tonal, quality of voice. In the last few years, I have become increasingly interested in voice in theater, and some of my most exciting work recently has been with voice in the theater. To me, voice is something physical, but it leads directly to the relational. To have a voice is to be human. To have something to say is to be a person, but speaking also depends on listening and being heard. It is an intensely relational act. Thus voice reveals a psyche connected to both the natural and the social world.
	It is this relational aspect of speaking and listening that I find so interesting. The inability to speak—the inability to connect one's inner world of thoughts and feelings with an outer world—comes from a problem in relationships. I became very interested in how people lose—or simply don't develop—the capacity to represent themselves, to speak their inner world. So voice to me is a part of being human, and problems in speaking, problems in voice, are then problems in relationship.
Hinman:	What role then does voice play in ethics?
Gilligan:	Its role is absolutely fundamental. Think of ethics as a conversation. Historically, this conversation has been limited by at least two factors: Some people have been excluded entirely from the conversation, and others have been unable or unwilling to articulate their inner world within the context of that conversation because they could not be heard.
	Let me give you an example of the second point first. When I started my research many years ago, I remember a particular conversation with a woman whom I was interviewing. I was asking her the kinds of questions that as a

psychologist I had been trained to ask. There was a moment in the interview when she looked at me and said, "Would you like to know what I think, or would you like to know what I *really* think?" Here was someone who could articulate her inner world but wasn't sure whether I wanted her to do so within this conversation. At other times, you find individuals who initially cannot even give voice to that world when they are encouraged to do so.

Returning to the first point, think of the history of ethics as an ongoing conversation. Historically, for many reasons, women's voices have been excluded almost entirely from that conversation until the last few decades. We are now in the process of adding new voices, that is, adding the voices that have been missing from this history, specifically the voices of women, and also voices of other people who have been outside this mainstream of the ethical conversation, that is because of their ethnicity, culture, or race. This offers the possibility then of changing the conversation and looking more deeply into this story.

Hinman: How do you see this as changing the shape, or tone, of ethics?

Gilligan: Just think of the new issues that emerge when women's voices become part of the conversation and when they are heard in ways that do more than simply assimilate them to men's voices. New moral issues emerge as significant—think of the contribution of women's voices to our understanding of issues such as violence, pornography, discrimination, and poverty. Also think of the ways in which women's voices have increased our awareness of neglected but very positive elements of morality such as love, compassion, caring, and the like. As women and other excluded groups are drawn increasingly into the conversation of ethics, and as their voices are heard increasingly on their own terms, the conversation becomes richer, fuller, and more helpful to all of us.

Hinman: Much has been written in recent years about the relationship between an ethic of justice and an ethic of care. Your work is usually identified with an ethic of care. Where do you stand on this issue?

Gilligan: That's an important issue, but to answer it we have to look first at the context of the question.

It's helpful, first of all, to distinguish between a feminine ethic of care and a feminist ethic of care. When care is seen as part of a feminine ethic, it usually involves special obligations and relationships, duties imposed on women to be selfless and self-sacrificing. The inner world of women is rarely allowed expression in the outer world, and women's voices are often silenced. This fits in as part of a larger patriarchal structure in which care and justice really are separate: Those who are told to be caring are rarely those who are given justice. Needless to say, this is not the kind of ethic of care that I am talking about.

A feminist ethic of care is quite different. Here, inner voices are allowed to surface and to resonate, to come into relationships. Connection is primary in this world, but it is connection unrestrained by traditional patriarchal structures. Not only is this different from a feminine ethic of care, it is also different from "equality feminism." Equality feminism rightly maintains that women should not be seen in any way as less than men, but it understands being equal as being like men. This, too, separates women from their own voice, constraining the expression of women's unique inner experiences in the outer world.

One of the most startling examples of equality feminism occurred a few years ago at the height of the war in Bosnia, when the new media were running countless stories of men killing other men and raping and killing the women in Bosnia. In an article in *The Nation,* Katha Pollit criticized those who thought women were less violent than men. Equality seems to mean not seeing or speaking about differences.

The feminist ethic I am articulating could be called "difference feminism." It recognizes that women may have different points of view and different voices. This is not to deny that women can be made to think and act and even kill like men, but it hardly sees this as an ideal. Difference feminism supports the integrity and importance of women's experiences and therefore refuses to reduce those experiences to the experiences of men. Only in this way can women's voices be heard as providing valuable contributions to the ongoing discussion that constitutes ethics.

Gilligan's Recent Work: Rethinking the Foundations of Ethics

In recent years, Gilligan has continued to pursue a series of empirical investigations, concentrating increasingly on the development of adolescent girls, including their moral development. As this work has progressed, several themes have moved from the background of her work increasingly into the foreground.

Ethics as Conversation

Moral discourse, to Gilligan's ear, is primarily *conversation*. This reflects her earlier criticisms of Kohlberg and the methodological shift that characterizes her work. Kohlberg began by presenting his subjects with the now well-known Heinz dilemma. Heinz's wife is critically ill with a rare form of cancer. The only druggist who has a possible cure is charging an outrageous amount of money, which Heinz just doesn't have. The question that Kohlberg poses is: Should Heinz steal the drug? Why or why not? Kohlberg expected an answer and a reason (e.g., human life is more valuable than property), but not a conversation. Indeed, one of the disturbing things (from the Kohlbergian standpoint) was that girls wanted to talk about the situation. They asked questions, looked for more details, tried to find hidden alternatives, and so forth. As a result, their responses often didn't fit the framework established by Kohlberg. These girls were, in effect, offering a different view of moral discourse. Kohlberg's view was that moral discourse is about taking a position and giving reasons in support of it. Gilligan's respondents were telling her that ethical discourse has a different form: It is primarily a conversation, an interchange.

Inclusive Conversations

After moral discourse comes to be seen as a conversation—a venerable tradition, to be sure, stretching from Plato's dialogues to Gadamer's *Truth and Method* (1975)—it is a short step to seeing that the conversation must be an inclusive one. In Gilligan's recent thinking, she increasingly emphasizes the idea that the conversation must be opened up to include everyone. Voices that had previously been excluded or muffled—notably the voices of women and many people of color in the United States—must become equal participants in the discussion. Again, recall the Heinz example: The voice of the wife is completely absent. Certainly one very appropriate response, which has little place on the Kohlbergian scale, is that Heinz should ask his wife what she wants him to do. Indeed, we hear nothing of the druggist's voice, either.

New Voices, New Issues

Gilligan thus begins to rethink the foundations of ethics by seeing ethics primarily as conversation rather than as theories and arguments and by suggesting that more inclusive conversations are better than ones that exclude some people's voices. The third step in this rethinking is to see the way in which, with the introduction of new moral voices, new moral issues come to the fore. Think, for example, of issues such as domestic violence, child abuse, family leave, and responsibilities toward elderly parents. These are pervasive moral issues, hardly ones confronted by only a few isolated individuals, yet they have received scant attention in the standard philosophical anthologies on contemporary moral issues.

The Use and Abuse of Moral Notions

Finally, Gilligan's recent work offers us a cautionary note: Beware of the ways in which so-called morality can be used to justify violence. Wars are an obvious example: All too often, countless people are killed in the name of honor. Domestic violence is often seen as justified in the eyes of the abusers to maintain their honor, and the appeal to moral values is often used to justify the suppression of those who do not agree with our version of morality.

Caring and Act Utilitarianism

Interestingly, there are some similarities between an ethics of caring and act utilitarianism. They are both, generally speaking, consequentialist theories; that is, both see morality primarily as a matter of consequences. Both are concerned with weighing the consequences of projected actions, and both see those consequences—broadly speaking—in terms of the pleasure or pain that they might cause.

But the differences are equally instructive. The act utilitarian usually employs some kind of calculus, some method of computing the total amount of pleasure and pain that would result from various courses of action. Gilligan's ethics of caring is consequentialist, but it differs from act utilitarianism both in (1) what kinds of consequences count and (2) how they are measured. The care ethic focuses primarily on two kinds of consequences: (1) the extent to which people might be *hurt* by a particular decision and (2) the degree to which a particular decision might diminish the *sense of connectedness* among the participants in the situation. Connectedness itself becomes a moral value. Moreover, the method by which these consequences are determined has a strongly intersubjective component. Whereas utilitarian calculators might well attempt to weigh consequences in the isolation of their offices, the caring person attempts to weigh consequences by talking with the participants and allowing them to participate actively in the process. For those assuming the standpoint of an ethic of care, there is an essentially intersubjective moment to the decision-making process. Both *what* is valued and *how* it is valued have a strong intersubjective dimension.

Emotions play a much more significant role in the ethics of caring than they do in the utilitarian calculus. First, in an ethics of caring, emotions (especially compassion and empathy) are necessary in order to know how much pleasure or pain a particular action causes. How can you know how much pain a particular action may inflict on friends if you do not listen to what they say about their feelings and try to understand those feelings? This process of listening and understanding is not just a purely intellectual one, but also involves an emotional, or affective, component.

Second, there is another emotive dimension to the ethics of caring that is absent from act utilitarianism. Caring simply has an irremediably emotive component to it. To care about someone is not just to act in particular ways; it is also, and necessarily, to *feel* in particular ways. There would be something odd if a parent tried to add up impersonally all the hedons and dolors for a particular choice that will affect the family. Part of caring is to feel something for the other person. (There is also a double evaluation going on: understanding how much the other person values a particular action of ours, and understanding how much we value the other person.)

This suggests a way of understanding the relationship between act utilitarianism and the ethics of caring. In an impersonal context where we are dealing with large numbers of people who are strangers to us, act utilitarian considerations may well be relevant. In personal contexts where we are dealing with people we know and care about, the ethics of caring may well better capture the moral insights that utilitarianism captures in the other, larger-scale contexts.

FEMINIST MORAL THEORY: EMERGING MORAL ISSUES

Feminine and Feminist Ethics

Moral theorists often distinguish between feminine ethics and feminist ethics. In general, *feminine ethics* is seen as emphasizing what is characteristic of women's moral voices. Often, following Gilligan, this is developed into an ethic of care. *Feminist ethics,* on the other hand, begins more directly with an awareness of women's oppression and argues more directly for policies that would rectify past injustices and establish genuine equality. In an influential treatment of feminist ethics, Alison Jaggar has argued that there are four minimum conditions that an ethical theory must meet to count as a feminist theory:

1. It must be sensitive to gender inequalities, never beginning with the assumption that men and women are similarly situated.
2. It must understand individual actions within the larger context of broader social practices.
3. It must be able to provide guidance to issues that traditionally have been seen as within the private domain, such as personal relationships and family issues.
4. It must "take the moral experience of all women seriously, though not, of course, uncritically."

In this account, feminist ethics is always aware of the ways in which issues of gender involve issues of power as well and the ways in which seemingly isolated issues exist within a larger social context of gender inequalities.

This is certainly a controversial distinction, and not everyone would agree with how the line of demarcation is drawn. In her article in *Hypatia* (1995) that was part of the Symposium on Care and Justice, Carol Gilligan distinguished between a feminine ethic of care and a feminist ethic of care. A *feminine ethic of care* urges women to pursue traditional virtues of selfless-ness, subservience, humility, and self-sacrifice, and Gilligan clearly distances herself from this position. A *feminist ethic of care,* in contrast, maintains the importance of relationships but refuses to cooperate with any efforts to con-fine women within traditional patriarchal power relationships.

However this distinction is drawn, the fact remains that some feminist moral theorists have been much more radical in their critique of the gender bias of traditional ethics, and they have often seen these issues in starker political terms than we have used so far. As philosophers take the moral ex-periences of women seriously, they begin to see that there are a number of previously neglected moral issues that merit attention. In many cases, these can be understood through the application of traditional moral concepts in new contexts. Here are just a few examples.

The Distinction between Public and Private

One of the crucial distinctions in traditional moral theory is between the public and private realms. Whereas moral scrutiny was focused on interac-tions in the public realm, the private realm was rarely seen as a suitable ob-ject of moral investigation. The private realm corresponded in traditional societies with the realm of women and children, and the net effect of this distinction was to place women and children beyond the protection of the moral umbrella. Moral issues such as the division of childrearing responsibil-ities between mothers and fathers received scant attention. Similarly, there was little moral consideration of topics such as incest, child abuse, or domes-tic violence. These issues are by no means confined to women, but they tend to be issues that are experienced more directly by the relatively powerless and disenfranchised in our society: children, women, persons of color, and persons with disabilities.

Justice and Family Issues

After this distinction between the public and the private is called into ques-tion, new areas of moral concern come into view. Family issues now merit more direct moral concern. Traditional moral philosophy is notable for the ways in which it has simply ignored the moral issues that arise within the family, despite the fact that these are pervasive and serious. Susan Moller Okin, for example, has raised a number of questions in her *Justice, Gender and the Family* (1991) about the necessity for justice within the family. What, Okin asks, would count as a just distribution of responsibilities within the family in regard to raising children? She suggests a Rawlsian experiment, asking us what policies about marriage and family we would agree to if we did not know in advance whether our particular role in society would be male or female. The ways in which responsibilities and rewards are appor-tioned would be significantly different, and we would be much more likely to have equity between men and women.

The radical character of feminist ethics begins to emerge in works such as Okin's. After the voices of women (and others who have been excluded from the moral conversation) are heard and taken seriously, a number of things in society need to be reordered. Traditional moral theory—at least when viewed in retrospect—seems to have provided an endorsement of the status quo in many instances, yet this endorsement has been maintained only through selective blindness. Okin's work does not introduce fundamentally new moral ideas; instead, she applies accepted ideas to situations that had previously been ignored. Thus she takes the idea of justice *within* the family seriously, and the result is a reordering of our moral understanding of that domain and of its place within the larger society.

After the idea of justice is taken seriously in these contexts, we are quickly compelled to restructure some traditional moral notions. Take, for example, the notion of justice as equal treatment. On its surface, this notion of equality seems simple enough: People are treated equally when they are treated the same. What does it mean for women to have equal opportunity in the workplace? Treating people the same becomes more suspect when we begin to realize that in general men and women are not in the same initial position in society in regardto jobs. Typically, when evaluating job candidates, employers will look at employment histories. All other things being equal, candidates who show a steady employment history (and perhaps steady movement up the employment ladder) will be preferred to those who have spotty employment records or who have advanced less at the same age. Yet in our society men and women face different family pressures and expectations in this area. Women are more likely to be encouraged to postpone career advances for the sake of the family. Those women who choose to pursue both career and family simultaneously often experience much more conflicting pressures than do their male counterparts.

Background gender differences often undermine seemingly gender-neutral criteria. For example, imagine a couple who decides that decisions about relocating for employment offers will be made in a gender-neutral fashion. They say, "We'll go wherever the highest paying job offer is, whether it be for the man or the woman." This appears to be completely gender neutral. Closer inspection, however, yields a more complex picture. Overall, women are still paid less for comparable positions than their male counterparts, although this has improved over the years. Moreover, in married couples, husbands are usually three or four years older than their wives on average— and thus further advanced in their career paths. These are two of the factors that make it more likely that, even with such an apparently gender-neutral criterion such as "highest paying job," couples are more likely to follow the husband's career path than the wife's. Of course, if this is done once, it then puts the wife at a further disadvantage.

Examples such as the preceding one illustrate two points about feminist ethics. First, they show that ethical reflection must pay attention to background conditions that may affect seemingly neutral moral rules and practices. Second, and more generally, they illustrate the way in which ethical theory for many feminists is much more concrete than it is for many traditional moral theorists.

Violence and Powerlessness

Feminist moral theorists show an awareness of the experiences of women, experiences that have often either escaped the notice of their male counterparts or been misinterpreted by them. Consider the example of violence against women. Whereas traditionally this issue received virtually no attention at all, in recent years feminist ethical theorists—male as well as female—have focused a critical eye on the ways in which women (and others in positions of relative powerlessness) have been objects of violence. Rape and domestic violence are two of the principal ways in which this occurs.

Revealing the Problem

There are several dimensions to feminist moral considerations of violence. The first of these is simply the effort to make the problem visible. In traditional moral theories, the tacit assumption is that moral problems, if they need to be solved, will present themselves as demanding attention. Yet this assumes that those who are suffering are able to voice their concerns loudly enough to attract attention. However, this is often not the case in either domestic violence or in rape. In situations of domestic violence, women are often afraid to press charges for fear of reprisals. Moreover, they often hope that the relationship can be salvaged and see an appeal to their rights as reducing the chances of salvaging the relationship. In the past (and to some extent still today) women also feared an indifferent or even hostile reception at the hands of police and prosecutors. Rape presents comparable considerations. It is one of the few offenses in which the victim is often subject to much greater scrutiny than is the perpetrator. This is particularly the case in areas of date rape and spousal rape, where the protection of the law is less clear cut and the criticism of the victim all the greater. Thus, feminist ethical theory, through its consideration of issues such as violence and rape, tells us something very important about the nature of moral problems. Some problems, it demonstrates, hide themselves from view, and the first moral task is simply to bring them out into the open.

Understanding the Problem

The second dimension is the attempt to understand the nature of violence better. Although there is certainly much to be said for emphasizing the physical dimensions of violence, the story hardly ends there. Violence has a psychological dimension, and indeed the significance of physical violence may often be found in the psychological dimension. Consider an act such as knocking a person over. It may be quite different, even though the physical dimensions are the same, if the act (1) takes place in a football game, (2) is intended to thwart a robber from fleeing, or (3) is the act of a husband abusing his wife. Indeed, when one sees the world primarily in terms of relationships, it makes sense that the core of violence will consist in the destruction of relationships. This is a good example of the way in which feminist ethical theory prompts us to reconsider the nature of some common moral problems.

Dominance and Patriarchy

A central theme emerges from these considerations: power and powerlessness. It is easy to see the way in which feminist moral theory leads quickly into a critique of power structures that dominate specific groups, especially women. (These groups need not be composed of just women—think of same-sex rape of men in prison, another case of powerlessness that is largely ignored in our society.) Feminist moral theory, situated in a society such as ours, inevitably leads to a critique of the structures that historically have dominated women. These structures are usually grouped under the general heading of "patriarchy."

Seeking Solutions

The final step in all of this for feminist ethical theorists is the development of ways of improving the situation. This has often been the most difficult step insofar as most remedies bring significant liabilities with them. The goal is to establish a society in which groups of individuals are not dominated by power relationships that diminish them. Legislation certainly provides an important component of the answer here. Laws prohibiting violence toward women (and others who are relatively powerless) play an important role here, and such laws need to exist within a justice system that is supportive of the larger ends of equality to which feminism is committed.

Rights to Self-Determination

Are Rights the Right Perspective?

There has been a tension within feminist ethics about the importance of the concept of rights and its proper role in the moral life. As we saw in our discussion of Carol Gilligan's work, some feminists have argued that the concept of rights has its natural home in a patriarchal framework; rights, at least, belong to the domain of the impersonal and anonymous world. However, many feminist moral philosophers have recognized that the concept of rights has played a pivotal role in the improvement of the conditions of women throughout the world. Without the leverage provided by the concept of rights, it would be much more difficult to bring about change in the oppressive conditions that women experience.

Reproductive Freedom

One of the areas in which the question of rights becomes important is that of reproductive freedom. Feminist moral theorists have been deeply concerned with freeing women from those structures that have in the past dominated them and restricted their freedom. One of the central ways in which that freedom has been restricted or denied is in the domain of reproductive choices, and much of the defense of abortion rights arises precisely out of the affirmation of women's right to be free from oppression. No one, feminist moral theorists argue, should be forced to bear a child against her will. A discussion of the morality of abortion would take us far beyond the scope of this work about moral theory, and no attempt will be made here to decide this difficult question once and for all. What is important in this context, however, is to see the way in which the question of abortion rights for feminist moral philosophers fits into a larger picture of freeing women from coercion. It is this moral concern that many feminist philosophers find overriding.

Considerations of power and the elimination of domination are by no means confined to this single issue. Let's look at several such issues that fall under the category of sexism, sexual harassment, and pornography—structures of domination that distort our moral experience.

Sexism, Sexual Harassment, and Pornography

The experience of discrimination is something that almost by definition escapes the notice of those who control the power in society. Until the voices of those being discriminated against are heard, discrimination appears on the surface to be a minor issue at best. However, after we begin to hear the voices of the oppressed, a very different picture emerges.

Sexism

Feminist moral philosophers see the pervasiveness of *sexism,* an attitude that tends to stereotype women and to devalue their moral experience. Sexist attitudes portray women as less capable than men, and these attitudes then serve as the basis for decisions and actions that disadvantage women. For example, sexist perceptions in hiring new employees and promoting current ones may well result in women's careers being hindered. Sometimes such discrimination is blatant, at other times much more subtle and difficult to discern and correct.

Language

Language provides interesting examples of some of the ways in which sexism is embedded into our culture. Think of the ways in which the same behavior might be portrayed in positive terms for men—"assertive"—and negative terms for women—"aggressive." Our prejudices are built into our language. To call a boy a "sissy" or a "girl" is strong criticism, whereas calling a girl a "Tomboy" is much less serious. Take another example. Think of English slang verbs for sexual intercourse. As several philosophers have pointed out, such verbs generally call for a male as the subject of the sentence and a female as the object; furthermore, most of these verbs are also synonymous with the verb *to hurt*. This suggests a disturbing picture of sexual intercourse as a hurtful activity that men inflict onto women.

Sexual Harassment

Sexism involves seeing and treating women differently simply because they are women. *Sexual harassment* is different because it seeks in most cases to extract sexual "favors" from the person (usually a woman) being harassed and uses threats as the basis for forcing compliance. In some instances, the threats are direct; in other instances, given the power differential between a boss and an employee, they may be unspoken but nevertheless quite powerful. The greater the power differential, the greater the possibility for abuse.

When women are sexually harassed, they are often silent for several reasons. They may feel shamed, even though they did nothing to elicit the harassment. Second, they may doubt whether their allegations will be believed or seen as important. (Think about the Clarence Thomas confirmation hearings and Anita Hill in this regard.) Third, they may feel, sometimes quite rightly, that speaking out will call forth recriminations. Once again, feminist moral theory is concerned with bringing the problem to light—and then looking for ways of alleviating the problem.

After those who have been sexually harassed are assured that they can come forth without recriminations, it is often astounding to see the breadth and depth of sexual harassment. Scandals in the U.S. armed forces in recent years illustrate the conspiracy of silence that has concealed these issues for so long.

Pornography

Feminist moral theory aims not only to uncover problems, but also to develop ways of responding to them. Nowhere has the search for remedies been so divisive as in regard to pornography. There is little question that pornography reinforces sexist attitudes and encourages sexual harassment. However, feminist philosophers are often deeply committed to the principle of free speech, and the debate centers on the question of whether pornography deserves protection as free speech. Although most feminists are in agreement that pornography is offensive, they are divided about how to respond to this. Some, such as Catharine MacKinnon, have argued that pornography is a type of action and thus not shielded by freedom of speech laws. Others have argued that, no matter how distasteful pornography is, it is best seen as free speech and thus should not be suppressed.

The Feminization of Poverty

One of the characteristics of feminist ethical theory is that it does not begin with the assumption that men and women are similarly situated in society. It may arrive at this as a conclusion in some cases, but it does not start out with it as a premise. This is most clear in the area of poverty, which is increasingly a condition that women are more likely to encounter than are men.

How, feminist ethical theorists ask, can men and women be treated equally in financial terms? Certainly equal pay for equal work, but the matter goes beyond this. Should there be equal pay for comparable work, especially because some areas of work that are traditionally reserved for women are paid much less than the corresponding areas for men? And, if the answer to this question is an affirmative one, how should this be accomplished? Should the government act in ways that would bring this about, or is it best seen as a matter of private initiative?

Pensions

Consider just one example of the type of inequalities that feminist theorists consider. How are pensions to be apportioned for married couples who are getting divorced? If one spouse stayed at home and raised the children while the other worked for money outside the home, do both have an equal claim to the outside pension? If not, are women (usually the ones who raise the children) going to find themselves as a group economically disadvantaged during their retirement years? What is fair in a situation such as this? This type of issue takes us to the very heart of our conception of such fundamental moral notions as fairness and justice.

Global Poverty

When we consider the issue of women's poverty on a global level, the picture is much more distressing than the situation in the United States alone. Here an interesting tension develops, which we shall examine in more detail in the next chapter: The demands of multiculturalism often seem to encourage a nonjudgmental attitude toward practices in other cultures that appear to be quite harmful to women.

Environmental Concern and Ecofeminism

When women's moral voices become part of the ethical conversation, the boundaries of the moral domain begin to expand as well. One of the most influential movements in contemporary feminist moral theory has been the extension of feminist concerns to the environment.

There is a natural movement here from feminine and feminist ethics, especially the ethics of care, to environmental concerns. Although by no means antitechnology, the ethics of care is certainly mistrustful of "technological fixes" that seek to resolve problems through the brute application of technology to the environment. Indeed, it is likely to see technology as part of a patriarchal structure of domination. Feminists seek to explore relationships with the natural world that do not involve domination and mastery, but rather harmony and balance and peace.

Ecofeminist philosophers see a deep connection between the ways in which women and nature have been understood and treated in the West.

Karen J. Warren, one of the leading proponents of ecofeminism, has pointed out the ways in which both women and nature have been subjected to oppression. We often use terms relating to animals to describe women, usually in unfavorable ways, and we tend to talk about nature in feminine terms. Ecofeminist philosophers see feminism and environmentalism as mutually entailing each other: one is not complete without the other. We cannot end the domination of nature without simultaneously overcoming the domination of women, and vice versa. Consider the traditional (male) attitude toward mountain climbing, in which the climbers are seeking to "conquer" the mountain. Climbing for them is a relationship of domination. The ecofeminist climber, on the other hand, sees climbing as a way of coming to know the mountain and also as a process of self-knowledge, and in both dimensions "knowing" is as much a matter of feeling as of concepts.

CONCLUSION

We all live in the same world. The moral challenge facing us is to decide how to do this in a way that promotes respect, understanding, and community. Taking women's moral voices seriously, as we have seen in this chapter, involves reassessing traditional moral theory, expanding our stock of fundamental moral concepts, and recognizing the existence of a wide range of previously unacknowledged moral issues. In doing these things, feminist moral theory opens up the possibility of a richer, more diverse moral conversation.

DISCUSSION QUESTIONS

1. Recall your answer to **statement 41** ("Men and women often view morality differently"). After reading this chapter, have your views on this statement changed at all? If so, in what ways? If so, what was the single most influential idea that prompted you to change your position on this issue?

2. **Statements 42 and 43** concern the relationship between emotions and rules in the moral life. Have your ratings of these two statements ("Emotions have no place in morality" and "Morality is primarily a matter of following the rules") changed at all? In what ways? What accounts for the change?

3. What's the difference (if any) between "guy talk" and "girl talk," or between the ways that men speak to each other, the ways that women speak to each other, and the way(s) that men and women speak to each other? Do these differences matter morally, or only socially? Are they fixed, or can we change them?

4. Suppose a visitor from another planet came down to earth and didn't understand why gender was even an issue for so many members of our species. What would you say to explain (or excuse) it? What might the "alien" say in return?

5. **MOVIE** The actress Sigourney Weaver, for example, often plays film roles (for example, in the *Alien* series or *Gorillas in the Mist*) that are high in both femininity and masculinity. Whom can you think of among males who ranks high on both scales?

BIBLIOGRAPHICAL ESSAY

A number of **journals** are devoted to feminist issues. Among those that regularly have articles on feminism and ethics are *Hypatia,* which is of particular relevance to philosophy, and *Signs,* an interdisciplinary journal of feminist studies. For **companions** to feminist philosophy, see Alison M. Jaggar and Iris Marion Young, eds., *A Companion to Feminist Philosophy* (Cambridge: Blackwell, 1998); and Miranda Fricker and Jennifer Hornsby, eds., *The Cambridge Companion to Feminism in Philosophy* (Cambridge: Cambridge University Press, 2000).

For an invaluable **overview** of various theories and positions, see Rosemarie Tong, *Feminist Thought: A More Comprehensive Introduction* (Boulder, CO: Westview Press, 1998) and *Feminine and Feminist Ethics* (Belmont, CA: Wadsworth, 1993). Also see the excellent review of the literature by Samantha Brennan, "Recent Work in Feminist Ethics," *Ethics* 109 (July 1999): 858–893; also see Jean Grimshaw, "The Idea of a Female Ethic," in Peter Singer, ed., *A Companion to Ethics* (Oxford: Blackwell, 1991), pp. 491–499; Alison M. Jaggar, "Feminist Ethics," in Hugh LaFollette, ed., *The Blackwell Guide to Ethical Theory* (Cambridge: Blackwell, 2000); Alison M. Jaggar, "Feminist Ethics: Projects, Problems, Prospects," Claudia Card, *Feminist Ethics* (Lawrence, KS: University of Kansas Press, 1991), 78–104; "Feminist Ethics," in Lawrence C. Becker and Charlotte B. Becker, eds., *Encyclopedia of Ethics* (New York: Garland, 1992), pp. 361–370.

Among the earlier works in feminist philosophy, see Genevieve Lloyd, *The Man of Reason: "Male" and "Female" in Western Philosophy* (Minneapolis: University of Minnesota Press, 1984). More recently, see especially Iris Marion Young, *Justice and the Politics of Difference* (Princeton: Princeton University Press, 1990), which presents a strong case for affirming, rather than minimizing, social group differences; Alison M. Jaggar, ed., *Living with Contradictions: Controversies in Feminist Social Ethics,* (Boulder, CO: Westview Press, 1994); Dana E. Bushnell, ed., *"Nagging" Questions: Feminist Ethics in Everyday Life* (Lanham, MD: Rowman & Littlefield, 1995); Patrice DiQuinzio and Iris Marion Young, eds., *Feminist Ethics and Social Policy* (Bloomington, IN: Indiana University Press, 1997), which contains all the essays in the Hypatia Symposium on Feminist Ethics and Social Policy plus four additional essays; Claudia Card, ed., *On Feminist Ethics and Politics* (Lawrence, KS: University of Kansas Press, 1999). For the work of **Annette Baier** on ethics and women, see especially her *Postures of the Mind* (Minneapolis: University of Minnesota Press, 1985); *Moral Prejudices* (Cambridge, MA: Harvard University Press, 1995), especially "What Do Women Want in an Ethical Theory?" and her Carus lectures, *The Commons of the Mind* (Chicago: Open Court, 1997).

Several **anthologies** contain a number of important papers on **feminism and ethics**: Eva Feder Kittay and Diana Meyer's *Women and Moral Theory* (Savage, MD: Rowman & Littlefield, 1987); Cass R. Sunstein, ed., *Feminism and Political Theory*, (Chicago: University of Chicago Press, 1990); Claudia Card, *Feminist Ethics* (Lawrence, KS: University of Kansas Press, 1991); Eva Browning Cole and Susan Coultrap-McQuin, eds., *Explorations in Feminist Ethics* (Bloomington, IN: Indiana University Press, 1992); Elizabeth Frazer, Jennifer Hornsby, and Sabina Lovibond, eds., *Ethics: A Feminist Reader,* (Oxford: Blackwell, 1992); Mary Jeanne Larrabee, eds., *An Ethic of Care: Feminist and Interdisciplinary Perspectives* (New York: Routledge, 1993); and Virginia Held's anthology, *Justice and Care: Essential Readings in Feminist Ethics* (Boulder, CO: Westview Press, 1995). Claudia Card's anthology also has an excellent bibliography.

Lawrence **Kohlberg**'s major works on moral development are contained in the two volumes of his *Essays in Moral Development* (New York: Harper & Row, 1981, 1984). Carol **Gilligan**'s *In a Different Voice* (Cambridge, MA: Harvard University Press) appeared in 1982, and since then has continued to have a profound impact in a wide range of disciplines, including psychology, religious studies, philosophy, sociology, communications, and literature. It has become the best selling paperback that Harvard University Press has ever published and has been translated into eleven languages. The 1993 edition has a new introduction. Gilligan's most recent work can be found in *The Birth of Pleasure* (New York: Knopf, 2002) and in the collection of essays that she coedited with Janie Victoria Ward and Jill McLean Taylor, *Mapping the Moral Domain* (Cambridge, MA: Center for the Study of Gender, Education and Human Development, 1988); in Lyn Mikel Brown and Carol Gilligan, *Meeting at the Crossroads: Women's Psychology and Girl's Development* (Cambridge, MA: Harvard University Press, 1992); and in Jill McLean Taylor, Carol Gilligan, and Amy M. Sullivan, eds., *Between Voice and Silence: Women and Girls, Race and Relationship* (Cambridge, MA: Harvard University Press, 1995). For the distinction between feminine and feminist ethics of care, see Gilligan's "Hearing the Difference: Theorizing Connection," *Hypatia* 10, no. 2 (Spring 1995): 120–127. Nel Noddings' *Caring* (Berkeley: University of California Press, 1984) and *Women and Evil* (Berkeley: University of California Press, 1989) have also had a significant impact in articulating a specifically feminine voice in ethics. My presentation of Gilligan's position is strongly indebted to the (largely unpublished) work of Michelle Dumont and to a two-day workshop on Ethics and Gender conducted by Carol Gilligan at the University of San Diego, January 27–28, 1997. I owe my familiarity with the Bem scale to Linda A. M. Perry.

The work of Gilligan and others has stirred up a healthy debate among philosophers about the implications of her work, and of feminism in general, for ethics. Several journal exchanges are also of particular relevance here, most of which have appeared in *Ethics*: the Kohlberg-Flanagan exchange on "Virtue, Sex, and Gender" *Ethics* 92, no. 3 (April 1982): 499–532; Lawrence Blum's "Gilligan and Kohlberg: Implications for Moral Theory" *Ethics* 98, no. 3 (April 1988): 472–491; and the symposium on "Feminism and Political Theory," *Ethics* 99, no. 2 (January 1989). Owen Flanagan's *Varieties of Moral Personality* (Cambridge, MA: Harvard University Press, 1991) contains several excellent chapters (esp. chapters 9–11) on this issue. Also see Susan J. Hekman, *Moral Voices, Moral Selves: Carol Gilligan and Feminist Moral Theory* (University Park, PA: Pennsylvania State University Press, 1995). Virginia Held's anthology, *Justice and Care: Essential Readings in Feminist Ethics*

(Boulder, CO: Westview Press, 1995), contains an excellent selection of very strong papers.

The influence of feminism in **bioethics** has been extensive. For an excellent overview, see Rosemarie Tong, *Feminist Approaches to Bioethics: Theoretical Reflection and Practical Applications* (Boulder, CO: Westview Press, 1997). For a genuinely cross-cultural perspective, see Rosemarie Tong, Gwen Anderson, Aida Santos, *Globalizing Feminist Bioethics: Crosscultural Perspectives* (Boulder, CO: Westview, 2000); Anne Donchin and Laura M. Purdy, eds., *Embodying Bioethics: Recent Feminist Advances* (Lanham, MD: Rowman & Littlefield, 1999); Susan Sherwin, *No Longer Patient: Feminist Ethics and Health Care* (Philadelphia: Temple University Press, 1992); and Anita Silvers, David Wasserman, and Mary B. Mahowald, *Disability, Difference, Discrimination: Perspectives on Justice in Bioethics and Public Policy* (Lanham, MD: Rowman & Littlefield, 1998). On the issue of abortion, see most recently Laurie Shrage, *Abortion and Social Responsibility: Depolarizing the Debate,* Studies in Feminist Philosophy (New York: Oxford University Press, 2002); On the way in which metaphors shape our thought in bioethics, see Susan Sherwin, "Feminist Ethics and the Metaphor of AIDS," *Journal of Medicine and Philosophy* 26, no. 4 (August 2001): 343–364.

Feminism has also had an impact on **environmental ethics.** See Karen J. Warren, *Ecofeminist Philosophy: A Western Perspective on What It Is and Why It Matters* (Lanham, MD: Rowman & Littlefield, 2000) as well as Warren's anthology, *Ecological Feminist Philosophies* (Bloomington, IN: Indiana University Press, 1996). I am indebted to Rosemarie Tong's fine treatment of ecofeminist in her *Feminist Thought,* pp. 246–277.

On feminism and race, see especially Patricia Hill Collins, *Black Feminist Thought,* 2nd ed. (New York: Routledge, 2000).

THE ETHICS OF DIVERSITY: RACE, ETHNICITY, AND MULTICULTURALISM

We live in an age of diversity. That is hardly news, and it is certainly not new. The United States has always been a country of immigrants—and of those whom the immigrants have sought to displace. Our history is in many ways the history of diversity. However, what is new is the unprecedented level of *interest* in diversity. A visit to any large bookstore will quickly reveal a wide range of books on "diversity," impassioned attacks against multiculturalism on a shelf next to equally impassioned defenses of it. As a nation, we talk about diversity now more than we ever have in the past.

This chapter cannot address the many issues that surround the discussion of race, ethnicity, and culture today. Its focus is much narrower: the relationship between moral theory and race, ethnicity, and culture. I shall concentrate on three main issues. First, I shall examine the "identity argument." In a nutshell, this argument maintains that race, ethnicity, or culture—the distinctions among these will be discussed shortly—is central to the identity of the moral agent, and that the identity of the moral agent partially determines what is morally right for that individual. Second, we shall consider the issue of minority rights and the question of whether minorities possess any special rights not belonging to the population as a whole. Finally, we will turn to a consideration of the question of what virtues we ought to possess to live well in a multicultural society and see how these virtues fit into our pluralistic approach to morality. However, before looking at those three issues, I would like to look briefly at the way in which the issues in this chapter continue some of the themes developed in Chapter 2.

Relativism, Pluralism, and Multiculturalism

In Chapter 2, we sketched out a middle ground between relativism and absolutism, a position we called ethical pluralism. In doing so, we wanted to recognize several important insights. First, ethical relativism is correct in emphasizing the importance of tolerance and understanding toward other cultures. Second, ethical absolutism is correct in maintaining that cross-cultural moral judgments are possible, even though absolutists may be prone to making such judgments too quickly, too often, and with little self-examination. Judging other cultures requires a lot of understanding, both of the other cultures and of ourselves. **Ethical pluralism,** as a middle ground between these two extremes, **maintains that cross-cultural moral judgments are possible but that we should engage in such judgments carefully and with self-scrutiny and that we should attempt to leave as much room for tolerance as possible.**

Our consideration of rights further developed this account of ethical pluralism, by suggesting that the limits of tolerance can be drawn by a notion of fundamental human rights. Basic human rights, in other words, establish the moral "floor" below which we cannot sink or allow others to sink. Our discussion of justice showed how pluralism can incorporate a notion of justice that is both sensitive to local conditions and at the same time cross-cultural. Finally, in our chapter on Aristotle and virtue theory, we sketched out an account of practical wisdom (*phronēsis*) that provides a practical framework within which we can make use of the insights of the various ethical theories discussed in this book. The person of practical wisdom is the individual who knows how and when to apply particular insights gained from ethical theories.

We now return to the issue of cross-cultural judgments, this time within the context of recent discussions of multiculturalism. There is no single definition of multiculturalism. Like most *isms,* it is subject to many uses and misuses by both supporters and critics. However, in the philosophical discussion of the term, *multiculturalism* has come to signify an inclusive, largely nonjudgmental attitude toward other cultures and a belief that other cultures are worthy of understanding and respect. The crucial issue here is the place of cross-cultural judgments, as we shall see in this chapter.

Ethical pluralism differs from multiculturalism in two respects. First, it accepts the legitimacy and, at least in some cases, the necessity of cross-cultural judgments. When ethical pluralists encounter practices such as female genital mutilation, they are willing to make moral judgments about them. Second, ethical pluralism accepts the cross-cultural judgments go in both directions (which absolutists generally do not emphasize), and are willing to look at practices in their own country and culture where some of the same issues might be raised. Thus, ethical pluralists would also be willing to examine the morality of practices (such as cosmetic surgery, body piercing, tattooing, and branding) in their own society which raise similar moral issues.

Within this context, let's now turn to some of the specific arguments about ethical theory and multiculturalism, beginning with the identity argument.

THE IDENTITY ARGUMENT

The basic structure of the identity argument is comparatively simple. It maintains that race, ethnicity, or culture is so central to a person's identity that it justifiably affects what a person ought to do. Morality, so this argument implies, depends (at least in part) on race, ethnicity, or culture. Before we examine this argument in more detail, let's look at the notions of race, ethnicity, and culture because these notions play such an important role in the discussion.

The Structure of the Identity Argument

Background Premise: The Critique of Impartiality

There are two aspects to the identity argument. The first is a critical one that centers on showing the inadequacies of standard appeals to the impartiality of the moral agent. Impartiality, according to this critique, is a sham. The moral point of view was never an impartial one—it was simply the standpoint of those who were in power who tried to pass their own point of view off as a universal standpoint. Such universality, the critics of impartiality argue, is an illusion. The appeal to impartiality is simply an attempt to provide further justification for the standpoint of the power elite.

Indeed, it is easy to understand why a majority would see its standpoint as impartial, simply as the way things are, whereas minorities never experience their standpoints that way. Members of ethnic minorities usually feel the difference between their own culture and the dominant culture of the country. Some of this is the result of active discrimination; some is simply the result of a tacit presumption that in the public arenas of power the dominant culture will be that of the majority. Thus, members of ethnic minorities grow up with a sense of themselves as an ethnic group. Members of the majority culture are less likely to experience themselves as a group; rather, their group identity is transparent to them. They simply experience themselves as themselves. They are not discriminated against because of this identity—or, in the isolated cases in which this occurs, they simply wonder what is wrong with those who are discriminating against them. Similarly, they do not experience themselves as outsiders in their own culture. Indeed, they see no difference between their culture and culture.

In the United States, for example, when white people go to the supermarket and find hamburger buns and ground beef prominently available on the shelves, they do not experience the store as catering to their needs as white persons. They simply see it as selling the basics of life. On the other hand, when Vietnamese in the United States go to the grocery store in a place where there is only a small Vietnamese population, they will experience themselves as a minority. Either the store will carry such things as Nam Pla, a salty fish sauce, or it won't. If it does, Vietnamese shoppers will typically experience this as a store that caters to Vietnamese. If it doesn't, those same shoppers will usually experience it as a store that is indifferent to the needs of Vietnamese. Either way, they will experience themselves as Vietnamese in a way that average white American shoppers would not experience themselves as white or American when they shop. In fact, if white American shoppers went to the supermarket and found that it did not sell hamburger buns, they would wonder what was wrong with the store, but it would not be likely to intensify their self-identification as white. For those in the majority, self-identification often permits their racial or ethnic identity to be transparent.

The Argument

After the critique of impartiality has been completed, the other aspect of the argument is a positive one, and it is the principal focus of our interest in this section. The identity argument has the following structure.

- *Premise 1* What is morally right depends (at least in part) on one's identity as a moral agent.
- *Premise 2* One's race (or ethnicity or culture) is central to one's identity as a moral agent.
- *Conclusion* Thus what is morally right depends (at least in part) on that person's race, ethnicity, or culture.

The first premise, although certainly open to dispute, could be accepted in some form by most major moral theorists. Kant accepts it, but sees the identity of the moral agent as purely rational. This argument has a number of controversial points. Thus he would reject the second premise very strongly. Utilitarians would not be inclined to accept either premise as stated, but they would certainly be willing to admit that factors significant to overall welfare may vary from group to group. Rights theorists would typically be most opposed to this line of argument insofar as it threatens the universality of rights, although the special issue of minority rights is an interesting one that will be discussed later. Finally, virtue theorists would certainly in principle be open to strong links between identity and what is morally right, although again the sticking point may well be the second premise.

In order to evaluate this argument in more detail, we need to look at several issues. First, the references to race are blurred by having being tied to race and ethnicity as well. The relationship among these concepts must be clarified. Second, we must look at the claim of how identity as a moral agent is dependent on race, ethnicity, and culture. Finally, we shall look at what follows from this argument if it is sound.

Race, Ethnicity, and Culture

The Initial Distinction

On the surface, the distinctions among race, ethnicity, and culture seem comparatively easy to draw. Here is the standard way of drawing these distinctions. Race has been regarded **primarily as a *biological* phenomenon** that manifests itself in characteristics such as skin color, hair texture, body shape, and the like. Ethnologists generally distinguish among three or four main racial groups: Caucasoid, Negroid, Mongoloid, and sometimes Australoid. The U.S. Census Bureau adds the racial category of Native American to the first three.

Ethnicity, in contrast, **is primarily a *cultural* phenomenon with a biological dimension.** It refers principally to individuals' identification with a particular cultural group to which they are biologically related. There are many more cultural groups than there are races, and often differences in cultures are overlooked by outsiders. There are, for example, many Southeast Asian cultures, but non-Asians often lump them all together as "Indochinese." This would be roughly equivalent to lumping the English, the Irish, the Portuguese, the Finns, the Spanish, the Italians, the Lithuanians, the French, and the Germans together as "Europeans." Although it is true that they all come from countries in Europe, they often perceive themselves primarily in terms of national and ethnic identities. They are Europeans only to outsiders.

Culture refers to a set of beliefs, values, and practices that define a group's identity. Although culture may overlap with ethnicity and race, it is in principle distinct. An infant born to Thai parents in Thailand and raised in that country will be racially Mongoloid, ethnically Thai, and culturally Thai. An infant boy born of Italian parents but immediately adopted by a Thai couple living in Thailand would be racially Caucasoid but culturally Thai; his ethnicity would be problematic because he would lack the biological aspect of Thai ethnicity and would lack the cultural aspect of Italian ethnicity.

The Complications

This initial picture becomes more complicated as we begin to look more closely at the concept of race. Initially, it appears to be a purely biological phenomenon. Indeed, race is often associated with skin color. But this will hardly do because we can easily find people of one race whose skin color is closer to that of some other race. Skin color hardly suffices as a sufficient or even necessary condition of racial identity. So if racial identity is biologically based, then we must look more deeply. Yet when we look for clear biological markers to describe race, we find that there is a tremendous amount of variation within racial groups and a significant amount of overlap among them as well, as the biologist Steven Jay Gould has shown in *The Mismeasure of Man* (1999). There is no clearly defined set of biological or genetic characteristics shared by all members of a particular race and only by members of that race.

These variations are intensified by interracial reproduction, both past and present. One of the reasons that it is impossible to find unique genetic markers for racial groups is that no races are genetically completely isolated from all other races. Virtually everyone is, to some extent, of mixed race, but no one knows for sure how much of which races contributes to the mixture.

Yet the situation is even more puzzling than this. Whatever may be involved in the search for biological or genetic markers of race, there is a sense in which this search is oddly irrelevant. Let's imagine, for example, that some obscure genetic marker for race was eventually discovered. What is the relationship between that marker and what people usually think of as race? Human beings have identified with, and fought over, race for centuries, but it is clear that no one involved in those struggles was thinking of some genetic marker.

Race, it turns out, has some superficial biological basis, but the concept of race is in fact a construction, a human projection that, instead of being acknowledged as a projection, is attributed to biology. Kwame Anthony Appiah makes a similar point in his essay, "Illusions of Race," when he argues that, "The truth is that there are no races: there is nothing in the world that can do all we ask race to do for us." His objection is based not on a denial of the importance of biology, but rather on the ways in which appeals to "race" pretend to offer a biological foundation to what in truth is cultural. "Talk of 'race' is particularly distressing for those of us who take culture seriously," he writes, "for, where race works—in places where 'gross differences' of morphology are correlated with 'subtle differences' of temperament, belief, and intention—it works as an attempt at a metonym for culture, and it does so only at the price of biologizing what is culture, ideology." Appeals to race, in other words, often appear to be appeals to biology, but actually they are appeals to culture.

Example: The Census

The complications, political as well as scientific, associated with these distinctions emerge in many ways. Consider, for example, the U.S. Census, which illustrates many of Appiah's points. Until Census 2000, respondents to census surveys in the United States had to choose a single race. This requirement was in sharp contrast to the practice of many other countries, such as Canada, that permitted individuals to check all the categories that apply to them. Even the official categories themselves are peculiar. The official categories (revised by the Office of Management and Budget in 1997) for race are: American Indian or Alaska Native, Asian, Black or African American, Native Hawaiian or Other Pacific Islander, and White. This is supplemented by two categories for ethnicity: "Hispanic or Latino" and "Not Hispanic or Latino." The so-called "racial" categories do not correspond exactly to those commonly recognized by scientists in the field. Moreover, many people of Latino or Hispanic ethnicity found it odd that they had to check "White" as their racial category. The concepts of race and ethnicity, in other words, often carry a lot of baggage—including political implications— that have nothing to do with whatever scientific meaning they have.

Thus, we must treat appeals to race with an element of care. Often, what is being appealed to is culture, or at least culture plus race. This is particularly important for the following reason. Race, insofar as it is seen as biological in character, is (1) immutable and, because we did not choose our race, (2) something for which we are not responsible in the way that we are responsible for our choices and actions. Yet after we recognize that race is at least in part a social construct, we begin to see that it is indeed subject to change and that it is something for which we bear responsibility. With this in mind, let's turn to a consideration of the identity argument itself.

How Are Race, Ethnicity, and Culture Central to Moral Identity?

The second premise of this argument claims that race, ethnicity, and culture are central to one's identity as a moral agent. Let's first look at some possible examples of this claim, then distinguish two ways—internalist and externalist—in which these factors can be seen as central to moral identity. Then we can conclude by looking at several ways of responding to this identity argument—separatist, supremacist, assimilationist—and examining how these relate to models of multiculturalism.

The Facts of Diversity

If the identity argument is sound, then different cultures should have distinctive moral identities. Do different cultures have distinctive moral voices? The obvious answer is, "Of course they do." In our consideration of descriptive moral relativism in Chapter 2, we saw that distinctive voices are clearly the case, at least in regard to (1) the particular actions that a given culture sanctions or condemns, and (2) the peripheral values that it accepts. Whether there is disagreement on central values is another question, and we have seen good evidence to suggest that there is widespread (but not total) agreement on certain values, such as respect for innocent life.

To say that moral voices are distinctive is not to say that they are necessarily incompatible. We might encounter a much stronger emphasis on the concept of honor in Japanese society than we encounter in contemporary American society, but that does not necessarily make them incompatible, only different. Incompatibility, at least in the strict sense, occurs only when there are clearly opposing value judgments such as "honor is good" and "honor is bad." (For strict incompatibility, there must also be rough equivalence in the meaning of shared terms such as *honor.* Cross-cultural comparisons of this type presuppose that understanding and judgment between cultures are possible; such comparisons also often demand a high degree of sensitivity to the nuances of another culture's worldview.) Differences alone do not constitute incompatibility. Often the relevant question is not whether different cultures have distinctive moral voices, but rather whether they can learn to sing harmoniously together when necessary.

Let us turn to a concrete example of the way in which a culture has distinctive voices so that we can understand more fully the nuances of the issues involved.

The Moral Voices of African-Americans

Consider the diversity of voices that is included in the African-American experience. Martin Luther King Jr., Malcolm X, Alice Walker, and Maya Angelou are among the most powerful African-American moral voices of the late twentieth century. These voices have many distinctive characteristics, but here I shall concentrate on just one element that is found in all four of these voices: *the moral voice of the affirmation of self-respect in the face of oppression*. Self-respect is a value found in virtually all cultures, as is opposition to oppression. In this respect, African-American culture is not unique. However, the affirmation of self-respect in the face of daunting oppression is a moral value that ranks higher on the scale in African-American culture than it does in, say, white American culture, where the same ongoing experience of oppression is not present. The speeches and writings of Dr. King and Malcolm X resonate with a deep affirmation of the self-respect of African Americans, an opposition to any attempts to deny the worth of black Americans, and a commitment to bringing about the social, political, and legal changes necessary to sustain and enhance that sense of self-worth among African Americans. Martin Luther King's "Letter from Birmingham Jail" eloquently details the ways in which segregation "distorts the soul and degrades human personality" for all involved—those who perpetuate segregation as well as those toward whom segregation is directed. Malcolm X's *Autobiography* is a superb example of moral autobiography, a description of his journey toward an increasingly well-founded sense of self-respect.

The novels, poetry, and journals of Alice Walker and Maya Angelou demonstrate a similar commitment. They have given voice to those African Americans whose suffering had previously been endured in silence. In *The Color Purple*, (1982) for example, Alice Walker traces the journey toward self-respect of an African-American woman whose life began in oppression and moved gradually toward autonomy. In a similar way, we find an account of the journey from oppression to increasingly full self-respect and self-determination in Maya Angelou's autobiography *I Know Why the Caged Bird Sings* (1983).

Against this rich background of diverse African-American moral voices, we now can understand better the conceptual issues involved in linking ethnicity to ethics. There are two ways of forging this link, one considerably stronger than the other.

Flip Schulke

Dr. Martin Luther King Jr. (1929–1968) was one of the strongest moral voices speaking for racial equality.

Externalist and Internalist Accounts of Ethnicity and Ethics

The first way of linking ethnicity and ethics, the *externalist account,* is through a shared set of social experiences and problems that are seen as largely independent of the identity of the persons in question. In the case of African Americans, the heritage of slavery and the ongoing presence of racism in American society figure prominently among the shared experiences of African Americans. The argument here would be that African Americans have to deal with a set of moral problems that are not usually encountered (at least in the same way) by the dominant white, male population of the United States. This way of understanding the link between ethnicity and ethics suggests that the connection is largely an external one. The analogy that suggests itself here is with professional groups that face particular moral problems not shared by the population as a whole. Physicians and psychologists, for example, must deal with questions of confidentiality and trust not shared in the same way by the population as a whole. African Americans face a certain set of external problems not shared by the population as a whole; consequently, they develop distinctive moral voices to deal with those problems.

The drawback of this first account is that it draws a comparatively sharp distinction between the group and the special moral problems it faces and consequently misses the ways in which specific moral problems partially constitute the identity of a particular group. The problems themselves are seen as largely external to the identity of the group itself. The distinctiveness of the voice derives primarily from the problems that it addresses, not from the members of the group themselves. The externalist account seems to miss the intimate connection between those problems and the very identity of the members of the group.

Ethics and ethnicity can be linked in a second, more intimate way through an *internalist account*. For example, the heritage of slavery and the experience of racism are powerful factors that are partially constitutive of the identity of African Americans. Their voices are partially shaped by these factors, and it is misleading to think of African Americans' identity as something completely external to them. A particular sensitivity to the affirmation of self-respect in the face of oppression is one of the distinctive characteristics of African-American moral voices, and an internalist account of the link between ethics and ethnicity recognizes the extent to which this sensitivity is partially constitutive of the identity of African Americans at this point in history.

Thick and Thin Conceptions of the Moral Self

Internalist and externalist approaches differ significantly in regard to the conception of the self that underlies each. The first approach is characterized by a *thin* conception of the self that sees the identity of the person as largely independent of empirical factors such as environment and ethnicity. As we saw in Chapter 6, Immanuel Kant strongly exemplifies this attitude. For Kant, the self is constituted primarily by reason and will; empirical conditions are generally excluded from the core identity of the moral agent. In our critique of Kant, we suggested a *thicker* conception of the self that includes more empirical factors as central to an individual's identity. In such thicker conceptions of the self, ethnicity may become an important part of identity. One's identity as a person, in other words, may in part be constituted by certain experiences largely unique to one's ethnic or racial group.

Ethnic identity is constituted by shared experiences. In the case of African Americans, one of the most significant of these shared experiences is that of being subjected to racial discrimination. In other words, an important part of their ethnic identity is precisely the experience of having their ethnic identity devalued and degraded. It is, as African-American philosophers such as Laurence Thomas have pointed out, an experience that has a profound impact on self-respect and self-esteem. The affirmation of self-worth against a background that denies or diminishes that self-worth is a particular value for any group that has been the object of systematic and long-standing oppression. Among African Americans, the experience of racism is certainly an experience that is partially constitutive of their identity, and this common experience partially shapes their distinctive moral voices. Their ethnic identity is part of who they are, part of their personal identity as moral agents, and ought to be affirmed in part because it was the object of discrimination in the past.

Normative Responses to the Identity Argument

We have now seen one of the ways in which different cultures may have (partially) different values. The central normative question we face is how we should act in light of this fact.

Separatists

Again, we can begin our discussion by noting two extreme positions. On one hand, we have the voice of the *separatists*, who maintain that cultures ought to retain their own voices by isolating themselves from the cultures around them. The drive toward separatism is particularly strong when the gap between cultures is wide and the difference in power is great. Separatists often fear being swallowed up by the larger culture and losing their identity in the process. Indeed, they feel that there is much to be gained from having a community of people with shared values, experiences, interests, and history. Such a community not only provides security, but also eliminates the need to start over in every conversation. Persons of color do not need to prove that racism still exists or show that it still has pernicious effects when talking with those who have shared their experiences. For example, recent Vietnamese immigrants share understandings of cultural alienation in their new homeland. They can take such common ground for granted and move on to a discussion of further issues within this shared context.

Yet *strict separatism* is rarely a long-term viable option because it usually will increase the power differential between the larger and smaller culture. Eventually this option leads to an even greater marginalization of the smaller, less powerful culture, in some instances leading even to its extinction. There are groups in America that still pursue this path, of course. Amish communities in Pennsylvania and other states are a highly visible example of a largely separatist tradition that has managed to survive and in certain respects flourish. Some Native American communities, such as the members of the Acoma pueblo, also have pursued a largely separatist course, preserving traditional values in comparative isolation from white society. African-American leaders such as W. E. B. Du Bois advocated the value of separatism in part as a way of preserving the uniqueness of the African-American tradition. The long-term prospects for such communities remain unclear, especially in an increasingly technological and computerized society.

If the prospects for strict separatism appear cloudy, the same cannot necessarily be said for *limited separatism*. Many groups in our society have long pursued a course of limited separatism, interacting with the larger culture yet simultaneously retaining a distinctive sense of group identity. Religious groups, fraternal organizations, and ethnic clubs are but a few types of such communities. They often flourish in part by maintaining a place within the larger community but at the same time retaining a limited sense of their own separate identity.

Interestingly, we would rarely consider separatism to be an acceptable option for the dominant group in society, presumably in part because we recognize that such a course of action would cut the smaller cultural groups off from valued goods and resources to which they have a right. We recognize that there may be a value in having traditionally African-American colleges in America, or organizations for Latino students on campus, but we would be hesitant to endorse the same options for Caucasians alone. There are at least two reasons for this. The first is one that we have already discussed. There is a special moral justification for the affirmation of ethnicity among groups that have been discriminated against precisely because of their ethnicity. For such groups, the affirmation of self-respect necessarily involves the affirmation of their ethnicity in a way that is not true for groups that have not been discriminated against on the basis of ethnicity or that even have been the perpetrators of discrimination.

The second reason for this difference is historical. Dominant ethnic groups often have functioned unjustly to disenfranchise and to disempower minority groups. Historical examples of this phenomenon are all too common. The Turkish attempt to exterminate the Armenians, the German attempt to wipe out the Jews and the Gypsies and enslave other ethnic groups such as the Poles, and recent Bosnian calls for "ethnic cleansing" are but a few of the most prominent examples of this tendency in our own century. Presumably separatist minority groups do not serve this same function. They do not attempt to disenfranchise or to disempower the majority group because such minority groups do not control the distribution of power in the same way that the majority group does. If they were to function in this way, they, too, would be morally suspect because they would turn into supremacist groups.

Supremacists

On the other hand, *supremacists* argue that (1) there is one culture that is morally superior to all others, and that (2) the superior culture is their own. In American society, we have seen this attitude in both white supremacist movements like the Aryan Nation and Posse Comitatus and the Ku Klux Klan and in some ethnic supremacist movements as well.

The supremacist attitude is suspect on several counts. Historically, it often has been associated with hatred, intolerance, and cruelty. This has certainly been the case with white supremacist movements in the United States.

Supremacists see other ethnic and racial groups as inferior, thus as less deserving of respect. Consequently, abuse of such groups appears as less objectionable to supremacists. Indeed, they will often convince themselves that abuse and suppression of minorities are positive moral duties for them, thereby cloaking their bigotry and hatred under the mantle of apparent moral respectability.

Philosophically, claims of supremacy are obviously suspect. Usually, the implicit claim is that everything about one race (or ethnicity or culture) is better than everything about the minorities. Yet this is obviously false. Claims of limited superiority in one or more areas function differently, yet rarely are these a part of any genuine comparison. Supremacists rarely believe that they have anything to learn from other cultures.

Most disturbing of all, supremacists depend on discrimination precisely in order to obtain a sense of their own self-worth. Jean-Paul Sartre, in his brilliant essay "Anti-Semite and Jew," saw this clearly in the case of anti-Semitism. Anti-Semites establish their own sense of self-worth at the expense of those they hate. This same point was made in another context in the movie *Mississippi Burning,* where the southern-born sheriff (Gene Hackman) recounts the story of his father and the neighbor's cow. Growing up as a poor white farmer in the South, the father continually was bothered by the fact that his neighbor, a black farmer, had a cow and was more prosperous. One day that cow died, and Gene Hackman came to realize that his father had poisoned it. "If you can't be better than a black man," his father told him, "who can you be better than?" The father's identity and sense of self-worth rested on his feeling of superiority. Consequently, if he felt that he was no longer superior to black farmers, he had to do something to them to reduce their situation and thus to regain his feeling of superiority. This is why persecution, lynchings, burnings, and so forth follow from a supremacist attitude: In order to ensure one's own superiority, it is necessary to diminish that of the other.

Integrationists and Assimilationists

In between these two extremes are various integrationist and assimilationist models. The integrationist model in regard to ethnic and cultural diversity has a somewhat different shape than it does in regard to gender. Although we recognized that both males and females can have both masculine and feminine voices, there is still a strong and pervasive cultural pressure to identify people as either male or female. For example, English grammar forces us to classify individuals as male or female but not as Latino or French. The pressure in regard to ethnic and cultural identification is weaker. Moreover, individuals obviously could be from more than one ethnic tradition—for example, both Irish and Jewish. Such diversity in regard to being male or female is, at best, a much more subtle matter.

There are several possible models of integration, and these can be ranked according to the degree of sameness they seek to achieve. Some strive for assimilation and uniformity, whereas others emphasize cooperation within a context of at least minimally shared rules of interaction. One of the principal criticisms of integrationist and assimilationist approaches is that they threaten to obliterate minority identities but to preserve at least the cultural identity of the majority.

Pluralists

The middle ground between these extremes is essentially the same one described at the end of our chapter on relativism: a *cultural pluralism* that sees diversity as a source of strength, emphasizes the value of *dialogue,* and approaches such dialogues with a *fallible* attitude. It is a pluralism that sees value in limited separatism but also recognizes that we need to learn to live together while honoring our differences. We have much to learn from other cultures, just as they have much to learn from us. As pluralists, we can recognize that there are many ways of being right without giving up the possibility of taking a stand in those instances when we are convinced that something is seriously wrong.

Consider the value of affirming self-respect in the face of oppression. As we have seen, it is hardly surprising that this is an important value in African-American culture, given historical conditions. Among groups that have not suffered such discrimination, the affirmation of self-respect may be a much less prominent value and may not involve an affirmation of ethnicity as part of self-respect. Thus, although white Americans also value self-respect, they may well not value it to the same extent or in the same way as do their African-American counterparts. This is an excellent example of *value pluralism,* one in which different groups have partially different (but not necessarily incompatible) values. The advantage of a pluralistic approach to values is that it is able to understand and appreciate such differences in values without resorting to an attitude of "anything goes." However, not all differences in values are as easily understood and appreciated as this one is. We shall consider how we live with diversity, and especially how we deal with moral conflicts in a pluralistic society, later in this chapter. Before turning to that issue, let us consider one last source of diversity.

Pluralism and Multiculturalism

Now we can return to the issue of pluralism and see more specifically the ways in which it relates to multiculturalism. Pluralism provides a strong foundation for a robust notion of multiculturalism. Recall the four principles that pluralism seeks to preserve from Chapter 2 and see how these fit into a notion of multiculturalism.

The Principle of Understanding

Certainly one of the principal insights of multiculturalism has been the way in which it has urged us to understand other cultures. All too often, we have simply dismissed other cultures, assuming that they are wrong or trivial.

Multiculturalism urges us to understand other cultures, and indeed one of the principal impacts of multiculturalism in education has been precisely an increased effort to understand other cultures.

The Principle of Tolerance

Our discussion of racial, ethnic, and cultural identity helps us now to see an additional reason for tolerance. This principle gains an added weight in this context from the following argument. A culture is a lot like an ecosystem, each individual element existing in a myriad of often imperceptible relationships with other elements in the system. Interfering with one element can often have unforeseen ripple effects throughout the rest of the culture. Add to this the fact that many minority cultures have a precarious existence, and we can see that tolerance has a special value.

The Principle of Standing Up to Evil

Tolerance, as we have seen, is an important value, but it has its limits. In certain circumstances, particularly those of great injustice, it is important to speak out against wrongdoing. Think of the persecutions, tortures, and killings that have plagued Eastern Europe in recent years. It would hardly be appropriate, in the name of tolerance or multiculturalism, to fail to speak out against the atrocities that have occurred there.

The Principle of Fallibility

Finally, throughout all of this, it is important to keep our own fallibility in mind and to seek to learn about ourselves from those outside of our culture. We approach other cultures with a spirit of humility, recognizing how difficult the task of genuine understanding is, and with an awareness of our own faults. The principle of fallibility encourages us to be aware of our own short-sightedness and to proceed with appropriate caution.

MINORITY RIGHTS

As we saw in Chapter 7, the notion of human rights is by its very nature thought to be universal. Indeed, the notion of special rights for particular groups seems to contradict the very core of our notion of human rights, namely, the notion that within a rights perspective no group is singled out as special.

Kymlicka, Liberalism, and Minority Rights

In *Liberalism, Community, and Culture* (1989) and, more recently, in *Multicultural Citizenship* (1995), Will Kymlicka has argued that liberalism, when properly understood, entails a commitment to minority rights. Kymlicka begins with the premise that many countries are now a single political entity but contain several distinct cultures.

The Argument

Kymlicka's argument begins with a notion taken from John Rawls's *A Theory of Justice,* namely, that the ability to develop and revise one's life plan—what in the U.S. Constitution is called "the pursuit of happiness"—is a very important good. Culture, Kymlicka suggests, is a necessary condition of pursuing one's life plan. Indeed, it is the very context within which such plans are formed and carried out. In the case of minority cultures, there is often a danger that, without special protection, they will be overwhelmed by influences from the outside. Thus, those cultures must be given special protections (i.e., special rights) to ensure their continued existence, thereby allowing minority members of a culture the same chance at pursuing a life plan that majority members already possess. The overall structure of the argument is straightforward:

- Developing and pursuing a life plan is a primary good.
- One's own culture is a necessary condition of pursuing a life plan.
- Many minority cultures need special protections if they are to continue to exist and not be overwhelmed by the majority culture.
- Thus, minority cultures must be afforded special protection so that all members of the society have an equal opportunity to pursue the primary good of developing and pursuing a life plan.

From this it follows that minorities, because of the possibility that pursuing a life plan would otherwise be threatened by the larger surrounding culture, have special rights necessary to the preservation of their racial, ethnic, or cultural identity.

Minorities are not all of the same type, and we can divide our discussion into several groups. Certainly the rights of indigenous people who have been conquered by outsiders form a distinct group, as do the rights of former slaves who were transported against their will to a new country. Both of these types of minorities are to be distinguished from minorities who travel to a new country for economic opportunity, greater freedom, and the like. Let's look at this first type of case in some detail and then briefly consider the other two.

The Rights of Indigenous People

Throughout the world many groups of indigenous people have seen outsiders take over their land and make it their own. The indigenous residents were variously pushed onto less desirable land, enslaved, or otherwise subjugated. In the United States and Canada, this was certainly the case with Native Americans. The original residents of this country, they were often conquered by force, captured and killed, and confined to life on reservations. They were forbidden to practice their religion, and in mission schools they were often not allowed to speak in their native languages. Just as their land was taken forcibly from them, so their culture was systematically stripped from them, and at the same time they were often condemned to an existence apart. Similar stories occurred throughout the world. In Australia, in South Africa, in South America, and in various other places around the world, we have witnessed a similar course of events.

Compensatory Justice

There is certainly an issue of compensatory justice for indigenous peoples. What does the majority, which has often benefited greatly from the subjugation of indigenous peoples, owe those people in recompense for the wrong that the majority has inflicted on them? This is a very important question, but there is nothing about it that stretches the boundaries of traditional ethical theory. Compensatory justice, though widely ignored in these cases, is fairly clear in principle and could easily occur without any special recognition of minority rights.

However, considerations of compensatory justice may strengthen claims about minority rights in the following way. Imagine two scenarios. In both of these, a minority culture is dying out. Its language and religion are disappearing, its members are marrying outside the culture, its stories are not being passed on to the next generation, and so forth. Now imagine that in one scenario this is occurring because members of that culture had been systematically persecuted for their culture—their religion and language banned, their economic welfare threatened when they lived together, and so forth. Contrast this to a scenario in which the demise of the culture is not due to any outside malevolence—children (and even parents) may move away because they are attracted to other ways of life, natural resources on which they depend may become scarce, and so forth. Many of these factors contributing to the demise of the minority culture in the second scenario must be caused by the majority culture, but there is no malevolence present. Are the moral obligations of the majority culture toward the minority culture different in the two scenarios? It seems reasonable to argue that the majority culture has moral obligations in the first scenario that are not present in the second one precisely because it intentionally tried to destroy the minority culture. Considerations of compensatory justice, in other words, might provide additional moral grounds for the establishment and protection of minority rights.

The Rights of Indigenous Peoples

What rights, if any, do indigenous peoples have? The basic principle in this type of argument would seem to be that indigenous peoples have a right to sufficient protection and privileges necessary to the preservation of their culture. This right includes things such as protection for religion and language. It might also include guaranteed representation in legislative bodies and regulatory agencies.

The details of these rights raise complex considerations that are beyond the scope of this discussion. However, it may be helpful to see an example of this complexity. Consider the question of religion for many Native Americans. Extensive attempts were made to obliterate Native American religions during and after the decades of active conquest of Native Americans by European invaders. They still suffer from the long-term effects of those attempts. In addition to this, as we saw in Chapter 3, Native American religions were often not respected simply because the dominant culture did not even recognize that they were religious. Recall the example of Blue Lake, a sacred Native American place that until recently was a public hiking trail. This is not unlike using a major church or synagogue or mosque as a place for children to play hide-and-seek, yet few in the U.S. government were willing to recognize the parallels because Blue Lake is a natural place and churches are made by human beings. (In a religion much more attuned to the natural world, it is hardly surprising that its "church" would in fact be a natural place.)

Native American religious practices also run afoul of other legal restrictions. Consider the Protection of Endangered Species Act, which bans the capture, killing, or use of certain endangered species, including the eagle. Yet eagle feathers play an important role in some Native American religious practices. Such a ban, which has now been partially lifted for Native Americans, restricts religious freedom in a way that does not occur with the majority religions. Or, to consider a second example, think of forced relocations of Native American populations. This is, in part, a religious and cultural issue. For many Native Americans, their sense of themselves is closely tied to the land. Among the Navajo, for example, people not only have a special connection to where their ancestors are buried, but they also have a connection to the place where their own afterbirth is buried. Being relocated for Navajo and many other Native Americans involves a deep sense of being torn from their roots, roots that are often essential to their sense of identity and the pursuit of their life plans.

Even more vexing, however, is the issue of freedom of religion. This is certainly a fundamental freedom in our Constitution, and we are forbidden to discriminate against people on the basis of religious beliefs. However, in some Native American traditions, religious affiliation is a necessary part of community membership. The notion of the separation of church and state, so fundamental to the Constitution of the United States, has little place in many other cultures, including most Native American cultures. The crucial issue then becomes whether the guarantee of minority rights extends to guaranteeing practices that would be seen as contradictory to the majority's notion of basic rights.

The Rights of Formerly Enslaved People

The issue of the rights of formerly enslaved people—in the United States this refers principally to African Americans—has certain similarities to the case of indigenous peoples. However, instead of having their land taken away from them by invaders, African Americans were taken away from their homeland, brought to a different land, stripped largely of their language and culture (insofar as this was possible), and treated as less than human. Eventually given some degree of freedom, they found themselves often condemned to the periphery of society, exploited by the larger society and at the same time excluded from it.

Once again, considerations of compensatory justice certainly seem relevant, although there continue to be controversies about what could be called "moral inheritance." Do the children of the perpetrators of injustice inherit a moral obligation to compensate for the wrongs inflicted by their ancestors—wrongs from which they may well have benefited? Similarly, do the children of the victims of such injustices inherit a moral right to be compensated for the injustices suffered by their ancestors—even if they themselves have succeeded personally in overcoming those injustices? These questions, needless to say, are not intended to imply that there are no longer any continuing injustices—the effects of old injustices linger, and new ones occur every day. But there is still a moral burden of past wrongdoing that we must somehow come to terms with. In addition to issues of compensatory justice, the wrongs perpetrated against formerly enslaved people also raise questions of minority rights. Here we will consider only two examples: hate crimes and adoption.

Hate Crimes

We all are familiar with crimes done for gain, such as a robbery done to get money. Objectionable as those crimes are, they still stem in part from motives that we may condone, even though we obviously condemn the means used to realize those motives. Hate crimes, on the other hand, not only are objectionable acts, but they also are done for motives that we find morally repulsive. Hate crimes single out their victims on the basis of their race (or some other identifying characteristic) and seek to harm both the individual victims and the larger group of which they are members.

In some cases, the actions performed, such as murder and assault, are clearly criminal actions anyway. Hate crime legislation may seek to impose an additional penalty in order to protect threatened minority groups, and presumably the premise of such protection is that the group as such, not just its members, has a right to continued existence. The issue becomes more complex when the actions are primarily symbolic, such as burning crosses on front lawns. To call this "symbolic" is not to suggest that it is any less real; and the harm that it causes, although not primarily physical, is deeply real. Finally, minority rights to protection sometimes conflict with other rights, most notably the right to free speech. The courts and the legislature are charged with the delicate balancing act of adjudicating these competing rights.

Group Reparations

One of the most controversial issues to arise in this area in recent years has been the question of group reparations for past official injustices. This issue applies to both indigenous peoples and to formerly enslaved peoples. It may also apply to other groups, such as Japanese Americans who were unjustly interred during World War II. The issue here is about wrongs done by the government rather than by specific individuals, for these are wrongs done in the name of all the citizens, done under the color of the flag. Moreover, the issue of reparations is not limited to the United States. They have been an issue in several European countries in the aftermath of the Holocaust. In the United States, both Native Americans and Africans brought here involuntarily into slavery have clear cases for group reparations.

Group reparations have both a monetary and a symbolic value. On the symbolic level, reparations involve the acknowledgment of harm and of a debt owed as a result of that harm. For many who have been the object of that harm, whether directly or indirectly, the acknowledgment of responsibility is itself an important step toward healing past injustices. On the practical, monetary level, reparations are often a complicated business, not only in assessing harm but also in giving reparations to the descendents of those who were directly harmed.

The Rights of Immigrant Minorities

Finally, let's consider the issue of minority rights where the issue of compensatory justice plays little role: immigrant minorities who have immigrated for the promise of a better life. Sometimes, the promised new life is better in economic terms; in other cases, it is politically better, with the promise of more freedom than was available in the home country.

This issue arises in a variety of specific forms. Consider the question of language. For many groups, cultural identity is preserved through language. Historically, public life in the United States has been conducted primarily in English. Providing assistance in learning English, both in schools and in adult classes, is uncontroversial and easy enough to justify in terms of the common good. However, the more controversial issue is whether the state should act in ways that support the continued existence of languages other than English. This may occur in a variety of ways. For example, election ballots may be available in various languages. Education might be offered in languages other than English. Measures such as these may, at least in principle, be subject to the kind of justification that Kymlicka offers for minority rights in general, although Kymlicka himself is much more reluctant to extend group rights to immigrant groups that have immigrated voluntarily.

Let us conclude this discussion with a final comment because the emphasis on rights may distort the moral picture here. Some minority groups may be more interested in assimilation than others, and this is more likely to be the case with immigrant minorities who have come voluntarily to the United

States because it represents the kind of life they want for themselves. It is important to realize that they may be much more interested in achieving assimilation and success than in maintaining their own culture as a separate entity. This is both a tension within specific minority groups and between groups.

Group Rights and Women's Rights

In a recent essay entitled "Is Multiculturalism Bad for Women?" Susan Moller Okin raised the question of whether respect for minority group rights leads at times to condoning practices and policies that are harmful to women. Are women being subjected to continued oppression under the guise of multiculturalism? Okin gives an interesting example. During the 1980s, France began allowing polygamous families from Africa and the Middle East to immigrate to France to such an extent that there are now about 200,000 polygamous families in Paris alone. In effect, they extended to these families, out of deference to different cultural practices, a group right to polygamous marriages that was not available to the population as a whole. These families, however, exist in vastly different conditions than they would have had in their homeland, where each wife might have had separate quarters. In an urban environment, they are often forced to live together in small spaces. The result is hostility among the wives and between wives and the children of other wives. When French authorities began interviewing the women, they discovered that the women often found the practice unavoidable in their homeland, even though they did not approve of it; in the French context, they found it "intolerable," according to Okin.

Here is a case, Okin contends, when multiculturalism results in continued and worsening oppression of women. The situation only became worse when the French, concerned about high welfare costs for such large families, reversed its policy on polygamy and nullified all but the first marriages. This effectively left the remaining wives stranded in a foreign land with no legal standing.

The more general issue that Okin raises is this: The subjection and oppression of women is one of the central characteristics of many cultures. She cites several practices, including polygamy, forced clitoridectomy, forced marriage, marriage of young girls, and practices concerning rape. In many countries, a rapist can escape punishment by marrying, or even offering to marry, his rape victim. In some countries, women who are victims of rape become victims again when they report the rape and find themselves accused of unlawful sex outside marriage. The issue Okin highlights is whether multiculturalism encourages us to assume a "hands-off" policy toward such practices.

The public-private distinction plays an important role here. Many countries, including the United States, have begun to take a stance against public, official policies that discriminate against women, but often the practices described here occur in private. Will Kymlicka, for example, draws this type of distinction. But Okin argues that it is insufficient to protect women from widespread oppression. In his reply to Okin's article, Kymlicka distinguishes between two kinds of group rights: one defending internal restrictions and the other establishing external protections. In the name of group traditions, some groups may attempt to restrict individual freedoms, especially the freedoms of women and children. On the other hand, they may also claim protection against the larger society in order to preserve their cultural traditions and practices from being overwhelmed by the outside society.

Kymlicka is clear that his position does not entail defending internal official restrictions that would discriminate against women, but Okin's point is that many of these restrictions are relegated to the private sphere. While Kymlicka acknowledges the need for more subtle distinctions in this area, he contends that this is not a sufficient reason for jettisoning the notion of minority group rights entirely. It simply is a reason to employ the notion with greater caution and subtlety.

Living with Moral Diversity: Ethical Pluralism and the Virtues of Living in a Multicultural World

Valuing Individuality

Individuals are the *loci,* the meeting points, of diversity. We have already seen some of the principal influences on an individual's identity: gender, ethnicity, and culture. Each of these factors—often along with other influences such as our religious background and our socioeconomic class—helps to shape who we are. What role does individuality play in the moral life?

Negative and Positive Morality

Morality is sometimes seen as having negative and positive elements. The negative elements are prohibitions that establish the *moral minimum* that is acceptable. To be concerned only with the moral minimum is like taking a course on a pass/fail basis: We are primarily concerned with what we need just to get by, to pass with a *C*-. Although being concerned with the moral minimum is preferable to not being concerned at all, it is still a long way from moral excellence. The positive element of morality focuses on *moral excellence.* Individuality finds its true place in the realm of the search for moral excellence because there are often many different individual ways in which we can excel.

Moral Excellence

Genuine saints need not be cardboard figures. Consider the great moral figures of the twentieth century. Each is characterized by the quest for excellence in a certain area. Gandhi showed us the power of nonviolence in the twentieth century. He was, if anything, tenaciously, insistently nonviolent. Think of Mother Teresa. Her compassion, her spontaneous and joyful love, set her apart from the rest of us and constituted her moral individuality. Yet it would be inaccurate to think of either of them as an extension of a theory or application of some single principle. Their lives show a richness, a vibrancy, that is a sign of robust moral health.

Moral excellence is not restricted to public figures. We all know, or perhaps are, people with a special moral excellence. Think of the friend who truly can be depended upon, even under the toughest of circumstances. That's a moral excellence, and it is one that we might choose to strive to embody. Or think of the friend who is able, even in the most difficult of circumstances, to put defensiveness aside and to listen genuinely to the concerns of the other person. This, too, is a moral excellence. Or the person who is always fair, even in the face of great pressures in the opposite direction. Or the person who can always be counted on to respond in a caring and compassionate manner to the suffering of others. Moral excellences come in many different shapes and sizes.

Forging Our Moral Identity

We all are born as human beings into particular moral communities and traditions. We are not impartial, purely rational moral agents lacking in particularity. We are individual women and men, born at a particular time and place, having a particular ethnic and cultural background, specific likes and dislikes, individual hopes and dreams. The task for us as moral individuals is to forge our own moral identity.

Ethical pluralism suggests that there is room for choice and creativity in the shaping of our individual moral identity, our moral values. In other words, although our moral values set some minimal limits within which we must act, we have a considerable degree of latitude within those limits to shape our own moral identity. Ethical pluralism establishes the negative limits on behavior and points out possibilities for us, but it is our own individual choice to create our own identity. It is here that virtue ethics is of particular relevance because it provides the most guidance to us in answering the question, "What kind of person do I want to be?" The guiding concern here is not that our moral identity be unique in the sense that it be different from anyone else's; rather, the guiding concern is that it be *ours*, that is, a freely chosen embodiment of the persons we want to be.

The formation of our individuality involves more than just our moral values; it also involves striking a balance between our moral values and our nonmoral values. Many of our choices in life about career, family, friends, and leisure involve nonmoral values as well as moral ones. Finally, it is important for us to note that the formation of individuality does not take place in a vacuum. We are always concrete individuals, situated in a particular time and place, members of various groups and communities. We can think of a community as a moral arena in which we have the opportunity to aspire to moral excellence.

There is a richness in the diversity of theory as well as the diversity of experience that we (especially philosophers) have been too ready to ignore. One of the principal aims of this book has been to recognize and to value such diversity. Yet this is easier said than done because moral conflicts—both real and imagined—present roadblocks on the path of the moral life. In order to complete our pluralistic account of moral values and to show the ways in which we can live with genuine diversity, we need an account of how to deal with moral conflicts. There are several ways in which we can respond to moral diversity and apparent moral conflict.

- We can live with diversity.
- We can seek imaginative ways of resolving conflicts.
- We can seek a compromise that all parties can live with.
- We can change our own behavior without demanding that others act differently.
- We can refuse to compromise and demand that others change.

Before examining these options, a cautionary word is in order about the way in which internal conflicts come to be perceived as purely external ones.

External and Internal Diversity

In discussing cases of moral conflict, it is easy to focus on *external* moral conflicts between two or more people with differing and conflicting value commitments. Although these are the more visible type of conflict, we should be aware that there are also *internal* conflicts in which a single individual experiences the pull of conflicting values.

There is a danger, especially in situations of sharp conflict, that internal conflicts come to be seen as purely external in character. In situations such as the abortion debate in which external conflicts are starkly polarized, participants can easily lose sight of the degree to which they also experience the conflict as an internal one. Pro-choice advocates might lose sight of their own moral qualms about abortion, just as pro-life advocates might neglect their own feelings of empathy for some women with unwanted pregnancies. The danger is that people on each side will ignore their own reservations because the other side is already advocating them so strongly. Psychologically, what happens in polarized situations such as these is that people allow their opponents to carry the burden of their own dissenting convictions. Most of us have had the experience of strongly defending a position, having our opponent capitulate, and then having doubts about our own position. This is not merely the product of some perverse desire to take the opposite side in every issue. It may also be the result of letting the opposition carry the minority side of our own feelings. When we are able to acknowledge the full and sometimes conflicting range of our own values and feelings, we may well find that there is more common ground between ourselves and those "on the other side" than we thought.

Living with Moral Diversity

In Peter Weir's 1985 film *Witness,* we are presented with an interesting example of moral diversity. The movie skillfully plays off two ways of life, both moral within their own traditions and yet apparently mutually exclusive. Harrison Ford plays a police detective, John Book, who must live in disguise in an Amish community during his pursuit of a killer. The movie portrays Book sympathetically as a detective genuinely committed to seeing justice done. If violence is necessary to accomplish this goal, Book does not shrink from it; but neither does he pursue violence for its own sake. The members of the Amish community, on the other hand, eschew violence; their commitment to pacifism lies at the core of their religious and moral identity. To betray that commitment would be to betray their deepest selves.

In one of the more striking scenes of the movie, a member of the Amish community named Daniel is confronted in town by several bullies who proceed to taunt him. Daniel does not fight back, but Book finally steps in and flattens one of the bullies. Most nonpacifists would cheer, at least silently, when the bully gets what is coming to him. Yet I think that we can step back from a scene such as this and draw several conclusions.

First, even if we are not pacifists, we might be glad that there are pacifists in our world. Even if we are happy to see Book punch the bully in the nose, we might still feel that our world is a better place because there are also people like Daniel in it. Daniel reminds us of another moral ideal, perhaps not one that is our own, but one that we can appreciate. Indeed, if there were more people like Daniel in the world, perhaps there would be both less violence and less need for violence. Daniel's presence in our own world may well prompt us to look harder for nonviolent alternatives before we resort to violence. We need not agree with Daniel in order to be happy that he is in our world.

Second, although there is an obvious moral conflict here about the moral value of violence, there is also a widespread area of agreement. If there is disagreement about whether justice can ever be brought about through violence, there is agreement that justice should be fostered. Indeed, there is also fairly widespread agreement about what counts as justice. Similarly, there is significant agreement about such issues as truthfulness, cooperation, and respect. Much moral diversity takes place within the larger context of moral agreement.

There is an added reason for valuing such diversity. It takes little reflection for us to realize that our values are not perfect. All we need to do is to look at virtually everyone else's values throughout history in order to see that none of them was without any moral blind spots at all. So, too, we can be assured that we are not immune to moral myopia, distortion, and blindness. We can be certain that some of our moral perceptions and judgments are off the mark—but the difficulty is that we cannot know *which* ones are. It is here that we depend on the values of others because their blind spots may not be the same as ours. We count on others to help us see what we miss.

Thus we see the first way in which we can live with moral diversity: We can acknowledge it and encourage it, glad that there are others who see the world differently than we do. We might not agree with them, but *we may feel* that our moral life as a whole could be more secure because they are part of our world.

Moral Imagination

The second way in which we can respond to moral diversity is imaginatively to seek new ways of acting that synthesize the diversity of apparently conflicting values. Some situations appear to be cases of moral conflict, but the conflict exists only because we lack the creative insight to devise a course of action that resolves the conflicting interests and values. Often a moral conflict has the following structure. One side says to do *A* because of value *x;* the other side says to do *not-A* because of value *y.* A morally imaginative solution would involve finding a course of action, *B,* which is compatible with both *x* and *y.*

Consider the following example, which *may* be a successful example of moral imagination. For the past several decades, our country has been experiencing a conflict that centers on the issue of poverty. On one hand, some in our society—we'll call them liberals for the convenience of the label—feel that the government must intervene to break the cycle of poverty. On the other hand, others in our society—we'll stay with the standard labels and call them conservatives—feel that individuals are (or at least should be) responsible for their own lives and that government has no business intervening in the private sector and creating dependency on government by giving people food and other necessities of life. Recently, there have been attempts to develop a third possibility (in addition to welfare or no support at all) that *may* synthesize these apparently conflicting values. Workfare, as it is currently known, would be a government program that provides the standard support usually associated with welfare but (in cases where this is appropriate) only for a limited time and under conditions that include job training and eventual employment. Undoubtedly many liberals and conservatives would perceive workfare as a compromise, that is, as temporarily setting aside some of their values for the sake of reaching a wider consensus on a course of action. Others, however, might experience it as a morally imaginative solution that does not involve giving up any of their values, a third alternative where previously they had seen only two alternatives. If such an alternative could be worked out properly (and this is not a small *if*), it might provide for some individuals on both sides of the issue just the kind of morally imaginative synthesis we have been discussing here. The interests and values of liberals would be satisfied insofar as the program helped to break the cycle of poverty and provided a compassionate response to the economically less fortunate in our society. The interests and values of conservatives would also be satisfied insofar as the program reduced dependency, encouraged personal responsibility, and was directed toward minimizing the government's intervention in the private sphere. Much, of course, would depend on how well developed the program was and how sensitively it could be administered. The success of the program would also depend on how well it dealt with recalcitrant cases, that is, those people who apparently could develop work skills but in fact did not do so, despite apparent opportunities. Finally, success would depend upon how well the program responded to the issue of the suffering of children, none of whom had a choice about the economic or social conditions of the family into which they were born.

One of the results of moral imagination is that it allows us to forge a new course of action that incorporates previously apparently conflicting values. When this occurs, the participants in the situation are not compromising because they are not going against any of their values. Instead, they are revising their values and wholeheartedly committing themselves to a course of action that they now perceive as consistent with their values.

Moral Compromise

Sometimes, in the face of moral conflict, we are unable to find a morally imaginative solution that synthesizes the conflicting values of the various parties. Compromise becomes necessary. Although "compromise" sometimes carries the connotation of "betrayal" or "selling out," not all compromises are betrayals. A compromise is an agreement that partially preserves the interests of all parties in a consensus that all can live with. There are times when moral compromise is appropriate and morally praiseworthy.

In his book *Splitting the Difference* (1990), Martin Benjamin has elaborated a number of the reasons why it is often appropriate to reach a compromise. First, compromise fosters the continuation of a communal life. Disagreements, including disagreements in values, are inevitable. Unless we are able to compromise in at least some of the cases, our common life will grind to a halt. Second, we may be more willing to compromise because we are not absolutely certain about what the right course of action is. This uncertainty may stem from either of two sources. There may be factual uncertainties. For example, how we act—especially if we are utilitarians—often depends on what we anticipate the results of our action to be. Yet these results are notoriously difficult to predict. We could find that a given situation is so morally complex that we are not completely sure about how we should act. Benjamin compares these situations to judging an Olympic figure skating competition. There may be as many as seven judges, with each judge evaluating a performance to the best of his or her ability. Generally we recognize that there is room for legitimate disagreement, and the final score is a compromise among the various scores. These are judgment calls in which compromise is eminently reasonable. Third, we may compromise because *some* decision has to be taken immediately, and there simply is not time to find an alternative that does not involve compromise. Finally, we may find ourselves in a situation of scarce resources that force compromises on us that, in situations of more ample resources, would not be necessary.

When Not to Compromise—and How

There are times when compromise is simply unacceptable. The moral price is too high, the suffering too great. There has been no shortage of such situations: The various genocidal programs of the twentieth century offer one set of examples, but they are not the only ones. Cases of child abuse offer another set of examples, ones that are often closer to home than is genocide. The moral theories we have examined help to articulate the moral minimum below which we should not allow ourselves or others to sink.

When discussing situations in which compromise is not acceptable, it is helpful to distinguish two types of cases. The first involves situations in which we will not compromise by acting, or agreeing to act, in ways that violate our moral values. Here the focus is on our own actions, on our refusal to co-operate with a possible compromise. In a second kind of situation we not only refuse to cooperate, but also actively try to stop other people from engaging in the objectionable activity. If we were to use abortion as an example, those in the first category would refuse to get abortions themselves if they were pregnant. Those in the second category would not only refuse to get abortions themselves if pregnant, but also would try to prevent others from getting abortions. Both are refusals to compromise, but the second involves an active intervention in a way that the first does not.

In both of these types of situations, it is important to reflect on *how* we refuse to compromise. Three points are noteworthy here. First, it is important to find ways of refusing to compromise that minimize polarization. We must look for ways of remaining connected with those with whom we disagree. This is often extremely difficult to do, but not always impossible. Often in such situations it is helpful to distinguish between people and their actions. We may refuse to cooperate with someone's actions, but we try to keep open other modes of communication and emotional connectedness with that person.

Second, we can refuse to compromise, but do so *with respect*. Such respect was one of the striking characteristics of Gandhi's eventual refusal to cooperate with British rule of India. He refused to compromise on the large issue of Indian independence, and he always agreed to compromise solutions on intermediate goals, but he never treated the British with disrespect. For a second example, recall the example of the villagers of Le Chambon given at the beginning of Chapter 9. One of the startling aspects of their refusal to cooperate with the Nazis is that they were concerned with the welfare of the German soldiers as well as that of the Jews they sheltered. They wanted to be sure that *no one* was killed, including the German soldiers.

Third, we can refuse to compromise, but do so *imaginatively,* perhaps even *cleverly.* As the example of the villagers of Le Chambon shows, sometimes we can refuse to compromise without resorting to violence. When we resist, we hope to find ways of resisting that will eventually convert our adversaries to our viewpoint rather than beat them into submission.

LIVING MORALLY

Let me conclude with a different kind of metaphor in terms of which we can understand the issues of diversity—diversity in culture, in gender, and even in age. Think of ethics as being architecture. Certainly there are occasionally matters of clear-cut right and wrong in architecture. From time to time, poorly constructed buildings do fall down, and people are accidentally killed or injured. Yet most of the time, questions other than those mathematical relations of size, weight, shape, and stress are much more interesting and relevant. After we decide that a given group of buildings will not fall down, we can move on to more interesting questions about what life would be like in such a place. For example, what kind of balance is implied between communal living and individual privacy in the architecture? Buildings with few walls put a premium on communal life, perhaps at the expense of individual privacy. Buildings composed primarily of small, isolated rooms with no communal areas give relatively little value to a shared life and emphasize the isolated individual as the primary unit. Our architecture reflects our values. For example, note the shift in American building away from large houses to small apartments and the implications for family life, both nuclear and extended.

We can learn about the moral life by studying different cultures in the same way that we learn about our everyday life by studying different architecture. Together, we might be able to build moral homes in which we all can live with dignity and mutual respect and in which each of us can flourish.

DISCUSSION QUESTIONS

1. Recall your rating of **statement 46** ("Morality should reflect an individual's ethnic and cultural background").
   (a) Has your rating of this statement changed after reading this chapter? If so, in what way? If your rating has not changed, are your reasons for your rating any different now than they were when you first responded to this statement?
   (b) Does your own ethnic or cultural background affect your moral views? If so, in what ways? Do you think that this is appropriate?
2. Recall your rating of **statement 48** ("Moral disagreement is a good thing in society").
   (a) Has your rating of this statement changed after reading this chapter? If so, in what way? If your rating has not changed, are your reasons for your rating any different now than they were when you first responded to this statement?

(b) Give an example of a moral disagreement that proved to be a good thing for society. Give an example of one that was harmful to society. What accounts for the difference between the two outcomes?

3. Recall your rating of **statement 50** ("Minorities have special rights by virtue of their status as minorities"). Have your views on this issue changed after reading this chapter? Discuss.

4. Each of us has a moral voice—or, more likely, several moral voices. Try to describe your own moral voice. In part, the theories presented in this book may help you to identify different voices: the voice of the egoist, the voice of the utilitarian, the voice of the religious believer, the voice of rights, and the voice of duty. Yet often what is most distinctive about our individual moral voices may not be captured by the theory that they embody. Try to describe the timbre, the tone, the texture of your voice. Try to isolate that which is distinctively *you*. It might help to imagine that you are trying to help another person get to know you morally.

This may be difficult because it is often much harder to hear ourselves than it is to hear others clearly. Let me suggest something that might help. Remember the first time you heard a tape recording of your voice. Did you think it sounded like you? Did other people's voices sound more natural to you? We may encounter the same thing in regard to our moral voices. We may find that they sound different from the inside than they do from the outside. Ask your friends and family what they think your moral voices sound like. Do they hear you as strict, harsh, tentative, sympathetic, blaming, indecisive, bullying, and so forth? Do they hear you as more rule-oriented or feeling-oriented? Do they hear your voice as primarily one of care or one of justice? Do they hear your individuality? Do they hear your culture, your ethnicity?

5. Here's an even more difficult assignment: Try to describe your *immoral* voices. This is harder because these voices are usually silent—we act on them, but we rarely express them in a public way.

6. We have discussed the issue of moral compromise at some length. Recall your response to **statement 49** ("Compromise is bad") in the Ethical Inventory.
   (a) Has your rating of this statement changed after reading this chapter? If so, in what way? If your rating has not changed, are your reasons for your rating any different now than they were when you first responded to this statement?
   (b) What values are so important to you that you would never compromise them by cooperating with others? What values are so important that you would go out of your way to actively prevent other people from engaging in behavior that violates those values?

7. **MOVIE** The movie *Rosewood* (1997) depicts racial hatred at its most extreme. What does it tell you about the nature of racism? In what ways does this movie contribute to our understanding of the invisibility of the oppression of the powerless?

BIBLIOGRAPHICAL ESSAY

Recently philosophers have become increasingly concerned with the issue of **ethnic and cultural diversity,** although much of traditional ethics—with its emphasis on universality and its "thin" notion of a moral agent—has minimized the value of such diversity. The *Philosophical Forum* took the lead in this area. See the double issue on "Philosophy and the Black Experience," *Philosophical Forum* 9, nos. 2–3 (Winter-Spring 1977–78) and the triple issue on "African-American Perspectives and Philosophical Traditions," *Philosophical Forum* 24, nos. 1–3 (Fall-Spring 1992–93). Also see the papers by Anthony Appiah, Maria C. Lugones and Thomas Wartenberg presented at an APA Symposium on Gender, Race, Ethnicity: Anthony Appiah, "'But Would That Still Be Me?' Notes on Gender, 'Race,' Ethnicity, as Sources of 'Identity'", *The Journal of Philosophy*, 87, no. 10 (October 1990): 493–499 and the commentaries by Lugones and Wartenberg. Also see the papers on multiculturalism and philosophy in *Teaching Philosophy* 14, no. 2 (June 1991), especially Larry Blum's "Philosophy and the Values of a Multicultural Community," pp. 127–134. For a recent discussion of some of these issues from a sociological standpoint, see Anthony J. Cortese, *Ethnic Ethics: The Restructuring of Moral Theory* (Albany: State University of New York, 1990). Also see Kwame Anthony Appiah, *In My Father's House* (Oxford: Oxford University Press, 1992); Craig Calhoun, ed., *Social Theory and the Politics of Identity* (Oxford: Blackwell, 1994); Cornel West's work, especially *Race Matters* (Boston: Beacon Press, 1993); and, most recently, *Color Conscious: The Political Morality of Race,* by Amy Gutmann and K. Anthony Appiah (Princeton: Princeton University Press, 1996). For a good, short overview of philosophical work on the issue of race, see Bernard B. Boxill, "Racism and Related Issues," in Lawrence C. Becker and Charlotte B. Becker, eds., *Encyclopedia of Ethics* (New York: Garland Publishing, Inc., 1992), Vol. II, pp. 1056–59. Discussions of the multiculturalism abound, but one of the philosophically most sophisticated is Charles Taylor, *Multiculturalism and 'The Politics of Recognition'* (Princeton: Princeton University Press, 1992) and the essays in Amy Gutmann, ed., *Multiculturalism* (Princeton: Princeton University Press, 1994).

On the question of **minority rights,** see especially **Will Kymlicka,** *Liberalism, Community and Culture* (Oxford: Oxford University Press, 1989), *Multicultural Citizenship* (Oxford: Oxford University Press, 1995); Will Kymlicka, *The Rights of Minority Cultures* (Oxford: Oxford University Press, 1995); *Politics in the Vernacular: Nationalism, Multiculturalism and Citizenship* (New York: Oxford, 2001); and Kymlicka and Ian Shapiro, eds., *Ethnicity and Group Rights: Nomos XXXIX* (New York: New York University Press, 2000). For a critique of Kymlicka, see John Tomasi, "Kymlicka, Liberalism, and Respect for Cultural Minorities," *Ethics* 105, no. 3 (April 1995): 580–603. **Susan Moller Okin**'s critique appears in several places. Her essay "Is Multiculturalism Bad for Women?" has been reprinted in a book by that name, edited by Joshua Cohen, Matthew Howard, and Martha C. Nussbaum (Princeton: Princeton University Press, 1999). Many of these pieces are available online at The *Boston Review,* where they originally appeared; see http://bostonreview.mit.edu/ BR22.5/. Also see Okin, "Mistresses of Their Own Destiny: Group Rights, Gender, and Realistic Rights of Exit," *Ethics* 112 (January 2002): 205–230. Her earlier work is to be found in her *Gender, Justice and the Family* (New York: Basic Books, 1994).

A number of works have recently appeared on **moral conflict.** For two influential arguments in favor of the plurality of moral values and the consequent unavoidability of moral conflict, see Bernard Williams, "Conflicts of Values," *Moral Luck* (Cambridge: Cambridge University Press, 1981), pp. 71–82 and Thomas Nagel, "The Fragmentation of Value," *Mortal Questions* (Cambridge: Cambridge University Press, 1979), pp. 128–141. Also see Stuart Hampshire, "Morality and Conflict," *Morality and Conflict* (Cambridge: Harvard University Press, 1983), pp. 140–170. For a discussion of the problems that moral conflict poses for liberalism, see Steven Lukes, "Making Sense of Moral Conflict," in Nancy L. Rosenblum, ed., *Liberalism and the Moral Life* (Cambridge, MA: Harvard University Press, 1989), pp. 127–142. John Kekes, "Pluralism and Conflict in Morality," *The Journal of Value Inquiry* 26 (1992): 37–50 argues in favor of pluralism but against the claim that our everyday moral lives are characterized by fundamental moral conflicts. For a contextualist account of the resolution of moral conflicts, see James D. Wallace, *Moral Relevance and Moral Conflict* (Ithaca, NY: Cornell University Press, 1988). Richard W. Miller's *Moral Differences: Truth, Justice and Conscience in a World of Conflict* (Princeton: Princeton University Press, 1992) is a well-argued defense of a limited version of moral realism. For a nuanced treatment of the issue of fundamental moral disagreements in a democratic society, see Amy Gutmann and Dennis Thompson, *Democracy and Disagreement* (Cambridge, MA: Harvard University Press, 1996). More recently see Elliot Turiel, *The Culture of Morality: Social Development, Context, and Conflict* (Cambridge: Cambridge University Press, 2002).

There also has been an increase in work on **ethical pluralism.** The Symposium on Pluralism and Ethical Theory in *Ethics* 102, no. 4 (July 1992) contains a number of important papers on pluralism. The issue of *Social Philosophy & Policy* 11, no. 1 (Winter 1994) is devoted to "Cultural Pluralism and Moral Knowledge," and contains a number of important papers. On the benefits of moral diversity, see Amélie O. Rorty, "The Advantages of Moral Diversity," *Social Philosophy & Policy* 9, no. 2 (Summer 1992): 38–62. Also see the works on pluralism discussed in the bibliographical essay at the end of Chapter 2. The most interesting, and perhaps also the most difficult, philosophical treatment of this issue is Michael Stocker's *Plural and Conflicting Values* (Oxford: Clarendon Press, 1990).

The issue of pluralism raises important questions about **pluralism and the limits of the liberal state.** For a provocative position on this issue, see Charles Taylor, *Multiculturalism and "The Politics of Recognition,"* with a commentary by Amy Gutmann, Steven C. Rockefeller, Michael Walzer, and Susan Wolf (Princeton: Princeton University Press, 1992); John Kekes, "The Incompatibility of Liberalism and Pluralism," *American Philosophical Quarterly* 29, no. 2 (April 1992) and John Kekes, *The Morality of Pluralism* (Princeton: Princeton University Press, 1993). Michael Walzer's *Spheres of Justice* (New York: Basic Books, 1983) defends a pluralistic account of the demands of justice; also see the excellent collection of essays in David Miller and Michael Walzer, eds., *Pluralism, Justice, and Equality* (New York: Oxford University Press, 1995). James Davison Hunter's *Culture Wars* (New York: Basic Books, 1991) contains an interesting chapter on "Ethical Pluralism and the Democratic Ideal." For a general defense of pluralism, see Nicholas Rescher, *Pluralism: Against the Demand for Consensus* (Oxford: Clarendon Press, 1993).

On the notion of **moral compromise,** see Martin Benjamin, *Splitting the Difference: Compromise and Integrity in Ethics and Politics* (Lawrence, KS: University of Kansas Press, 1990) and David Wong's "Coping with Moral Conflict and Ambiguity," *Ethics* 102, no. 4 (July 1992): 763–784 for a related discussion of moral accommodation.

On moral imagination, see Mark Johnson, *Moral Imagination* (Chicago: University of Chicago Press, 1993); S. Babbitt, *Impossible Dreams: Rationality, Integrity, and Moral Imagination* (Boulder, CO: Westview, 1996); and Martha Nussbaum, *Love's Knowledge* (New York: Oxford University Press, 1990).

References. Susan Wolf offers a perceptive discussion of the movie *Witness* and ethical pluralism in her article, "Two Levels of Pluralism," *Ethics* 102, no. 4 (July 1992): 792 ff. The quotations from Kwame Anthony Appiah are from his book, *In My Father's House* (Oxford: Oxford University Press, 1992), p. 45. The quotation from Dr. King's "Letter from Birmingham Jail" is found in Martin Luther King, Jr., *Why We Can't Wait* (New York: Mentor Books, 1964), p. 82. Susan Okin's comments on Kymlicka and his reply are to be found in the *Boston Review* exchange cited earlier.

CONCLUSION: TOWARD A GLOBAL ETHIC OF PEACE

Throughout this book, we have sketched out major theories and concepts and controversies in ethics, largely (though not always) leaving personal views to the side in favor of surveying the territory as impartially as possible. In this conclusion, I would like to step outside this role as a guide to the domain of ethical theories and speak in my own voice about issues of peace, justice, and the prospects for a global ethic. In doing so, I am not claiming to offer a detached or definitive account of these issues, but rather a personal vision of where the future of ethics is to be located.

Global Ethics and Pluralism

Throughout this book, we have been developing an account of ethical pluralism as a way of understanding how conflicting ethical theories relate to one another. This strategy has been motivated by a belief that different though these theories are, they have been developed by thoughtful individuals of good will and have, each in different ways, stood the test of time. Good, intelligent people have believed these theories, and that is *prima facie* evidence that we have important things to learn from each of these theories. They are deserving of moral as well as intellectual respect, the recognition that even when we disagree with them, these theories are worth our attention. It is in this spirit that this book has been written.

A Note about Limited Vision

My own vision is limited, and those limits have affected this book. This book is, first and foremost, a book in Western moral philosophy. True, the book discusses non-Western traditions at a number of points, and this is certainly to the good, but the basic structure of the book is Western. This is my tradition; it is not only the tradition in which I was educated, but it is the tradition that has formed many of the people around me. Yet more, much more, lies beyond this tradition. This is the issue to address here.

Moreover, this is not a matter solely of the limitations of this author's own vision. There is a tradition of Western ethics, a long conversation in which major philosophers address the ideas of their predecessors and contemporaries. Each major tradition in ethics talks with the other traditions in the West. However, there are far fewer conversations between Western ethics and other traditions, whether they be indigenous traditions in America or other parts of the world or major traditions in Asia and elsewhere. F. Max Müller's *Sacred Books of the East* was published in the 1870s, and before this landmark series Western thinkers had little access to the classics of Eastern philosophy. Oxford and Cambridge exerted a tremendous influence in Asia by educating the sons of the elite throughout Asia, but there was no comparable influence in the other direction. Few Western scholars pursued their academic degrees, especially in philosophy, in universities in China, India, and elsewhere in Asia.

As a result, we are only just beginning to see a coherent discussion developing in the West that involves both Eastern and Western traditions, and even now that conversation remains on the outskirts of mainstream scholarship in ethics. If we look at major journals in ethics, such as *Ethics* or *Philosophy and Public Affairs*, we find well-articulated discussions between, say, Kantians and virtue theorists, between utilitarians and communitarians, and the like. But there are no similar conversations between, say, Confucians and utilitarians. There may be an occasional reference, but there is not yet a community of discourse within which serious work about global ethics can proceed. Occasionally, we find the beginnings of a cross-cultural dialogue centering around a thinker such as Mencius, but this is still the exception to the rule. The result is that serious cross-cultural ethical reflection often has to start from the beginning without presupposing a shared world of discourse that encompasses East as well as West.

The central argument of Chapter 2 was that even though moral relativism might have been a helpful doctrine in the nineteenth century, it offers us little guidance for the twenty-first century. We live in what some have called a shrinking world. It is a world in which increasingly our actions and interactions extend beyond traditional boundaries. We no longer live in small, isolated, and self-contained worlds, impervious and indifferent to our neighbors around the globe. Trade, manufacturing, and communications have all contributed to a world of interlocking relationships. The World Wide Web is but the most recent step in a process that has brought us increasingly in contact with others who are far beyond our boundaries.

Awakening

The terrorist attacks of September 11 brought this home most vividly. In the seventeenth century, John Donne wrote that "no man is an island, entire of itself . . . any man's death diminishes me, because I am involved in mankind; and therefore never send to know for whom the bell tolls; it tolls for thee" (Meditation XVI, from *Devotions upon Emergent Occasions*). Injustice and disharmony halfway around the globe can—and did—have a profound impact on our shores. Many other people gain different insights from this tragic event, but for me it brought home the realization that we must strive for justice throughout the world if we are to have peace at home. Isolationism is no longer an option.

If isolationism is no longer an option, then we must come to understand those beyond our borders, whether the borders be drawn by nationality or race or ethnicity or some other local factor. In particular, we must develop a global ethic, one that can lay claim to moral allegiance around the world, not just within our Western tradition. This is the challenge that lies before us.

The Shape of a Global Ethic

What would such a global ethic look like? It's perhaps easiest to begin with what it would not look like. A genuine global ethic cannot be simply the imposition of one local and partisan viewpoint on the entire world. A global ethic will not be some variant on a *pax Americana* or any other provincial standpoint raised to a global level.

Respect

A global ethic will begin with respect—respect for differences, respect for the multiplicity of ways in which individuals strive to live lives of integrity. Indeed, despite talk of relativism and difference, we see that almost every culture in the world has some notion of respect. True, there are differences in the proper objects of respect and the appropriate ways of manifesting respect, but almost all cultures have some notion of respect.

One of the more fruitful cross-cultural discussions would be an extended inquiry into respect across cultures. Who or what deserves respect? Think of differing stances on the question of whether animals are deserving of respect. In the Western Christian tradition, there is a sharp line of demarcation between human beings and animals. After all, God became incarnate as a human being, not an animal; and human beings have immortal souls, whereas animals do not. Yet in the Hindu traditions, where there are many Gods and some of them (like Ganesh, the elephant God) have the form of animals. Moreover, souls transmigrate after death, and may move from a human being to an animal or vice versa. (In one remote Tibetan monastery, the dogs guarding the monastery were thought to be the spirits of failed monks.) The line between human and animal is much more blurred in these cultures, and we see a resultant difference in the extent to which animals are shown respect.

Just as many cross-cultural differences exist about the proper objects of respect, so too there are significant differences in how respect is shown. Recall our discussion of respect in Chapter 2. In white cultures in the United States, children show respect to their elders by looking them in the eye when the elders are speaking to them. In many traditional Native American cultures, respect is shown by looking downward; looking someone in the eyes in that situation would be considered insolent. If we are to understand one another, we must understand that the same values are sometimes manifest in quite different forms of behavior.

Respect is important for another reason here: It provides the foundation for cross-cultural dialogue. Without respect, there is little chance of genuine understanding. Equally important, without respect for the ideas of the other, we are unlikely to question the adequacy of our own views. When we respect others and find that their views on an important issue are quite different from our own, we are likely to question ourselves as well as them about the strengths and weaknesses of both views.

Pluralism

The account of pluralism that has been sketched out in this book provides a conceptual framework within which we can pursue this kind of cross-cultural discussion and within which we can gradually develop a global ethic. Pluralism recognizes that there are many truths, but it also acknowledges that there are many mistakes. The pluralist framework defends the possibility of cross-cultural communication and understanding, but acknowledges that such understanding does not come easily. Moreover, pluralism is *self*-reflective— that is, in the face of deep cultural differences, it encourages us to reflect on the adequacy of our own beliefs and practices, not just those of the other culture. Understanding others and self-understanding are intimately linked, for the process of coming to understand other people and cultures challenges us to reflect on our own culture and its limits as well as its strengths.

War, Peace, and Justice

Consider, in conclusion, the link between peace and justice and the question of war. Both the chapter on theories of justice and this conclusion on a global ethic of peace were added in this new edition. The two go hand in hand, for justice—economic as well as social and political—provides the foundation for genuine peace.

We learned many different lessons from the terrorist attacks of September 11th. For me, one of the most important lessons was the realization that isolated injustices are much less likely to remain isolated in the twenty-first century. Conflict and injustice in the Middle East, in this instance, touches us halfway around the world. Increasingly, it is insufficient to think about justice in local terms. As we live more and more in a single world, justice must be global if it is to flourish locally. As Dr. Martin Luther King, Jr., said, "Injustice anywhere is a threat to justice everywhere."

The path to peace is global justice, and this includes economic as well as social and political justice. This is not a proposition that can be proven here, at least not in any short and simple way. Test it against your own experience, your own beliefs, and see to what extent it rings true. Peace is not merely the absence of armed conflict, but a positive state of well-being.

Does a commitment to peace exclude the possibility of going to war? This is a question that cannot be settled here, but one thing is clear: Intelligent, decent people of good will are divided on the answer to this question—and that alone should tell us something. When we encounter such deep disagreement, we can be sure that both sides are seeing something that is real and important, something which the opposing side either does not see as clearly or does not value as highly. Their disagreement can be a strength, for it is likely that each helps to keep the other honest, at least to the extent that they genuinely listen to one another.

It is also important to realize that both supporters and critics of war may share a commitment to the same fundamental values but may differ about how best to protect those values. Recently I was involved in a dialogue between two men, one a decorated hero in the Vietnam War and the other a conscientious objector to that war from Kansas. What was most striking was not only the mutual respect they had for each other (each realized the other had also chosen a difficult path), but also the extent to which they share a love of their country. Their differences were not about *whether* to love their country, but about the best way of doing so.

We must also realize that the purpose of war should be peace, and the pursuit of war should be guided by a clear sense of the long-term objective of establishing a just peace. Two implications follow from this position. First, if we pursue war, we must do so in a way that maximizes the possibility of an eventual just peace. Think of the contrast between the actions of President Lincoln and General Sherman during the Civil War. Lincoln tried to guide the conduct of the war in a way that would make eventual reconciliation possible, whereas Sherman simply fought to vanquish the enemy. Lincoln's way is much more likely to lead to a lasting peace, and it is peace that must remain the goal of war. Second, if we pursue war, we must be willing simultaneously to pursue other courses of action as well. Wars typically arise out of conditions of injustice. In responding to aggression, we must not narrow our vision to such an extent that we fail to see the larger injustices lurking in the background that may have contributed to the conflict. To say this is not to condone the resulting wars or to justify the enemy's attacks. It is, however, to say that we must eventually address and attempt to rectify the underlying conditions of injustice that may have given rise to the war in the first place. Even in waging war, the focus of our efforts must be on eventually creating a lasting and just peace.

Conclusion

We live in perilous times, times in which there is even fundamental disagreement about what the perils are. Pluralism teaches us that wisdom in difficult times is to be found, first and foremost, in our ability to listen and understand one another, even when we are in deep disagreement. It is precisely this shared understanding that provides the first step toward peace. Our developing sense of justice—economic as well as social and political—then provides the guidance for that next step toward peace, just as our shared understanding of human rights will mark out the limits beyond which we cannot go. True peace just be built on the firm foundation of justice, and in the twenty-first century both peace and justice must be global if they are to be truly stable. The challenge to ethics is twofold: to help us to see clearly that peace with justice is our ultimate goal, and to help us discern wisely how best to move closer to that goal.

ETHICAL INVENTORY: ASSESSING CHANGES IN YOUR MORAL BELIEFS

Strongly Agree / Agree / Undecided / Disagree / Strongly Disagree

Relativism, Absolutism, and Pluralism

1. ❑ ❑ ❑ ❑ ❑ What's right depends on the culture you are in.

2. ❑ ❑ ❑ ❑ ❑ No one has the right to judge what's right or wrong for another person.

3. ❑ ❑ ❑ ❑ ❑ No one has the right to intervene when he or she thinks someone else has done something morally wrong.

4. ❑ ❑ ❑ ❑ ❑ It's hopeless to try to arrive at a final answer to ethical questions.

5. ❑ ❑ ❑ ❑ ❑ Ultimately, there is one and only one right standard of moral evaluation.

Religion and Ethics

6. ❑ ❑ ❑ ❑ ❑ What is right depends on what God says is right.

7. ❑ ❑ ❑ ❑ ❑ There is only one true religion.

8. ❑ ❑ ❑ ❑ ❑ What my religion says (in the Bible, the Qur'an, or other sacred scripture) is literally true.

9. ❑ ❑ ❑ ❑ ❑ All major religions have something important to tell us about what is right and what is wrong.

Strongly Agree
Agree
Undecided
Disagree
Strongly Disagree

10. ❑ ❑ ❑ ❑ ❑ We do not need to depend on religion in order to have a solid foundation for our moral values.

Psychological and Ethical Egoism

11. ❑ ❑ ❑ ❑ ❑ Everyone is just out for himself or herself.

12. ❑ ❑ ❑ ❑ ❑ Some people think that they are genuinely concerned about the welfare of others, but they are just deceiving themselves.

13. ❑ ❑ ❑ ❑ ❑ People are not really free. They are just products of their environment, upbringing, and other factors.

14. ❑ ❑ ❑ ❑ ❑ Everyone should watch out just for himself or herself.

15. ❑ ❑ ❑ ❑ ❑ You can't be both altruistic and selfish at the same time.

Utilitarianism

16. ❑ ❑ ❑ ❑ ❑ When I am trying to decide what the right thing to do is, I look at the consequences of the various alternatives open to me.

17. ❑ ❑ ❑ ❑ ❑ The right thing to do is whatever is best for everyone.

18. ❑ ❑ ❑ ❑ ❑ If someone tries to do the right thing but it works out badly, they still deserve moral credit for trying.

19. ❑ ❑ ❑ ❑ ❑ Pleasure is the most important thing in life.

20. ❑ ❑ ❑ ❑ ❑ Happiness is the most important thing in life.

Kant, Duty, and Respect

21. ❑ ❑ ❑ ❑ ❑ If someone tries to do the right thing but it works out badly, that person still deserves moral credit for trying.

22. ❑ ❑ ❑ ❑ ❑ It is important to do the right thing *for the right reason.*

23. ❑ ❑ ❑ ❑ ❑ What is fair for one is fair for all.

24. ❑ ❑ ❑ ❑ ❑ People should always be treated with respect.

25. ❑ ❑ ❑ ❑ ❑ We should never use other people merely as a means to our own goals.

Rights Theories

26. ❑ ❑ ❑ ❑ ❑ Morality is basically a matter of respecting people's rights.

27. ❑ ❑ ❑ ❑ ❑ Some rights are absolute.

Strongly Agree
  Agree
    Undecided
      Disagree
        Strongly Disagree

28. ❑ ❑ ❑ ❑ ❑ I have a right to do whatever I want as long as it does not impinge on other people's rights.

29. ❑ ❑ ❑ ❑ ❑ People have a right to health care, even if they can't afford to pay for it.

30. ❑ ❑ ❑ ❑ ❑ Animals have rights.

Justice

31. ❑ ❑ ❑ ❑ ❑ Justice is the most important characteristic of a society.

32. ❑ ❑ ❑ ❑ ❑ Might makes right.

33. ❑ ❑ ❑ ❑ ❑ Justice consists of treating everybody exactly the same.

34. ❑ ❑ ❑ ❑ ❑ A just society is one in which everyone has the maximal amount of liberty.

35. ❑ ❑ ❑ ❑ ❑ Sometimes strict justice is bad for society.

Virtue Ethics

36. ❑ ❑ ❑ ❑ ❑ Morality is mainly a matter of what kind of person you are.

37. ❑ ❑ ❑ ❑ ❑ Sometimes courage seems to go too far.

38. ❑ ❑ ❑ ❑ ❑ Compassion for the suffering of others is an important character trait.

39. ❑ ❑ ❑ ❑ ❑ It's important to care about yourself.

40. ❑ ❑ ❑ ❑ ❑ Virtues are the same for males and females.

Gender and Ethics

41. ❑ ❑ ❑ ❑ ❑ Men and women often view morality differently.

42. ❑ ❑ ❑ ❑ ❑ Emotions have no place in morality.

43. ❑ ❑ ❑ ❑ ❑ Morality is primarily a matter of following the rules.

44. ❑ ❑ ❑ ❑ ❑ The more masculine someone is, the less feminine that person is.

45. ❑ ❑ ❑ ❑ ❑ There are often unjust relationships in the modern family.

Race, Ethnicity, and Ethics

46. ❑ ❑ ❑ ❑ ❑ Morality should reflect an individual's ethnic and cultural background.

47. ❑ ❑ ❑ ❑ ❑ Some ethnic and racial groups deserve reparations for the wrongs done to them in the past.

Strongly Agree
Agree
Undecided
Disagree
Strongly Disagree

48. ❑ ❑ ❑ ❑ ❑ Moral disagreement is a good thing in society.

49. ❑ ❑ ❑ ❑ ❑ Compromise is bad.

50. ❑ ❑ ❑ ❑ ❑ Minorities have special rights by virtue of their status as minorities.

GLOSSARY

absolutism   In ethics, the belief that there is one and only one standard of morality and that it is unconditionally binding.

absolute rights   Rights that cannot be overridden by any other considerations at all, including other rights.

atheism   The belief that God does not exist. In the last two centuries, some of the most influential atheistic philosophers have been Karl Marx, Friedrich Nietzsche, Bertrand Russell, and Jean-Paul Sartre.

autonomy   The ability to freely determine one's own course in life. Etymologically, this term goes back to the Greek words for *self* and *law*. It is most strongly associated with Immanuel Kant, for whom it meant the ability to give the moral law to oneself.

autonomy of ethics   A theory that claims that ethics is completely independent of religion. It maintains that human reason alone is sufficient for ethics.

calculus   A means of computing something. A **moral calculus** is simply a means of calculating what the right moral decision is in a particular case. Typically, this terminology is associated with utilitarianism.

categorical imperative   An unconditional command. For Immanuel Kant, all of morality depended on a single categorical imperative. One version of that imperative was, "Always act in such a way that the maxim of your action can be willed as a universal law."

compatibilism   The belief that both determinism and freedom of the will are true; religion and reason are compatible with each other and do not conflict.

consequentialism   Any position in ethics that claims that the rightness or wrongness of actions depends on their consequences.

cultural relativism   See **relativism, cultural.**

deductive   A deductive argument is an argument whose conclusion follows necessarily from its premises. This contrasts to various kinds of *inductive arguments*, which offer only a degree of probability to support their conclusion. See **inductive.**

deontology   Any position in ethics that claims that the rightness or wrongness of actions depends on whether they correspond to our duty or not. The word derives from the Greek word for duty, *deon.*

determinism   In ethics, the belief that our actions and moral values are causally determined.

distributive justice   See **justice, distributive.**

divine command theory   Any position in ethics that claims that the rightness or wrongness of actions depends on whether or not they correspond to God's commands.

dolors   Utilitarian unit of pain or displeasure. Its opposite is a hedon, a unit of pleasure.

ecumenical tradition   In various religions, this tradition is characterized by an openness to other religious traditions and a willingness to explore overlapping areas of faith; this tradition is often contrasted with fundamentalist and absolutist traditions in religion.

emotivism   A philosophical theory that holds that moral judgments are simply expressions of positive or negative feelings.

enlightenment (1) An intellectual movement in modern Europe from the sixteenth until the eighteenth centuries that believed in the power of human reason to understand the world and to guide human conduct. (2) For Buddhists, the state of Enlightenment or *nirvana* is the goal of human existence.

ethical egoism A moral theory that in its most common version (*universal ethical egoism*) states that each person ought to act in his or her own self-interest. Also see **psychological egoism.**

ethics The explicit philosophical reflection on moral beliefs and practices. The difference between ethics and morality is similar to the difference between musicology and music. Ethics is a conscious stepping back and reflecting on morality, just as musicology is a conscious reflection on music.

ethnicity A person's ethnicity refers to that individual's affiliation with a particular cultural tradition that may be national (i.e., French) or regional (i.e., Sicilian) in character. Ethnicity differs from race in that ethnicity is a sociological concept whereas race is often viewed as a biological phenomenon.

eudaimonia The word Aristotle uses for "happiness" or "flourishing." It comes from the Greek *eu*, which means "happy" or "well" or "harmonious," and *daimon,* which refers to the individual's spirit. See **utilitarianism.**

flourishing See **eudaimonia.**

fundamentalism In various religious traditions, this is the belief that correct religious belief and practice are determined by how close they correspond to basic texts and dogmas. In fundamentalist traditions, basic texts and rules are often interpreted very literally.

gender A person's affiliation with either male or female social roles. Gender differs from sex in the same way that ethnicity differs from race; gender is a sociological concept, while sex is a biological one.

hedon Utilitarian unit of pleasure. Its opposite is a dolor, a unit of pain or displeasure. The term *hedon* comes from the Greek word for pleasure.

hedonistic Of, or pertaining to, pleasure. See **utilitarianism.**

human rights See **rights.**

hypothetical imperative A conditional command, such as, "If you want to lose weight, stop eating cookies." Some philosophers have claimed that morality is only a system of hypothetical imperatives, while others—such as Kant—have maintained that morality is a matter of categorical imperatives. Also see **categorical imperative.**

ideal utilitarianism A form of utilitarianism that maintains that we ought to act to maximize the realization of certain ideals, such as truth or beauty. This theory was first advanced by G. E. Moore (1873–1958).

impartiality In ethics, an impartial standpoint is one that treats everyone as equal. For many philosophers, impartiality is an essential component of the moral point of view.

imperative A command. Philosophers often distinguish between **hypothetical imperatives** and **categorical imperatives;** see the entries under each of these topics.

inclination The word that Kant used (actually, he used the German word *Neigung*) to refer to our sensuous feelings, emotions, and desires. Kant contrasts inclination with reason, viewing inclination as physical, causally determined, and irrational and reason as nonphysical, free, and obviously rational.

integrationist   Any position that attempts to reconcile apparently conflicting tendencies or values into a single framework. Integrationist positions are contrasted with *separatist* positions, which advocate keeping groups (usually defined by race, ethnicity, or gender) separate from one another.

jus ad bellum   The moral considerations of justice that determine when it is permissible to enter into a war.

jus in bellum   The moral considerations of justice that govern a nation's conduct during a war.

jus post bellum   Also known as **justice in peace.** The moral considerations of justice in establishing a peace after a war is concluded.

justice, compensatory   A theory about how to compensate people who have been wronged.

justice, distributive   A theory about how best to allocate the benefits and burdens of society among individuals.

justice, retributive   A theory about how best to respond to injustice in society.

lex talionis   Literally, "law of retaliation" in Latin; often referred to as the principle of "an eye for an eye," which calls for imposing punishment that is the same as the crime itself, especially for imposing the death penalty for murder.

maxim   According to Kant, a maxim is the *subjective rule* that an individual uses in making a decision.

means   Philosophers often contrast *means* and *ends.* The *ends* we seek are the goals we try to achieve, whereas the *means* are the actions or things that we use in order to accomplish those ends. A hammer provides the means for pounding a nail in a piece of wood. Some philosophers, most notably Immanuel Kant, have argued that we should never treat human beings merely as means to an end.

moral ballpark   The domain of actions, motives, traits, and the like that are open to moral assessment, that is, can be said to be morally good *or* morally bad.

moral isolationism   The view that we ought not to be morally concerned with, or involved with, people outside our own immediate group. Moral isolationism is often a consequence of some versions of moral relativism.

moral luck   The phenomenon that the moral goodness or badness of some of our actions depends simply on chance. For example, the drunk driver may safely reach home without injuring anyone at all or may accidentally kill several children that run out into the street. How bad the action of driving while drunk is in that case depends partly on luck.

moral realism   The belief that moral disagreements can, at least in part, be resolved by appeals to facts about the natural order of things.

moral rights   See **rights, moral.**

morality   The first-order beliefs and practices about good and evil by means of which we guide our behavior. Contrast with **ethics,** the second-order, reflective consideration of our moral beliefs and practices.

narcissism   An excessive preoccupation with oneself. In mythology, Narcissus was a beautiful young man who fell in love with his own image reflected in a pool of water.

natural law   In ethics, believers in natural law hold that (a) there is a natural order to the human world, (b) this natural order is good, and (c) people therefore ought not to violate that order.

natural rights   See **rights, natural.**

naturalistic fallacy   According to G. E. Moore, any argument that attempts to define the good in any terms whatsoever, including naturalistic terms; for Moore, good is simple and indefinable. Some philosophers, most notably defenders of naturalism, have argued that Moore and others are wrong and that such arguments are not necessarily fallacious.

negative rights   See **rights.**

nihilism   The belief that there is no value or truth. Literally, a belief in nothing (*nihil*). Most philosophical discussions of nihilism arise out of a consideration of Friedrich Nietzsche's remarks on nihilism, especially in *The Will to Power.*

noumenal   A Kantian term that refers to the unknowable world as it is in itself. According to Kant, we can only know the world as it appears to us, as a **phenomenon.** We can never know it as it is in itself, as a **noumenon.** The adjectival forms of these two words are *phenomenal* and *noumenal,* respectively.

particularity   Specific attachments (friendships, loyalties, etc.) and desires (fundamental projects, personal hopes in life) that are usually seen as morally irrelevant to the rational moral self. In recent discussions, ethicists have contrasted particularity with universality and impartiality and asked how, if morality is necessarily universal and impartial, it can give adequate recognition to particularity.

phenomenal   See **noumenal.**

pluralism   The belief that there are multiple perspectives on an issue, each of which contains part of the truth but none of which contain the whole truth. In ethics, ethical pluralism is the belief that different moral theories each capture part of the truth of the moral life, but none of those theories has the entire answer.

positive rights   See **rights, positive.**

preference utilitarianism   A moral theory that says we ought to act in such a way as to maximize the satisfaction of everyone's preferences.

prima facie   In the original Latin, "at first glance." In ethics, this phrase usually occurs in discussions of duties. A *prima facie* duty is one that appears binding but that may, upon closer inspection, turn out to be overridden by other stronger duties.

***prima facie* rights**   These are rights that are initially taken as binding until and unless some other right comes to be recognized as stronger. The term "prima facie" was made popular by W. D. Ross (1877–1940) in his discussion of duties in *The Right and the Good* (1930).

psychological egoism   The doctrine that all human motivation is ultimately selfish or egoistic.

relativism   In ethics, there are two main types of relativism. **Descriptive ethical relativism** simply claims as a matter of fact that different people have different moral beliefs, but it takes no stand on whether those beliefs are valid or not. **Normative ethical relativism** claims that each culture's (or group's) beliefs are right within that culture and that it is impossible to judge validly another culture's values from the outside.

retributive justice   See **justice, retributive.**

rights   Entitlements to do something without interference from other people (**negative rights)** or entitlements that obligate others to do something positive to assist you (**positive rights**). Some rights (**natural rights, human rights**) belong to everyone by nature or simply by virtue of being human; some rights (**legal rights**) belong to people by virtue of their membership in a particular political state; other rights (**moral rights**) are based in acceptance of a particular moral theory. See also **absolute rights** and *prima facie* **rights.**

rights-conferring properties These are characteristics of a being that entitle that being to claim certain rights. Typical rights-conferring properties may include sentience (the ability to feel pain), the ability to use language, and the ability to think.

satisfice A term utilitarians borrowed from economics to indicate how much utility we should try to create. Whereas maximizing utilitarians claim that we should strive to *maximize* utility, satisficing utilitarians claim that we need only try to produce *enough* utility to satisfy everyone. It's analogous to the difference between taking a course with the goal of getting an *A* and taking it pass-fail.

skepticism This term has two senses: In ancient Greece, skeptics were inquirers dedicated to the investigation of concrete experience and wary of theories that might cloud or confuse that experience. In modern times, skeptics are wary of the trustworthiness of sense experience. Thus classical skepticism primarily distrusted theories, whereas modern skepticism primarily distrusts experience.

subjectivism An extreme version of relativism, which maintains that each person's beliefs are relative to that person alone and cannot be judged from the outside by any other person.

supererogatory Literally, "above the call of duty." A supererogatory act is one that is morally good and that goes beyond what is required by duty. Some ethical theories that demand that we always do the act that yields the *most* good, such as certain versions of utilitarianism, have no room for supererogatory acts.

teleological suspension of the ethical This is a term introduced by the Danish philosopher Søren Kierkegaard (1813–1855) to refer to those instances in which normal ethical duties are overridden by a command from God. Kierkegaard's principal example of this is God's command to Abraham to sacrifice his son Isaac.

transcendental argument A type of argument, deriving from Kant, that seeks to establish the necessary conditions of the possibility that something is real. For example, we have to believe that we are free when we perform an action; thus belief in freedom is a necessary condition of the possibility of action.

universalizability A Kantian term applied to the maxims, or subjective rules, that guide our actions. A maxim is universalizable if it can consistently be willed as a law that everyone ought to obey. The only morally good maxims are those that can be universalized. The test of universalizability ensures that everyone has the same moral obligations in morally similar situations. See **maxim.**

utilitarianism A moral theory that says that whatever produces the greatest overall amount of pleasure (*hedonistic utilitarianism*) or happiness (*eudaimonistic utilitarianism*) is morally right. Some utilitarians (*act utilitarians*) claim that we should weigh the consequences of each individual action, whereas others (*rule utilitarians*) maintain that we should look at the consequences of adopting particular rules of conduct.

vice A weakness of character that prevents individuals from flourishing. According to Aristotle, vices typically consist of having either too much or too little of a proper virtue. Thus courage is the mean between foolhardiness (too much) and cowardice (too little).

virtue A strength of character, usually acquired through habit, that promotes human flourishing. According to Aristotle, virtues represent a middle ground between the two extremes of too much or too little.

PHOTO CREDITS

INDEX